T0325643

Human Interaction with Technology for Working, Communicating, and Learning:

Advancements

Anabela Mesquita
ISCAP/IPP, Portugal

Managing Director:	Lindsay Johnston
Senior Editorial Director:	Heather Probst
Book Production Manager:	Sean Woznicki
Development Manager:	Joel Gamon
Development Editor:	Mike Killian
Acquisitions Editor:	Erika Gallagher
Typesetter:	Michael Brehm
Print Coordinator:	Jamie Snavely
Cover Design:	Nick Newcomer, Greg Snader

Published in the United States of America by
Information Science Reference (an imprint of IGI Global)
701 E. Chocolate Avenue
Hershey PA 17033
Tel: 717-533-8845
Fax: 717-533-8661
E-mail: cust@igi-global.com
Web site: http://www.igi-global.com

Library of Congress Cataloging-in-Publication Data

Human interaction with technology for working, communicating, and learning : advancements / Anabela Mesquita, editor.
     p. cm.
  Includes bibliographical references and index.
  Summary: "This book provides a framework for conceptual, theoretical, and applied research in regards to the relationship between technology and humans"--Provided by publisher.
  ISBN 978-1-61350-465-9 (hardcover) -- ISBN 978-1-61350-466-6 (ebook) -- ISBN 978-1-61350-467-3 (print & perpetual access) 1. Social media. 2. Human-computer interaction. 3. Technology--Social aspects. 4. Social interaction.
I. Sarmento, Anabela.
  HM742.H86 2012
  302.23'1--dc23
                              2011044138

British Cataloguing in Publication Data
A Cataloguing in Publication record for this book is available from the British Library.

Table of Contents

Detailed Table of Contents

Chapter 1

Philip D. Carter, Auckland University of Technology, New Zealand

In this paper, the author is concerned with "stories" society makes about "the machine". A story that holds consensual elements is of great interest if one accepts the premise that story in itself has a strong influence on what we seek to create. Given that many popular stories present nightmare scenarios, a self-fulfilling prophesy would not want to be created. The psychodramatic method was used to produce several unscripted enactments of people's feelings, thoughts and experiences concerning the machine. Certain elements of setting, character, metaphor and action were then drawn from the enactments and formed into a story.

Chapter 2

*Claire Gauzente, Institute of Political Sciences of Rennes, France & ESC Rennes
School of Business, France*

This study explores mobile users' perceptions about SMS advertising. The empirical study uses a double methodology. First, a qualitative study using the Q-method is conducted. Qualitative analysis reveals that negative attitudes are commonly shared, and that ad-clutter is perceived critically. Therefore, in a second step, a quantitative study is adopted to assess the impact of attitudes towards SMS advertising and perceived ad-clutter on reading behaviour. The main test is conducted over a representative sample of 302 mobile owners. From a behavioural standpoint, the results show ambivalent behaviour in most cases. In particular, the role of perceived ad-clutter is ascertained. Implications for practice and directions for future research are discussed.

Chapter 3

Shari R. Veil, University of Oklahoma, USA

To lessen the threat of an intentional or naturally occurring livestock disease, the Animal Plant Health Inspection Service of the United States Department of Agriculture introduced the National Animal

Identification System (NAIS), encouraging the use of innovative tools such as radio frequency identification (RFID) tags to track cattle across the country. In this study, the author examines the barriers to adoption of NAIS and RFID technology as risk-reduction tools. Diffusion of innovation literature is used to analyze a case study of a state livestock association advocating the rejection of NAIS and RFID technology. Implications for the diffusion of risk reduction tools are provided.

Chapter 4

Flow theory has been widely applied in the context of information technology and is useful in understanding users' behavior; however, few studies empirically examine what factors influence players' flow, and what the facets and consequences of flow are in the context of electronic games (e-games). In this study, the author reviews previous flow-related literature to develop the proposed model to explore these research questions. The proposed model is empirically evaluated using survey data collected from 277 users responding about their perception of e-game. Results of this empirical study show that perceived ease of use, immediate feedback, skill and challenge are antecedents of flow, while enjoyment is the most salient facet of flow. The results provide further insights into e-game design and development.

Since most e-recruiting portals suffer from outdated applicant profiles and receive little user return as soon as applicants have found a new job, in this study, the authors explore how to motivate applicants to keep their profiles up-to-date and stay connected with one specific recruiting portal throughout their careers. The authors interviewed applicants, system analysts and programmers of an Austrian e-recruiting portal. Narratives showing striking differences between these three stakeholders' interpretation of system requirements for long-term usage are discussed. The identified requirements point to niche recruiting: integrating social network and community features for specified user segments sharing a similar social identity and fostering pre-existing offline ties among users for career purposes. Implications are sketched for more sustainable e-recruiting research, design and development.

Chapter 6

This paper presents the results of a longitudinal exploratory survey based on a sample of French firms. Different contexts of Intranet, as well as introduction, development stages, performance and Intranet content are presented. Three approaches are in existence: corporate Intranet, specialized Intranet and

HR Intranet. These can be linked to different stages of development: communication, functional support, and knowledge management. The HR Function will be successful if it integrates Intranet in its management process, if the players are aware of the stakes and they behave as "real change agents". Research shows the importance of strategic alignment between human resource management (HRM) and Intranet as well as the relevance of technological infusion, therefore, this paper's result in showing a configurative approach that allows the integration of more variables and in turn leads to a systemic model contains great significance.

The purpose of this paper is to explore the acceptance and the appropriation of videoconferencing-mediated training during real training situations in a French company. The authors compare the acceptance and appropriation by 60 employees of two videoconferencing-mediated training systems: the virtual class (desktop videoconferencing) and the remote class (where learners are gathered together in the same room while the trainer is located at distance). In considering the acceptance of these videoconferencing-mediated training systems, a link was confirmed between perceived usefulness and the intention to use, but no relationship was established between the levels of acceptance and the required effort. The intention to use videoconferencing was associated with the expected benefits and not with the expected effort. Regarding appropriation, learners did not report a perception of technological distance. Moreover, this paper shows that learners and the trainer preferred the virtual class rather than the more classical remote class. The authors' findings contradict the media richness theory, according to which the remote class, which is the "richer" medium in their research, should have been preferred.

This paper examines HR Management issues in Environmental Scanning (ES) process. Although literature claims that selecting information in this kind of processes is central, the authors are using the concept of "intelligent filters" (Simon, 1983) to understand how human attention can be managed for selecting strategic information in a complex environment. The author examines HR executives and the way they deal with issues related to ES and focuses on an empirical study in a big technological firm, where the use of an internal reporting and communication system (the weekly) was studied. This author finds that this particular system can be considered as an "intelligent filter", requiring both human and technological resources. Finally, suggestions that the system is used by HR executives in order to organize communication and coordination in an ES process but also to increase the participation and involvement of all employees in such a process are made.

This paper falls into five main parts. Part one, offers a critical analysis and evaluation of Luciano Floridi's
metaphysical theory of information ethics (IE). Drawing on part one, part two provides a discussion of
what I consider to be the main conceptual and practical difficulties facing Floridi's IE theory. Although
in agreement with the overall motivation and objective that informs Floridi's IE position, namely, that
"all entities, qua informational objects, have an intrinsic moral value..." and that "there seems to be no
good reason not to adopt a higher and more inclusive, ontocentric [moral] perspective" (Floridi, 2007,
10), part three of the paper proposes an alternative New-Gewirthian approach to Information Ethics that
avoids some if not all of the difficulties facing Floridi's own position. Part four then examines the implications for Floridi's metaphysical theory of information ethics and finally, offers a conclusion in part five.

Chapter 10

The vocational colleges in Taiwan regard professional certifications as a badge of skills achievement. To
enhance student learning in this specific context, the authors conducted a quasi-experiment to explore
effects of web-mediated self-regulated learning (SRL) with feedback, blended learning (BL) and their
combinations on enhancing students' skills of using Microsoft Word. Four classes in successive years,
with a total of 190 freshmen, were divided into 2 (SRL with Feedback vs. SRL without Feedback) × 2
(Blended vs. Traditional) experimental groups. Results were generally positive. The results showed that
students in the group of BL and SRL with feedback had better skills and higher pass rate on certification
exams than those in the control group. It is hoped that the lesson learned is also useful for those teachers
engaged in e-learning, specifically, in vocational colleges.

Chapter 11

In theory, usability work is an important and well-integrated activity in developing software. In practice,
collaboration on improving usability is ridden with challenges relating to conflicting professional goals,
tight project schedules, and unclear usability findings. The authors study those challenges through 16
interviews with software developers, usability experts, and project managers. Four themes that are key
challenges to successful interaction between stakeholders are identified: poor timing when delivering
usability results, results lacking relevance, little respect for other disciplines, and difficulties sharing
important information. The authors review practices that have successfully addressed these challenges
and discuss their observations as encompassing multiple perspectives and as a collaborative cross-
professional learning process.

Users of information technology (IT) frequently encounter "exception messages" during their interactions with computing systems. Exception messages are important points of communication with users of IT and are similar in principle to compliance and warning messages that appear on consumer products and equipment (e.g., cigarettes, power tools, etc.), in various environments (e.g., around machinery), and on chemicals. This study reviews the normative elements and information that are included in product, chemical, and environment compliance and warning messages and combines these with recommendations in the IT literature to propose that five elements and information should be included in IT exception messages with a standard format. It is argued that including these elements in the proposed format will improve the consistency and effectiveness of exception messages. Also reported are the results of an investigation of a sample of actual exception messages to determine their degree of conformity with the proposed elements. Results indicate that IT exception messages lack descriptive content.

Chapter 13

The history of human resource information systems stretches to the 1960s, when human resource data were separated from payroll systems. In the 1980s, researchers and practitioners became more interested in human resource information systems, and in the 1990s several studies, articles, user experiences, opinions and descriptions were published in journals, magazines and on the internet. Still, despite the number of literature, no survey or framework exists that constructs a synthesis of the fragmented issues of human resource information systems from both of these viewpoints, that is, information systems and human resource management. In this paper, an initial framework for human resource information systems is introduced to underline the importance and the need for consolidating the knowledge on the phenomenon.

This article addresses the issue of geographically distributed work teams that carry out new product development projects. These are task-oriented, goal-driven, temporary teams that use ICTs. This exploratory study measures the moderating affect of team *distributedness* on the relationships between organizational and workforce management best practices and two measures of project success (efficacy and effectiveness). Data were obtained from real teams working in Canadian companies in diverse high-tech industries. The results show a moderating effect of team distributedness, which is interesting in that the distributedness factor is examined from a different perspective, that is, as a moderating rather than an explanatory dimension.

Ewan Oiry, Université de la Méditerranée, France
Roxana Ologeanu-Taddeï, Université Montpellier II, France
Tanya Bondarouk, University of Twente, The Netherlands

The concept of appropriation is frequently used in IT implementation research. Rooted in the analysis of the diffusion of innovation, this concept is usually linked with characteristics of an organization's structure, size, and sector. Since the 1980s, appropriation has been actively studied by IT researchers, who linked it with technological attributions and characteristics of users. In this paper, the authors observed the application of the appropriation concept developed from the extreme of giving full credit to technology, and the other extreme of fully crediting end-users. The authors argue that to capture a full range of benefits from technology and human interaction, researchers cannot ignore organizational structure. By presenting three case studies, this paper shows that it is necessary to reintroduce this "side" to have a complete analysis of appropriation.

Alysson Bolognesi Prado, State University of Campinas, Brazil
Carmen Freitas, State University of Campinas, Brazil
Thiago Ricardo Sbrici, State University of Campinas, Brazil

In the growing challenge of managing people, Human Resources need effective artifacts to support decision making. On Line Analytical Processing is intended to make business information available for managers, and HR departments can now encompass this technology. This paper describes a project in which the authors built a Data Warehouse containing actual Human Resource data. This paper provides data models and shows their use through OLAP software and their presentation to end-users using a web portal. The authors also discuss the progress, and some obstacles of the project, from the IT staff's viewpoint.

Preface

INTRODUCTION

This publication – *Human Interaction with Technology for Working, Communicating and Learning: Advancements* – comprises some of the best articles published in the *International Journal of Technology and Human Interaction*. It is our purpose to offer the reader the most up to date research and discussions providing an overview of the trends and advancements in this area.

IJTHI

The first issue of the International Journal of Technology and Human Interaction appeared in 2005 due to the recognition that an increasing amount of research was being done in the area where technology and human meet. Several studies came to the conclusion that the success or even the failure of the implementation of technologies were not due to the technology itself but to the interaction between the technology and the user. Furthermore, this problem of technology and human interaction covers all the fields and aspects of our lives, such as education, profession, private, leisure time, just to mention a few.

Taking this into consideration, the journal provides a platform for leading research that addresses issues of human and technology interaction in all the domains. The research that the journal intends to publish should therefore be interdisciplinary and include aspects from a wide variety of disciplines. These disciplines may range from more technical ones such as computer science, engineering or information systems to non-technical descriptions of technology and human interaction from the point of view of sociology, psychology, education, communication, management, marketing or even philosophy. The journal also aspires to provide a publication outlet for research questions and approaches that are novel and may find it difficult to be published in established journals following a rigid and exclusive structure. It is open to all research paradigms, be they empirical or conceptual, but requires that they be accessible and reflected. We also encourage the submission of high quality syntheses across research in different specialties that are interesting and comprehensible to all members of the information systems community and related disciplines.

The journal is opened to several topics that may include (but are not limited to) the following:

- Experiential learning through the use of technology in organizations
- Influence of gender on the adoption and use of technology
- Interaction and conversion between technologies and their impact on society

- Intersection of humanities and sciences and its impact on technology use
- Perceptions and conceptualizations of technology
- Relationship of theory and practice with regards to technology
- Social impact of specific technologies (e.g. biometrics, SCM, PGP, etc.)
- Social shaping of technology and human interaction research
- Technological risks and their human basis
- Value of intellectual capital in knowledge management

and all other issues related to the interaction of technology and humans, either individually or socially.

Special Issue

The IJTHI is also attentive to the trends and changes in the society and from time to time organizes special issues that cover, discuss and deal with special and particular topics. This is why one of the next issues will comprise researches concerning green technologies and human interaction. Green technology is, by definition, environmentally friendly, and aims to conserve natural resources as well as the environment itself. "Green technology" provides us with processes of generating energy by way of environmentally non-toxic products. Our major goal is to provide a "Low" environment which includes Low carbon emission, Low pollution, and Low water waste. This special issue focuses on the field of new, innovative green technology to make changes in human daily life. We are looking for papers discussing bio-energy, curriculum research and development in green technology, climate change education and water resources, green chemistry, green energy, scientific progress of green technology, just to name a few. For these special issues we invite guest editors, experts in the field that help to draw the most important lines concerning these novelties. For the edition of Green Technology the editors will be Keng-Shiang Huang and Chun-Yen Chang.

However the topics that need to be explored are not confined to those mentioned above. Everyday new technologies and applications emerge in the market. These are applied in all the different dimensions of our lives, namely in working, communication and learning. In the next paragraphs I will focus on a development that may have impact in these 3 dimensions. This is the mobile industry with particular emphasis on the apps and their application in the touristic market. I also point out the trends in the market as well as the challenges that are or will be faced by those that want to be successful in this field.

THE MOBILE, THE APPS AND THE TOURISM

Traditionally, the mobile industry tried to innovate improving performing handsets and faster transmission speeds for data traffic. Now all the energy spent is around mobile operating systems and software applications while handsets become a commodity. This development had an impact on the use and consumption of tourism services. For instance, the internet has changed the way people acquire information about tourism destinations, make their reservations and interact with players in the tourism industry (Leo, 2010). In the US 34% of tourists use mobile phones to find travel information, 29% to check reservations and 25% to book accommodation (*op. cit.*).

At the time of the introduction of UMTS[1] systems in the market, many operators were on a quest to find the "killer application" for this new technology. This conduced to an increasing competition through new entrants in the market, resulting in significant price reductions that lead to increased mobile broadband access and internet usage over mobile devices. At this time, Europe was the region with the "largest mobile penetration and rather broad mobile internet usage caused by low prices due to strong competition and strict regulation" (Leo, 2010). This scenario has changed due to the ongoing software revolution that shifted the centre of activity from Europe to US. Apple entered the market and introduced iPhone. The advantage of this device was the user interface that fully exploited the touch principle. The excellent usability of the phone made it a huge success with customers and changed the paradigm for mobile phones substantially (op. cit.).

Tabel 1 shows the evolution in the smarthphones brands. The iPhone is by far the leading device; however 7 of the top 10 smartphones run on Android.

These figures show that there is a potential market for this kind of products. Moreover, a survey done in February 2010, based on 963 respondents, revealed that Android and iPhone users download ~9 new apps[2] / month, ~12 iPod touch, ~6 webOS. Twice as many iPhone users regularly download paid apps as Android and webOS users. For instance, iPod touch users that purchase paid apps spend \$11,39 vs. \$9,55 webOS, \$8,36 android and \$8,18 iPhone. Andoid users that purchase paid apps download 5.0/ month vs 4.6 iPod touch, 3.6 iPhone and 2.5 webOS (Admob metrics, 2010).

As for the behavior and habits of consumers, Android users have similar download habits as iPhone users as shown in Figure 1 (Admob metrics, 2010).

At the end of 2008 there were approximately 10,000 apps in the App Store. By the end of 2009 there were over 100,000 apps delivering approximately 1 billion downloads in the last 9 months alone. This scenario, seen before as a promise of technology convergence, has become a reality and for the tourism industry, this represents an unprecedented opportunity to deliver "in-destination visitor information, hyper-localised and hyper-personalised to the individual and where they happen to be" (New Mind, 2011).

Table 1. Evolution in the number of smarthphones between 2008 and 2010 (Source: Admob metrics, 2010)

Top Smarthphones, May 2008			Top Smarthphones, May 2009			Top Smarthphones, May 2010		
Brand	**Model**	**% requests**	**Brand**	**Model**	**% requests**	**Brand**	**Model**	**% requests**
Nokia	N70	10.8	Apple	iPhone	47.9	Apple	iPhone	39.9
Palm	Centro	5.4	Nokia	N70	3.9	Motorola	Droid	6.8
Nokia	N73	4.9	HTC	Dream	3.5	HTC	Magic	2.9
Nokia	6600	4.8	Nokia	6300	3.0	Nokia	N70	2.5
RIM	Blackberry 8100	4.4	Nokia	N80	2.6	HTC	Hero	2.4
Nokia	6300	4.0	Nokia	N73	2.4	Nokia	6300	2.3
Apple	iPhone	3.5	Nokia	N95	2.1	HTC	Dream	2.1
Nokia	N80	3.4	Nokia	6120c	2.0	Motorola	CLIQ	1.8
Nokia	6630	3.3	Nokia	6600	1.7	HTC	Droid Eris	1.8
Nokia	N95	3.3	RIM	Blackberry 8300	1.6	Samsung	Moment	1.5

Figure 1. Comparison between paid and free apps (Source: Admob metrics, 2010)

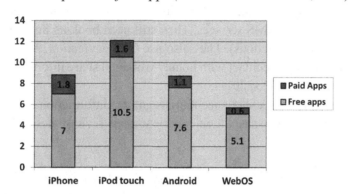

THE TOURISM INDUSTRY

Our behavior, as consumers, has changed – we are more informed, more demanding, we want to engage with the content, with the brand, we want stories, emotions, relationships. We are more and more mobile. Four in five business travelers would like to have mobile applications offering recommendations for restaurants and bars close to a hotel location (Psarros, n/d). We travel for work and leisure. We prepare our trips and like to share them with friends. We recommend hotels, restaurants and places to visit. Before travelling, tourists educate themselves about what they are looking at. They read books, hire a tour guide or they can read every plaque and sign on the premises – they prepare themselves beforehand. They are described as "self made tourist" or "active tourist" (Evjemo et al. 2009). As far as smartphones are concerned, more than 40% of owners of such technology, already get destination information, and 34% of business travelers and 26% of leisure travelers use them to make booking during their trip (Psarros, n/d).

Tourism industry is currently an extremely sensitive hybrid industry and incorporates distinct features of information society. Although the core product in the industry is physical service, which is produced and consumed in the physical world, it is dominated and achieved though information services. The perfect integration of information and physical services is the challenge for the contemporary tourism industry across the globe. Hence it is largely a information product.

Usually the touristic activity can be divided in 3 phases:

- **the pre visit phase:** this phase can usually start with information search and online research, word of mouth (via online review sites, social media and face to face accounts) and continues with conversations both online and offline with other consumers which can recommend places to visit, to stay and to eat. Consumers use the technology for booking and ticketing (transport, dinner, accommodation and attractions) as well as for other preparations (Simons, 2005). At this stage what do customers want from travel websites? 52% say they look for information about the destination which can be useful when choosing a holiday, while 38% say they look for maps showing the location of the airport and resort (Psarros, n/d) (data obtained from the econsultancy digital marketers united). Consumers also look for photos of the destination and accommodation since these help them to choose a holiday. Reviews are also useful before making a decision.

- **the visit phase:** the experience that started in the pre visit phase is extended throughout the travel. At this stage, consumers still look for information and routing using digital guidebooks, digital guides using GPS or SMS services. They still need booking and ticketing (transport, dinner, accommodation and attractions). They also use GPS navigation, get around with RFID, take pictures / movie clips, stay in contact with home / work and share information with other travelers (Simons, 2005; acoupleofchicks, 2011).
- **the post visit phase:** after the experience tourists gathers information about the place visited and if they liked it they are likely to share their experiences via review sites and social media (Simons, 2005; acoupleofchicks, 2011).

The use of the devices depends on the services being offered by the touristic market. And this means that this market needs to know exactly what the consumer wants in order to satisfy their needs with adequate products and services. The five main sectors of the tourism and travel industry and for which consumers are looking for information are (Middleton and Clarke, 2001): (1) Accommodation; (2) Attraction; (3) Transport; (4) Travel organisers' sector and (5) Destination organizations. It is here that suppliers must keep their eyes on and make their offers.

TRENDS AND CHALLENGES

In the next paragraphs we briefly present some of the trends and challenges in the mobile industry and apps applied to tourism.

Maybe enabled by the technologies (or because of them) we can no longer imagine the leisure industry without mobile devices. The free internet via wifi access is also blooming and has a catalyzing effect on the development of digital applications which will, by its turn, to reform the tourist landscape (RCCT, 2011).

Moreover, one knows that internet is becoming more and more important in the pre-holiday phase, when the tourist looks for information about the place to visit, where to eat, sleep, what to do and see. According to RCCT (2011), 52% of the potential travelers visit three or more websites before making a booking. Also, more and more users book their own custom-made trip (dynamic packaging). But despite the growing dexterity in using the internet, many people still have problems to book and/or pay the desired product due to customer unfriendly sites and applications. People would abandon a travel purchase online if the pricing is unclear and if there are hidden charges. Moreover, this will also happen if there is lack of information or if they experience difficulties in searching for holidays (Psarros, n/d). This means that there is still a lot to do in order to facilitate to reserve, book and pay the product / service.

Another trend, according to the Trendwatching.com, is related to real-time reviewers. Nowadays, whatever one sells or launches is viewed and discussed widely, live and 24/7. People want to read reviews about all sort of products and services and be able to share their comments with their peers.

Related to the need to look for information and have recommendation there is the F-Factor (Trendwatching, 2011). Consumers are increasingly tapping into their networks of friends, fans and followers to discover, discuss and purchase goods and services, in ever-more sophisticated ways. The five ways that the F-Factor influences consumption behavior are (op. cit.):

- **F-Discovery:** How consumers discover new products and services by relying on their social networks.
- **F-rated:** How consumers will increasingly receive targeted ratings, recommendations and reviews from their social networks.
- **F-feedback:** How consumers can ask their friends and followers to improve and validate their buying decisions.
- **F-together:** How shopping is becoming increasingly social, even when consumers and their peers are not physically together.
- **F-me:** How consumers' social networks are literally turned into products and services.

Almost everybody has a mobile phone and in a few years we will have smartphones. Power of multimedia technology storytelling together with digitalization trends and diffusion of handy mobile devices support changes. All these developments are transforming the mobile phone into a multimedia device. However, there are still some problems that need to be solved such as the communication costs and network coverage (Evjemo et al. 2009). We also acknowledge that more and more there is an emphasis on relationships. Consumers want to engage with the products / services and brands. This is why cultivating relationships online will dominate value in content, links and promotion (Psarros, n/d).

Another technology that can have some impact in the tourism is the use of QR Codes or "Quick Response" codes. The code is a specific matrix barcode (or two-dimensional code), readable by dedicated QR barcode readers and camera phones. How does this work? Users scan the code into a smartphone and then they are taken to a friendly web based page or mobile app where they can find more information about the product / service / monument and engage with the brand while they are in the market and experiencing travel. In order to be successful the QR codes must be used at the point of consumption or close to the travel buying cycle.

However, one also has to consider the cost of development of application. As a matter of fact, to develop an application costs thousands of dollars, depending on the functionality the client wants. It is also important always provide updated information for visitor, which means having the information always updated. Furthermore, there will also come into question whether or not one should charge for the app (Lively, 2011). Usually they are available for free but now some suppliers are already charging for it.

Another issue that needs to be discussed is the need for speed. Consumers need to get what they want even faster. They do not want to wait too long.

Usability will also be the key success factor saving those deep, cumbersome websites from instant dismissal by users (Psarros, n/d). This means that websites must be simple. A visual appealing website is a site that is easy to read, easy to navigate and where one can find relevant information.

Finally, content is the king. This means that qualitative and diverse information, trip planning tools, attractive visual material including video and photo sharing applications, multilingual content, B2B and press sections are all must elements of a successful DMO website (Psarros, n/d).

In the next section some ideas on how the technology can help to improve the trip of the tourist are presented.

HOW TECHNOLOGY CAN HELP THE TOURIST TO IMPROVE THE TRIP

In the next paragraphs it is specified ways in which technology can help the tourist to improve his / her trip (Bashara, 2010):

1. **Identifying tourist problems:** The common problem among tourists is to decide where to go and what to do. To overcome this problem, travelers are relying on smartphones and tablets and do not typically browse websites from mobile devices. Anyway, special apps helping to identify popular spots are needed to be developed. The next step is to help tourists to know how to get to their final destinations and coordinate travel with availability of certain attractions.

2. **Identifying tourist solutions:** The possibility to document and share a trip is something that the tourist wants. The user wants to bring something with him / her back to his / her life. It could be a photosharing or leaving a digital trail full of blogs.

3. **Indispensable travel apps:** There are several apps that improve the travelling experience. Nevertheless, users will only download an app that provides value. It is necessary to give them a reason to use the app while they are visiting a destination and encourage consumers to share experiences while they are in the destination. In the next paragraphs some tools are presented.

    a. **Google maps:** a map is one of the mostly needed tool together with guidebooks during a trip.

    b. **Guidebooks and itineraries:** tourists look for sources where they can find all sorts of reviews and information about any attraction.

    c. **Translators:** frequently, tourists need translations and here the iPhone seems to reign with its app iLingual. This app replaces the mouth of the user with an animated mouth generated from photo reference that speaks the inquiries to whoever one is requesting information from.

    d. **Layar:** this app is about augmented reality. This application allows finding fellow Twitter users, or café's to spend time while one checks up on what is going on back at home. It is also possible to get information about the building the tourist passes by asking the app to identify the places around. How can this be done? Just need to hold up the mobile phone in front of the user and receive annotation on the screen on top of the visual coming through the camera lens from the real world. It is also possible to narrow down the information by selecting categories such as bars, restaurants, hotels, etc. The user will see dots in the screen that will tell him / her which direction is relative to his / her position as well as how far they are. The software relies on knowing the user's position rather than recognizing the scenery. As long as the user can receive a GPS signal and have a compass, gyroscope and accelerometer in his / her device, then the app will know which way the person is facing, the orientation at which he / she is holding the phone and where all the POIs are relative to his / her location (Sung, 2011).

    e. **Tracking transactions:** There are some apps that help tracking transactions and facilitate the expenses report portion of any business trip. The user just needs to point the camera to the receipt, shoot and file the report away for later.

    f. **Tracking the journey:** tourists also enjoy tracking their journey. There are several solutions for this. One of them is Foursquare.

    g. **Staying in touch:** there are several chat programs that allow communicating with family and friends.

CONCLUSION

The *International Journal of Technology and Human Interaction* is concerned with research that explores the link between men and technology. Being the technology present in all the dimensions of our lives it is natural that all sort of disciplines may contribute for this publication. Furthermore, the journal also publishes special issues where a certain topic is fully discussed and presented. One of the next special issues will cover "green technology". Besides that, one acknowledges that in the mobile industry and tourism market several developments have occurred in the last years, bringing changes in the way people look for information at all the travelling stages. Users want to engage with brands, they want to be stimulated and get emotionally involved with the experience. Taking this into consideration, some trends were identified and presented. However, there are also some challenges that need to be overcome and these were also discussed.

Anabela Mesquita
ISCAP / IPP, Portugal

REFERENCES

Acoupleofchicks (2011). QR codes and mobile Apps: what can they do for destination marketing? In Tips from the list (Blog). http://www.tipsfromthetlist.com/37096.html.

Admob Mobile Metrics. (2010). *Metrics highlights*, May 2010, Admob. URL: http://metrics.admob.com/wp-content/uploads/2010/06/May-2010-AdMob-Mobile-Metrics-Highlights.pdf.

Bashara, R. (2010). *Indispensible Tourist Apps | Mobile Phone Tourist Apps*. http://www.softcity.com/contribution/3IDMyEzN/view/indispensible-tourist-apps-mobile-phone-tourist-apps).

Evjemo., et al. 2009. *Piloting tourist guides in a mobile*. InTech context. URL: http://www.intechopen.com/source/pdfs/8962/InTech-Piloting_tourist_guides_in_a_mobile_context.pdf.

Lively, K. (2011). *Phone Apps Help Tourism Businesses Keep Travelers Informed*. http://ezinearticles.com/?Phone-Apps-Help-Tourism-Businesses-Keep-Travelers-Informed&id=3471483.

Mag, P. C. (2011). *Encyclopedia: definition of app*. http://www.pcmag.com/encyclopedia_term/0,2542,t=app&i=37865,00.asp.

Middleton, V., & Clarke, J. (2001). *Marketing in travel and tourism* (3rd ed.). Butterworth-Heinemann.

Mind, N. (2011). *Mobile apps for tourism*. http://www.newmind.co.uk/site/technology/mobile-apps.

RCCT. (2011). *Trends and developments*. Research Center for Coastal Tourism. http://www.kenniscentrumtoerisme.nl/en/trends-en-ontwikkelingen.

Simons, R. (2005). *Mobile communication technologies in tourism – possibilities for the future*. Thesis. NHTV University of Professional Education. December. http://brochures.nhtv.nl/scriptiebank/documenten/Mobile%20communication%20technologies%20in%20tourism-Simons,%20R.pdf.

Sung, D. (2011). Augmented *reality in action - travel and tourism*. http://www.pocket-lint.com/news/38806/augmented-reality-travel-tourism-apps.

Trendwatching (2011). *The F-Factor*. http://www.trendwatching.com/briefing/.

ENDNOTES

[1]   Universal Mobile Telecommunications System (UMTS) is a third generation mobile cellular technology for networks based on the GSM standard.

[2]   The term has been used as shorthand for "application" in the IT community for decades. However, it became popular for mobile applications in smartphones and tablets, especially due to the advent of Apple's iTunes App Store in 2008. It is just as correct to say "iPhone application" as it is "desktop computer app;" although app is shorter (PC Mag, 2011).

Chapter 1
The Emerging Story of the Machine

Philip D. Carter
Auckland University of Technology, New Zealand

ABSTRACT

In this paper, the author is concerned with "stories" society makes about "the machine". A story that holds consensual elements is of great interest if one accepts the premise that story in itself has a strong influence on what we seek to create. Given that many popular stories present nightmare scenarios, a self-fulfilling prophesy would not want to be created. The psychodramatic method was used to produce several unscripted enactments of people's feelings, thoughts and experiences concerning the machine. Certain elements of setting, character, metaphor and action were then drawn from the enactments and formed into a story.

INTRODUCTION

The work described in this paper is concerned with the stories we are making about 'the machine'. The premise of the work is that the emergent story which is being consolidated under the gaze of communal interest will be predictive of the actual technology we create in the future. The historical analyses by Lewis Mumford (1966, 1970) offers compelling illustrations of how the

projected material of the mind, such as in story and ritual, have been the primary provocation and inspiration for our human inventions. The paper begins with a description of Mumford's perspective. This description is embedded within an expression of the spirit of the building momentum of our technical inventions, their seductions, and present costs. The paper seeks to respond to Mumford's invitation for us to become much more conscious of the cultural and political forces that cluster around the creation and use of technology. The psychodramatic method of unscripted drama

DOI: 10.4018/978-1-61350-465-9.ch001

is used so as to access the affective, kinaesthetic and cognitive aspects of people's experiences with the machine. Rather ambitiously, a condensed and selective version of these dramas is presented as a short story. Central and surprising dynamics in the story are discussed.

ON THE ORIGINS AND EVOLUTION OF TECHNICS

The critical moment was man's discovery of his own many-faceted mind, and his fascination with what he found there. Images that were independent of those that his eyes saw, rhythmic and repetitive body movements that served no immediate function but gratified him, remembered actions he could repeat more perfectly in fantasy and then after many rehearsals carry out. (Mumford, 1966, p. 45)

The ape still bashes the nut with a stick, the bird twigs its nest; not one of the instinctual habits of mammal or dinosaur has ever concocted a screw, a water wheel, or a knitting needle. "Technics has been deeply modified at every stage of its development by dreams, wishes, impulses, religious motives that spring directly, not from the practical needs of daily life, but from the recesses of man's unconscious… It was initially through the fabrication of the mind, through dream and symbol, not alone through the cunning of his hands, that man learned to command his own bodily organs, to communicate and cooperate with his kind, and to master so much of the natural environment as would serve his actual needs and ideal purposes" (Mumford, 1970, pp. 415-416).

Our inner impulses met the physical world in art, symbols, ritual, machines, architecture and institutional structures. The knitting needle, the pipe and the screw; lathes, looking glasses and the compass scriber - incredible things were invented. We designed watches and printing presses and in one stupendous leap of inspiration, a weav-

ing loom was conceived with the patterning of the cloth replicated into a card that directed the sequence of the weaving operations; an astonishing synthesis of engineering with symbol. It was then a short trip down the cascade of creativity to the new breed of thing that is language and logic mechanised - the computer. We appear to have achieved the ultimate God-act and made in our own image; and, we work to give it eyes and ears and skin so it may take in more. As a seed guides the impulse that springs into the magnificence of a tree, so a spontaneous momentum, of perhaps more distant origins than we can easily imagine, coagulates around the infancy of this computer artefact, the nature of its growth to maturity we can only just begin to perceive.

We are well aware of the double-edged nature of new things: when the foot has a boot and the footpath is flat, the ankles become weak; when the calculator is handy, the brain doesn't get exercised as it once did; when the cellphone connects us at every place to every other place, it seems even harder to be present at any one place. Cars destroy street football; speed shrinks space and the dross-scape spreads. The world won't be tidy and uniform. No two pine trees are the same, no snowflake, no galaxy; and so it seems too, every piece of technology resists all efforts to reduce its presence in the world—COBOL lives on, plugs, data compression algorithms, digital formats and hardware devices—all, proliferate.

Still it is claimed that technology will release us from mindless, repetitive drudgery; and, the next product imminent will ease our burdens and save us from the messes we have made. As long as blood runs in our veins, we will invent and innovate our way forwards. And more so, as Mumford (1970) declares, it is our essential nature to transcend the limits of our biological nature "and to be ready if necessary to die in order to make such transcendence possible" (p. 434).

Mumford alerted us to the grave peril of the megamachine; a pentagon of power, prestige, property, productivity and profit. He takes us on a historical journey to illustrate its genesis in Egyptian pyramid building; human work units as bits in a vast production. Fifty years on from Mumford's warning and these historic forces still have clout.

Safety is pursued for its own sake and so is not safe because difficult problems are avoided, worst case fantasies run riot in the vacuum of anonymity, and simplistic and premature solutions cause more madness. The media meddles with power. Bureaucrats won't deal directly with real people. Democracy is imposed as a global fix-it all and education is equated with moral superiority. We push freedom of speech without responsibility for speech or freedom of hearing. We are spectators to our own images and labelled antiquated if we are not frantic with busyness. Work has been made a dirty word; craftsmanship archaic; apprenticeship replaced by learning grubs that no human hand need contaminate. The professional can't be trusted.

It is easy to list such a wild litany of ills. Much is debatable. Different criteria could be raised, a different lens of selective inattention applied, and quite a different view constructed. It is presumptuous to have confidence in any assessment on the state of things when we don't know what we don't know, nor the extent of things that have been washed out of the collective habit: the vitality of the body when hardened feet and strong ankles meet the ground; the vision of a starry night sky without the buzz of a single light bulb; the science of the dimension in depth; the satisfaction of craftsmanship; the reverence of mildness, the art of going slow, the valuing of the emotional life of a single word. To believe that the current monstrosity of facts is proof of increased knowledge only indicates that a new and puerile ideology has displaced worn out superstitions in the slice of the brain that appears to need such things.

Some would blame technology and our absorption in it for our loneliness and unnatural plight but Mumford (1970) does not: "I have emphasized the technodrama, it is not because I have accepted the technocratic belief that the command of nature is man's most important task, but because I regard technology as a formative part of human culture as a whole" (p. 415). Mumford's eloquence of analysis impels the interested reader to recognise that technology per se is intimately integrated within the creative and humane elements of civilisation. He called for a detachment and withdrawal that would "lead to the assemblage of an organic world picture, in which the human personality in all its dimensions will have primacy over its biological needs and technological pressures" (p. 423). He did not say this was simple: "To describe even in the barest outline the multitude of changes necessary to turn the power complex into an organic complex, and a money economy into a life economy, lies beyond the capacities of any individual mind."

As one response to Mumford's challenge, the work described in this paper forms an inquiry into the stories we are making about the machine. Joseph Campbell held that of all the significant things within the human experience, only technology had not yet a story that had stabilised into a myth or archetype. Mumford (1970) suggests such a formulation would be challenging as "Man's marvellous achievements in projecting his subjective impulses into institutional forms, aesthetic symbols, mechanical organizations, and architectural structures....defies any extensive description, since it involves nothing less than the entire history of mankind" (p. 420).

In recent years, the science fiction movie has captured the greatest public attention. Philip K. Dick's stories were an early inspiration for the movie makers. His stories are a continuation of the age-old story of the slaves' uprising, re-worked into a vision of the future where the subservient machine turns master blaster. In the Matrix, humans are farmed to juice the machine. In Terminator, Blade Runner, Star Trek, Star Wars, I-Robot and many others, the luminal space between human and machine identity is enacted in many varied forms. We have the machine as cute juvenile, bumbling savant, cold fact compiler, and monolithic terroriser. In many of these stories, the future is presented as very frightening and inhumane. It would be unnecessarily cruel to fuel that and create any kind of self-fulfilling prophesy. It is, therefore, worthwhile to see if we can tap the emergent story if only to fill the moment with awareness and so more effectively analyse the potentialities and be more conscious and purposeful in our acts of creativity. Rilke whispers words of advice:

You must give birth to your images.

They are the future waiting to be born.

Fear not the strangeness that you feel.

The future must enter you long before it happens.

Mumford (1970) says, "to pass from what is internal, unconscious, and private, to a public world which can be shared by other men is the next stage in materialization. At this point, the nascent idea, well before it can find words to express itself, first does so in the language of the body." (pp. 422).

In order to tap the affect and kinaesthetic urges as well as the cognitive elements that are surfacing in the common person, unscripted drama was used.

THE ENACTMENTS

I put out an invitation through different networks for people to meet up and co-create unscripted dramas relating to what 'the machine' meant to them. Three groups met. Each group had a mixture of gender, age and attitude to technology. As a psychodramatist, I led the group and emphasised a rolling production where group members responded to the unfolding drama and took up new roles as whim, motivation, and imagination took them.

The productions resembled sociodramas in that they focused on the identification of values and relationship dynamics expressed within group as relating to a topic area. They differed from typical sociodramas in that there was no framing of the situation as a problem area and therefore one needing solutions. There were, however, explorations of different perceptions and interventions.

Sociodrama is part of the psychodramatic method invented by J. L. Moreno (1953) at the beginning of the 20th Century. Moreno wanted a practical means for the evoking, experiencing and sustaining of spontaneity. He saw that it is spontaneity that mobilises the emotions and intelligence and breathes life into the soul. He saw it as a force that pre-dated objects, space and time and is non-conservable and non-casual.

On the psychodramatic stage, expression occurs through different techniques of dramatic production. This has several advantages. Expression can be integrative of thoughts, feelings and physical action. Any aspect can be singled out and emphasised. Action can be emphasised and ponderous thinking thwarted. The producer may encourage the protagonist like this: "Express yourself now, right away, without thinking, again, express immediately what your experience is; don't pre-empt it, express what is arising in you now, and now, again and again." Other times, the process is slowed down or paused and precise, fine grained thinking is emphasised. The inner world is produced in sculptures and images. This production can be worked with in ways not accessible in internal processes: perspective can be generated, elements moved around and rearranged, relationships played with and changed, new elements introduced or transferred from other situations.

I used this method to produce several dramas with the three groups. I then took various metaphors, images, actions and characters from the dramas and created a story. The story contains elements that were common across the dramas but is not inclusive of all that was produced. There are also elements in the story that were not present in the dramas; these were drawn from my thinking, reading, and work over some years (Carter, 2002a, 2002b, 2007).

The construction of a story from psychodramatic productions is not typically part of the psychodramatic method. It could be considered a hybrid with the ethnotheatre tradition which *focuses on giving a live performance of significant selections of narrative collected during research* (Saldaña, 2005). In this case, the material was collected from several psychodramas. This appears to be the first instance of these two related approaches being used together in this way.

The story is presented not only as entertainment and material for analysis and reflection, but also as an invitation to participate. Please take the bits you like, change bits if you want, add your own bits; make a story that is satisfying to you. That, said J.L. Moreno, is the value of an art work; it's ability to inspire further acts of creativity.

THE STORY

A family were going to a picnic in a car.

'Look, what was that?' Dad asked. 'Was it a Porsche? Maybe a Jag?'

But Daughter was texting and Son was playing a computer game.

'What?' Dad said. 'Aren't you interested in cars? When I was young, we used to have so much fun in the car. We'd guess the brands of cars. Were Morrie Minors the most popular or Volkswagens? Some thought Cadillacs were the best. In my day we had great times in the car. We used to sing songs and squabble.'

They went off the main road onto a country road. Mother saw a bird in a tree.

'You don't have cars like you used to. They used to have character back then,' said Father. 'Now they're all the same.'

'Sometimes I think you love cars more than me,' said Mother.

He turned to look at her, the car went off the road and hit a rock. It wouldn't start again. They all got out. Father walked around the car.

'Fix it then.' Mother said.

But he couldn't. He called for help. It wasn't going to come until the next day. That night they slept in the car best they could. The next morning the sun came up. They wound down the windows but it was still very hot.

A Repairman came. He put his toolbox down three steps in front of the car. He paced around the car. He brought out a large piece of paper and opened it out. 'This is not the car that has been scheduled to be fixed.'

'Can't you fix it anyway?' Father looked at the toolbox.

The Repairman shook his head.

'It's a long way to come out,' said Father.

'Exactly.' He folded his schedule and put it in his toolbox.

'What about us?' said Mother.

'We can't take responsibility for you.' He picked up his toolbox and left.

The next morning, the sun came up like a very large eye. Another Repairman came. He put his toolbox down three steps in front of the car. He paced around the car. He brought out the schedule and opened it out. 'What happened?'

'It won't start,' said Father.

'But it has not ended its warrantee. It cannot be a problem of the car but a problem of the way it was used.'

'We hit a rock,' said Son.

'Ah ha,' said the Second Repairman. He folded up his schedule and picked up his toolbox.

'But you can't go,' said Mother.

'I cannot fix a car that isn't broken.'

'That's ridiculous,' said Father.

'Do I look happy?' said the Second Repairman. 'How do you think it is all on my own out here?'

'We have been here for two days,' said Mother.

'Does the sun ever go down on the machine? Does a machine ever complain? We have no right to be weak, we must grit our teeth and do our duty.'

'The machine is to serve us,' said Mother. 'To help us with the washing, to get us to picnics.'

'To make us go fast,' said Father.

But there was no way to convince the Second Repairman to stay and fix the car. There was not a cloud in the sky. He left. It was very hot and dry.

That night, the moon was full. Daughter dropped the apple she was eating. She picked it up and took a bite all the way through the skin to the core.

The next morning, the sun came up. Of course, it was bigger and hotter and drier. A man came. He had a rope.

'What's the rope for?' asked Daughter.

'It a comfort thing.' The Man had the rope around his foot like a sling. 'It keeps me amused.'

'Can I use it for a clothesline?' asked Mother.

'Sure,' said Ropeman.

'Can you repair cars?' asked Father.

'Yes, but I need oil.'

'I have a litre in the back.'

'I need four.'

'You can have my Son as an Apprentice,' said Father. 'He isn't good with words. He's not gifted as a guard, he doesn't want to be a doctor, let him learn how to fix the machine. What other kind of work is there?'

'To work is senseless because money cannot be obtained through work but through exploitation of others. If we cannot exploit as much as we wish, at least let us work as little as we can. For the weak work for the strong, and if they have no strength or will to work, then let them steal or let them die.'

'What!'

'I believe neither in the morality of man, nor in the morality of systems.'

'Do you believe in cars?'

'Machines give me comfort; to fix them is worship.'

'Then fix ours.'

'We have to synchronize the gears. We must work out how to mesh the gears. Can you help me? Can you humour me? Could you become the different parts of the car?'

'I don't know,' said Mother, but she did anyway.

One person was a rod, another a gear, someone else a wheel, someone a piston. They jostled and poked, turned and moved around. They laughed a lot and almost fell in a heap. This was what Father had in mind for the picnic all the time. Even Mother was having a good time.

'Even you are having a good time,' Father said.

'Yes, so strange. I feel free,' said Mother.

A Researcher appeared with a questionnaire on service satisfaction. He made them read the consent forms and he told them they always had a choice; they didn't have to contribute to knowledge and human progress if they didn't want to. They signed the consent forms and filled in the questionnaire.

'I will be recommending improvements,' said the Researcher. 'Do you know they are developing an engine that speaks to you; an engine that can fix itself. Imagine that?'

'We want it to work for us now,' said Mother.

'We are even working on a replacement for the…' The Researcher winked at Father. 'Something that will never complain.'

But Father didn't say anything.

'It is our tools that have made us great,' said the Researcher. 'If we can, then we must.'

'We just want to get to the beach for a picnic,' Mother said.

'Oh, don't you know?' The Researcher picked up a rock. 'This is the beach. This is the old shoreline.'

'Where's the water?' said Daughter.

'It's been split into fuel and burnt. Unfortunate.'

'The planet has been bled?' said Father.

'What about the fish and everything,' said Daughter.

'We're the last living things left.'

Father fell to his knees and cried. 'We should have listened. We should have paid attention to the signs.'

'All I've tried to do is look after everyone and make them safe,' said Mother.

'Nothing left?' said Daughter. 'Not even crabs?'

'Crabs,' said Son who was piling rocks into a pile.

That gave Ropeman a different idea. He made a new thing out of bits. He whistled while he worked to give it a body and legs. He put it down on the dried-out beach.

'Look!' said Son. 'A crab.'

And Daughter laughed and played with it too.

Father was standing with his head and arms raised to the whole round world. 'We have got to get into relationship.'

Simple are the legs of the crab, and the mind of the crab, but complex the terrain. The children played with the crab because eternity is a very long time.

DISCUSSION

Life

The most surprising thing to myself and many of the participants was the life that arose in the people enacting the actual machine. In most cases, the humans in the system – repairmen, drivers, schedulers – were low in vitality. They were working on their own, isolated and unsupported. This was in contrast to the people enacting the machine - whether it was a vending machine or a car – each one was typically 'concretised' by many people. This was done without direction; it emerged.

The impact of movement was also very noticeable in the enactments. Life came to people when they moved, and movement came when a machine was being enacted.

A third factor in this dynamic was voiced in the de-brief at the end of the enactments. One participant said, 'I was so surprised when I became the vending machine. It was fun. I didn't expect that because normally I don't like machines, but

I had such fun. It was like a holiday. I didn't have to think or prove anything. I could have gone on like for a long time. There was no fatigue.' Others described it as an ego-free state, lacking pressure, a release from the burden of being human.

There are signs of an impulse becoming manifest that is perhaps a new persona for the machine that is different from the existing forms that have been presented in film and books. Perhaps this portrayal of the machine is a maturing of the cute, childlike and naive robots as portrayed in Lost in Space and Star Wars. There is a similar blend of freedom, movement and friendliness.

Why would these things - movement, freedom and community - be projected onto and associated with the machine? Interestingly the car was a central part in two enactments. Many psychodramatic enactments of important family events are also situated in the car (Clayton & Carter, 2004). The car has joined the dining table as a common location for the family get together and so would be firming up this association with the machine. The initial scene in the story of a family in a car was inspired by a participant saying that the purpose of technology was to help families go on picnics. This is in contrast to the dominant rhetoric that has the original and sustaining purpose of technology as control and meeting survival needs.

The experience of relief in being a machine also appears to be a convenient escape from the burden of responsibility that comes with being the modern human being. Perhaps a return to what Mumford (1966) saw as our more rational and humble animal inheritance.

THE NATURE OF THINGS: THE MOON, THE SUN AND THE HUMAN BEING

The scene of Daughter eating an apple is offered as an image of our understanding of the nature of things. The apple is dropped at the same time the moon is full. It was Newton's fascination with the moon's path that made the falling apple evocative of his epiphany of the laws of motion in a constant space and time universe. The description of her taking *a bite all the way through the skin to the core* is provoked by a saying of Goethe—*nature has neither core nor skin: she's both at once outside and in*—a poetic forerunner of Einstein's finding that the centre of the universe is at every point. In the story, the apple metaphor is not obvious and is not given any importance in terms of plot. This reflects the enactments where no definitive formulation on the nature of things was produced.

Joseph Campbell (1972) describes a key event in the recent evolution of our consciousness.

Along with – and as a consequence of – this loss of essential identity with the organic divine being of a living universe, man has been given, or rather has won for himself, release to an existence of his own, endued with a certain freedom of will. And he has been set thereby in relationship to a deity, apart from himself, who also enjoys free will. The gods of the great Orient, as agents of the cycle, are hardly more than supervisors, personifying and administering the processes of the cycle that they neither put in motion nor control. But when, as now, we have a deity who, on the contrary, can decide on his own to send down a flood because the people he has made have become wicked, himself delivering laws, judging, and administering punishment, we are in a totally new situation. A radical shift of consciousness has bathed the universe and everything in it in a new, more brilliant light – like the light of a sun, blotting out the moon, the planets, and the other lights of the stars. And this new light, in the centuries then following, penetrated and transformed the whole world westward of Iran (p. 76)

The sun is a regular presence in the story. Through the words of the technical evangelist repairman, the machine has replaced England as the empire that the sun never sets on. The sun

gets hotter each day. And the final scene is of a dried-up beach.

The centrality of a sun consciousness to the megamachine was stressed by Mumford (1970). He describes that when Copernicus re-asserted the sun as central source and Newton fixed absolutism, order was given beauty, the universe was considered mechanical and interdependent of man. The sun cult was resurrected, the megamachine re-assembled and immense concentration has been given to the mastery of earthly life, exploration, invention, conquest, colonization and immediate satisfaction. Change and progress were the royal commands. "Change itself became not merely a fact of nature – as it is – but an urgent human value; and to resist change or to retard it in any way was to 'go against nature' – and ultimately to endanger man by defying the Sun God and denying his commands. On these assumptions, since progress was ordained by Heaven, regression was no longer possible" (p. 208).

The story highlights the ideology of progress by having the Researcher embedding it in ethical practice and using choice and consent as weapons of moral condemnation. *He made them read the consent forms and he told them they always had a choice. They didn't have to contribute to knowledge and human progress if they didn't want to.*

As in the enactments, the story offers no strong candidate for an orientating and effective political structure for the future. Interestingly, nationalistic pride was linked with car brands in two of the three groups of participants. The Father expresses nationalism through car brands at the beginning but no other character in the story is interested. The emergent global consciousness is hinted at in the Father gestating to the whole world at the end. However, no other character is drawn towards that either.

Mumford (1970) comments on the difficulty inherent in democracy when it is applied on a large scale: democracy "is in every respect the precise opposite of the anonymous, de-personalised, mainly invisible forms of mass association, mass communication, mass organisation. But as soon as large numbers are involved, democracy must either succumb to external control and centralised direction, or embark on the difficult task of delegating authority to a cooperative organisation" (p. 236).

In the story, the Mother's lament about her one goal having been the safety of the family is an illustration of the actual result of the half-hearted risk avoidance and survival focus that has colonised institutional ethics. These products of threat-possessed ideologies can be compared with the results of adventure, companionship and creativity that arise such as in the last scene.

The Evolution of the Creator

Much of the last scene is taken directly from the end of an enactment: an old beach was found, a child pointed out that there weren't crabs, a maverick built a crab, the children played with it, and a character raised his hands to the whole world lamenting about the lack of relationship even as that very thing was occurring beneath his nose. The creation of the crab and the children's response is the climax of the story. Creation is of central importance in the story.

We have in our descriptions of God throughout history, our highest concerns and most revered sense of ourselves. Beginning with a God primarily dedicated to justice and might, we then found a God who was the Word, then a God of compassion, and now She appears to be the Creator. J. L. Moreno, the inventor of psychodrama, argued that God the Creator could not exist without having put Himself into the form of His creation. "More important than the evolution of creation is the evolution of the creator". Moreno saw that the dignity of humankind had been degraded through the taking on findings of science in certain ways. We had taken Copernicus and Galileo to mean that the Earth was out on the periphery, that Darwin had us descending from apes, that Mendel revealed a lottery, and Freud gave us the final degradation in saying we were mere victims of unconscious

sexual impulses. Moreno wanted humans back in the centre of things again as I-Gods.

The Ropeman is the creator in the story. The source for the Ropeman was an enactment where a participant introduced the role of a playful and resourceful maverick with a fascination for mechanical things and a kind of humorous cynicism. I took the element of cynicism to an extreme by giving Ropeman some of the words of Tadeusz Borowski (1976). Borowski is unusual in writers of the modern horror of the concentration camp, in that he has been able to describe the realms of the inmate who has gained some leverage of power or small privilege in return for doing some abhorrent task. The Ropeman was given this level of cynicism to see if he will be accepted as having creative and generative qualities. I am motivated by the commitment to a future where all will be included and none will be excluded. It is the spirit of the psychodramatic stage. It is an explicit attempt to counter all forms of exclusion, moral superiority, elitism and scapegoating in which untold atrocities on families have been justified. Inclusion must be tested and it must be tested with the very ones we find it hardest to include.

The Dignity of Work

The story attempts a movement towards a restoration of the dignity of work. Work is first portrayed by the Repairmen; uninvolved and unconcerned with real humans. The Father summarises the types of work, apart from drone, that are available in a stripped down world as has been documented by survivors of the Lager and the Gulag. 'But he isn't good with words. He's not gifted as a guard, he doesn't want to be a doctor, let him learn how to fix the machine. What other kind of work is there?'

The Father sees the Ropeman as someone who can offer an apprenticeship to his son. We do not find out if the Ropeman accepts this but we do see him whistle while he works. He enjoys his work. He is inspired by the children. So, although deeply cynical and isolated, he responds. The creative act emerges from a friendly social field.

Relationship and Dwelling

The value of relationship is emerging as an underlying impulse that has inspired many profound scientific revelations of recent times. Darwin's primary perception evoking the theory of evolution was that everything in nature grows from relationship. Martin Buber even lays claims for relationship in a domain that the physicists think is under their sole, specialist care: *All real living is in the meeting. Meeting is not in time and space, but space and time are in meeting.* When Einstein proved the centre was everywhere, we were back in the very centre of things again but with everything else there as well.

In the story, the crab is born from a social impulse. It comes into its being and behaviour in an environment; what Tim Ingold (2000) calls dwelling. *Simple are the legs of the crab, and the mind of the crab, but complex the terrain* is the line in the story that hints at the intricacy and breadth of knowledge that grows when the self interacts with something other than the self. It is the first breeze that awakens the form of movement in a butterfly's new wings (Simon, 1996). It appears that even the 'social self', the neural template upon which each individual experiences their social worlds, is hardwired in response to their first social field (Schore, 1994).

This simple truth of things places a tight boundary on the answer to the question of machine intelligence and consciousness. With such an impoverished sensitivity to other things that aren't, so few elements of the environment can be taken in. Not until we give it holes—eyes, ears, skin, heart—does the machine begin to even approach the sophistication of a fly. It will remain for sometime closest to the consciousness of a rock, a binary movement of swelling with heat and shrinking with cold.

Of course, the complexity of the environment must also be matched within as evidenced by Mesulan's (1998) description of the human brain:

Sensory information undergoes extensive associative elaboration and attentional modulation as it becomes incorporated into the texture of cognition. This process occurs along a core synaptic hierarchy which includes the primary sensory, upsteam unimodal, downstream unimodal, heteromodal, paralimbic and limbic zones of the cerebral cortex. Connections from one zone to another are reciprocal and allow higher synaptic levels to exert a feedback (top-down) influence upon earlier levels of processing...The resultant synaptic organisation supports parallel as well as serial processing, and allows each sensory event to initiate multiple cognitive and behavioural outcomes (p. 1013)

Mumford (1970) put it that "no machine, however complex its structure or ingenious its human inventor, can even theoretically be made to replicate a man, for in order to do so it would have to draw upon two or three billion years of diversified experience" (p. 91).

And if the soul exists, then the complexities are not just compounded but we are dealing with an altogether different kind of thing. With increasingly sensitive instruments, perhaps one can expect in the coming years a dedicated study of the soul-body interface. Like the physical parts of a radio set, such things as the DNA might be discovered as one of the many mechanisms of transformation and not the driver.

If soul is the case, a test of machine consciousness could be: *when dropped, does it try to fly?* Has soul found the mechanism in the thing that welcomes embodiment?

Life Again

The remarkable thing in the enactments was the life and vitality there was in those playing the machine; and this occurred for people who have no great affection for computers, cellphones, or cars.

Life is not able to be suppressed, controlled, or even bargained with. It is renewal itself. It must transform. Life springs forth on the inside of nuclear reactor chimneys and deep down in toxic dumps. In *The Immense Journey,* Loren Eiseley describes what happened when warm blooded beasts began to suckle their young and flowers and grasses spread out all over the earth. Nectars, pollens, seeds, fruits and succulent leaves dilated the senses, quickened the appetite and exhilarated the mind. He argued that such floral beauty cannot be justified on purely utilitarian grounds. They exist for their own sake and transcend the organism's earlier limitations.

If survival were all that mattered, life might well have never crept out of the primeval ooze. If safety, surety and predictability where the main motivators, then the very first thing did not need to be differentiated or divided. There would be one thing only, whatever it was, that would be it. Something else was more attractive: the delight of surprise, the need for relationship, the joy of homecoming? We continue to search for the answer perhaps because, as Swimme and Berry (1992) present in *The Universe Story,* the mind that searches for contact with the Milky Way may well be the very mind of the Milky Way in search of its own inner depths. The co-evoked, emergent and irreversible nature of the universe is getting presented to us in its deep mystery by scientists. It is the scientists and the writers who now offer pathways for the experience of reverence and awe. The shaman and the priest have been replaced. Mumford (1966) shines light on the dark side of the human impulse:

a broad streak of irrationality that runs all through human history, counter to man's sensible, functionally rational animal inheritance. As compared even with other anthropoids, we might refer without irony to man's superior irrationality. Certainly human development exhibits a chronic

disposition to error, mischief, disordered fantasy, hallucination, 'original sin,' and even socially organized and sanctified mis-behavior, such as the practice of human sacrifice and legalized torture. In escaping organic fixations, man forfeited the innate humility and mental stability of less adventurous species. Yet some of his most erratic departures have opened up valuable areas that purely organic evolution, over billions of years, had never explored (pp. 10-11)

It might seem that the human being is so complex to evade replication...

WRAP UP

Only a few aspects of the enactments made it to the story and only a few aspects of the story have been discussed. The paper is an opener. The test of its value will be in the engagement and response of the readers; what it provoke or evokes in them; whether it encourages the generation of another story.

The computer might have grown out of the landscapes of the imagination but it is now external, living on its own, and so it returns to the imagination a new thing, a fresh source of inspiration and fantasy. William Blake's question must now be turned on us: *Did he who made the Lamb, make thee?* There is a new space between, a new kind of reciprocity that has life because life and motivation rise from within when there is movement, engagement and participation.

The main message of the enactments is that 'the machine' has life for us. The human fascination with the machine is not over. Technology per se is not equated with isolation from nature, domination, or destruction of life. We have a companion of our own making and it may well result in us seeing ourselves clearer and shedding unwanted habits. The future is wide open within the vehicle history is propelling us forwards in.

REFERENCES

Borowski, T. (1976). *This Way for the Gas, Ladies and Gentlemen*. New York: Penguin.

Campbell, J. (1972). *Myths to Live By*. New York: Penguin Compass.

Carter, P. (2007). Liberating usability testing. *Interaction, 14*(2), 18–22. doi:10.1145/1229863.1229864

Carter, P. D. (2002a). *Encounters with computers: A psychodramatic adventure*. Unpublished psychodrama thesis, Auckland University of Technology, Australian and New Zealand Psychodrama Association.

Carter, P. D. (2002b). Building Purposeful Action: Action Methods and Action Research. *Educational Action Research: An International Journal, 10*(2), 207–232. doi:10.1080/09650790200200180

Clayton, G. M., & Carter, P. D. (2004). *The Living Spirit of the Psychodramatic Method*. Auckland, New Zealand: Resource Books.

Eiseley, L. (1946). *The Immense Journey*. New York: Vintage.

Ingold, T. (2000). *The Perception of the Environment: Essays on livelihood, dwelling and skill*. London: Routledge.

Jung, C. J. (1954). *Answer to Job*. London: Routledge.

Mesulan, M. (1998). From sensation to cognition. *Brain, 121*, 1013–1052. doi:10.1093/brain/121.6.1013

Moreno, J. L. (1953). *Who shall survive?* New York: Beacon House.

Mumford, L. (1966). *The Myth of the Machine: Volume One: Technics and Human Development*. New York: Harcourt.

Mumford, L. (1970). *The Myth of the Machine: Volume Two: The Pentagon of Power*. New York: Harcourt.

Saldaña, J. (2005). An introduction to Ethnodrama. In Saldaña, J. (Ed.), *Ethnodrama: An anthology of reality theatre* (pp. 1–36). Walnut Creek, CA: AltaMira Press.

Schore, A. N. (1994). *Affect regulation and the origin of the self: The neurobiology of emotional development*. Hillsdale, NJ: Erlbaum.

Simon, H. A. (1996). *The Sciences of the Artificial* (3rd ed.). Cambridge, MA: MIT Press.

Swimme, B., & Berry, T. (1992). *The Universe Story*. New York: Harper Collins.

This work was previously published in International Journal of Technology and Human Interaction, Volume 6, Issue 2, edited by Anabela Mesquita & Chia-Wen Tsai, pp. 1-12, copyright 2010 by IGI Publishing (an imprint of IGI Global).

Chapter 2

Does Anybody Read SMS–Advertising?
A Qualitative and Quantitative Study of Mobile Users' Attitudes and Perceived Ad–Clutter

Claire Gauzente
Institute of Political Sciences of Rennes, France & ESC Rennes School of Business, France

ABSTRACT

This study explores mobile users' perceptions about SMS advertising. The empirical study uses a double methodology. First, a qualitative study using the Q-method is conducted. Qualitative analysis reveals that negative attitudes are commonly shared, and that ad-clutter is perceived critically. Therefore, in a second step, a quantitative study is adopted to assess the impact of attitudes towards SMS advertising and perceived ad-clutter on reading behaviour. The main test is conducted over a representative sample of 302 mobile owners. From a behavioural standpoint, the results show ambivalent behaviour in most cases. In particular, the role of perceived ad-clutter is ascertained. Implications for practice and directions for future research are discussed.

INTRODUCTION

"SMS ads? Nobody reads them!" This assertion seems taken for granted in public opinion. And yet, marketers still consider it a promising marketing and advertising avenue. SMS—short message service—advertising is part of the larger picture of mobile advertising, which is defined as "a form of advertising that is communicated to

DOI: 10.4018/978-1-61350-465-9.ch002

the consumer/target via a handset. This type of advertising is most commonly seen as a Mobile Web Banner, Mobile Web Poster.../.... Other forms of this type of advertising are SMS and MMS ads, mobile gaming ads, and mobile video ads" (MMA Global, glossary version 068). A definition of SMS advertising is provided by Barwise and Strong (2002), who describe it as a "text-based advertisement on cell phone". Although unsophisticated, text messaging has "found itself centre stage in contemporary social life" (Taylor & Vincent, 2004), as well as in the advertising arena.

Global mobile advertising spending is expected to reach $2.4 billion in 2009, up from $1 billion in 2008 (strategyanalytics.com, August 2008). Similar research from eMarketer goes much further by accounting for the growing economies of Brazil, Russia, India, and China. It expects total mobile advertising expenses (including creative, IT, and other related spending costs) to reach $6.44 billion in 2009, rising to $19.15 billion in 2012 (emarketer.com). In this context, SMS appears to be the most attractive medium for advertising (Mobile Marketing Association, MMA, 2009), along with Multimedia Message Service (MMS). Whatever the exact figures, they demonstrate high expectations. Average response rates are considered to be high (around 10%) (Nokia Network, 2008), which is far better than alternative media but also means that 90% of these messages get no response from mobile users. That is why it is crucial to understand users' reactions to mobile phone advertising and, more specifically, to its main form: SMS advertising.

Taking into account the type of ad (simple versus rich text) and the pull- or push-orientation of the campaign (whereas push message are unidirectional messages, pull messages call the receiver to action), Barnes (2002) indicates that SMS is a simple ad tool that is preferentially used in push marketing. Despite its basic and push characteristics, SMS entails several advantages from both the consumer and marketing standpoints. From the marketer's point of view, SMS is a fairly cheap means of contact. The automation of a campaign makes it easy to distribute messages to the target audience. Even if there is some delay in message delivery, up to 6 hours according to Scharl et al. (2005), the technology is considered reliable and rapid. Two other characteristics of interest are time and space independence, in the sense that there is no restriction on the time when SMS are sent and geographical distance is not an issue—SMS can be sent to anywhere from anywhere in the world.

This means that a campaign can be launched at any time (although certain experts consider the time of sending to be important, Scharl et al., 2005) and will be received wherever the consumer may be. From the consumer's standpoint, SMS has the potential to be well accepted, provided that advertisers have received permission to send the ads. So, once consent is granted to the sender, consumers will receive messages supposedly tailored to their needs. SMS messaging is nonintrusive, as people are not obliged to answer immediately; it leaves consumers free to discover the message where and when they want. As messages are short by nature, the consumer may not feel overwhelmed by SMS advertising. With SMS messages, a consumer is not forced to engage in social interaction, as is the case with telephone campaigns.

These advantages are clearly recognised by firms and other multinational actors as an opportunity to build their brands (Okazaki & Taylor, 2008). However, their hopes can be realised only if consumers accept SMS advertising, read it, and perceive it positively. It is therefore of primary importance to understand consumer perceptions of SMS advertising. The number of research articles dealing with mobile marketing and advertising has increased tremendously since 2002. However, to the best of our knowledge, few qualitative studies of the perceptions of SMS advertising are available. At the same time, informal observations often yield conflicting conclusions about consumer acceptance of SMS advertising. An in-depth study of consumer subjectivity about SMS advertising is thus needed to guide further investigation.

The present study delivers qualitative knowledge about SMS advertising perceptions. It emphasises not only the role of attitude, which is a classical variable in the study of behaviour, but also the role of perceived ad-clutter, a variable originating from the field of advertising research and defined as the belief that the amount of advertising is unwarranted. The remainder of the paper is organised in four main parts. First, it reviews the available literature about mobile and

SMS advertising. Second, it describes a qualitative study that uses the Q-method to investigate mobile users' subjectivity. Third, it builds on the results of this qualitative study to test quantitatively the role of the variables identified via the Q-study. Lastly, it discusses the limits of the study and the managerial and research implications of both the qualitative and quantitative results.

LITERATURE REVIEW

Although the theoretical key success factors have long been known, there is still a gap in our understanding of why most mobile users do not read SMS advertising, and many even avoid it.

Theoretical Key Success Factors

Developing successful mobile marketing models is essential for practitioners (Becker et al., 2005; Scharl et al., 2005). The identification of key success factors and the assessment of their impact within mobile marketing is still of interest.

A synthetic view suggests that there are five types of variables that contribute to mobile campaign success: sender characteristics, receiver characteristics, message characteristics, and media and technology characteristics.

Sender characteristics refer to the source of the message (Milne & Rohm, 2003; Tsang et al., 2004; Rettie et al., 2005). The success of a mobile campaign depends on the interest in the branded product or service, the brand's reputation and credibility, and its privacy policy. Receiver characteristics pertain to individual factors, such as demographics, personality, motives, and attitudes (Barwise & Strong, 2002; Bruner & Kumar, 2003; Tsang et al., 2004; Kleijnen et al., 2004; Rettie et al., 2005; Tähti et al., 2005; Bauer, 2005; Merisavo, 2007; Peters, 2007; Gauzente et al., 2008; Wei, 2009). Message characteristics refer to the message's content and form: whether it is simple or rich, entertaining, informative, push- or pull-oriented (Barnes, 2002; Tsang et al., 2004; Kleijnen et al., 2004; Scharl et al., 2005; Rettie et al., 2005). Media and technology characteristics correspond to both technical and perceived features (Buellinger & Woerter, 2002; Scharl et al., 2005). The technical features on some phones may allow certain types of advertising that other devices do not, because of display limitations, for instance. The fact that not all users are equipped with up-to-date devices should be taken into account. In addition to this, the ease of use and perceived complexity of their devices also affect the way users accept and behave when receiving SMS advertising. Finally, environmental characteristics have also been proved to be of importance (Barnes, 2002; Drossos et al., 2007; Merisavo et al., 2007). Users respond differently to a message depending upon when and where it is received.

All of the aforementioned variables are essential in understanding mobile marketing success or failure, and they are also relevant for the study of user reactions to SMS advertising. However, of these variables, the following have been empirically tested and proved significant in most quantitative studies: complexity and compatibility (Kleijnen et al., op. cit.), perceived risk (Kleijnen et al., op. cit.; Bauer, 2005), and utility and sacrifice (Merisavo et al., op. cit.). Gratification is also important (Peters, op. cit.; Wei, 2009); it entails aspects such as entertainment (Tsang et al., op. cit.; Bauer, op. cit.), information (Bauer, op. cit.), and social benefits (Bauer, op. cit.).

The role of these variables has been reported within the context of "standard" models. As a matter of fact, most, if not all, underlying theoretical models are hierarchical models of the following type: attitude→ intention→behaviour. They are derived from the Technology Acceptance Model (Davis, 1989) or Theory of Reasoned Approach and Theory of Planned Behaviour (Fishbein & Ajzen, 1975; Ajzen, 1985). In the extant literature, these models have all been applied to the same underlying research question, that is, what drives the success of SMS advertising and user acceptance? It would also be interesting to investigate what drives resistance and avoidance behaviour. More generally, taking into account the whole range of the behavioural repertoire towards SMS advertising and investigating what guides different types of behaviour remains necessary.

Understanding Low Response Rates: The Need For Qualitative Inquiry

Even if integrative models of user reaction to mobile solicitations can be sketched, the click-through rate for mobile advertising remains rather low: 10% at best (see Nokia Media Network, 2008). This suggests that users avoid mobile phone advertising most of the time. One explanation may originate from the lack of a deep understanding of user reactions and perceptions. As mentioned previously, most studies of user reactions to mobile marketing have been derived from theoretical models and tested quantitatively (as shown in Table 1), which may result in the lack of a fine-grained understanding of other potentially interesting variables.

We hold that it is important to deepen our qualitative understanding of consumer reactions to mobile marketing. To date, Ling (2005) has been one of the few researchers to carry out qualitative analysis (quantitative sociological knowledge has been produced as well; see Reid & Reid, 2004) of the sociological role of mobile phones in the teen population. However, his research is restricted to teenage users and comes from a sociological standpoint; we need to obtain a similar understanding from a consumption standpoint. The study conducted by Peters et al. (2007) is the only one that addresses this point with a sample of 20 students. Its focus is on wireless advertising, which is a broader subject than SMS advertising, and the interview guide was looking for the perceived advantages of WAM (wireless advertising messages). The results indicate that WAM may be of interest to users who want to be "kept aware" and to feel part of a group or in touch with a company. However, participants would not pay to receive WAM. We intend to proceed in a different way. We do not seek what is potentially advantageous in users' eyes, but what they think about existing SMS ads. Therefore, our questions are: What are the representations associated with SMS advertising as a marketing tool? Is it possible to shed light on the structure

Table 1. Empirical studies of consumers' reactions to mobile services and advertising

Authors	Main topic	Method
Barwise and Strong (2002)	Consumer response to permission based mobile marketing	Quantitative, N=500 Focus groups
Bruner and Kumar (2003)	Consumer acceptance of handheld Internet services	Quantitative, N=212
Kleijnen et al. (2004)	Consumer adoption of wireless services	Quantitative, N=99
Tsang et al. (2004)	Consumer attitude toward mobile advertising	Pre-test, N=30 Quantitative, N=380
Bauer et al. (2005)	Consumer acceptance of mobile advertising	Quantitative, N=1028
Rettie et al. (2005)	Response rates and brand effect of sms-advertising	Quantitative, N=5401
Tähti et al. (2005)	Consumer emotions elicited by mobile services	Qualitative, 3 tests (n=5; n=8, n=48)
Lee et al. (2006)	Customer perception of mobile advertising	Quantitative, N=358
Peters et al. (2007)	Consumers' perception of wireless advertising messages	Qualitative, N=20
Drossos et al. (2007)	Experimental study of SMS advertising	Quantitative, N=97
Merisavo et al. (2007)	Drivers of mobile advertising's acceptance	Pretest, N=90 Quantitative, N=4 062

of subjectivity this topic engenders? Can qualitative investigation orient our quantitative study of user behaviour when receiving SMS advertising?

STUDY ONE: SMS-ADVERTISING SUBJECTIVITY

Q-Method

The Q-method (for more details, see q-method. org and Brown, 1993), which is also called q-methodology, was developed by the psychologist Stephenson (1935; 1953). Contrary to other classical approaches in psychology, where the aim is to objectivise the inner state of an individual, he considered the subjective view most important. He conceived a method aimed at the study of subjectivity. Subjectivity is conceptualised as "statements that emanate from a particular vantage point" (Brown, online).

The Q-method rests on two important pillars: one is theoretical (concourse theory) and the other is methodological (q-sorting procedure and q-factorial analysis). Concourse theory suggests that meaning is dependent upon context and therefore not given *in abstracto*. Concourse can be defined as the volume of available statements on a topic. In other words: "concourse is the common coinage of societies large and small, and is designed to cover everything from community gossip and public opinion to the esoteric discussions of scientists and philosophers" (Brown, op. cit.). Even for one individual, a single word can have several meanings. Depending on circumstances and the individual's mind-set, one meaning will be meant specifically in one context at one moment. What is important to note is that these meanings partly overlap with other people's meanings, and this is what makes interpersonal communication possible.

Based on these considerations, Stephenson suggests that initial qualitative interviews or literature reviews should be conducted to generate

as many meanings (or statements) as possible concerning one topic. These statements can be kept in their original expression; they are called assertions. Altogether, assertions constitute the q-sample. Then, individuals are asked to rank-order assertions according to the degree to which they represent their subjective view of one object or topic (say, the mobile). This ranking procedure, called q-sorting, requires that only a small portion of assertions be selected as highly representative of one's personal vantage point, and only a small portion be selected as badly representative; the majority will be neither representative nor non-representative. The result of the q-sorting process is a q-sort.

Each individual can do several q-sorts. For instance, one individual can be asked to describe his or her view of the mobile, his or her view of his or her mother, and his or her view of his or her grandmother. This allows for case studies.

Factor analysis is then used to analyse the data. This is called q-factor analysis because instead of analysing individuals, statements are analysed. A map of the representations that people have is produced, which helps to identify the different visions that people share. Factor analysis is then used to identify "groups" of individuals (also called q-factors) that share the same vision. In the case of a single-case study, an identification of one individual's different facets of subjectivity concerning one topic is obtained.

In our particular study, we used the Q-method to analyse one q-sort per individual. The study was undertaken during a marketing research class, with 13 students aged from 21 to 24 years old.

Statements concerning SMS-advertising were generated using a focus group technique. They were asked to answer the following general questions: "Could you indicate which ideas SMS-advertising evokes for you?" and "How would/do you feel when receiving such messages on your cell phones?" Twenty-three statements were generated. In a second step, the group went through statements to see which assertions were virtually the same (that is, expressed identical ideas). The aim was not necessarily to reduce the number of assertions, but simply to rationalise, reword or refine certain statements. The number of statements was reduced to 19 through this process. The list of assertions is available in the appendix.

One week later, a q-sort sheet was prepared, and the student participants were asked to classify the 19 assertions concerning SMS-advertising using seven categories ranging from "very similar to my view" to "very unlike my view".

Results

The results can be read from two different standpoints. One is the classical typological point of view from which groups of individuals are interpreted in terms of characteristics linked to commercial SMS. This typological view would necessitate introducing individual descriptive variables, and thus it is not adopted here. Rather,

we focus on the main visions (rather than groups of people) that emerge from the analysis, each of which presents a specific, fine-grained structure of subjectivity. Three visions, also called q-factors, summarised 62 percent of the variance. Table 2 shows how individuals congregate along q-factors.

We are interested in the weight of each assertion in each q-factor. These weights allow us to see that individuals hold either very or slightly different views of SMS advertising. For instance, q-factor B (which comprises individuals 10, 13, and 2) represents a vision that differs dramatically from q-factors A and C, with A and C holding partially overlapping perceptions (see appendix A1, A2, A3).

The rejection of SMS advertising is common to visions A and C. However, it does not take the same form and exteriorisation. Vision A represents a passionate reaction with violent, visceral emotions: "It's unbearable" and "I feel it's harassment".

Table 2. Results of the Q factor analysis

	Factors		
	1	**2**	**3**
Ind08	.776		
Ind01	.767		
Ind05	.724		
Ind03	.696		
Ind06	.624		
Ind07	.531		
Ind11	.477		
Ind10		.869	
Ind13		.773	
Ind02		.636	
Ind12			.847
Ind09			-.673
Ind04			.566
Eigenvalue	3.543	2.703	1.85
% of Variance	27.25	20.789	14.229
Cumulative %	27.25	48.039	62.268

Extraction Method: Principal Component Analysis. Rotation Method: Varimax.

These individuals obviously felt overwhelmed by SMS advertising.

In contrast, vision C represents a more reasoned and justified type of rejection: "It's always an Orange ad" and "It isn't interesting". This position is also accompanied by rejection assertions: "It bothers me", "It's unbearable". A touch of scepticism or of irony surfaces in this vision: "It's only promotion" or "It's always an Orange[1] ad". Taken together, these two visions are shared by 10 out of 13 individuals (that is, 77%).

Vision B, shared by individuals 10, 13, and 2 (that is, only 23%), is much more marginal, but displays a more favourable attitude towards SMS advertising. However, this benevolent view is half-tinted with considerations about the uncontrollable and ill-targeted characteristics of SMS advertising. Despite these potential drawbacks, SMS advertising is seen as informative and useful. This vision is totally unconcerned about intrusiveness and privacy matters.

At this stage of the research, two main conclusions arise. First, the fun and entertaining dimension of certain SMS ads, which is something often described as key to viral effects and SMS advertising success, is not mentioned as adequately describing SMS ads. In the informal feedback and discussion, some of the respondents stressed that supposedly entertaining messages often miss their goal, as they are not humorous.

Second, a demarcation line appears clearly between those who accept SMS advertising and those who do not. This line has to do with perceived ad-clutter and resulting irritation. Both are linked to the frequency of messages, the media (for some respondents, the mobile phone is something very personal, almost intimate), and targeting problems. Here again, managerial evaluations of such limitations of mobile advertising should be developed.

These two main conclusions suggest that we engage in a more quantitative investigation of the behavioural consequences of (1) perceived ad-clutter and, more generally, (2) attitudes towards SMS advertising.

STUDY TWO: THE ROLE OF GENERAL ATTITUDES TOWARDS SMS ADVERTISING AND PERCEIVED AD-CLUTTER IN SMS-READING BEHAVIOUR

Attitudes Towards SMS-Advertising

Attitude towards advertising-in-general (Aag) is defined as *"the audience member's affective reaction to advertising in general"* (Lutz, 1983). Many of the seminal studies dedicated to examining attitudes towards Aag were conducted in the 1950s (Zanot, 1984), and in the main were conducted by institutes such as Gallup or Harris & Associate.

Subsequently, researchers such as Muehling (1987) have emphasised the need to recognise the multidimensional nature of Aag in that it entails not only judgments about advertising (see, for instance, Greyser & Bauer, 1968; Gaski & Etzel, 1986, 2005), but also judgments concerning the tools used to advertise. Researchers such as MacKenzie and Lutz (1989) have provided an integrative model to explain attitudes towards a specific advertisement (Aad), and have shown that Aag transfers to Aad. Additionally, based on their meta-analysis, Brown & Stayman (1989) emphasise that Aad is a powerful predictor of advertising effects. These effects have been shown to comprise not only behavioural consequences but also cognitive and affective consequences (see, for instance, MacInnis & Jaworski, 1989; Vakratsas & Ambler, 1999).

Building on the previous literature, attitudes towards SMS advertising can in general be defined as audience members' affective reaction to SMS advertising in general, and they are expected to influence reading behaviour. In line with hierarchy of effects models, it follows that positive attitudes towards SMS advertising should encourage acceptance behaviour, such as the intention to read the ad. Hence, our first hypothesis can be formulated as follows.

H1: Positive attitudes towards SMS advertising are significantly associated with acceptance behaviour (that is, reading).

Perceived Ad-Clutter

As noted in our qualitative study, a touch of scepticism and irony surfaces. The rise of generalised scepticism towards advertisements has become deeply rooted in modern society. Surprisingly, there are only a few studies focusing on this phenomenon. Obermiller and Spangenberg (2000) and Obermiller et al. (2005) have defined this scepticism as "the tendency to disbelieve the informational claims of advertising". They show that sceptical consumers tend to search for other information sources to make their choices. In addition to this, perceived ad-clutter (Ha & Litman, 1997; Li, Edwards & Lee, 2002; Cho & Cheon, 2004) and resulting perceived intrusiveness have been shown to nurture avoidance behaviour. Speck and Elliott (1997) define perceived ad-clutter as "a consumer's conviction that the amount of advertising in a medium is excessive". This is perfectly coherent with the results of our q-study of SMS advertising. Therefore, we propose the following hypothesis.

H2: The greater the perceived ad-clutter, the greater the SMS-advertising rejection (that is, avoidance or non-reading) behaviour.

Method

The literature pertaining to (1) attitude towards the ad in general (MacKenzie & Lutz, 1986) and (2) perceived ad-clutter (Cho & Cheon. op. cit.) has been used to build the survey instrument (see appendix A4).

Attitudes towards SMS advertising comprise three differential semantic items adapted from attitudes towards advertising in general (adapted from Ajzen, 1985). Perceived ad-clutter entails three items measured on 5-point Likert-type scales (Cho & Cheon, 2002).

A list of potential types of behaviour towards SMS advertising has been built using focus groups, as not all mobile devices have the same procedures for reading and deleting ads (five types of behaviour have been identified; three of them are used in the main test and two of them are eventually retained for predictive analysis). This has been conducted with the same participants as those in the q-study. Once assertions about SMS advertising had been generated, a roundtable was gathered to list the available types of behaviour when receiving SMS ads (open question: According to your device, what kind of action can you take when receiving an SMS ad?).

A pretest with a convenience sample of students (n = 93) is conducted. Students are aged from 19 to 25 years. They have all owned mobile phones, with the average length of use being 5.239 years (dev: 2.062), and they spend 27.59 minutes daily on their phones. The sample comprises 45 males and 48 females. From this pretest, the scale properties appear satisfactory. In particular, reliability analysis reveals a Cronbach's alpha of 0.87 for the attitude scale and of 0.67 for the ad-clutter scale.

The main test is run on a quota sample of 302 mobile phone owners. The survey participants were interviewed via CATI (computer-assisted-telephone-interview). The survey instrument is reproduced in the appendices. This sample is representative of the French population in terms of age, sex, and occupation (see appendix A5). The participants use their mobile phones approximately 15 minutes per day. A retest of the scale properties shows very satisfactory Cronbach's alphas of 0.96 for the attitude scale and 0.90 for the perceived ad-clutter. According to the factor analysis results, attitude and perceived ad-clutter represent two distinct concepts, an indication of the scales' divergent validity (see the factor loadings in appendix A6). Therefore, the factors are used in the subsequent analyses.

Results

Cluster analysis is used to establish a typology of usual reading behaviour. Three groups of behavioural types appear to be meaningful: reading, non-reading, and occasional reading. Out of 257 valid answers (45 respondents were unable to answer), the reading group accounts for 29.57%, the non-reading group 49.80%, and the occasional reading group 20.62%.

Hypothesis 1, which states that positive attitudes towards SMS advertising are significantly associated with acceptance behaviour (that is, reading), is tested using mean difference analysis (ANOVA). Hypothesis 2, which asserts that the greater the perceived ad-clutter the greater the SMS advertising rejection (that is, avoidance) behaviour, is also tested via ANOVA. The respective predictive power of these two variables is assessed through discriminant analysis.

The results of the mean difference tests indicate that both attitudes towards SMS advertising and perceived ad-clutter differ significantly from one group to another and can predict group belonging. Non-reading mobile users hold more negative attitudes towards SMS advertising and feel overwhelmed by it (See Table 3).

When stepwise discriminant analysis is performed on the three behavioural groups (N = 257), only attitude towards SMS advertising is entered. The percentage of correctly classified individuals is 62.6%, which is better than random classifica-

tion (33%), but still rather low. The lowest percentage of correctly classified cases is found for the occasional reading group. We therefore decided to exclude this group from further analysis, as their attitudes may not necessarily be a good predictor of their behaviour; indeed situational variables may be more fruitful in predicting this behavioural group.

When new discriminant analysis is conducted on only readers and non-readers (N = 204), the percentage of correctly classified individuals rises to 79.9% (see Table 8). Both attitudes towards SMS advertising and perceived ad-clutter are significant predictors of reading behaviour, therefore providing support to Hypotheses 1 and 2. However, attitudes towards SMS advertising are identified as the main predictor. This result suggests that perceived ad-clutter is not a direct antecedent to behaviour; rather we suggest that it may be posited as a belief in which this attitude is grounded. We suggest that future investigation engage in analysis and elaboration of the underlying beliefs that nurture attitudes towards SMS ads (See Table 4).

DISCUSSION AND FUTURE RESEARCH DIRECTIONS

Our research makes a number of academic and managerial contributions. First, the qualitative results concerning SMS-advertising subjectivity

Table 3. Anova test

Usual behaviour		Attitude twd SMS-ad.	Perceived ad-clutter
Reading (N=76)	Mean	.242	-.561
	Std dev.	.673	.775
Non-reading (N=128)	Mean	-.474	.002
	Std dev.	.333	.730
Occasional reading (N=53)	Mean	-.189	-.455
	Std dev.	.670	.513
F-test	Sign level	.000	.000

Table 4. Final discriminant analysis

Function	Eigenvalue	Variance %	% cumulated	Canonical correlation	Wilks Lambda	Chi-square	ddl	Sign.
1	.509(a)	100.0	100.0	.581	.663	82.750	2	.000

Structure matrix	Function
	1
attitude	1.000
clutter	-.514

Confusion matrix			Predicted		
			Reading	Non-reading	Total
Original	N	Reading	41	35	**76**
		Non reading	6	122	**128**
	%	Reading	53.9	46.1	**100.0**
		Non reading	4.7	95.3	**100.0**

79.9% of observations are correctly classified.

show that, although perceived utility is linked to more favourable attitudes, this understanding of SMS advertising is rather marginal. In both the qualitative and quantitative studies, only 23% and 29.57%, respectively, of the samples hold positive attitudes about SMS ads and read these ads. Although the qualitative sample is small, quantitative results based on a larger representative sample yield convergent conclusions, which is an indication of robustness.

The results suggest that although SMS advertising is theoretically interesting to consumers, they do not necessarily accept and perceive it as such. Our qualitative results are obtained using a student sample, and even in this type of sample (which is presumably more open to mobile technologies), reading behaviour is far from systematic. They thus arouse questions about the potential for SMS advertising and should raise serious concerns regarding large investments in mobile phone advertising, at least at this stage.

It should be noted that French consumers constitute the sample. A number of studies concerning privacy have shown that privacy is not uniformly appreciated across countries (Gurau et al., 2005). Cross-cultural studies of SMS advertising will certainly shed new light on reading behaviour.

A number of additional observations must be made. The participants in the study, whether they held positive or negative attitudes towards SMS ads, were all a bit sceptical of advertising in general and, consequently, of SMS advertising as well. This finding deserves attention, as it shows that scepticism is not necessarily linked to rejection behaviour. Consumer feelings, perceptions, and understandings cannot be equated directly with mere acceptance or rejection; a wide range of behaviour is possible. This is reflected in the occasional reading group that was observed in our quantitative study. This group represents 20% of the main sample, which is not negligible. This ambivalence towards SMS ads is both an opportunity and a threat. Ambivalent people may reject or accept SMS advertising, depending on conditions that need to be further investigated. Situational variables should clearly be investigated to better predict reading behaviour. In line with this, Drossos et al. (2007) suggest that time and location, interactivity, incentive, source credibility, appeal, and product involvement are key variables. We need to assess the role of these variables in relation to reading behaviour. For instance, incentives may be relevant only once an SMS receiver has read the message or if they are mentioned in the very first words of the message, and thus may not necessarily constitute an action variable.

The role of emotional (Tähti et al., 2005) appeal (Drossos et al., op. cit.) or humour is supposed to ease the adoption of advertising and accelerate its viral effects. However, our qualitative results indicate that although humour is noted as one of the characteristics of SMS advertising, it does not seem to be at the heart of its acceptance by young consumers. Instead, their judgments are rather harsh. SMS advertising is generally seen as awkward: "It's ill-targeted", "It's sent at odd hours". Again, a fine-grained study of situational variables should be undertaken to further our understanding, as these comments suggest that both time and location are important variables in reading behaviour. They also indicate that an appropriate and well-targeted message is a key factor in SMS advertising success. Although SMS technology is available, its advertising use still appears to be in its infancy. More efforts have to be made to make more effective use of this powerful and versatile tool.

Despite these important findings, the study suffers from certain limitations. In particular, additional qualitative studies are necessary to examine different age groups and to adopt a cross-cultural perspective. The Q-method helps to elicit complex perceptual structures, and we need to pursue this type of inquiry. In particular, beliefs about SMS advertising should be further investigated. The fact that perceived ad-clutter already occurs in relatively high levels in this sample (3.48 out of 5 on average) shows that marketers do not have much room to increase SMS ad pressure. This suggests that the managerial priority should be the smart use of SMS advertising, which is the most difficult use to achieve. Hence, from both a managerial and a theoretical standpoint, further investigation of perceived ad-clutter prolongations and antecedents—both subjective and objective—is needed.

Finally, in addition to the perceived ad-clutter variable included here, future research should integrate such variables as attitudes towards specific ads (Aad). Complementary studies are also necessary to assess the roles played by brand familiarity, product involvement, and message tone in reading behaviour.

CONCLUSION

The use of a double methodology in investigating consumer perceptions of SMS advertising is fruitful, as it yields useful results. Based on a qualitative sample and a quantitative representative sample, this study helps to explain the complex and sometimes ambivalent nature of users' perception of SMS advertising. It also shows that irony is part of mobile users' evaluation of such advertising and that this irony contributes to the perception of ad-clutter. Attitude is particularly predictive for behavioural groups that practise systematic types of behaviour (either systematic reading or the systematic deletion of SMS ads), but not necessarily for occasional reading ones. The identification and characterisation of occasional readers deserves priority in research.

REFERENCES

(2004). An SMS history. In Taylor, A., & Vincent, J. (Eds.), *Mobile World, Computer Supported Cooperative Work* (pp. 1431–1496). London: Springer.

Barnes, S. J. (2002). Wireless digital advertising. *International Journal of Advertising, 21*, 399–420.

Barwise, P., & Strong, C. (2002). Permission-based mobile advertising. *Journal of Interactive Marketing, 16*(1), 14–24. doi:10.1002/dir.10000

Bauer, H. H., Barnes, S. J., Reichardt, T., & Neumann, M. M. (2005). Driving consumer acceptance of mobile marketing: A theoretical framework and empirical study. *Journal of Electronic Commerce Research, 6*(3). Retrieved April 15, 2006, from http://www.csulb.edu/journals/jecr

Becker, M. (2005, December 6). Effectiveness of mobile channel additions and a conceptual model detailing the interaction of influential variables'. *MMA Global.* Retrieved October 13, 2007, from http://mmaglobal.com/modules/wfsection/article.php?articleid=131

Brown, S. P. (1993). A Q methodological tutorial. *Operant Subjectivity, 16,* 91-138. Retrieved October 3, 2005, from http://www.qmethod.org

Brown, S. P., & Stayman, D. M. (1992). Antecedents and consequences of attitudes toward the ad: A meta-analysis. *The Journal of Consumer Research, 19*(June), 34–51. doi:10.1086/209284

Bruner, G., & Kumar, A. (2005). Explaining consumer acceptance of handheld internet services. *Journal of Business Research, 58*(5), 553–558. doi:10.1016/j.jbusres.2003.08.002

Buellinger, F., & Woerter, M. (2004). Development perspectives, firm strategies and applications in mobile commerce. *Journal of Business Research, 57*(12), 1402–1408. doi:10.1016/S0148-2963(02)00429-0

Cho, C. H., & Cheon, H. J. (2004). Why do people avoid advertising on the internet? *Journal of Advertising, 33*(4), 89–97.

Drossos, D. (2007). Determinants of effective SMS advertising: an experimental study. *Journal of Interactive Advertising, 7*(2). Retrieved from http://www.jiad.org/article90.

Gaski, J. F., & Etzel, M. J. (1986). The index of consumer sentiment toward marketing. *Journal of Marketing, 50*(July), 71–81. doi:10.2307/1251586

Gaski, J. F., & Etzel, M. J. (2005). National aggregate consumer sentiment toward marketing: A thirty year retrospective and analysis. *The Journal of Consumer Research, 31*(March), 859–867. doi:10.1086/426623

Greyser, S. A., & Bauer, R. A. (1968). Americans and advertising: Thirty years of public opinion. *Public Opinion Quarterly, 30,* 69–78. doi:10.1086/267382

Gurau, C., Ranchhod, A., & Gauzente, C. (2003). To legislate or not to legislate – A comparative exploratory study of privacy/personalization factors affecting French, UK and US web sites. *Journal of Consumer Marketing, 20*(7), 652–664. doi:10.1108/07363760310506184

Ha, L., & Litman, B. R. (1997). Does advertising clutter have diminishing and negative returns? *Journal of Advertising, 26*(2), 31–42.

Kleijnen, M., de Reyter, K., & Wetzel, M. (2004). Consumer adoption of wireless services: discovering the rules while playing the game. *Journal of Interactive Marketing, 18*(2), 51–61. doi:10.1002/dir.20002

Lee, S. F., Tsai, Y. C., & Jih, W. J. (2006). An empirical examination of customer perception of mobile advertising. *Information Resources Management Journal, 19*(4), 39–55.

Li, H., Edwards, S. M., & Lee, J. H. (2002). Measuring the intrusiveness of advertisements: scale development and validation. *Journal of Advertising, 31*(2), 37–47.

Ling, R., & Pedersen, P. E. (Eds.). (2005). *Mobile communications: re-negotiation of the social sphere.* Surrey, UK: Springer.

Lutz, R. J. (1985). Affective and cognitive antecedents of attitude toward the ad: A conceptual framework. In Alwitt, L. F., & Mitchell, A. A. (Eds.), *Psychological processes and advertising effects: Theory, research and application.* Hillsdale, NJ: Lawrence Erlbaum Associates.

MacInnis, D. J., & Jaworski, B. J. (1989). Information processing from advertisements: toward an integrative framework. *Journal of Marketing, 53*(4), 1–23. doi:10.2307/1251376

MacKenzie, S. B., & Lutz, R. J. (1989). An empirical examination of the structural antecedents of attitude toward the ad in an advertising pre testing context. *Journal of Marketing, 53*(2), 48–65. doi:10.2307/1251413

Merisavo, M. (2007). An empirical study of the drivers of consumer acceptance of mobile advertising. *Journal of Interactive Advertising, 7*(2). Retrieved from http://www.jiad.org/article92.

Milne, G. R., & Rohm, A. J. (2003). The 411 on mobile privacy. *Marketing Management, 12*(4), 40–45.

Mobile Marketing Association. (2009). *Mobile Advertising Overview, January.* Retrieved May 12, 2009, from http://www.mmaglobal.com/mobileadoverview.pdf

Muehling, D. D. (1987). An investigation of factors underlying attitude-toward-advertising-in-general. *Journal of Advertising, 16*(1), 32–41.

Nokia Media Network. (2008). Retrieved November 13, 2008, from http://www.nokia.com/A4136001?newsid=1190110

Obermiller, C., & Spangenberg, E. R. (2000). On the origin and distinctiveness of skepticism toward advertising. *Marketing Letters, 11*(4), 311–322. doi:10.1023/A:1008181028040

Obermiller, C., Spangenberg, E. R., & McLahan, D. L. (2005). Ad skepticism – the consequences of disbelief. *Journal of Advertising, 34*(3), 7–17.

Ozaki, S., & Taylor, C. R. (2008). What is SMS advertising and why do multinationals adopt it? Answers from an empirical study in European markets. *Journal of Business Research, 61,* 4–12. doi:10.1016/j.jbusres.2006.05.003

Peters, C., Amato, C. H., & Hollenbeck, C. R. (2007). An exploratory investigation of consumers' perception of wireless advertising. *Journal of Advertising, 36*(4), 129–145. doi:10.2753/JOA0091-3367360410

Reid, D., & Reid, F. (2004). Insights into the social and psychological effects of SMS text messaging. *160characters.org,* February. Retrieved May 12, 2009, from http://www.160characters.org/documents/SocialEffectsOfTextMessaging.pdf

Rettie, R., Grandcolas, U., & Deakins, B. (2005). Text message advertising: response rates and branding effects. *Journal of Targeting. Measurement and Analysis for Marketing, 13*(4), 304–312. doi:10.1057/palgrave.jt.5740158

Scharl, A., Dickinger, A., & Murphy, J. (2005). Diffusion and success factors of mobile marketing. *Electronic Commerce Research and Applications, 4*(2), 159–173. doi:10.1016/j.elerap.2004.10.006

Speck, P. S., & Elliott, M. T. (1997). Predictors of advertising avoidance in print and broadcast media. *Journal of Advertising, 26*(3), 61–76.

Stephenson, W. (1935). Correlating Persons instead of Tests. *Character and Personality, 4,* 17–24.

Stephenson, W. (1953). *The study of behavior: Q-technique and its methodology.* Chicago: University of Chicago Press.

Tähti, M., Väinämö, S., Vanninen, V., & Isomursu, M. (2004). Catching emotions elicited by mobile services. In *Proceedings of the Australian Conference on Computer-Human Interaction.* Wollongong, Australia (CD-ROM).

Tsang, M. M., Ho, S. C., & Liang, T. P. (2004). Consumer attitudes toward mobile advertising: an empirical study. *International Journal of Electronic Commerce, 8*(3), 65–78.

Vakratsas, D., & Ambler, T. (1999). How advertising works: what do we really know? *Journal of Marketing, 63*(1), 26–43. doi:10.2307/1251999

Zanot, E. (1984). Public advertising towards advertising. *International Journal of Marketing, 3*, 3–15.

APPENDICES

A1. Perceptual structure of vision A concerning SMS-advertising (shared by individuals 8, 1, 5, 3, 6, 7, 11) (See Figure 1)

Figure 1.

#	Original statement	Translation	mean
16	Cela me dérange, c'est pénible.	It bothers me, it's uncomfortable.	2,0635
5	C'est incontrôlable.	It's uncontrollable.	1,2898
7	C'est mal ciblé.	It's ill-targeted.	1,1865
12	C'est trop fréquent.	It's too frequent.	0,7663
3	C'est du harcèlement.	It's harassment.	0,659
6	C'est insupportable.	It's unbearable.	0,5152
4	C'est envoyé à des horaires « étranges ».	It's sent at odd hours.	0,2572
14	Ce n'est que de la promotion.	It's only promotion.	0,245
8	C'est pas intéressant.	It's not interesting.	0,1436
13	C'est une violation de ma vie privée.	It's a violation of my privacy.	0,1194
10	C'est régulier.	It's repeated.	0,0887
9	C'est pratique pour connaître les offres.	It's practical for discovering offers.	-0,1283
1	C'est ambigu : on ne sait pas exactement quelle est l'offre faite.	It's ambiguous: you don't understand exactly what the offer is.	-0,2565
19	Personne ne les lit (ou ne les lira).	Nobody reads it.	-0,4046
18	On paie plus cher pour l'offre faite.	You pay more for this.	-0,9651
2	C'est des messages accrocheurs.	It's attractive messages.	-1,0918
17	Les messages sont drôles, fun.	It's fun messages.	-1,3058
15	Cela donne des informations utiles.	It provides useful information.	-1,3947
11	C'est toujours une pub Orange.	It's always an Orange ad.	-1,7875

Highly characteristic of my vision.

Very unlike my vision

A2. Perceptual structure of vision B concerning SMS-advertising (shared by individuals: 10, 13, 2)

#	Original statement	Translation	Mean
9	C'est pratique pour connaître les offres.	It's useful for discovering offers.	1,5739
15	Cela donne des informations utiles.	It provides useful information	1,2357
14	Ce n'est que de la promotion.	It's only promotion.	1,2053
7	C'est mal ciblé.	It's ill-targeted.	1,0912
5	C'est incontrôlable.	It's uncontrollable.	0,5888
4	C'est envoyé à des horaires « étranges ».	It's sent at odd hours.	0,5839
12	C'est trop fréquent.	It's too frequent.	0,5338
10	C'est régulier.	It's repeated	0,3952
8	C'est pas intéressant.	It's not interesting.	0,2687
11	C'est toujours une pub Orange.	It's always and Orange ad.	0,2634
2	C'est des messages accrocheurs.	It's attractive messages.	-0,244
17	Les messages sont drôles, fun.	Messages are fun.	-0,3204
16	Cela me dérange, c'est pénible.	It bothers me, it's uncomfortable.	-0,3649
1	C'est ambigu: on ne sait pas exactement quelle est l'offre faite.	It's ambiguous: you don't understand what the offer is.	-0,4049
19	Personne ne les lit (ou ne les lira).	Nobody reads it.	-0,5196
6	C'est insupportable.	It's unbearable.	-0,9428
18	On paie plus cher pour l'offre faite.	You pay more for the offer.	-1,1949
13	C'est une violation de ma vie privée.	It's a violation of my privacy.	-1,7995
3	C'est du harcèlement.	It's harassment.	-1,9489

A3. Perceptual structure of vision C concerning SMS-advertising (shared by individuals 12, 9, 4)

#	Original statement	Translation	Mean
11	C'est toujours une pub Orange.	It's always an Orange ad.	2,3559
6	C'est insupportable.	It's unbearable	1,1313
8	C'est pas intéressant.	It's interesting.	1,0902
16	Cela me dérange, c'est pénible.	It bothers me, it's uncomfortable.	1,0896
14	Ce n'est que de la promotion.	It's only promotion.	0,7186
19	Personne ne les lit (ou ne les lira).	Nobody reads it.	0,4829
4	C'est envoyé à des horaires « étranges ».	It's sent at odd hours.	0,4224
7	C'est mal ciblé.	It's ill-targeted.	0,0987
18	On paie plus cher pour l'offre faite.	You pay more for the offer.	-0,0192
3	C'est du harcèlement.	It's harassment.	-0,3177
15	Cela donne des informations utiles.	It provides useful information.	-0,322
13	C'est une violation de ma vie privée.	It's a violation of my privacy.	-0,3434
1	C'est ambigu: on ne sait pas exactement quelle est l'offre faite.	It's ambiguous: you don't understand exactly what the offer is.	-0,3463
9	C'est pratique pour connaître les offres.	It's practical to discover offers.	-0,3866
10	C'est régulier.	It's repeated.	-0,475
2	C'est des messages accrocheurs.	It's attractive messages.	-0,9317
12	C'est trop fréquent.	It's too frequent.	-1,2509
5	C'est incontrôlable.	It's uncontrollable.	-1,2594
17	Les messages sont drôles, fun.	Messages are fun.	-1,7376

A4. Measurement scales

Attitude toward SMS-advertising (adapted fromLutz, 1985, Ajzen, 1991)

Overall, what do you think of commercial messages that are sent to you cell phone:

A1. It is a good or bad thing
A2. It's pleasant / unpleasant
A3. I'm favourable / unfavourable

Usual behaviour

What is your usual behaviour on receiving commercial messages on your mobile?

Av1. I read it
Av2. I delete it directly
Av3. I occasionally read it.

Perceived ad clutter (Cho and Cheon, 2004)

When you receive commercial messages on your mobile phone, you find that:

C1. It's excessive
C2. It's exclusive
C3. It's irritating

A5. Main sample characteristics

Age			Sex			Occupation			Region		
Less than 25	41	14%	male	145	48%	Higher level	44	15%	Paris and region	110	37%
25 to 34	71	24%	female	157	52%	Intermediary	49	17%	North	20	7%
35 to 44	58	19%				Lower level	109	37%	East	30	10%
45 to 54	53	18%				Retired	54	18%	West	40	13%
55 to 64	41	14%				Unemployed	39	13%	South-West	33	11%
65 to 74	25	8%							Centre-East	33	11%
75 and more	13	4%							Mediterranean region	36	12%
TOTAL	295	98%*		302	100%		302	100%		302	100%

* approximately 2% of survey participants did not answered this question

A6. Factor analysis of measurement scales: Attitude toward SMS advertising and Perceived ad-clutter

N=302 KMO: .773	Rotated factor matrix	
	1	2
Attitude toward SMS advertising		
SMS/MMS advertising is a good thing	0.962	
SMS/MMS advertising is pleasant	0.962	
I am favourable to SMS/MMS advertising	0.946	
Perceived ad-clutter		
SMS/MMS advertising: It's excessive		0.933
SMS/MMS advertising: It's exclusive		0.911
SMS/MMS advertising: It's irritating		0.881
% of explained variance	46.51	41.99

[1] Orange has historically been the phone operator in France.

This work was previously published in International Journal of Technology and Human Interaction, Volume 6, Issue 2, edited by Anabela Mesquita & Chia-Wen Tsai, pp. 13-29, copyright 2010 by IGI Publishing (an imprint of IGI Global).

Chapter 3
Adoption Barriers in a High-Risk Agricultural Environment

Shari R. Veil
University of Oklahoma, USA

ABSTRACT

To lessen the threat of an intentional or naturally occurring livestock disease, the Animal Plant Health Inspection Service of the United States Department of Agriculture introduced the National Animal Identification System (NAIS), encouraging the use of innovative tools such as radio frequency identification (RFID) tags to track cattle across the country. In this study, the author examines the barriers to adoption of NAIS and RFID technology as risk-reduction tools. Diffusion of innovation literature is used to analyze a case study of a state livestock association advocating the rejection of NAIS and RFID technology. Implications for the diffusion of risk reduction tools are provided.

INTRODUCTION

As the Taliban and al-Qaeda forces retreated from their caves and safe houses, American troops found "hundreds of pages of US agricultural documents that had been translated into Arabic" (Doeg, 2005, p. 167). Most alarming, a "terrorist's training manual was reportedly devoted to agricultural terrorism such as the destruction of crops, livestock, and food processing operations" (pp. 167-168). Approximately $17.5 billion are lost each year because of unintentional infestations resulting

in diseased livestock and poultry (ARS, 2002). While even a massive outbreak of plant or animal disease would not cause famine, a successful agroterrorist attack could have severe consequences on the $201 billion farm economy (Piller, 2004), the most substantial of which would be the loss of international markets (Wheelis, Casagrande & Madden, 2002). A then isolated case of mad cow disease (bovine spongiform encephalopathy or BSE) in 2003 revealed both the vulnerability of American agriculture to disease and the economic disruption that could result. U.S. exports declined by approximately 50% (Cox et al., 2005), and more than $3 billion in annual exports were shut

DOI: 10.4018/978-1-61350-465-9.ch003

down in a matter of days (Sparshott, 2004). Even a limited occurrence of disease and a temporary suspension of trade can cause severe economic loss to the agriculture industry. Thus, terrorists need not bring about an epidemic to cause significant economic harm (Casagrande, 2002).

In April of 2005, the Animal Plant Health Inspection Service (APHIS) of the United States Department of Agriculture (USDA) released a draft of the Strategic Plan for the National Animal Identification System (NAIS) (APHIS, 2005). Using innovative tools such as radio frequency identification (RFID) tags that can be scanned when passed by an electronic reader, the plan called for animal trace-back within 48 hours to mitigate a naturally occurring disease or an agroterrorist attack. Since the release of the draft strategic plan, USDA-APHIS has extended the deadlines for implementation of NAIS and agreed to further review tracking mechanisms and privacy concerns. USDA has also extended Federal Relations Grants to agriculture-based universities to research the potential for RFID to track cattle. Prototype RFID tags are being tested, scanned, and mapped using university extension research facilities (NDSU, 2005). RFID individually identifies each ruminant and can then identify each ruminant scanned at the same location during a specified timeframe. If the United States experiences an outbreak of a highly communicable disease like foot-and-mouth (FMD), individual identification and quick location of all cattle that has come into contact with an infected ruminant could prove to be essential information in reducing the risk of further disease.

As research continued on the technology, the plan was released on the USDA website, allowing organizations involved in the industry to comment. In July 2005, the executive vice president of the North Dakota Stockmen's Association (NDSA) submitted comments criticizing the plan. As the state legislature appointed brand inspection agency in North Dakota, NDSA traces cattle that are fire branded in North Dakota across the country without the assistance of RFID tags or the proposed government mandates of NAIS. While evidence of 48-hour trace-back ability is limited, the brand records kept by NDSA do allow cattle to be source verified.

In the comments posted to the USDA-APHIS website, NDSA admonished USDA-APHIS for its "failure to address cost, confidentiality, flexibility and the integration of current ID programs that are proven" (NDSA, 2004). At the North Dakota Stockmen's Association Annual Meeting on September 22–24, 2005, just two months after NDSA leadership posted comments, open-ended questionnaires were distributed to attending members to learn their perceptions of the adoption or rejection process of RFID technology.

Technology has become an essential component in the resolution of terrorism threats (Wulf, Haimes & Longstaff, 2003). This study examines the barriers to adoption of NAIS and RFID technology as risk-reduction tools. Specifically, this study analyzes the responses of NDSA members surveyed two months after NDSA leadership posted their criticisms of the plan. First, diffusion of innovation literature is reviewed. This review is followed by a detailed explanation of the methodological procedure and a comprehensive analysis of the barriers to adoption identified as awareness, interest, and influence. Finally, implications for the diffusion of NAIS and RFID technology as risk reduction tools are provided.

Diffusion of Innovation

An innovation is an idea, product, or process that is new to an adopter (Hage & Aiken, 1967; Rogers, 2003; Zaltman, Duncan & Hoibek, 1973). Diffusion is "the process in which an innovation is communicated through certain channels over time among the members of a social system" (Rogers, 2003, p. 5). While the original idea of diffusion was first expounded on by Tarde in 1903, the first application of the diffusion model can be traced to the agriculture industry (Rogers, 2003). Focusing on the adoption of hybrid seed corn in Iowa, Ryan and Gross's (1943) influential study provided the basic framework for diffusion research. Diffusion of innovation research has since been used to evaluate the adoption process of innovations as diverse as cancer treatment and internet use in industries as diverse as civic planning and fashion.

Most relevant to this study, specific contributions in agriculture diffusion acknowledge the slow adoption process in the industry. Ashby et al. (1996) found many farmers were slow to adopt new practices even though they understood the practices would help improve the land. While Saltiel, Bauder and Palakovich (1994) found that negative farmer perceptions regarding any one element or combination of elements in an innovation can limit the adoption of new practices. Saltiel et al. (1994) also suggest that the diverse goals and wide range of practices in the industry make the current frameworks for explaining adoption in agriculture inadequate. Examining opinion leaders and change agents in the industry, Röling, Ascroft and Chege (1976) found that even within the agriculture industry, social status impacts the diffusion process since change agents can accomplish more by doing less if they focus on producers with larger farms.

Regardless of the industry, diffusion of innovation research typically follows the original process established by Ryan and Gross (1943) using retrospective surveys to determine the rate of adoption over time. The rate of adoption traditionally forms an S-shaped curve as a few individuals adopt the innovation at first before the adoption rate accelerates and then tapers off once most individuals have adopted the innovation (Ryan & Gross, 1943). The point of adoption is determined in the decision-making process of (1) knowledge, (2) persuasion, (3) decision, (4) implementation, and (5) confirmation during which individuals evaluate the attributes of the innovation. Since this study specifically evaluates an innovation during the adoption process

and not after, the attributes of the innovation are described in more detail.

Innovation Attributes

Throughout the decision making process, individuals evaluate the attributes of the innovation. While studies in educational settings (Holloway, 1977), information technology (Kearns, 1992; Moore & Benbasat, 1991); healthcare (Goldman, 1992) and agriculture (Kremer et al., 2001) have examined and even added to the list of attributes, the five attributes defined by Rogers (2003) including (1) relative advantage, (2) compatibility, (3) complexity, (4) trialability, and (5) observability, continue to be used as the base from which attribute categories are expanded.

The first and most influential attribute is relative advantage (Rogers, 2003). Relative advantage is the degree to which an innovation is perceived as better than the idea it replaces (Rogers, 2003). Whether an individual or organization receives an actual benefit from an innovation does not determine the rate of adoption. If an individual or organization perceives the innovation to provide advantages over the current system, the innovation will be adopted. According to Rogers (2003) "The greater the perceived relative advantage of an innovation, the more rapid its rate of adoption will be" (p. 15). Relative advantage is often expressed as economic profitability since an innovation is not likely to be adopted if the costs outweigh the benefits of the idea. Incentives, specifically financial incentives, help encourage adoption of an innovation when costs are a major concern of potential adopters (Rogers, 1973).

Compatibility is the degree to which an innovation is perceived as being consistent with existing values, experiences, and the needs of potential adopters (Rogers, 2003). If an innovation is not compatible with the norms of a social system, adoption of a new values system is often required in order for the innovation to be considered. An innovation that fits in the social norms of an organization will be adopted more rapidly than an innovation that is not compatible with the existing practices of the organization. As Rogers (2003) notes, "The rate of adoption of a new idea is affected by the old idea that it supersedes" (p. 245). The rate of adoption may be impeded if the innovation is not compatible or is simply too different from the system currently in place.

Complexity is the degree to which an innovation is perceived as difficult to understand and use (Rogers, 2003). If the innovation requires a new skill set in order to be used effectively, the learning curve in attaining the skills may delay the innovation adoption. The innovation must be user friendly, not just to those who propose the innovation, but to the end users. In this sense, complexity can act as a barrier to adoption when a technology-based innovation is introduced to a non-technical field (Rogers, 2003). In addition, potential adopters must also understand what purpose the innovation will serve. As Rogers (2003) states, "Some innovations are clear in their meaning to potential adopters while others are not" (p. 257). The innovation will be rejected if potential adopters do not understand the consequences of using of the innovation.

Trialability is the degree to which an innovation may be experienced on a limited basis (Rogers, 2003). If potential adopters are able to test the innovation to determine how it functions and if it works, adoption becomes more likely as uncertainty about the innovation is reduced. Trying an innovation before adopting it also allows potential adopters to make meaning of the innovation thereby reducing the complexity surrounding the innovation (Rogers, 2003). If the potential adopters have a negative experience when trying the innovation, the adoption rate will diminish. For example, if the innovation does not work as it is designed to work in the trial period, there would be no reason to adopt the innovation when it is formally disseminated.

Observability is the degree to which the results of an innovation are visible to others (Rogers, 2003). Potential adopters who are able to see the innovation working in a real-world setting are more likely to adopt the innovation. The more individuals see other people using an innovation, the more likely they are to adopt the innovation as well. Innovations that are used privately, cannot be seen, or have ambiguous results have a slower adoption rate than those that are highly visible and have obvious results. Preventative innovations have a particularly slow rate of adoption because the desired outcome is to prevent a future event (Rogers, 2003). Because the event has not occurred and may not occur, the results may never be visible.

How potential adopters perceive the five attributes of an innovation affects the relative speed with which an innovation is adopted. How the attributes are presented as information is diffused and sought in the decision-making process is another essential element in the diffusion model. Mass media channels are usually the most rapid and efficient means of sharing information with an audience; however, because diffusion of innovation takes place in a social system, interpersonal channels are actually more effective in persuading an individual to accept a new idea (Rogers, 2003). The role of opinion leaders in the social system can greatly influence the adoption process of an innovation (Severin & Tankard, 1997).

Opinion Leaders

Katz and Lazarsfeld (1955), who first defined the concept, describe opinion leadership as a transparent role that exists in informal relationships. Opinion leaders are influential people within a peer group who serve as pacesetters (Turnbull & Meenaghan, 2001). As models for the innovation behavior of their followers, opinion leaders can either speed up or slow down the diffusion process by adopting or rejecting an innovation (Rogers, 2003; Turnbull & Meenaghan, 2001). Opinion leaders tend to be more educated, innovative, wealthy, and have a higher social status than those who follow their leadership (Rogers & van Es, 1964; Rogers & Svenning, 1969). Opinion leaders also tend to have a high-perceived level of leadership (Weir, 1999).

While the leadership role of an opinion leader is usually inconspicuous (Katz & Lazarsfeld, 1955), Mancuso (1969) suggests that status, along with mobility and confidence, are the main characteristics of an opinion leader. Wasson, Sturdivant and McConaughty (1970) propose that the opinion leader is the most prestigious member of the group. The dual role of an opinion leader in an organizational leadership role can further influence the adoption process. Leaders who become advocates for or against an innovation can become change agents or champions in the process (Rogers, 2003). Rogers (2003) suggests that a weakness in organization-based studies is that the influence of leadership has not been taken into account.

Another weakness noted by Rogers (2003) is that most diffusion studies are conducted retrospectively after an innovation has been accepted; therefore, few rejected innovations are studied to determine why the innovation was not adopted. The focus on time as a major factor also encourages researchers to only conduct studies at the end of the process. Conducting research as an innovation is being diffused rather than after the fact could provide insight as to the motivations for adopting or rejecting an innovation (Rogers, 2003). This process would allow for specific questions concerning the relative advantage, compatibility, complexity, trialability, and observability of an innovation in order to determine the argument needed to influence change. This study surveyed members of NDSA within six months of the release of the NAIS Strategic Plan and two months of NDSA leadership's posted criticisms of the plan.

Method

Questionnaires have been used extensively in diffusion studies (Rogers, 2003), following the

original process established by Ryan and Gross (1943) to determine the rate of adoption over time. In reviewing the utility and value of diffusion of innovations over the last 40 years, Haider and Kreps (2004) noted the reliance on recall data from questionnaire respondents as central to the development and application of the theory. Questionnaires have also been used effectively to study risk perception and behavior related to the diffusion process (Singhal & Rogers, 2003).

At the North Dakota Stockmen's Association Annual Meeting on September 22–24, 2005, open-ended questionnaires were distributed to attending members to learn their perceptions of the adoption or rejection process of RFID technology. The method was naturalistic (Lincoln & Guba, 1985) in that the researcher adopted "strategies that parallel how people act in the course of daily life" (Taylor & Bogdan, 1998, p. 8). Participants were already attending the meeting, and panels had already been scheduled during the meeting to discuss NAIS, allowing for an environment in which the participants would feel comfortable revealing related information (Taylor & Bogdan, 1998).

Participants

The participants were all adults and members of NDSA attending the NDSA Annual Meeting. As members picked up their registration packets and before and after each general session, they were asked to complete a questionnaire. Participation in the survey was voluntary and the decision about whether to participate in the study did not affect the standing of the participants in NDSA. If individuals decided not to participate, they were free not to complete the questionaire or to stop at any time. Those partipating in the survey signed an informed consent form allowing the information to be studied.

Of the 316 individuals registered for the meeting, 24 did not attend; 75 were vendors; approximately 50 were spouses who did not participate in

Figure 1. Number of Years Ranching Graph shows how long participating producers have been ranching

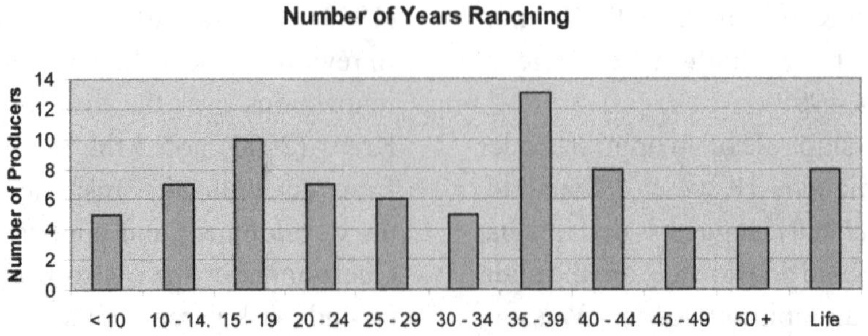

Number of Years Ranching

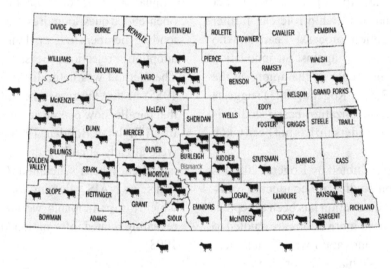

Figure 2. Producer Participant Map shows the counties in which respondents ranch

= Producer Participant

the procedings; 8 were staff members of NDSA; 5 were members of the press; 5 were presenters; and 2 were the researcher and research assistant for this study (NDSA staff, personal communication, September 2005). Approximately 147 participants were qualified to take part in the survey, and 92 participants returned questionaires for a 63% response rate. Of the 92 respondents, 76 were producers: 68 of whom had no other affiliation in the industry and 8 of whom listed themselves as both producer and another affiliation; and 16 listed a title other than producer such as veterinarian, extension researcher, brand inspector, etc. Producers were also classified by length of time in the industry (Figure 1) and by the county in which

they ranch (Figure 2) for description purposes. In the instance that a producer ranched in more than one county, the first county listed was documented.

Survey Environment

The organizational setting of the Annual Meeting was determined to be conducive to the process of encouraging members of NDSA to elaborate on their opinions, questions, and concerns regarding a topic of discussion at the meeting (Taylor & Bogdan, 1998). The researcher stayed at the meeting hotel and attended the general sessions and meals to observe the interaction of members as they completed the questionnaires and discussed the issue. Based on observation and personal communication with participants, questionnaires were completed at the registration table, during the course of meetings, during discussions with other participants at lunches and banquets, and in the privacy of hotel rooms.

Survey Instrument

The questionnaire consisted of three description questions, one Likert-type scale to gauge the respondent's likeliness to adopt the technology, and eight open-ended questions pertaining to the reasoning for the proposal of NAIS, advantages and disadvantages of RFID technology, perceptions of USDA-APHIS and the role of NDSA, and recommendations for animal identification procedures. Questions were composed based on feedback from members of an extension research team testing RFID tags. The questions were then pre-tested and revised based on feedback from the executive vice president of NDSA.

Data Collection

Questionnaires were distributed at the registration table as participants picked up their registration packets and entered the general assembly meetings each day. Before receiving a questionnaire, participants were asked if they had already completed a questionnaire to avoid duplication. Participants were able to complete the questionnaire at their leisure over the course of the three-day convention. In exchange for completing the questionnaire, respondents received a vented cap with the researcher's university extension center logo. In speaking with members of NDSA before the meeting, extension services are seen as a supportive entity to producers.

Data Analysis

Frequency measures were used to analyze responses to questions regarding the role of NDSA

in the adoption/rejection process of RFID technology, whether USDA-APHIS was effectively addressing the concerns of producers, the purpose of NAIS, and recommendations for tracking cattle. Frequency measures were also used to analyze the likelihood of members to voluntarily adopt RFID technology for cattle tracking purposes. Responses to the questions regarding the advantages and disadvantages of the innovation and the respondent's conditions for adoption were coded following Coffey and Atkinson's (1996) clustering of themes for organization. The themes were organized by the underlying construct (Boyatzis, 1998) of the five attributes that affect the adoption process. Intercoder reliability was calculated using Scott's Pi (1955) and was found to be acceptable for all three questions regarding advantages ($\pi =$ 1.00, intercoder agreement 100%), disadvantages ($\pi = .91$, intercoder agreement 93%), and recommendations ($\pi = .81$, intercoder agreement 86%).

Results

When asked what role respondents thought NDSA should play in the adoption/rejection of RFID technology, the respondents' devotion to NDSA was evident in that 90% (n = 83) of the respondents felt NDSA should be involved in the process. Suggestions ranged from having the organization be involved in the education process to managing the system. A 19-year producer from McKenzie County wrote, "I see NDSA as the most informed entity and look to them for current information. Would most likely go with what NDSA supports." A 23-year producer from Ransom County supported the admiration for the organization in saying, "I'm proud how NDSA has stepped forward to be the state major voice on this issue." Other respondents looked to NDSA as the bridge to USDA and identified the organization as housing the opinion leaders of the industry. A 13-year producer from McHenry County wrote:

They can educate and increase acceptance by producers and lead them into this new era. NDSA can help USDA establish real world standards for the technology. Their members are leaders in their individual neighborhoods and can help determine the success or failure of the system.

In contrast to the overwhelming support for NDSA, many respondents were unsure as to how well concerns are being addressed by USDA-APHIS. Some wrote USDA was addressing their concerns fairly well; however, 60% (n = 55) of respondents felt USDA was not listening to their concerns. A 33-year producer from Logan County wrote, "USDA is blind to the concerns of the producers and see things only one way (their way)." A 17-year producer from Stutsman County supported the comment in saying "I don't think they are being addressed much at all. These individuals don't know how ranching and feeding operations work." Other respondents showed more contempt for government systems in general. A 14-year producer from Slope County wrote, "It's a government agency—they will screw it up," and a retired producer from Grand Forks County agreed: "They will probably bungle it like most other projects."

Respondents referred to specific events as the motivation for proposing NAIS. Participants that mentioned BSE as reasoning for the new system represented 73% (n=67) of the total sample, while 22% (n = 20) specifically mentioned FMD and 12% (n = 11) mentioned 9/11 or the potential of agroterrorism. While these numbers could indicate that NDSA members understood the system was being introduced to protect the food supply, the comments suggest another understanding. A 21-year producer from Divide County classified the reasoning simply as "Fear mongering," while others pointed out that BSE, the most referred to reason for the new system, does not require a 48-hour traceback. A 17-year producer from Stutsman County wrote, "BSE-this is not an

infectious disease and I feel this should not have prompted the NAID."

Respondents were asked to rate their likelihood to adopt on a Likert scale. Of the 84 who responded, 7% (n = 6) had already adopted RFID, 49% (n = 41) were likely to adopt, 24% (n = 20) were undecided, 15% (n = 13) were unlikely to adopt, and 5% (n = 4) indicated they will not adopt RFID technology (Table 1). A lifetime producer from McIntosh County wrote that he "would quit cattle first." While the majority of the respondents indicated they were likely to adopt RFID tagging, of the 41 respondents who were likely to adopt, 78% (n = 32) listed conditions that would need to be in place to adopt the technology. Respondents who either have adopted or are likely to adopt without certain conditions being met represented 19% (n = 16) (Table 1).

Despite concerns over the reasoning behind the implementation of NAIS and some reservations in adoption, 76% (n = 70) of respondents were able to list advantages for adopting RFID technology for animal identification. Advantages included disease mitigation, increased consumer confidence, increased revenue, streamlined industry trace-back for all livestock, speed of trace-back, speed of commerce, improved record keeping, owner verification outside the state, and carcass information from the packers. Some comments were very positive. A 10-year producer from Burleigh County commented, "It would

Table 1. Likelihood to adopt RFID technology

Likelihood	Number of Respondents
Likely to adopt – under conditions	32
Undecided	20
Unlikely to adopt	13
Likely to adopt – no conditions	9
Already adopted	6
Will not adopt	4

n = 84.

create a system to track almost every head of livestock in the nation." While a 13-year producer from McHenry County wrote the advantages are as follows:

Export market health/sanitation assurances, protection of national health of cattle industry, consumer confidence in source verification all under an electronic framework that is rapid, automatically database, and more easily managed with RFID technology.

Other respondents had mixed feelings and added stipulations to the advantages they listed. An auction market affiliate commented, "On a mandatory basis. .. very little or no advantages, for producers. On a voluntary basis. .. access to export market, production and possible feed and slaughter information." A lifetime producer from Billings County wrote, "Identifying and keeping complete records on our cattle is very advantageous in many ways. My concern is who has those records." A 28-year producer from Logan County addressed the differences in state-to-state tracking:

For states with existing tracking capabilities I see very little advantage—until they leave the state. For states without existing systems it will allow them to source verify their animals and track them throughout the system.

While 76% of respondents were able to identify advantages to RFID tagging, 98% (n = 90) were able to identify disadvantages to the technology. Many respondents listed multiple disadvantages for a total of 151 comments. Using the theoretical lens of diffusion of innovation, disadvantages of the system and recommendations for the NAIS were categorized and coded into the five attributes that affect the adoption process (Rogers, 2003).

Relative Advantage

Before anyone will replace a product or system, the advantages of the new product or system must be demonstrated. The advantages must also be worth the additional costs. A 35-year producer from Stark County and university employee stated, "Cost would need to be less than the financial gain I receive as a producer." At the time of the survey, USDA had not addressed who would be responsible for paying for any additional costs. Respondents who mentioned disadvantages regarding relative advantage or cost represented 43% (n = 40) of the total sample (Table 2), while 37% (n = 34) indicated that relative advantage was a condition that would have to be met before adoption (Table 3). A lifetime rancher involved in livestock auction felt not enough research had been done. "Government has not clearly outlined funding for an animal ID system.. ... It seems in its current direction that the government is all to eager to put in place a program and let everybody else pay for it." A 25-year producer and health representative from Brown County, SD, agreed: "It appears all of the expense is going to be born by the producer and most of the benefit will be to those up the chain in the industry and society at large."

Some respondents were open to the technology, but concerned about the producer's bottom line. A 16-year producer from Burleigh County

Table 2. Classification of disadvantages

Disadvantage	Number of Respondents
Trialability	41
Relative Advantage	40
Complexity	37
Observability	17
Compatibility	9
Other	7
None	2

n = 153

Table 3. Classification of conditions for adoption

Condition	Number of Respondents
Relative Advantage	34
None	29
Trialability	24
Other	24
Complexity	16
Observability	5
Compatibility	4

n = 136.

wrote "Someone who feels that they want/need this information to be the ones to pay for it—adoption of the technology doesn't bother me…paying for it and adding this cost—which will have no monetary return to my operation—does concern me." An 8-year producer from Ransom County agreed, "In the majority of the cattle operations I can only see problems if the cost to the producer affects the bottom line. RFID technology is a good idea only if the cost is minimal to producers."

Compatibility

Comments related to a need to integrate the new technology with the current system of brand identification were classified as concerns regarding compatibility. Respondents that mentioned compatibility in that either branding should be the only tracking system or that whatever system is implemented needs to be integrated with branding represented 10% (n = 9) of the total sample (Table 2), while 4% (n = 4) indicated that compatibility was a condition that would have to be met before adoption (Table 3). A 33-year producer from Logan County felt "The brand would be just as good" while a 9-year producer from Mercer County suggested, "It [RFID] needs to be used in conjunction with existing procedures already in place like brand inspection."

Many members felt the tracking should be specific to states and integrate the programs used by each state. A Billings County producer felt branding should continue to be used for tracking. He wrote, "It is proven and it works and the cost isn't a factor. Let the non-brand states do whatever system works for them, but we have one that works already." A 35-year producer from Dunn County agreed, "If all states had branding and brand inspection like we do we wouldn't need another tracking system. Ours works within 24 hours of a problem the animal is tracked back to the original owner." A 10-year producer from Burleigh County recognized that the system might have to adapt as cattle cross state boarders, "Since it is an animal health issue, let each state develop a program that suits its needs. When cattle are moved to another premise in another state they would then be under that state's system."

Complexity

Concerns regarding complexity in user friendliness, compliance, and confidentiality were mentioned by 40% (n = 37) of respondents (Table 2), while 17% (n = 16) indicated that complexity was a condition that would have to be met before adoption (Table 3). The concern over the ease of using the information was summed up in a comment from a producer of over 40 years from Ward County regarding a potential disadvantage as "unintelligent people trying to use the system." The animal ID coordinator from NDSA even acknowledged, "The program at USDA to assign numbers is not very user friendly."

While a few comments centered on compliance, including one from 35-year Dunn County producer saying simply, "Some producers will do it, others won't," most comments regarding the complexity of the technology concentrated on the level of privacy for the information. A 37-year producer from Morton County felt a disadvantage to RFID was "Confidential information made available to government and/or private organizations," while an 18-year producer from Sioux County was concerned about "Information getting to the wrong people." An extension worker at a research center in Adams County was also concerned about "who controls the data" and would be concerned "[i]f information put in national database, if info will have public access or if remain in private hands." A lifelong Billings County producer wrote, "My cattle are all permanently identified, but the records are all in my file and that is where they should be – not in Washington or Denver or wherever."

Trialability

Comments related to trialability or testing the technology and demonstrating that it will work were made by 45% (n = 41) of respondents (Table 2), while 26% (n = 24) indicated that trialability was a condition that would have to be met before adoption (Table 3). Many questions arose regarding whether the technology will work in colder climates. A 17-year producer from Stutsman County asked, "Will the readers work in -30 degree weather and what percentage will be allowed as slippage?" Other questions emerged regarding the potential for tags to be lost. An extension center researcher asked, "What happens if RFID tag comes out of ear—is there a visual tag that corresponds to RFID tag so imputed info won't be lost?" A producer and veterinarian asked, "Is reading only 90% of tags going to be acceptable for an animal health program on interstate movement? Will state veterinarians accept that less than 100% of animals in a load are accounted for?"

For other respondents, passed experience with identification methods altered their view of the new technology. A 25-year producer from Morton County wrote, "I have worked with button tags for 25 years and they don't stand up. Some years I have 7% loss, and our brand has yet to fall off. So it's going to be a mess." A producer of 10 years from Burleigh County plainly stated, "Technology isn't proven to be effective enough to implement," While a 13-year producer from

McHenry County acknowledged, "RFID, like all computer based application, has the potential to malfunction or crash."

Observability

Comments of concern that centered on if the respondents could see the technology working at the speed of commerce represented 18% (n = 17) of the total sample (Table 2), while 5% (n = 5) indicated that observability was a condition that would have to be met before adoption (Table 3). Some respondents did not see how RFID could work outside the test system. A lifetime Ward County producer who had adopted RFID wrote, "RFID is not yet 'state of the art,' it doesn't scan the first time usually which will cause delays." A 28-year Logan County producer's concern is that "[t]he speed of commerce will be slowed severely," while a lifetime producer from outside ND wrote the only way he would adopt is if there is "[t]echnology that is adequate enough not to impede commerce." A lifetime McIntosh County producer summed up the concerns in writing: "It would seem it is completely unworkable in the real world."

Other

Not all the disadvantages listed by respondents were encompassed by the elements of the adoption process. Respondents with concerns other than what fit into the categories comprised 8% (n = 7) of the total sample (Table 2), while 29% (n = 24) indicated another condition would have to be met before adoption (Table 3). Other disadvantages listed included: program was unnecessary, producers lacked information, technological age gap, and segmented investing. Additional conditions that would need to be in place before adoption included mandatory enrollment, those who want the information to be the ones to pay for it, and a standard system for all livestock across the country.

Of the 151 disadvantages to RFID technology listed by respondents, 95% (n = 144) were categorized into relative advantage, compatibility, complexity, trialability, and observability of the innovation (Table 2), while of the 107 conditions for adoption listed, 78% (n = 83) were categorized into elements of the adoption process replicating the barriers identified by NDSA leadership (Table 3). In fact, the researcher identified exact comments and phrases used by NDSA leadership in the response to USDA-APHIS including concerns regarding "cost, confidentiality, flexibility and the integration of current ID programs that are proven" (NDSA, 2004, para. 1).

When asked what the respondents recommend for an animal identification process, 47% (n = 43) recommended the continuation of branding, 9% (n = 8) recommended RFID technology, 3% (n = 3) recommended another form of identification (leg bracelet, metal ear tags, or computer chip); 2% (n = 2) recommended eliminating identification programs; and 17% (n = 16) did not provide recommendations (Table 4). Of the respondents, 20 did not specify a type of identification but provided recommendations for the kind of system needed. A 35-year producer from McHenry Country recommended a "system which is easily applied, tamper proof, and uniformly adopted "nationally." While a veterinarian from McKenzie County recommended, "Whatever method proves to be the most accurate over a tested time period." Noting the importance of implementing a workable system, a lifetime Kidder County producer wrote "Before it's implemented it really needs to be used on a ranch or station so that the flaws can be ironed out. Ranchers can be set in their ways and if something doesn't work – they will feel negative about the entire program."

Analysis

Despite respondents' understanding of the need for trace-back, 47% specifically recommended continuing the brand identification system com-

Table 4. Recommendations for animal identification

Recommendation	Number of Respondents
Branding	43
Workable System	20
No-Recommendation	16
RFID	8
Other	3
No Animal ID	2

n = 92.

pared to 9% specifically recommending RFID technology (Table 4). Similar to past studies, adoption in agriculture may be slower even if the innovation may lead to improvements (Ashby et al., 1996), as negative perceptions regarding any one element or combination of elements in an innovation can limit the adoption (Saltiel et al., 1994) Based on the results of this study, barriers to adoption of NAIS and RFID technology were evident in the description of the case. These barriers are described here as awareness, persuasion, and influence.

Awareness

In order for adoption to occur, an individual or organization must be aware of the innovation and gain an understanding of how it works. Since knowledge is limited by selective exposure, individuals are not likely to acknowledge information about an innovation unless they first feel a need for the innovation (Rogers, 2003). The occurrence of BSE was the most common reason provided by producers for the proposal of NAIS and RFID technology. However, as a 17-year producer from Stutsman County commented, "BSE-this is not an infectious disease and I feel this should not have prompted the NAID." The argument for the new system could be seen as irrelevant because the brand inspection program is already able to address what producers discern as the reason for the introduction of the technology. Producers who do not see a need for the innovation will not expose themselves to messages concerning the technology.

In addition, the knowledge required to implement adoption may also act as a barrier. As Rogers (2003) suggests, if an innovation is complex, "the amount of how-to knowledge needed for adoption is much greater," and without adequate how-to knowledge before adoption, "rejection and discontinuance are likely to result" (p. 173). The government agents proposing the system are educated and likely work with technology on a regular basis. Meanwhile, livestock producers who are not accustomed to technology may not feel that they will be able to work with RFID tags. As noted, a producer of over 40 years from Ward County regarded a potential disadvantage of the program as "unintelligent people trying to use the system."

Interest

Once aware, information on the innovation will still have little effect if an individual does not feel the innovation is relevant to his/her needs or if the innovation is not consistent with the established belief system (Hassinger, 1959). Branding has become a way of life for livestock producers in the Midwest (L. Schuler, personal communication, June 2005). A brand is the identifying symbol for a cattle operation and is one of the many practices past down through generations on family farms. In discussing the purpose of the state brand book, the chief NDSA brand inspector commented, "besides the book's obvious use to verify the ownership of livestock, you can bet some family member in future generations will treasure it for its historical value if they have one" (NDSA, 2006a). To introduce technology that would take the place of a symbol similar in many aspects to a family crest does not coincide with the established belief system of many livestock producers.

The attributes of the innovation are very important during the persuasion or interest stage of the adoption because the perception of the innovation is established. Noting the lack of messages from USDA-APHIS specifically addressing relative advantage, compatibility, complexity, trialability, and observability, many producers may not take the proposal seriously because they do not feel the system will actually be implemented. Within this barrier, producers feel it would be a waste of time and energy to evaluate a program that will never work. A lifetime producer from McIntosh County summed up this obstacle in writing: "It would seem it is completely unworkable in the real world."

Influence

Change agents seek the acceptance of opinion leaders in order to accelerate the adoption process, however, opinion leaders apposed to the adoption can instead act as a barrier that can stall or even halt the learning process. Rogers' (2003) explanation of diffusion of innovation classifies the adoption of an innovation by opinion leaders as the tipping point in the adoption process. As the self proclaimed "state's spokesperson for the beef cattle industry" (NDSA, 2006b, para. 3), NDSA leadership spoke for its members in the response submitted to USDA-APHIS: "We are extremely disappointed. .. we find it ridiculous.. . we are not convinced. .. we question. .. " Many members are likely to follow the leadership as indicated by responses stating the members will do whatever NDSA recommends. Based on the influence of NDSA leadership identified in the articulation of barriers to the adoption process as categorized into relative advantage, compatibility, complexity, trialability, and observability of the innovation (Rogers, 2003), membership will likely not adopt RFID technology unless supported by NDSA leadership. In effect, NDSA leadership became a change agent for the rejection of NAIS and RFID Technology.

Conclusion and Implications

This study provided an example of how barriers to adoption are articulated during the diffusion process. The following implications are outlined to provide direction to help overcome these barriers and encourage research in the diffusion process of risk reduction tools.

1. Organizations proposing risk reduction tools cannot assume that reducing the risk is perceived to be worth the time, money, and effort to adopt a new process. The innovation attributes were all identified by the membership as disadvantages and conditions of acceptance. USDA-APHIS must address these concerns with producers to further the adoption of NAIS and RFID. Since the plan was released, USDA-APHIS has had to backtrack. They have had to provide for more time and leeway for NAIS. Had they addressed each of the innovation attributes in the plan, the reception may have been better. Organizations proposing new risk reduction tools should prepare the informative/persuasive messages to address each of the innovation attributes.

2. Organizations proposing risk reduction tools cannot assume that reducing the risk is perceived to be necessary. Suder and Inthavong (2008) suggest that risk reduction depends on the public perception of risks. Participants thought NAIS and RFID were introduced because of BSE. Since source verification for BSE is already accomplished through branding, participants did not see a need for the new tools. Organizations proposing new risk reduction tools must effectively convey the need before proposing the innovation to address the need.

3. Organizations proposing risk reduction tools must consider the significance of maintaining the status quo in the culture of the population. Branding is more than a means for identifying cattle. A brand identifies the family in much the same way as a family crest. For some producers, to replace branding with tags is to reduce the family identification to a number. Proposed risk reduction tools are more likely to be adopted if they are compatible with the belief system of the population. Before the launch of any innovation, the culture of the population must be analyzed.

4. Lastly, while original work in diffusion of innovation does acknowledge the role of opinion leaders in speeding up the adoption process, more research is needed to examine the role of opinion leaders in the rejection of an innovation. The organizational rhetoric submitted by NDSA leadership provided attribute limitations that needed to be addressed. These limitations were mirrored in the member responses. Kuzma and Ahl (2006) in assessing the risk of BSE suggested that it would be reasonable to include representatives of the industry in the decision making process. Organizations proposing risk reduction tools must determine the concerns of opinion leaders and address them before the opinion leaders become change agents advocating the rejection of the innovation.

While the implications described here can provide direction to most organizations diffusing innovative risk reduction tools, this study specifically examined the barriers to adoption of NAIS and RFID technology as risk-reduction tools. Barriers were identified as awareness, interest, and influence, requiring further research regarding innovation attributes. In addition to intense competition from international trade and fluctuating markets, the agriculture industry also faces impending loss each year due to devastating weather, overpopulation of pests, and naturally occurring diseases. The threat of an agroterrorist attack only adds to the turbulent future of the high-risk agriculture industry. To counteract the terrorist's training manual devoted to agricultural terrorism, USDA-APHIS must write its own manual on how to diffuse innovative risk reduction tools. The risk in this case is not having an effective system in place, not if, but when the next crisis strikes.

ACKNOWLEDGMENT

This research was funded by a USDA Special Grant for Agrosecurity: Disease Surveillance and Public Health, and by the U.S. Department of Homeland Security (Grant number N-00014-04-1-0659), through a grant awarded to the National Center for Food Protection and Defense at the University of Minnesota. Any opinions, findings, conclusions, or recommendations expressed in this publication are those of the author(s) and do not represent the policy or position of the Department of Homeland Security.

REFERENCES

Agricultural Research Service, United States Department of Agriculture. (2002). *ARS national programs, animal health.* Retrieved May 20, 2002, from http://nps.ars.usda.gov/programs/programs.htm?npnumver=103

Animal Plant Health Inspection Service. (2005, April 25). *National Animal Identification System draft strategic plan.* Retrieved March 14, 2006, from http://animalid.aphis.usda.gov/nais/about/pdf/NAIS_Draft_Strategic_Plan_42505.pdf

Ashby, J. A., Beltrán, J. A., Guerrero, M. P., & Ramos, H. F. (1996). Improving the acceptability to farmers of soil conservation practices. *Journal of Soil and Water Conservation, 51*, 309–312.

Boyatzis, R. E. (1998). *Transforming qualitative information: Thematic analysis and code development.* Thousand Oaks, CA: Sage.

Casagrande, R. (2002). Biological warfare targeted at livestock. *Bioscience, 52*(7), 577–581. doi:10.1641/0006-3568(2002)052[0577:BWTAL]2.0.CO;2

Coffey, A., & Atkinson, P. (1996). *Making sense of qualitative data: Complementary research strategies.* Thousand Oaks, CA: Sage.

Cox, L. A., Popken, D. A., VanSickle, J. J., & Sahu, R. (2005). Optimal tracking and testing of U.S. and Canadian herds for BSE: A Value-of-Information (VOI) Approach. *Risk Analysis, 25*(4), 827–840. doi:10.1111/j.1539-6924.2005.00648.x

Doeg, C. (2005). *Crisis management in the food and drinks industry: A practical approach* (2nd ed.). New York: Springer.

Goldman, K. D. (1994). Perceptions of innovations as predictors of implementation levels: The diffusion of a nationwide health education campaign. *Health Education Quarterly, 21*, 433–444.

Hage, J., & Aiken, M. (1967). Relationships of centralization to other structural properties. *Administrative Science Quarterly, 69*, 32–40.

Haider, M., & Kreps, G. L. Forty years of diffusion of innovations: Utility and value in public health. *Journal of Health Communication, 9*, 3–11. doi:10.1080/10810730490271430

Hassinger, E. (1959). Stages in the adoption process. *Rural Sociology, 24*, 52–53.

Holloway, R. E. (1977). *Perceptions of an innovation: Syracuse University's Project Advance.* Syracuse, NY: Syracuse University.

Katz, E., & Lazarsfeld, P. F. (1955). *Personal influence.* New York: The Free Press.

Kearns, K. P. (1992). Innovations in local government: A sociocognitive network approach. *Knowledge and Policy, 5*(2), 45–67. doi:10.1007/BF02692805

Kremer, K. S., Crolan, M., Gaiteyer, S., Tirmizi, S. N., Korshing, P. F., & Peter, G. (2000). Evolution of an agricultural innovation: The N-Track Soil Nitrogen Test: Adopt, and discontinuance, or reject? *Technology in Society, 23*, 93–108. doi:10.1016/S0160-791X(00)00038-5

Kuzma, J., & Ahl, A. (2006). Living with BSE. *Risk Analysis, 26*(3), 585–588. doi:10.1111/j.1539-6924.2006.00768.x

Lincoln, Y. S., & Guba, E. G. (1985). *Naturalistic inquiry*. Beverly Hills, CA: Sage.

Mancuso, J. R. (1969). Why not create opinion leaders for new product introductions? *Journal of Marketing, 33*, 20–25. doi:10.2307/1248476

Moore, G. C., & Benbasat, I. (1991). *An examination of the adoption of information technology by end-users: A diffusion of innovations perspective* (Working paper 90-MIS-012). Vancouver, BC, Canada: Department of Commerce and Business Administration, University of British Columbia.

North Dakota State University. (2005). *Agrosecurity: Disease surveillance and public health (Brochure)*. Fargo, ND: Knight Printing.

North Dakota Stockmen's Association. (2005). *Comments submitted on the National Animal Identification System Strategic Plan*. Retrieved August 25, 2005, from http://www.ndstockmen.org/images/animal%20id%20comments.htm

North Dakota Stockmen's Association. (2006a). *Stockmen's Association publishes new brand book*. Retrieved October 12, 2006, from http://www.ndstockmen.org/images/Brandbook.htm

North Dakota Stockmen's Association. (2006b). *Welcome*. Retrieved March 12, 2006, from http://www.ndstockmen.org

Piller, C. (2004, September 12). US agriculture adds defenses against terrorism; some microbes or poisons could ruin confidence in U.S. food and devastate the farm economy. *Orlando Sentinel*. p. G1.

Rogers, E. M. (1973). *Communication strategies for family planning*. New York: Free Press.

Rogers, E. M. (2003). *Diffusion of innovations* (5th ed.). New York: Free Press.

Rogers, E. M., & Svenning, L. (1969). *Modernization among peasants: The impact of communication*. New York: Holt Rinehart & Winston.

Rogers, E. M., & van Es, J. C. (1964). *Opinion leadership in traditional and modern Columbian peasant communities*. East Lansing, MI: Michigan State University.

Roling, N., Ascroft, J., & Chege, F. Y. (1976). The diffusion of innovations and the issue of equity in rural development. *Communication Research, 3*, 155–170. doi:10.1177/009365027600300204

Ryan, B., & Gross, N. C. (1943). The diffusion of hybrid seed corn in two Iowa communities. *Rural Sociology, 8*, 15–24.

Saltiel, J., Bauder, J. W., & Palakovich, S. (1994). Adoption of sustainable agricultural practices: Diffusion, farm structure, and profitability. *Rural Sociology, 59*, 333–349.

Severin, W. J., & Tankard, J. W. (1997). *Communication theories: Origins, methods, and uses in the mass media* (4th ed.). White Plains, NY: Longman Publishing Group.

Singhal, A., & Rogers, E. M. (2003). *Combating AIDS: Communication strategies in action*. New Delhi, India: Sage.

Sparshott, J. (2004, February 24). Outbreak points out vulnerability of U.S. food supply. *The Washington Times*. p. A01.

Suder, G., & Inthavong, S. (2008). New health risks and sociocultural contexts: Bird Flu impacts on consumers and poultry businesses in Lao PDR. *Risk Analysis, 28*(1), 1–12. doi:10.1111/j.1539-6924.2008.00997.x

Taylor, S. J., & Bogdan, R. (1998). *Introduction to qualitative research methods* (3rd ed.). New York: John Wiley & Sons.

Turnbull, P. W., & Meenaghan, A. (2001). Diffusion of innovation and opinion leadership. *European Journal of Marketing, 14*(1), 3–33. doi:10.1108/EUM0000000004893

USDA-APHIS. (2008). *National Animal Identification System.* Retrieved April 16, 2008, from http://animalid.aphis.usda.gov/nais/

Wasson, C. R., Sturdivant, F. D., & McConaughy, D. H. (1970). The social process of innovation and product acceptance. In Britt, S. H. (Ed.), *Consumer behaviour in theory and in action* (pp. 252–255). New York: John Wiley & Sons.

Weir, T. (1999). Innovators or news hounds? A study of early adopters of the electronic newspaper. *Newspaper Research Journal, 20*(4), 62–81.

Wheelis, M., Casagrande, R., & Madden, L. V. (2002). Biological attack on agriculture: Low-tech, high-impact bioterrorism. *Bioscience, 52*(7), 569–576. doi:10.1641/0006-3568(2002)052[0569:BAOALT]2.0.CO;2

Wulf, W. A., Haimes, Y. Y., & Longstaff, T. A. (2003). Strategic alternative responses to risks of terrorism. *Risk Analysis, 23*(3), 429–444. doi:10.1111/1539-6924.00325

Zaltman, G., Duncan, R., & Holbek, J. (1973). *Innovations and organizations.* New York: John Wiley & Sons.

This work was previously published in International Journal of Technology and Human Interaction, Volume 6, Issue 2, edited by Anabela Mesquita & Chia-Wen Tsai, pp. 30-46, copyright 2010 by IGI Publishing (an imprint of IGI Global).

Chapter 4
Exploring the Player Flow Experience in E–Game Playing

Chin-Lung Hsu
Da-Yeh University, Taiwan

ABSTRACT

Flow theory has been widely applied in the context of information technology and is useful in under-standing users' behavior; however, few studies empirically examine what factors influence players' flow, and what the facets and consequences of flow are in the context of electronic games (e-games). In this study, the author reviews previous flow-related literature to develop the proposed model to explore these research questions. The proposed model is empirically evaluated using survey data collected from 277 users responding about their perception of e-game. Results of this empirical study show that perceived ease of use, immediate feedback, skill and challenge are antecedents of flow, while enjoyment is the most salient facet of flow. The results provide further insights into e-game design and development.

INTRODUCTION

Information technology is advancing so rapidly, it has extensively restructured people's leisure activities. A very popular leisure activity is the electronic game (e-game), which includes video games, computer games, and online games. A video game is comprised of a TV monitor and console machines such as Sony's PlayStation, Microsoft's Xbox, and Nintendo's Wii. Computer games require a personal computer (PC) platform

to play. Online game users can play not only with the PC, but also with other users connected via the Internet. Notably, people can play all e-games mainly for leisure and enjoyment.

People can play games for enjoyment (Hsu & Lu, 2007). Accordingly, there will be huge business opportunities in this field. According to eMarketer (2006), the global market for e-games which includes game-related hardware and soft-ware, computer games, console game, computer games and online game will rapidly expand from $ 29 billion in 2005 to $ 44 billion in 2011. Many e-game companies consequently invest far more

DOI: 10.4018/978-1-61350-465-9.ch004

resources to develop game products. Moreover, countries such as Taiwan, Singapore, and Korea have in recent years launched projects to speed up the digital entertainment industry; game-related manpower training and platform building are growing significantly. For example, Taiwan's government launched the Taiwan Digital Contents Industry plan, which includes both digital games and multimedia animation, to promote the whole e-games industry.

While many reports indicate that the e-games market will be huge, there has been relatively little research into this area. Notably, most studies to date have concentrated on online games user (Hsu & Lu, 2004; Choi & Kim, 2004; Voiskounsky et al., 2004). These studies show that users' flow experience is a critical factor of intention to use. When a user is in the flow state, he/she is completely immersed in it. This cognitive state has been defined as the flow experience. As this experience is intrinsically enjoyable, users always want to maintain this state. Furthermore, Johnson and Wiles (2003) also indicate that a game may be successful when it is able to create a sense of flow in the user. They use the concept of flow in computer games to inform affective user interface design. Therefore, it is important to understand the driving forces of users' flow experience in the context of e-games.

Over the past few years, a considerable number of studies have related the concept of flow to information technology (Trevino & Webster, 1992; Webster et al., 1993; Ghani & Deshpande, 1994; Hoffman & Novak, 1996; Webster & Ho, 1997; Chen et al., 2000; Koufaris, 2002; Konradt et al., 2003; Pilke, 2004). Flow has been identified as the key for attracting and retaining customers as well as obtaining competitive advantage on the internet. However, few attempts have been made with entertainment technology. Although studies have been made on games (Johnson & Wiles, 2003; Hsu & Lu, 2004), they seem not to explain what factors influence the players' flow experience. Remarkably, numerous attempts have

been made to explore the antecedents of flow but the results are still confusing mainly because different contexts, such as web sites (Novak et al., 2000; Korzann, 2003), e-commerce (Koufaris, 2002) and online games (Choi & Kim, 2004) are used. Moreover, while antecedents of flow have been examined in these studies, no research has been found to investigate the facets of flow. Therefore, the question this study has to ask is: what motivates users to create flow experience in the context of entertainment technology, such as e-games? In addition, what facets and consequences of flow in the context of electronic games need to be clarified?

The purpose of this study is to examine the antecedents, facets and consequences of flow in e-games. This study proposes that flow experience is important to the study of e-game users' behavior because it serves as a key antecedent to users' attitude and behavior to an e-game. Furthermore, it is also vital to understand the antecedents and facets of flow because by manipulating these factors, game developers can better create users' flow experience, and subsequently, suggest new ways to improve game use. In this study, structural equation analysis is applied to explore the theorized nomological network of flow.

FLOW EXPERIENCE

Csikszentmihalyi (1975) originally defined flow as "the holistic sensation that people feel when they act with total involvement". When in the flow state, people become absorbed in their activity. Flow is characterized by a narrowing of focused awareness, so that irrelevant perceptions and thoughts are screened out; a loss of self-consciousness; a responsiveness to clear goals and unambiguous feedback; and a sense of control over the environment. Recently, researchers have used this concept to understand people's behavior while using information technology. As stated by Novak et al. (2000), online executives note that creating a flow experience for cyber customers is the key to competitive advantage on the Internet.

Csikszentmihalyi (1990) identified clear goals and immediate feedback as a necessary condition of flow. In addition, the balance between perceived challenge and personal skill is also critical to reaching flow. A person is bored when the level of skill exceeds the perceived challenge. On the contrary, a person is frustrated when the perceived challenge exceeds the level of skills. Thus, a person's perceptions of challenge and skill affect the sensation of flow.

Chen et al. (1999) indicated that flow experience can be categorized into three stages: antecedents, experiences and effects. The first stage describes the qualifying factors of the activity itself to create the flow; the second stage describes the facets perceived by a person in flow; the final stage describes the possible effects after being in flow. In recent years, most flow studies have studied these stages of user's flow in contexts ranging from human-computer interaction, Internet, e-commerce, e-learning, and online games.

In the context of human-computer interaction, Ghani et al. (1991) showed that flow includes two facets: enjoyment and concentration. In addition, their findings indicated that perceived control and challenge can predict flow. In subsequent work, Ghani and Deshpande (1994) proposed that skill and challenge directly influence flow, and then influence users' exploratory behavior. However, Trevino and Webster (1992) described four facets of the flow experience: control, attention focus, curiosity and intrinsic interest. They modeled that antecedents of flow include computer skill, technology type, and ease of use. Webster et al. (1993) used this definition but combined curiosity and intrinsic interest into cognitive enjoyment, and described that specific characteristics of the software (flexibility and modifiability) and information technology use (future voluntary use) would create flow.

In the context of the Internet, flow is defined by Hoffman and Novak (1996) as "the state oc-

curring during network navigation which is: (1) characterized by a seamless sequence of responses facilitated by machine interactivity, (2) intrinsically enjoyable, (3) accompanied by a loss of self-consciousness, and (4) self-reinforcing." They modeled skill and control, interactive speed, challenge and arousal, focused attention, and telepresence and time distortion as antecedents of flow. In a subsequent study, Novak et al. (2000) used this model and empirically examined the relationship between the antecedents and flow. Additionally, Agarwal and Karahanna (2000) proposed cognitive absorption (CA) as the state of flow in the World Wide Web context. They treated flow as a multi-dimensional construct that includes temporal dissociation, focused immersion, heightened enjoyment, control and curiosity. The individual innovativeness and playfulness are important determinants of CA. Furthermore, recent works also used CA to explore online shopping and user's online learning behavior (Shang et al., 2005; Saade & Bahli, 2005).

In e-commerce research, flow has been applied to explore online customer behavior (Koufaris, 2002). His study shows that antecedents of flow include product involvement, web skill, value-added search mechanisms and challenges. Flow experience influences customers' intention to visit. Also, Korzann (2002) confirmed that flow experience influences both web exploratory behavior and attitude toward purchasing online.

In the context of entertainment technology, Hsu and Lu (2004) applied the technology acceptance model (TAM) that incorporates social influences and flow to predict users' acceptance of online games. Specifically, their result verified that flow directly influences users' intention to play. Choi and Kim (2004) argued that personal interaction and social interaction are two antecedents of flow, and found that these factors can predict flow. Their findings confirm that flow directly influences customer loyalty. Furthermore, flow seems to be critical in game design. To form a positive effect, a game designer should combine flow characteristics with user interface design (Johnson & Wiles, 2003).

The proposed research model based on flow is mixed, as presented in Table 1. As Koufaris (2002) argued, flow is too broad and ill defined because much still needs to be defined and tested. In addition, while the flow experience is a psychological variable within people, most researchers need users to remember their flow experience in order to meaningfully describe flow. In other words, flow is a latent variable (Webster et al., 1993). Therefore, based on Koufaris's (2002) suggestion, this study proposes flow's emotional (enjoyment and control) and cognitive components (concentration)

to measure the flow experience. The emotional responses also correspond to those of pleasure and dominance from environmental psychology (Mehrabian & Russel, 1974). In this study, flow is defined as an extremely enjoyable experience, where a user engages in an e-game activity with total involvement, enjoyment, control, concentration and intrinsic interest.

Additionally, researchers also proposed different antecedents of flow in a specific context. This study extends Csikszentmihalyi's work that incorporates perceived ease of use by exploring the antecedents of flow in the context of e-games, namely, clear goals, immediate feedback, skill,

Table 1. Previous flow studies

Authors (years)	Research Contexts	Antecedents	Facets	Consequences
Ghani, Supnick, and Rooney (1991)	Human-computer interaction	Skill, control, challenge	Enjoyment, concentration	
Trevino and Webster (1992)	Human-computer interaction	Computer skill, technology type, and ease of use	Control, attention focus, curiosity and intrinsic interest	Attitude, effectiveness, quantity and barrier reduction
Webster, Trevino and Ryan (1993)	Human-computer interaction	Perceived flexibility, perceived modifiability, experimentation, future voluntary use, actual use, perceived communication quality, perceived communication effectiveness	Control, attention focus, curiosity and intrinsic interest	
Ghani and Deshpande (1994)	Human-computer interaction	Control, challenge	Enjoyment, concentration	
Hoffman and Novak (1996)	Web sites	Skill/challenge, focused attention, telepresence, and interactivity	Flow	Increased learning, perceived behavioral control, positive subjective experience, distortion of time perception
Webster and Ho (1997)	Multimedia	Challenge, feedback, control, variety	Attention focus, curiosity, and intrinsic interest	
Novak and Hoffman (1997)	Web sites	Skill and challenge	Flow	
Chen, Wigand and Nilan (1999)	Web sites	Clear goals, immediate feedback, skill, challenge	Merging of action and awareness, concentration, control	A loss of self-consciousness, the sense of time distortion, experience which becomes autotelic

continued on following page

Table 1. Continued

Authors (years)	Research Contexts	Antecedents	Facets	Consequences
Agarwal and Karahanna (2000)	World Wide Web	Playfulness, personal innovation, self-efficacy	Cognitive absorption (control, focused immersion, curiosity, temporal dissociation, heightened enjoyment)	Perceived ease of use, perceived usefulness, intention to use
Novak et al. (2000)	Web sites	Skill/challenge, interactive speed, challenge/arousal, focused attention and telepresence/ time distortion	Flow	Exploratory behavior
Moon and Kim (2001)	World Wide Web	Perceived ease of use	Enjoyment, concentration, curiosity	Intention to use
Koufaris (2002)	Online purchase	Product involvement, web skills, value-added search mechanisms, challenge	Control, shopping enjoyment, concentration	Unplanned purchases, intention to return
Konradt et al. (2003)	Hypermedia learning	Skill, challenge	Flow	
Korzaan (2003)	Online purchase		Flow	Attitude, exploratory behavior
Skadberg and Kimmel (2004)	Web sites	Skill, challenge, telepresence	Flow	Increased learning, changes in attitudes and behavior
Hsu and Lu (2004)	Online game		Flow	Intention to use
Choi and Kim (2004)	Online game	Personal interaction, social interaction	Flow	Customer loyalty
Shang et al (2005)	Online shopping		Cognitive absorption	Perceived ease of use, Perceived usefulness, shopping online
Saade and Bahli (2005)	Online learning		Cognitive absorption (Temporal Dissociation, Focused Immersion, Heightened Enjoyment)	Perceived ease of use, Perceived usefulness, Intention to use
Wan and Chiou (2006)	Online game			Addiction

challenge and perceived ease of use. In fact, these five factors are common antecedents of flow proposed by past empirical studies (Csikszentmihalyi, 1993; Hoffman & Novak, 1996; Chen et al., 1999; Novak et al., 2000; Koufaris, 2002; Konradt et al., 2003; Pace, 2004; Skadbert & Kimmel, 2004). Additionally, understanding the consequences of flow is interesting and important. Literature suggests that satisfaction, intention to use and exploratory behavior may be the outcomes of flow (Ghani, 1991; Ghani & Deshpande, 1994; Novak et al., 2000; Korzaan, 2003; Hsu & Lu, 2004). While this study can verify flow significantly affect these factors, e-game developers should be strive to plan appropriate strategies to create flow experience of players to increase these consequences. Hence, these three factors are examined in this study.

RESEARCH MODEL AND HYPOTHESES

Research Model

Figure 1 illustrates the research model, which was built based on the literature review. It asserts that the flow experience is determined by perceived ease of use, clear goals, immediate feedback, skill, and challenge. Flow facets comprise enjoyment, perceived control, and concentration. The consequences of flow are satisfaction, intention to use, and exploratory behavior. The definition of constructs, network of relationships illustrated in the model, and the rationale for the proposed links are explained in the following section.

Hypotheses

Facets of Flow

Human behavior can be affected by both intrinsic and extrinsic motivation (Davis et al., 1992). While extrinsic motivation emphasizes performing a behavior to achieve specific goals/rewards (Deci & Ryan, 1987), intrinsic motivation refers to the pleasure and satisfaction from performing a behavior (Vallerand, 1997). Furthermore, perceived enjoyment is a form of intrinsic motivation. In the context of e-games, users always expect to enjoy the game. They play games mainly for their leisure and pleasure. Therefore, enjoyment is a key driver of behavioral intention to use. In this study, perceived enjoyment was defined as the degree to which the user perceives that playing an e-game will be pleasurable and fun. Moreover, Koufaris (2002) identified enjoyment as the facets of flow experience when people shop online. Past studies also indicate that the flow experience comprises enjoyment (Ghani & Deshpande, 1994; Hoffman & Novak, 1996; Chen et al., 2000; Agarwal & Karahanna, 2000; Hedman & Sharafi, 2004). Hence, we believe that enjoyment is an important component of flow in a game context.

In addition, Koufaris (2002) contends that the concentration is also related to flow experience. According to many studies, the characteristics of flow are: "Users are completely and totally

Figure 1. Research model

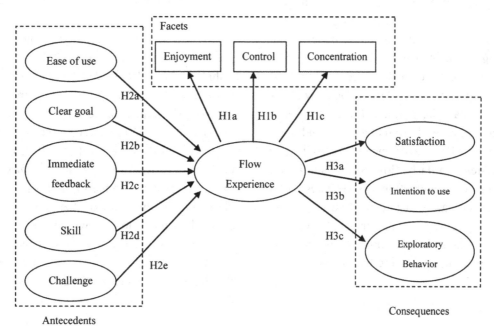

immersed in it" or "Complete involvement of the actor with his activity". As far as meaning is concerned, users always concentrate on their activity and feel in control of their environment when in a state of flow. Therefore, theses two factors can also play a critical role in flow characteristics. Concentration was defined as the degree of the intensity of the user's absorption in the game. Perceived control was defined as the extent to which the user perceives the level of one's control over the environment and one's actions. In the context of e-games, users need the ability to control the game and their actions; otherwise they will have trouble engaging in a game with total involvement. Additionally, concentration can help users complete interaction with an e-game more efficiently. In this state, users can easily be in flow. In summary, this study proposes the following hypothesis:

H1a-c: Flow comprises the facets of (1) perceived enjoyment, (2) perceived control and (3) concentration.

Perceived Ease of Use

Perceived ease of use was defined as the degree to which the user believes that using an e-game will be free of effort. It is a salient belief in the Technology Acceptance Model (Davis, 1989). Past research has shown that perceived ease of use is an important antecedent to the flow experience. For example, Hsu and Lu (2004) found that perceived ease of use had a direct and positive impact on flow experience in the context of online games. Similarly, flow-related studies on human-computer interaction and web sites found that perceived ease of use directly affects flow experience (Trevino & Webster, 1992; Moon & Kim, 2001; Chung & Tan, 2004). Therefore, this study proposes the following hypothesis:

H2a: Perceived ease of use will influence flow experience when playing an e-game.

Clear Goal and Immediate Feedback

Csikszentmihalyi (1975, 1993) identified that the antecedents of flow experience include clear goals and immediate feedback. Clear goals was defined as the extent to which the user perceives a specific target, such as building a civilization or conquering the enemy, and wants to achieve it during the game. Additionally, immediate feedback was defined as the extent to which the user perceives that task provides a seamless sequence of response while interacting with e-game. Empirical studies based on this viewpoint have found that these two factors positively affect an individual's flow experience (Chen et al., 1999; Pilke, 2004). Therefore, this study proposes the following hypotheses:

H2b: Clear goals will influence flow experience when playing an e-game.
H2c: Immediate feedback will influence flow experience when playing an e-game.

Skill and Challenge

These two factors are verified as the important predictors of flow by previous studies (Csikszentmihalyi, 1975b, 1993; Webster et al., 1993; Hoffman & Novak, 1996; Novak & Hoffman, 1997). To cause flow, the balance between personal skill and perceived challenge is necessary (Csikszentmihalyi, 1990). If the level of skill is below the challenge, a person is in a state of anxiety. On the contrary, a person feels bored if skill exceeds challenge. In the context of e-games, skill was defined as the extent to which the user judges one's capability to use an e-game. Challenge was defined as the extent to which the user perceives the challenge provided by the game. Users usually need a personal skill to meet the game's challenge. While playing can be perceived by a user as a challenge, the level of skill will decide their positive or negative experience. Therefore, this study proposes the following hypotheses:

H2d: Skill will influence flow experience when playing an e-game.
H2e: Challenge will influence flow experience when playing an e-game.

Consequences of Flow

The flow experience, which defined as the extent of enjoyment, control and concentration with which users engage in game activity, may cause users' behavior to change, such as higher user satisfaction (Ghani, 1991; Woszczynski et al., 2002), increased behavioral intention (Agarwal & Karahannal, 2000; Rettie, 2001; Moon & Kim, 2001; Koufaris, 2002; Hsu & Lu, 2004), and more exploratory behaviors (Webster et al., 1993; Ghani & Deshpande, 1994; Hoffman & Novak, 1996; Novak et al., 2000, Korzaan; 2003). Here, satisfaction was defined as the extent to which users believe the available game meets their playing requirements. Intention to play was the extent to which the user would like to play the game in the future. Exploratory behavior referred to the degree to which the user is eager to check out new games and find out about the latest game just out of curiosity. This study proposes the following hypotheses.

H3a: Flow experience will influence satisfaction toward playing an e-game.
H3b: Flow experience will influence intention to play an e-game.
H3c: Flow experience will influence exploratory behavior into e-games.

METHODOLOGY

Sample and Procedure

The research sample was taken from e-games users, who were collected by conducting an online field survey. The survey messages outlined the goal of this study and the hyperlink to the survey form were posted at e-game related web sites such as Gamebase (http://www.gamebase.com.tw), Bahamut (http://www.gamer.com.tw/), Yamgames (http://game.yam.com/) and game-related communities for two months. Notably, the discussion boards in these sites contain variety of game types which include video games, computer games, mobile game and online games. Participants were able to respond to the online questionnaire from perceptions of their favorite games. In survey site Javascript programming was developed to actually handle the data collection process, thereby ensuring that all items in the questionnaire were filled in completely. At the completion of the survey, this study offered respondents an opportunity to join a draw of 30 NT$300 bookstore certificates for a prize. Therefore, participants need to leave their email account to enter the drawing. To avoid participants' repeats on answering the questionnaire, duplicate IP addresses and email account were checked.

Overall, 277 completed responses were returned. Among them, 83% were male and 17% female; over 82% of them were below the ages of 25; 62% of respondents had a bachelor's degree. The data also indicates that 80% of respondents had over 3 years experience in playing e-games. Table 2 summarizes the profiles of the respondents.

Measurement of Variables

The items on the questionnaire, which were developed from the literature, are listed in Table 3. Those for perceived ease of use (2 items), clear goals (3 items), immediate feedback (2 items), skill

Table 2. Demographic attributes of respondents

	Frequency	Percentage
Gender		
Male	231	0.83
Female	46	0.17
Age		
Under 15	12	0.05
16-20	89	0.32
21-25	127	0.45
26-30	37	0.13
31-35	9	0.04
Over 36	3	0.01
Education level		
Junior high school	12	0.05
Senior high school	63	0.23
Bachelor's degree	171	0.62
Graduate degree (or above)	31	0.11
Years of playing experience		
Under 1 year	8	0.04
1-3 years	22	0.06
3-6 years	67	0.25
6-10 years	60	0.22
Over 10 years	120	0.43
Monthly expenditure on playing games (NT$)		
Under 100	74	0.26
100-300	48	0.18
300-600	78	0.28
600-1000	43	0.16
Over 1000	34	0.12
Time spent playing a game each time (hours)		
Under 1	10	0.04
1-3	131	0.47
3-6	105	0.38
Over 6	31	0.11
Weekly playing time (hours)		
Under 10	60	0.22
11-20	77	0.27
21-30	79	0.28
31-40	26	0.10
Over 41	35	0.13

(2 items) and challenge (2 items) were adapted in our model from TAM and previous studies on flow (Davis, 1989; Koufaris, 2002; Choi & Kim, 2004). The flow instrument developed by Koufaris (2002) is a second model that consists of three first-order factors measured by 7 items: enjoyment (2 items); concentration (3 items); control (2 items). The scales for satisfaction (2 items), intention to use (2 items) and exploratory behavior (2 items) are based on studies (Al-gahtani & King, 1999; Davis, 1989; Novak et al., 2000). Theses scales were slightly modified to suit the e-game context. The items were measured using a five-point Likert scale, ranging from "disagree strongly" (1) to "agree strongly" (5).

Before conducting the main survey, both a pre-test and a pilot test were administered to validate the instrument. The respondents in the pre-test were five e-game experts. The respondents were asked to comment on listed items that cor-

Table 3. Summary of measurement scales

Item	Measure	Factor Loading	Mean	SD	Composite Reliability	Average Variance Extracted
Perceived ease of use (PE)						
PE1	Learning to play a game is easy for me	0.88	4.21	0.70	0.87	0.77
PE2	It is easy to play	0.88				
Clear goal (GO)						
GO1	I know the specific target I want to achieve during the game	0.85	4.02	0.76	0.91	0.78
GO2	I clearly understand what mission should be accomplished	0.93				
GO3	The game clearly informs me of its goal at present	0.88				
Immediate feedback (IF)						
IF1	The game's response to my actions is fast	0.92	3.83	0.79	0.82	0.70
IF2	The game's response is without delay	0.75				
Challenge (CH)						
CH1	Playing a game challenges me to perform to the best of my ability	0.77	3.92	0.83	0.82	0.70
CH2	Playing a game provides a good test of my skills	0.90				
Skill (SK)						
SK1	I am very skilled at playing the game	0.87	3.96	0.79	0.82	0.69
SK2	I know how to find what I want on the game	0.80				
Perceived enjoyment (EN)						
EN1	I have fun playing the game	0.87	4.46	0.64	0.90	0.82
EN2	I find playing the game enjoyable	0.94				
Perceived control (PC)						
PC1	When I play the game, I feel in control	0.91	3.53	0.79	0.81	0.69
PC2	When I play the game, I do not feel confused	0.75				
Concentration (CO)						
CO1	When I play the game, I am absorbed intensely in the activity	0.92	3.88	0.87	0.95	0.88
CO2	When I play the game, my attention is focused on the activity	0.96				
CO3	When I play the game, I concentrate fully on the activity	0.94				
Satisfaction (SA)						
SA1	I am satisfied playing the game	0.87	3.80	0.92	0.86	0.76
SA2	Playing a game is a good decision for me	0.88				
Behavioral intention to use (BI)						
BI1	I will frequently play the game in the future	0.96	4.30	0.73	0.93	0.88
BI2	I am willing to play the game	0.91				
Exploratory behavior (EB)						
EB1	When I hear about a new game, I'm eager to check it out	0.81	3.69	0.95	0.82	0.70
EB2	I often find out about the latest game just out of curiosity	0.87				

Table 4. Discriminant validity

	1	2	3	4	5	6	7	8	9	10	11
1.PE	**0.77**										
2.GO	0.20	**0.78**									
3.IF	0.12	0.15	**0.70**								
4.CH	0.06	0.07	0.08	**0.70**							
5.SK	0.28	0.24	0.14	0.26	**0.69**						
6.EN	0.13	0.11	0.13	0.18	0.21	**0.82**					
7.PC	0.18	0.16	0.12	0.10	0.24	0.10	**0.69**				
8.CO	0.14	0.12	0.17	0.16	0.20	0.18	0.07	**0.88**			
9.SA	0.07	0.07	0.11	0.13	0.15	0.26	0.13	0.15	**0.76**		
10.BI	0.12	0.10	0.11	0.10	0.15	0.17	0.07	0.15	0.33	**0.88**	
11.EB	0.13	0.02	0.04	0.11	0.16	0.16	0.04	0.16	0.23	0.23	**0.70**

responded to the constructs, including the wording of the scales, the length of the instrument, the format of the questionnaire, and other comments on how the questionnaire could be improved. Finally, to ensure that the questionnaire adequately addressed the relevant issues and to reduce possible ambiguity in the questions, a pilot test was administered.

DATA ANALYSIS AND RESULTS

Descriptive Statistics

Descriptive statistics were calculated and are shown in Table 3. It was determined that, on average, users responded to e-games in a positive manner (the averages were all greater than 3.5). This reflects meaningful information. First, the score of perceived ease of use is very high; this confirms that subjects perceive the current e-game user interface as easy to use. Secondly, subjects usually have clear goals to interact with games which can respond to user's operation immediately. Third, the result shows that subjects are very experienced on playing games (as shown in Table 2, 65% of respondents have over 6 years experience playing games). Therefore, we can

infer that the subjects responded positively to skill in game playing. However, the surveyed players consistently perceive that modern games become more complicated and challenging. So, they need to use their best ability and skill to play. Fourth, regarding flow experience, respondents believe that enjoyment, control and concentration are perceived while playing games. Finally, subjects enjoy playing very much. This reflects their high satisfaction, intention to use and exploratory behavior.

Analytic Strategy for Assessing the Model

The test of the proposed model includes two stages: the measurement model and the structural model. The method of the first stage was to perform Confirmatory Factor Analysis (CFA) to evaluate overall fitness of the measurement model as well as to measure reliability and validity. Second, the structural model examines the strength and direction of the relationship among constructs.

The Measurement Model

The reliability and validity of all constructs were assessed by the CFA. The CFA was computed using

LISREL 8.3. As shown in Table 3, item reliability (loading) ranged from 0.75 to 0.92. All constructs were greater than 0.5, which indicated acceptable item reliability (Hair et al., 1992). Additionally, as shown in Table 3, for composite reliability, consistent with the recommendations of Fornell (1982), all scores exceeded the acceptable value of 0.6. The average variance extracted (AVE) for all constructs also exceeded the threshold value of 0.5 recommended by Fornell and Larcker (1981). These three results provided support for the adequate convergence reliability of the scales.

To assess the adequacy of discriminant validity, the shared variance among variables should be less than the AVE by the constructs. As shown in Table 4, discriminant validity was adequate for the measurement model, which indicated that constructs were empirically distinct. Thus, these results showed the test of the measurement requirements to be satisfactory.

As shown in Table 5, the measurement model test presented a good fit between the data and the proposed measurement. Results showed that Chi-square/df value was 1.56, slightly less than 3 as recommended by Hayduk (1987). GFI, NFI and NNFI exceeded the recommended 0.90 benchmark (Scott, 1994). In addition, RMSEA was lower than 0.05 as suggested by Bagozzi and Yi (1988). Therefore, all measurements indicated that the model fits the data.

Diagonals represent the average variance extracted, while the other matrix entries represent the shared variance (the squared correlations)

The Structural Model

In a structural model, the second-order CFA model was estimated to identify the relative importance of each flow facet. For ease of exposition, only loadings for the flow facets are shown in Figure 2. Results showing the loading of perceived enjoyment, perceived control and concentration were 0.67, 0.82 and 0.72 respectively. They all exceeded the acceptable value of 0.5, and thus support H1a-c. Therefore, this finding encourages the decomposition of the flow variable into its theorized facets. Moreover, the model explains 60% of the variance for perceived enjoyment indicating that the perceived enjoyment is the most salient concern in the context of e-games.

For the antecedents of flow, results showed that perceived ease of use, immediate feedback, skill and challenge play an important role in reaching flow experience (β=0.25, 0.34, 0.24, 0.44, p< 0.05). Together, the four paths account for approximately 59% of the observed variance in explaining flow experience. Notably, H2a, H2c-d were supported. However, clear goal was not found to influence flow experience. Therefore, H2b was not supported.

Finally, consistent with our expectations, the effect of flow on satisfaction, intention to use, and exploratory behavior was significant (β=0.76, 0.70, and 0.69, p< 0.001). Therefore, H3a-c was supported.

Table 5. Model evaluation overall fit measurement

Measure	Value
X^2/df (<3.0)	1.56
Goodness of fit index (GFI) (>0.9)	0.91
AGFI (>0.8)	0.88
Normed fit index (NFI) (>0.9)	0.93
Non-normed fit index (NNFI) (>0.9)	0.97
Root mean square error of approximation (RMSEA) (<0.05)	0.037

Figure 2. Results of structural modeling analysis

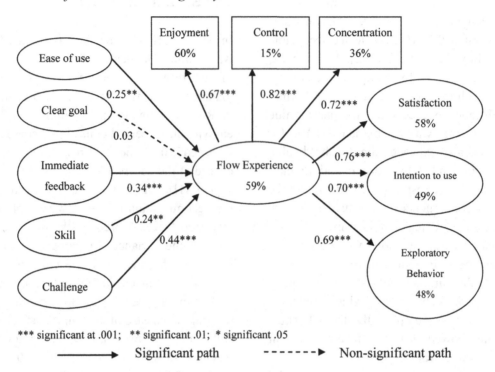

*** significant at .001;   ** significant .01; * significant .05

⟶ Significant path   - - - - - - ▶ Non-significant path

DISCUSSION AND IMPLICATIONS

This study quantitatively investigated user flow experience of e-games, with results that supported most of the proposed hypotheses. Organizations that launch e-game projects should be aware of these flow-related factors. The results support the following conclusions.

First, the results indicate that flow includes emotional (enjoyment and control) and cognitive (concentration) facets. When in the flow state, e-game users enjoy themselves intrinsically; they become concentrated on their activity, and they feel in control of their game world. Specifically, enjoyment appears to be the foundation of flow experience. This result confirms that users' game playing experience is shaped by pleasure, happiness, and fun. Therefore, game designers should actively seek ways to combine emotional components into game design. For example, an e-game may provide an entertaining story, humor, and surprise effect such as sound, graphics,

and animation. In a well-designed e-game, these characteristic should excite people's emotions and lead to the experience of flow.

Second, the findings reveal that the antecedents of flow including perceived ease of use, immediate feedback, skill and challenge significantly influence flow experience. To create a sense of flow in the user, game developers should include these factors in game design. For example, easy-of-use interfaces play an important role in forming flow experience. While playing the e-game, users' perception of ease of use may easily help them concentrate and feel in control. On the contrary, a complicated operation may decrease the likelihood of users experiencing flow. Therefore, ease of use is a salient factor that contributes to the flow experience of e-games. This finding also confirms Hsu and Lu's research on online games. Additionally, there is an existing significant difference between novices and experts of computer games (Hong & Liu, 2003). Hence, interface design should not only be more user-friendly, but also provide a special mode such as a hot key for experienced users to speed their operation.

In addition, users should get feedback immediately while interacting with the game. This result indicates that the more immediate feedback users receive, the more likely they are to focus their attention on the interaction, and thus be in a state of flow. Here, game managers may want to maintain stable and high quality systems. System quality such as response time and accessibility of the game are very influential factors in determining the users' belief in ease of use and interaction with the game. If interacting with the game is slow and tedious, it may be difficult for users to experience flow.

Unexpectedly, clear goals have no significant effect on flow experience. The result seems inconsistent with previous work by Choi and Kim who verified that a goal is an antecedent factor of flow in an online game. Nevertheless, the results of our analysis reveal that the score of clear goals is 4.02 on a five-point scale and variance is 0.76 (see Table 3). This shows that users still have clear goals to play games. Therefore, one possible explanation is that users focus totally on the present while playing games. It is possible that although users want to accomplish the goals or tasks in their mind, they just perceive the seamless sequence of responses at every moment in a flow state.

The results of this study also confirm that skill and challenge are important antecedents of flow. This finding is in line with the results of prior studies that indicated a strong link between these two factors and flow (Novak et al., 2000; Koufaris, 2002). Specifically, Barendregt et al. (2006) indicated that challenge is an important factor for the fun of a game when a user becomes more familiar with a game. From the viewpoint of flow, however, game designers should consider the balance between skills and challenge and how they relate to flow. Additionally, for users to remain in flow, designers may gradually increase the complexity of the activity by developing users' skills

in meeting new challenges. For example, in order to increase the level of skills, games can train their users to be more skilled and efficient on operating games. Moreover, designers should make sure that users have enough skills to overcome the different degrees of challenge in the game.

Finally, results reveal that flow experience may directly influence users' behavior in the context of e-games. This is in agreement with previous studies (Choi & Kim, 2004; Hsu & Lu, 2004). When in a state of flow, users are likely to get satisfaction and to develop intention to use. Furthermore, they are more likely to engage in exploratory behavior. Therefore, marketers should undertake efforts to remind users of their flow experience. For example, combining multimedia effect and enjoyment components can inspire users to experience the psychological state of flow. In addition, developers who are designing e-games should keep in mind the antecedent factors identified in this study that have been empirically shown to influence flow.

CONCLUSION AND LIMITATIONS

This study provides a research model to examine users' flow experience in the context of e-games. More specifically, the antecedents in terms of perceived ease, immediate feedback, skill and challenge explain 69% of the variance on users' flow experience. The key findings are:

1. Understanding the essence of flow experience is very informative for a game designer because flow significantly influences users' satisfaction, intention to use and exploratory behavior.
2. Flow experience can be facilitated by providing users enjoyment, concentration and control. Notably, an important point to emphasize is the fact that enjoyment is the main facet of flow in an e-game context. This shows that flow experience derives

from intrinsic motivation. If enjoyment can give users emotional satisfaction, they are more likely to fall in flow.

3. Antecedents of flow such as perceived ease of use, immediate feedback, skill and challenge play important roles in causing flow experience. Decreasing these factors is an obstacle to forming flow. In other words, if e-game designers ignore one of these factors, users will have trouble concentrating on and controlling the game, and then won't have fun.

The results of the present study need to be interpreted with caution for several reasons. First, statistical analysis provides only numerical relationships. Interpretation of results is an author's subjective appraisal. However, results consistent with theories and other studies, enhance confidence in the findings. Second, this study regarded the flow experience as a latent variable and thus proposed enjoyment and control, concentration to measure the flow experience. Generally, there are three major approaches including native/survey, activity/survey and experience sampling method (ESM) to measuring flow experience that have been taken in empirical study (Novak & Hoffman, 1997). This study used the narrative/survey for measuring flow. The other method such as activity/survey method is used in laboratory experiments which assigns samples participated in a selected activity and has them complete questionnaires measuring flow. The ESM is suited to measure flow in activities encountered in everyday by paging the respondent. This study also recommends additional e-game flow research employing these measurement methodologies.

Third, this study used internet users as respondents to implement an online survey. Thus, a bias exists because the sample was self-selected. Nevertheless, the demographic profile showed that players are relatively young and generally well educated. These demographic findings on respondents confirmed previous findings (MIC,

2004). However, further research such as gender differences in the context of e-game may be performed. Many studies had indicated that women and men differ in their perceptions of IT usage (Gefen et al., 1997; Venkatesh & Morris, 2000; Lucas & Sherry, 2003). Hence, this study suggests that future study should include gender in explaining e-game playing behavior.

Fourth, although there are many different game platforms (video game, computer game and online game) or game types (role-playing game, a first-person shooter, a strategy title and simulation) in e-game market, with a goal to better understand the e-game players' flow experience, this study did not differentiate the game types since many players usually play diverse games. This study mainly focused on the formation as well as effect of the flow in the context of e-games. However, future research may be needed to address this particular issue. For example, further analyses suggest that researchers investigate the flow experience of players in different game types such as a simulation game and first-person shooter.

Finally, this research mainly attempted to apply Koufaris's and Csikszentmihalyi's work to assess players' flow experience. Therefore, there can be additional factors such as social aspects and individual factors to predict a user's emotional and cognitive responses. For example, Weibel et al. (2007) examined different competitive experiences of with other human beings and/or computer-controlled components in the context of online game. Future research may investigate the influence of these additional variables to better understand the flow experience of e-game.

ACKNOWLEDGMENT

This study was supported by grants from the National Science Council of the Republic of China under Contract Number NSC 94-2416-H-212-001.

REFERENCES

Agarwal, R., & Karahanna, E. (2000). Time flies when you're having fun: cognitive absorption and beliefs about information technology usage. *Management Information Systems Quarterly, 24*(4), 665–694. doi:10.2307/3250951

Al-Gahtani, S. S., & King, M. (1999). Attitudes, satisfaction and usage: factors contributing to each in the acceptance of information technology. *Behaviour & Information Technology, 18*(4), 277–297. doi:10.1080/014492999119020

Bagozzi, R. P., & Yi, Y. (1988). On the Evaluation of Structural Equation Models. *Journal of the Academy of Marketing Science, 16*, 74–94. doi:10.1007/BF02723327

Barendregt, W., Bekker, M. M., Bouwhuis, D. G., & Bauuw, E. (2006). Identifying usability and fun problems in a computer game during first use and after some practice. *International Journal of Human-Computer Studies, 64*, 830–846. doi:10.1016/j.ijhcs.2006.03.004

Chen, H. (2000). Exploring web users' optimal flow experiences. *Information Technology & People, 13*(4), 263–281. doi:10.1108/09593840010359473

Chen, H., Wigand, R., & Nilan, M. (1999). Optimal experience of web activities. *Computers in Human Behavior, 15*(5), 585–608. doi:10.1016/S0747-5632(99)00038-2

Choi, D., & Kim, J. (2004). Why people continue to play online games: in search of critical design factors to increase customer loyalty to online contents. *Cyberpsychology & Behavior, 7*(1), 11–24. doi:10.1089/109493104322820066

Chung, J., & Tan, F. B. (2004). Antecedents of perceived playfulness: an exploratory study on user acceptance of general information-search website. *Information & Management, 41*, 869–881. doi:10.1016/j.im.2003.08.016

Csikszentmihalyi, M. (1975). *Beyond Boredom and Anxiety*. San Francisco, CA: Jossey-Bass.

Csikszentmihalyi, M. (1993). *The evolving self: a psychology for the third millennium*. New York: Harper & Row.

Csikzentmihalyi, M. (1990). *Flow, the Psychology of Optimal Experience*. New York: Harper & Row.

Davis, F. D. (1989). Perceived Usefulness, perceived ease of use, and user acceptance of information technology. *Management Information Systems Quarterly, 13*, 319–339. doi:10.2307/249008

Davis, F. D., Bagozzi, R. P., & Warshaw, P. R. (1992). Extrinsic and intrinsic motivation to use computers in the workplace. *Journal of Applied Social Psychology, 22*(14), 1111–1132. doi:10.1111/j.1559-1816.1992.tb00945.x

Deci, E. L., & Ryan, R. M. (1987). The support of autonomy and the control of behavior. *Journal of Personality and Social Psychology, 53*(6), 1024–1037. doi:10.1037/0022-3514.53.6.1024

Desanctis, & C. Beath (Eds.), In *Proceedings of the Twelfth International Conference on Information Systems (ICIS)* (pp. 229-237). New York.

EMarketer. (2006). *EMarketer*. Retrieved July 20, 2008, from http://www.find.org.tw/find/home.aspx?page=news&id=4512

Fornell, C. R. (1982). *A second generation of multivariate analysis methods: Vols. I and II*. New York: Praeger Special Studies.

Fornell, C. R., & Larcker, D. F. (1981). Structural equation models with unobservable variables and measurement error. *JMR, Journal of Marketing Research, 18*, 39–50. doi:10.2307/3151312

Gefen, D., & Straub, D. W. (1997). Gender differences in the perception and use of e-mail: An Extension to the technology acceptance model. *Management Information Systems Quarterly, 21*(4), 389–400. doi:10.2307/249720

Ghani, J. A., & Deshpande, S. P. (1994). Task characteristics and the experience of optimal flow in human-computer interaction. *The Journal of Psychology, 128*(4), 381–391.

Ghani, J. A., Supnick, R., & Rooney, P. (1991). The experience of flow in computer-mediated and in face-to-face groups. In Hair, J. F., Anderson, R. E., Tatham, R. L., & Black, W. C. (Eds.), *Multivariate data analysis with readings*. New York: MacMillan.

Hayduck, L. A. (1987). *Structural Equation Modeling with LISREL: essentials and advances*. Baltimore, MD: John Hopkins University Press.

Hedman, L., & Sharafi, P. (2004). Early use of Internet-based educational resources: effects on students' engagement modes and flow experience. *Behaviour & Information Technology, 23*(2), 137–146. doi:10.1080/0144929031000164825

Hoffman, D. L., & Novak, T. P. (1996). Marketing in Hypermedia Computer-mediated environments: conceptual foundations. *Journal of Marketing, 60*, 50–68. doi:10.2307/1251841

Hong, J. C., & Liu, M. C. (2003). A study on thinking strategy between experts and novices of computer games. *Computers in Human Behavior, 19*, 245–258. doi:10.1016/S0747-5632(02)00013-4

Hsu, C. L., & Lu, H. P. (2004). Why do people play on-line games? An extended TAM with social influences and flow experience. *Information & Management, 41*(7), 853–868. doi:10.1016/j.im.2003.08.014

Hsu, C. L., & Lu, H. P. (2007). Consumer behavior in on-line game communities: a motivational factor perspective. *Computers in Human Behavior, 23*, 1642–1659. doi:10.1016/j.chb.2005.09.001

Johnson, D., & Wiles, J. (2003). Effective affective user interface design in games. *Ergonomics, 46*(13/14), 1332–1345. doi:10.1080/0014013031000161086

Konradt, U., Filip, R., & Hoffmann, S. (2003). Flow experience and positive affect during hypermedia learning. *British Journal of Educational Technology, 34*(3), 309–327. doi:10.1111/1467-8535.00329

Korzann, M. L. (2003). Going with the flow: predicting online purchase intentions. *Journal of Computer Information Systems*, (Summer): 25–31.

Koufaris, M. (2002). Applying the technology acceptance model and flow theory to online consumer behaviour. *Information Systems Research, 13*(2), 205–223. doi:10.1287/isre.13.2.205.83

Lucas, K., & Sherry, J. L. (2003). *Sex Differences Among Young Adults' Video Game Use and Preference*. Paper presented at the Mass Communication Division, National Communication Association Annual Convention, New Orleans, LA.

Mehrabian, A., & Russel, J. A. (1974). *An Approach to Environmental Psychology*. Cambridge, MA: MIT Press.

Moon, J. W., & Kim, Y. G. (2001). Extending the TAM for a World-Wide-Web context. *Information & Management, 38*(4), 217–230. doi:10.1016/S0378-7206(00)00061-6

Novak, T. P., & Hoffman, D. L. (1997). Measuring the flow experience among web users. *Interval Research Corporation*. Retrieved from http://www.find.org.tw/find/home.aspx?page=many&id=78

Novak, T. P., Hoffman, D. L., & Yung, Y. F. (2000). Measuring the customer experience in online environments: a structural modeling approach. *Marketing Science, 19*(1), 22–42. doi:10.1287/mksc.19.1.22.15184

Pilke, E. M. (2004). Flow experiences in information technology user. *International Journal of Human-Computer Studies, 61*, 347–357. doi:10.1016/j.ijhcs.2004.01.004

Rettie, R. (2001). An exploration of flow during Internet use. *Internet Research, 11*(2), 103–113. doi:10.1108/10662240110695070

Saade, R., & Bahli, B. (2005). The impact of cognitive absorption on perceived usefulness and perceived ease of use in on-line learning: an extension of the technology acceptance model. *Information & Management, 42*, 317–327. doi:10.1016/j.im.2003.12.013

Scott, J. (1994). The measurement of information systems effectiveness: evaluating a measuring instrument. In *Proceedings of the Fifteenth International Conference on Information Systems,* Vancouver, BC, Canada (pp. 111-128).

Shang, R. A., Chen, Y. C., & Shen, L. (2005). Extrinsic versus intrinsic motivations for consumers to shop on-line. *Information & Management, 42*, 401–413. doi:10.1016/j.im.2004.01.009

Skadbert, Y. X., & Kimmel, J. R. (2004). Vistors' flow experience while browsing a Web site: its measurement, contributing factors and consequences. *Computers in Human Behavior, 20*, 403–422. doi:10.1016/S0747-5632(03)00050-5

Trevino, L. K., & Webster, J. (1992). Flow in computer-mediated communication. *Communication Research, 19*(5), 539–573. doi:10.1177/009365092019005001

Vellerand, R. J. (1997). Toward a hierarchical model of intrinsic and extrinsic motivation. *Advances in Experimental Social Psychology, 29*, 271–360. doi:10.1016/S0065-2601(08)60019-2

Venkatesh, V., & Morris, M. G. (2000). Why don't men ever stop to ask for directions? gender, social influence, and their role in technology acceptance and usage behavior. *Management Information Systems Quarterly, 24*(1), 115–139. doi:10.2307/3250981

Voiskounsky, A. E., Mitina, O. V., & Avetisova, A. A. (2004). Playing online games: flow experience. *PsychNology Journal, 2*(3), 259–281.

Wan, C. S., & Chiou, W. B. (2006). Psychological Motives and Online Games Addiction: A Test of Flow Theory and Humanistic Needs Theory for Taiwanese Adolescents. *Cyberpsychology & Behavior, 9*(3), 317–324. doi:10.1089/cpb.2006.9.317

Webster, J., & Ho, H. (1997). Audience engagement in multi-media presentations. *The Data Base for Advances in Information Systems, 28*(2), 63–77.

Webster, J., Trevino, L. K., & Ryan, L. (1993). The dimensionality and correlates of flow in human-computer interactions. *Computers in Human Behavior, 9*, 411–426. doi:10.1016/0747-5632(93)90032-N

Weibel, D., Wissmath, B., Habegger, S., Steiner, Y., & Groner, R. (2008). Playing online games against computer- vs. human-controlled opponents: Effects on presence, flow, and enjoyment. *Computers in Human Behavior, 24*(5), 2274–2291. doi:10.1016/j.chb.2007.11.002

Woszczynski, A. B., Roth, P. L., & Segars, A. H. (2002). Exploring the theoretical foundations of playfulness in computer interactions. *Computers in Human Behavior, 18*, 369–388. doi:10.1016/S0747-5632(01)00058-9

This work was previously published in International Journal of Technology and Human Interaction, Volume 6, Issue 2, edited by Anabela Mesquita & Chia-Wen Tsai, pp. 47-64, copyright 2010 by IGI Publishing (an imprint of IGI Global).

Chapter 5
Sustainable
e–Recruiting Portals:
How to Motivate Applicants to Stay Connected throughout their Careers?

Elfi Furtmüller
University of Twente, The Netherlands

Celeste Wilderom
University of Twente, The Netherlands

Rolf van Dick
University of Frankfurt, Germany

ABSTRACT

Since most e-recruiting portals suffer from outdated applicant profiles and receive little user return as soon as applicants have found a new job, in this study, the authors explore how to motivate applicants to keep their profiles up-to-date and stay connected with one specific recruiting portal throughout their careers. The authors interviewed applicants, system analysts and programmers of an Austrian e-recruiting portal. Narratives showing striking differences between these three stakeholders' interpretation of system requirements for long-term usage are discussed. The identified requirements point to niche recruiting: integrating social network and community features for specified user segments sharing a similar social identity and fostering pre-existing offline ties among users for career purposes. Implications are sketched for more sustainable e-recruiting research, design and development.

DOI: 10.4018/978-1-61350-465-9.ch005

INTRODUCTION

Communication between customers using a web service and the staff responsible for the service's development (such as system analysts, programmers, web designers, system testers, etc.), is oft absent although it is important in all phases of systems development. This communication is crucial, from a sustainability point of view, and is even more essential during requirements analysis. In its simplest form, requirements determination entails eliciting and encoding into the new system the requirements that potential and/or current users verbalize to system analysts. Usually, the analyst works with end users to establish an understanding of their needs, then designs system alternatives and writes up a documentation of those requirements for the programmers. One consistent finding in the literature concerned with IS (Information Systems) development is the communication difficulty between analysts and users (Bostrom, 1989). The communication between analysts and users is often problematic due to cognitive and vocabulary-type limitations (Byrd et al., 1992). Much interview-type research portrays a mismatch in the expectations of analysts, programmers and clients.

Several IS researchers argue that the interview remains the best elicitation technique for requirement analyses (Alvarez & Urla, 2002). Independent of the type of interview (e.g., structured or unstructured), this technique depends on interactional talk between those who (re-)design or further develop the service and those who use it. Since the obtained data is, in this sense, partly a function of the talk between a (potential) client and a system designer, the study of this talk is central to the understanding of how information is captured in this client-analyst link. While much attention has been given to the problematic nature of system analyst-to-client communication, very little of the extant research involves any intermediate communication among system designers, programmers and users; there is not much research that analyzes their different interpretations of requirement specifications and communications outcomes (Pfleeger & Atlee, 2010).

This paper seeks to make a contribution to the scholarship on requirements analysis in the context of sustainable e-recruiting services. Based on in-depth interviews with users, system analysts and programmers of a niche e-recruiting platform for engineers, we show how differently these three stakeholders interpret system requirements for long-term usage. We will argue, based on their insights, that so-called domain expert researchers (i.e., those professionals with expertise in a specific related field such as e-recruiting platform design) may add value (incl. unbiased requirement insights) from narratives of involved participants in a system-development project. Using such an intermediary expert researcher for purposes of interpreting and comparing focused communication outcomes may help in better recognizing, understanding, and ultimately making use of the experiences of involved parties. This type of captured tacit knowledge may enable e-recruiting providers to better serve their customers and help them to differentiate themselves from other providers. We first review the relevant literatures; we then present the research site and the collected data. Following, we illustrate the narrative analyses, results and derive concluding as well as future-study insights.

THEORECTICAL BACKGROUND

IS Requirement Analyses and User Involvement

The idea of involving users in IS development stems from the belief that involving users provides multiple benefits. As a result of their pre-involvement, potential users may form stronger intentions to actually use the new/revised service; it might even enhance their service experience. It will further increase user accountability for the system's design, thus resulting in higher user satisfaction, commitment and reduced resistance to renewing or innovating services (Amoako-Gyampah, 2007). Also, innovative and market-oriented development of new products and services has been associated with high-user involvement (von Hippel, 2007). High IT-service success has been shown already to be a function of the active involvement of members of the user community (Doherty et al., 2003). Moreover, development times have been shown to be shortened if continuous acceptance tests occur during service development (Iansiti & MacCormack, 1997). Exactly how and how extensively user involvement needs to be organized into the (re)design process of services and their organizations is unknown as of yet (Rondeau et al., 2006). Although it has been found that involving users can lead to innovative service ideas, sometimes the users' ideas are too difficult to create or too costly to realize. A general definition of user involvement is still lacking as well. It has been seen as synonymous with *contacting with users* (Grudin, 1991), *participation of users* (Ives & Olson 1992), *user-centred design* (Noyes et al., 1999), and *user engagement* (Wagner & Piccoli, 2007).

Research findings report that many system failures are due to the lack of clear and specific information requirements (Davis, 1982; Buchanan, 2007). Most development engineers have little or no experience as an end-user in the application domain for which they develop the software. As a result, development often tends to be technology (or solution) driven without a contextualized sense of the specific issues to be addressed. We tend to offer products and services to our customers not based on their actual needs but rather on what updated hardware and software packages allow engineers to do. In a study of information systems projects, Jenkins (1984) found that over half of the systems examined had problems and required the analysts to return to the requirements analysis phase. Moreover, if errors in requirements analysis are not found until later stages

of the implementation process, costs or failure rates can rise significantly (Marakas & Elam, 1998). Hence, determining accurate information requirements is important to both researchers and practitioners alike. Requirements analyses play an increasingly important role in software development because most persistent problems are caused by an incorrect analysis of customer's requirements. Information systems implementations are notoriously difficult. Of the variety of problems that present themselves, obtaining a robust set of system requirements is one of the most important as well as one of the most difficult tasks. Requirements analysis approaches are intensely interactive and demand effectual communication between the user and analyst. In its simplest form, requirements analysis during a systems development project entails encoding into the new information system any requirements that users verbalize. The primary means for obtaining data during requirements analysis interactions is the direct interview (Hotzblatt & Beyer, 1995). However, interviews are recognized as a potentially rich but notoriously difficult method of data elicitation (Moody et al., 1998). While some system analysts perceive user narratives collected in interviews as messy or uncodeable data, we find the insights they provide to be valuable. This may be especially true for e-recruiting service portals that, unlike other information systems, such as social networks (www.facebook.com) or business networks (www.LinkedIn.com), face more struggles to maintain active user (applicant) profiles. Hence, a better understanding of the stories, explanation and interpretations of users, system analysts and programmers for continued use of such portals is needed.

Narratives and IS Research

Narratives have been defined as tales, stories or the recital of facts, and usually are told in the first person. In this research tradition, stories and individuals' experiences rather than logical arguments are assumed to be the vehicle through which meaning is communicated (Sarbin, 1995). Narrative theory can also be seen as part of social construct theory, as meaning is assigned through definite processes of interaction. This account is also closely linked to Weick's (1995) emphasis on organizational sensemaking. The narrative approach stands in contrast to rationalist perspectives since events are not explained by establishing their causes; rather they are made understandable by integrating them within a sequence. Similarly, Czarniawska (1998) describes narratives as interpretations of events that reflect the significant issues that actors seek to dramatize and emphasize. In a similar vein, interviewees not only organize their world through these narratives, they also perform stories that are consistent with their expectations, values and identity.

In the area of information systems, research on narratives has recently begun to spread. For instance, Davidson (1997) used narrative analysis to examine sensemaking and interpretation during an IS development project. Further, Scarbrough (1997) explored the idea of *strategic IT* as a particular form of social labelling. Brown (1998) examined the use of narratives that organizational members produced to create meaning and gain political advantage during an IT implementation. In another case, Brown and Jones (1998) examined a failed IS project and the types of individual narratives that emerged after the project. Fincham (2002) explored a narrative perspective on success and failure in computer-systems development. Alvarez and Urla (2002) argue that in the field of information systems implementation, narrative analysis provides richer data than the data obtained by conventional systems requirements analysis. According to these authors, narratives do provide a window into the pragmatic and emic perspectives of information system users. They argue that these perspectives are valuable to the successful assessment and design of a new information system, and analysts need to become better skilled at conducting and interpreting interviews. Hence,

interviewers should actively engage in seeking stories from users, system analysts, developers, designers and testers and interpret them to reveal their encoded information. Requirement analyses would not only benefit from the improvement of interview techniques but also from methods for analyzing the rather messy qualitative data that interviewees provide. Also, Bartis and Mitev (2008) recently combined constructionist and critical approaches through a narrative methodology to discuss the launch of an information system.

Of particular interest to the art of conducting requirement-analytical interviews, we see the concept of identity construction as useful. During those interviews individuals express their thoughts, intentions, desires, feelings, values and attitudes. Put differently, in narrating our experiences and attitudes (etc.), we define ourselves as the implied subject of the narrative, and possibly at the same time as members of groups sharing a similar identity (such as Programmer, System Analyst or User Identity or Professional of a certain organization). Through the elicitation of requirements, the interviewees are regarded as the object of knowledge. In this sense, researchers have argued that through linguistic expressions the interviewees' identities are produced. The research findings presented in this paper seek to contribute to this growing research stream by analyzing user, system designer and programmer narratives to better understand and make use of different requirements produced by different interviewee groups. Interview-generated narratives from different involved stakeholders, mediated by a communicative or action researcher, are assumed to provide valuable insights into system-development projects.

Research on e-Recruiting

During the past 10 years, e-recruiting services have been spreading across the globe. Although research into e-recruiting is still sparse, surveys from professional organizations such as the Society for Human Resource Management (SHRM) frequently report the staffing/recruiting area and specifically online recruiting as one of the most critical HR duties. Until about five years ago, most studies focused on applicant reactions (e.g., Feldman & Klaas, 2002; Zusman & Landis, 2002; Dineen et al., 2007). Research in this area has been carried out also in order to find out why companies and recruiters decide to use e-recruiting (Parry, 2008). Further, Wolters' study on job boards found that there is a negative relationship between the amount of information given about the job and the percentage of suitable reactions (Wolters, 2006). The emerging importance of e-recruiting services to identify talent and meet staffing needs is quite pronounced. One could get the impression that too many e-recruiting portals are emerging, considering that, for instance, in the current German market a new e-recruiting portal announces their operating start approximately every two weeks.

Unlike social networks, one of the main problems e-recruiting portals have is that in general their registered users are not long-time active users. Usually, employees who are looking for a job tend to search through the published job ads and apply to the e-listed jobs. As soon as they have found a new job, there is hardly any reason to return to a site again. Consequently, large numbers of e-recruiting initiatives fail (Feldman & Klaas, 2002; Lin & Stasinskaya, 2002). It is difficult to design technical features of online services and seed at the same time new social practices for ongoing communications, in addition to the initially perhaps only instrumentally oriented users (Szmigin et al., 2005). Another struggle still tends to be the challenge of delivering semantically accurate search results when offering applicant-pool search functions. Besides this, posting resumes on job boards also calls for consideration of privacy and security issues. Often, both an applicant's and recruiter's name, address and phone number are displayed for anyone to see. Another problem e-recruiting portals are facing is the frequently reported dissatisfaction with slow responses from

applicant pools. Consider for instance business networks such as LinkedIn.com or Xing.com, where most of the registered users have jobs and are generally not easily motivated to switch jobs. While business networks are too slow in meeting urgent staffing needs, many general job boards are overloaded with job postings, hence minimizing the visitors per job ad. Further, many portals allow visitors of the recruiting sites to upload resumes or fill out pre-defined online resume forms and find information about suitable job openings. However, some recruiting providers advertise that they delete applicants' profiles after a certain period of time (e.g., every 6 weeks) so as to only offer up-to-date profiles. The latter practice is causing some frustration among many registered applicants who spent a significant amount of time filling out resume forms. Other providers accumulate masses of resumes and advertise having the most registered applicant profiles. However, in such resume databases, many of the profiles are not up-to-date anymore: the applicants have already found a job or their contact data has changed. This is especially important if recruiters can search in the applicants' pools. If company recruiters search in such pools, they may not have effective access to their desired candidates. Hence, a major challenge e-recruiting services are facing is to keep the applicants' profiles up-to-date. E-recruiting services also need to demonstrate their performance through high amounts of applicants visiting their sites and clicking on ads; high ratings on page impressions; a high accuracy of the matching between job ads and resumes; and by their ability to quickly suggest appropriate candidates to recruiters (Smith & Rupp, 2004; Zhao et al., 2007).

Increasingly, niche recruiting portals are entering the market. We assume that niche recruiting portals are similar to niche communities, which are based on shared interests and where the commonality of users will contribute to a higher sense of belonging to the platforms and a higher likelihood to remain and contribute to the shared goals of those portals. In general, communities depend on people visiting the sites, participating in social interactions, and on the loyalty of users (Kim, 2000). Although communities are conceptualized and studied in many diverse ways (Knoke & Kuklinski, 1982; Castells, 2000; Van Dijk, 2005; Boyd, 2007), many researchers agree that networked communities are defined on the basis of shared identity, interests, and commonality among their members (Turkle, 1995; Preece, 2000; Castells, 2004; Plickert et al., 2007). Further, offline activities have been found to increase the solidarity and cohesiveness of virtual communities, and to strengthen the ties between members (Wellman & Haythornthwaite, 2002; Wellman et al., 2002; Ellison et al., 2007). It may well be that these concepts apply to niche recruiting portals (i.e., career community platforms). Thus, there is enough justification for exploring actual user requirements that applicants, system analysts and programmers associate with sustainable e-recruiting services.

Given the paucity of academic research on these issues, our guiding research question is: What system requirements do e-recruiting services need to implement so as to motivate users to keep their applicant profiles up-to-date (even though they may have a job) and stay connected with one specific recruiting portal over their entire career?

METHOD

Research Site and Data Collection

The chosen e-recruiting company aims to become Austria's leader in intelligent online recruiting and career networking for engineers. Since its establishment in 2005, the company has developed many partnerships with engineering schools and companies across Austria and has obtained research grants for developing Web 2.0 technologies for e-recruiting services. The company's employees' regularly participate in

international conferences and are recognized within the www.drupal.org developer community. They also participate in international programming competitions and regularly assume mentor roles at the *google summer of code* event. The company actively collaborates with its registered applicants, recruiters and developers in an effort to capitalize and distribute knowledge for system design improvements (e.g., von Hippel, 2007). The organization was to determine its information requirements so as to enhance applicant retention.

Given the exploratory nature of our study, we adopted qualitative requirement interviews with registered applicants, system analysts and programmers. Our narrative research methodology focuses on understanding how interviewees deal with experience by constructing stories and listening to the stories (Riessman, 1993). All interviewed participants were asked about their ideas on system requirements to get users to return to the site throughout their careers and how to motivate them to keep their applicant profiles up-to-date.

We randomly selected (from the recruiting database) one registered user from each Higher Technical School (HTL) in Austria. The interviewees had a minimum of three years of work experience, and were telephone interviewed. Fifty-eight male engineers and two female engineers were interviewed, which represents the gender ratio for Austrian HTL engineers. On average, the interviews lasted 20 minutes. All telephone interviews were taped to capture the narratives. Also, during all interviews field notes of salient themes were taken. Further, several follow-up interviews were conducted when interviewees had too little time for the interview or needed time to think about answers to the questions. In addition, we interviewed six system analysts and eight programmers experienced in e-recruiting portal development. These 14 interviews lasted about an hour each. Narratives were recorded anonymously and with the consent of interviewees. Our aim was to gain their confidence in telling us their side of the story in a climate of trust. This was supported by the neutral investigation of a researcher instead of the usual direct requirement interviews done between system analysts and end-users. We noted several contradictions and overlaps of requirement specifications across subjects' narratives right after the first interviews. Also, meeting minutes from several status-update staff meetings with system analysts and programmers were compiled. It is a general policy that the system analysts record memos of their new ideas or requirements for system improvements. An administrative assistant usually types those memos once a week and the system analysts review, structure and publish the ideas on the company's project intranet site. We got access to the memos and studied the user-based system requirement comments. Programmers typically do not record memos but type their status updates on the same project intranet. On this project management site, programmers communicate textual messages via theme-oriented blogs, upload manuals, define milestones and schedule project tasks. We received a log-in account to get full access to the digital communications. We also had the opportunity to access the e-recruiting system, which provided us with a deeper understanding of the software's current features and functions. While interviewing, tracking digital data, observing meetings and asking questions, we kept a detailed record of field notes that enhanced the quality of later in-depth analysis. Researchers such as Van Maanen (1995) regard field notes as the *secret papers of social research* that comprise the most important observations.

Data Analyses

We followed the suggestion of Buchanan and Dawson (2007) that narratives should be analysed in relation to the sense-giving and sense-making of other stories and interpretations. In this vein, story analyses of certain groups of interviewees seek to accommodate the overlaps, ambiguities and contradictions that are part of the storytelling process

and audience interpretations. The challenge lies in analyzing components of data while also engaging in a meta-analysis that provides a synthesis that is both poly-vocal and represents coherently the meaning of the collected data. Hence, we followed the call for more informed studies that combine elements of a narrative research with contextual analysis. We did not rely only on stand-alone stories to understand the sensemaking and sense-giving associated with interviewee experiences. We also tried to understand the broader context in which repeated descriptions both account for and shape the processes of which they seek to make sense (Buchanan & Dawson 2007).

We first listened to all audio tapes of the interviews with the applicants, system designers and programmers. Then, we compiled narratives of salient parts of the interviews and compared them with the content of the field notes, meeting minutes and digital communications. Next, we identified broad themes in the data and reduced them to more precise categories (Miles & Huberman, 1994; Yin, 2003). We went back and forth between the different perspectives of the three groups of interviewees and altered existing requirement categories as other categories were created or eliminated (see Table 1). We found this first structural analysis helpful for the purpose of getting a broad overview of emerging themes, categories and sub-categories.

In order to enhance theoretical grounding and to more comprehensively understand the interview text, we analyzed the collected narratives. The emphasis during this stage of analysis was placed on stories and based on the language and interactions used to describe users' intentions for returning to an e-recruiting site and staying actively involved over time. Therefore, we included also intonation, volume, pacing and other qualities of speech to capture the feel of the interviews. Symbols used in the transcribed extracts are: Exclamation [!]; word emphasized by speaker [*Italics*]; pause [...]; hesitating [<<]; {nonlexical utterances}; [explanatory note]. Speakers are identified

Table 1. Summary of the interview results

Require-ment Specifica-tions	Users (Applicants)	System Analysts	Programmers
System Requirements	Fast loading of website Stable system availability Possibility for different profile views: for friends and public view Different options to determine privacy settings	Fast and strong server, stable system availability Strong hardware: when more users are online at the same time, Optimization of software Strong software High reliability Optimize back-up saving High security and privacy settings, invitation by friends necessary to register, make platform exclusive.	Accessible on every internet browser Strong hardware to be equipped when many users come, high server power Keep updating to new software versions so as to enhance possibilities for user When opening website, automatically move cursor to log in Include cookies so that user remain logged in and system recognizes returning users Ajax Privacy, SSL encrypted Define processes, interfaces e.g. HR-XML to link the recruiting platform to different companies and make the communication and data transfer more efficient e.g. applicant can directly apply to more companies at once by only filling out profile once SPI, SEO, SOA, WSDL, UDDI, SOAP Modular code structure, re-useable code and possibility to extend the code, documentation, tests, layering Balance between pre-defined standards e.g. within the specific software such as www.drupal.org but also develop customized solutions Code reliability, nodes relevance, debugging Multilingual capability
Information Requirements	Timeliness: latest news, latest and many relevant, customized job postings, structured content Send job updates How to prepare application documents Interview tips Infos on trainee programs Links to companies, internal contact persons Company Career Day info Online story pages First years as an engineers My worst and best career start Not overloaded Download section Salary calculator, Alumni calendar Career ABC, search for A (Audi), B (BMW) and link with users' experience reports Branch categorization Links to continuing education Technical blog	Timeliness: whenever re-visiting the page, provide new content and target specific information: new jobs exactly meeting my skill set and search specifications, new statistics about me: how do I score compared to others, automatic updates of contents, surprising news and experiences Concrete use meeting/exceeding expectation: leave data active for your next career move, communicate that the portal is accompanying your career throughout the life, stay online with your applicant profile so that you get better job offers, possibility to use free applicant page with individual address e.g., www.fh-absolventen.at/lastname_firstname Don't overload page: list only relevant jobs for user niche Classify contents carefully e.g., jobs and related jobs Job notification where only few people have applied + matches own skills Education & employer matching: which employer pays more for certain graduates/skills Show educational offers if skills are missing for a specific job ad	State-of-the art in all features compared to competitors Classification of content Relevance matching, multivariate ranking (e.g. show me only jobs from companies > 5000 employees) Video tutorial to show what page offers, how to register, navigate, connect with user, ask questions etc Faceted search and browsing Filter content using multiple taxonomy terms at the same time Search Engine Optimization (SEO) Push services add-ons (sms or email) rather than pull services

continued on following page

Table 1. continued

Require-ment Specifica-tions	Users (Applicants)	System Analysts	Programmers
Social Requirements	Community and Social Network features: possibility to connect with friends and FoF and follow each others' career paths, share pics, reports, exams etc. Entertainment/ Playfulness: Typical community features: inviting, blogging, tagging etc. Interest groups for shared hobbies, sports, music, companies, travel etc. Discussion board, social support from community how to deal with negative job experiences	Community and Social Network features: provide applicants the possibility to link to friends, common interest groups e.g. VIP club of Company XY, ccommonality of interests, goals API Interface to other social networks, open integration of contacts Entertainment/ Playfulness: e.g. Fun factor, applications to enable comparisons with others, registered users, friend compare etc., functions that applicants enjoy, curiosity, possibility for interactions (tagging etc.) with other registered users Indicate on users profiles who has visited their site	APIs, define applications for integration of other social network features Open ID integration Follow WCAG - Web Content Accessibility Guidelines for e.g. disabled users
Psychological Requirements	Reputation: word of mouth, who of my friends know and use the portal, experience reports about good internships, highly recognized jobs at certain companies Self esteem/competency features: games with other users on technical problems, rank best players Success rate of placements: return if I or my friends received good jobs via the portal Feel of control: many adjustment possibilities in privacy settings, different newsfeed selection options, moderated content	Reputation, credibility, high quality standards, blogs about experiences, word of mouth advertising, make site more known by e.g. search engine optimization, user reports of successful placements, transparency of information Self esteem/competency features: ontology extension e.g. molecular biology – offer applicants different terms and ask them to order into specific ontologies (crowd-sourcing). If one user becomes domain expert (e.g. 10 persons order it the same way in one field, give user credits and enable to use score for resume, invite former bosses to provide online recommendation Feel of control: many adjustment possibilities, moderated content Check your market value: challenge users with intelligence games, rank users, cause users to search for what job ad they are the top candidate, show me how I rank compared to other users, friends in my network, all graduates from a specific school etc. VIP/insider community of certain companies	No
Service Requirements	Responsiveness of recruiters to applications Responsiveness to questions posted in blog Active profiles of other users in the database Friendly emails and other communications even though I might not be their ideal candidate Range of possibilities (services)	Responsiveness of recruiters, customer representatives and other users to requests Communications: different channels: email, chat, phone, video interviewing, blogging etc. Customer representatives training, routines, fixed times to get back to applicants	Feedback forms Service representative contact forms RSS

continued on following page

Table 1. continued

Require-ment Specifica-tions	Users (Applicants)	System Analysts	Programmers
Ease of use	High usability Quick and easy registration Easy navigation Possibility to upload different files, i.e. resume and testimonials files (doc, pdf, jpg etc)	High usability Easy navigation; sub-menus, put similar contents together, different views for different user needs, e.g. structural or icon-based Appearance: harmonic colors, proportion of text and buttons Ongoing usability testing with users, FAQs, video tutorial, analyze website navigation and understanding of textual meaning for different user groups Design appropriate for target group (age group, branches etc.)	High usability

by I [Interviewer]; P [Programmer]; SA [System Analyst], U [User]. We also relate our analysis to Goffman's (1982) suggestions for requirement-analysis interviews. He defined *footing* as the relationship between speakers. This means speakers can take on several different social roles from which they can move in and out. For instance, in one moment a speaker may be a *User* of an information system and in the next moment a *Programmer* of a different system himself. As we speak, we shift footing which helps us to establish relationship with others such that the meaning of what we say can be better interpreted and understood. We found these social interactions —representing particular presentations of self and dynamic shifts between frames— useful for analyzing users', system analysts' and programmers' communication.

RESULTS

We present the results in line with our guiding research question: What system requirements do e-recruiting services need to realize so as to motivate users to keep their applicant profiles up-to-date (even though they may have a job) and stay connected with one specific recruiting portal over their career? We illustrate the results with quotes from system analysts, applicants and programmers to show the richness of our data.

A general trend among the three interviewee groups emerged. First, system analysts tend to talk about future requirements and hypothetical possibilities to achieve competitive advantage and differentiate the portal on the market. They tend to switch into different roles during the interview and better empathize with user needs than programmers do. Second, applicants describe system requirements in the form of past stories where the language is inviting and rich. Applicants also talked about their experiences with, and perceptions of, other effective and similar information systems they used. Finally, programmers describe requirements in a rather abstract and analytical way. Many times, they do not use full sentences to describe requirements but rather refer to standards, code requirements, integration and code adaptability optimization. Further, many interviewees describe system requirements closely related to system, service and information quality criteria of general website usage (DeLone & McLean, 2003). Table 1 presents a summary of the interview results. The following passages portray several conversations between the interviewer and the involved study participants.

Requirement Interview
with System Analyst

I: I want to find out what system requirements that e-recruiting services need to realize so as to motivate users to keep their applicant profiles up-to-date {um} and stay connected with one specific recruiting portal over their career stages.

SA: Well {um}; first of all, we have to make sure that we list as many jobs as possible; we need to list all jobs available in a specified region [!] This means, we need to develop a sophisticated job crawler that automatically collects new listed jobs from all existing websites in Austria that have job openings for our target group.

I: Why is this so important?

SA: If we have all the available open engineering jobs online for our niche group, then users might use our system rather than the general job boards which are overloaded with many irrelevant job postings. [SA shakes head, laughing].

I: {um} but if you have so many jobs, the clicks per ad may be fewer, no?

SA: You need to make the service more exclusive so that people feel good. << only registered users should be able to see all job postings. This way, we will get more people to sign up and make them curious and come back.

I: But why should the users keep their profiles up-to date just because you have many jobs for the specific niche and have them registered once?

SA: After you get the job crawler right, you need to give them accurate and customized search results. [...] Sure, users will most likely not return to our website and maintain their profiles if they get disappointed with our search.

I: So what does this mean?

SA: This means, we have to improve the semantic matching [!] and integrate users' voice by crowd-sourcing and build up adaptive skill ontologies. [...] If users get bad job search results and are overloaded with job offers that don't fit their applicant profile, they are more likely to lose trust in the quality and credibility of our platform. It's a waste of their time to look through irrelevant job postings. If our goal is to get them come back to the site, we should work to provide better search results than other providers".

I: Well, [...] I guess there are many platforms out there with good search results, so why exactly should the users re-visit your e-recruiting service for the long run. Many have already found a job, so why re-visit the site?

SA: It comes down to niche portals. They are arranged around users who have something in common, who share something << whatever this is, doesn't matter. << Our internal analysis shows << listen, what really matters is that recruiting portals should develop strong ties with specific niche communities, educational portals or branch networks {um} and get users to sign up when they still have offline ties to other potential users. If you get a whole network of people sign up together, {um} whole graduating classes this is the best[!] This will certainly have an impact on user return rate.

I: But {um} usually they already have alumni clubs, what's the advantage?

SA: The advantage is that they can simply keep in touch {um} and follow each other's career paths. [...] If they just sign up for the sake of getting a job and cannot connect with people online, the portal has little to offer other than at the time the applicant searches a job.

I: So why should they maintain the profile then?

SA: Just look at facebook, myspace or studivz [!] they maintain their profile because their friends do also, so if you get people who have connections with each other, they are more likely to continue these connections online, for whatever reason, if this is about jobs or something else. In our case it's jobs".

The interview opened with the basic introductory question on how e-recruiting portals can achieve an actively participating user base. The system designer responded with *("first of all")* what indicates to the listener that he will describe a series of events or actions over time in order to get users come back to the site, rather than what took place at a specific point in time. He spoke in the plural, indicating that he thinks and works in "we" instead of "I." Specific suggestions included listing all jobs available in a specified region and continuously updating the job offers for specific target groups or niches so that users see highly relevant content. The interviewer inquired into the importance of these suggestions. Then, the system analyst made hypothetical statements *("then users may rather use our system")* and blamed the inefficiencies of general job boards that list many irrelevant and no niche-specific job postings. The interviewer kept challenging the system analyst by more directly questioning his narratives. An argument to make the service exclusive followed *("only registered users should be able to see all job postings.")*. The interviewer reframed the interview by returning to the same question but reformulating it. Finally, the system analyst got back to the sequence that he started in line 2. *("After you get the job crawler right, you need to give them accurate and customized search results")*. He concluded by explaining how to improve the semantic matching and integrate users' voice by crowd-sourcing and building up adaptive skill ontologies. In this sense, he suggested that the registered user community should be an active part in the development and maintenance of the portal. The analyst further identified future requirements and derived hypothetical possibilities to achieve competitive advantage and differ-

entiate the portal on the market. The interviewer maintained a critical voice. Following, the system analyst came to the conclusion what really matters is receiving many users from niche communities who have strong offline ties with other potential users. However, the interviewer countered that some users may already be part of other alumni networks. The system analyst also made strongly emphasized claims *(whole graduating classes this is the best [!] This will certainly have an impact on user return rate")*, which should be presented as a hypothesis about what could prove to sustain recruiting portals. In the context of designing active communities, research has been conducted, for instance, on how to improve community-supporting systems design (see, e.g., Rheingold, 2000; Geib et al., 2005). Concluding, the analyst searched for universality of his responses *("If you get people who have connections with each other, they are more likely to continue these connections online, for whatever reason, if this is about jobs or anything else. In our case it's jobs")*.

Requirement Interview with User (Applicant)

I: Can you think about system requirements the e-recruiting portal where you recently registered would need to realize so as to motivate you to *keep your applicant profile up-to-date* [...] and also to *stay connected* with this specific portal over your career stages?

A: I was wondering {um} you must have many people registered in the engineering portal, and probably I know some people who are registered there. I have been out of school already a couple of years and lost touch with most of my former schoolmates. However, in your resume forms I had to fill out my graduating year and my school. So I would be interested what careers those people have now.

I: How could this be done?

A: You have all the data and the database behind. *Just open the platform for search* so that people see who is there.

I: What do you want to do, just find their profile and that's it?

A: Maybe they work in some interesting company where I am also interested, we could exchange experiences. [...] Or they went to some graduate school that I am interested in.

I: How could this system requirement be realized?

A: I don't know [...] maybe a forum, blog or something like that where people can discuss job-related stuff. I am on studiVz, there you can put up more stuff about yourself, not just stuff about your job, but fun stuff. All kinds of community or social network features would enhance the current e-recruiting platform.

I: Would you use the recruiting platform more intensely and for the long run if it included such community features?

A: I don't have much time. {um} I am already on several networks. On the other hand, << I spent 5 years in this school. I am an HTL engineer like many others. I would use it if there are people I know. I would not just link up with strangers. I have a job now, {um} so I would not use it for getting a job right now, maybe in the future. Currently, I would only like to see who else is there, how many folks from my former class, school are registered and then get in touch with them, it's also easier than calling.

I: Do you primarily communicate about job-related things in such a platform? {um} What are the information requirements, the necessary contents on the platform?

A: It is a starting point to talk about jobs. << This is a recruiting portal right, so you could blog how work is in different companies, how much they pay or how the work climate is. Maybe for the recent graduates some help in preparing application documents or interview tips. It is more authentic if it comes from fellow graduates than from some external agency.

I: What else could such a portal offer so that you and other registered applicants come back and re-use it?

A: Nowadays privacy is an issue. {um} How can you make sure {um} that my current boss will not find my profile in the database? I would prefer to have a private and a public profile, one for friends and one for the rest of people. Also, there needs to be the possibility to deactivate my profile, hence including many options of profile setting is an issue so that I would maintain my profile there.

I: What else matters to you?

A: *Most important is the job aspect.* I would find it interesting to follow others career paths. However, only talking about jobs is boring. I spend some time on games. Probably some possibility to play games with other users, maybe even solving some tricky technical question together, some intelligence games, I always liked to play games.

I: Now, when you think about rather technical system requirements, what comes into your mind?

A: First, the site needs to *load fast and be accessible all the time*, I need to find stuff that I am looking for, it needs to be easy to get my things done, if this concerns applying for a job or blogging or linking with other users. I already lost some resume data at other portals, *I certainly will never return to a site where I invested time and lost my data.*

The usefulness of networked online communities, as indicated in the interview above, has already been discussed in e-recruiting. Butler (2001), for instance, describes that online career services may be seen as virtual social communities rather than only instrumental career-move services. In this regard, Khapova (2006) argues that studies of online career services need to include the design principles of a traditional community as well as the incorporation of social network research, so as to understand the various ways people make use of online career services. Therefore, some researchers support the idea that innovative online career services require more "cross-fertilization" across users and those who design und sustain services (von Hippel, 2007; Khapova, 2006). There is ground to assume that e-recruiting platforms can only be sustainable if they evolve or transform into highly participative and continuously innovating e-community platforms organized around niches of users sharing a similar social identity. This requires more customer-centric and niche approaches to e-recruiting than the "one-size-fits-all" Monsterboard-type services. Hence, exchange-based e-recruiting platforms are challenged to transform into lasting career networks.

Many of the interviewed engineers noted that a common online career service for all HTL engineers across Austria is needed. In particular, an integrated social network and community features within career services have been frequently found to make it easier to keep in touch with and follow their fellow students' career paths. One engineer noted: *"When getting a job in a different location in Austria, it's great to search if any of my schools' graduates works in the same area or company."* In this sense, some researchers suggest that people use communities[1] by merely adding internet contact to existing telephone and face-to-face contact, or by shifting their means of communication to the internet (Wellman et al., 2001; Wellman et al., 2002). This also seems to apply to most of the interviewed applicants who want to get back in touch with former classmates and communicate with them via the platform. Engineers identified a wide range of ideas that they want to share and exchange online with other fellow engineers (see Table 1, Information and Social Requirement). They predominantly intend to communicate online with offline-known fellow

acquaintances from their schools or via extended networks (friends of friends). Interestingly, the interviewed engineers did not seem to be keen on developing or maintaining a strong network with fully unknown fellow engineers. Fifty-six of the sixty interviewed engineers reported that they would use an online career service for the long run if specifically targeted at engineers' needs. Most of the interviewed users are not inclined to sign up at a general online job board that attracts many different job searchers; General jobs boards are seen as exchange-based career tools for finding a job when needed, but among the interviewed users it was not desirable to connect online in such job boards with unknown users.

Social presence theorists (Biocca et al., 2003) describe that the presence of other members (which can be complemented by offline interactions) may foster the ties of community members to their online community. Hence, we assume that determinants of long-term sustainability of online career communities need to range from understanding how users judge online features, such as the quality of a career community's service, its system, and the provided information (DeLone & Mclean, 2003), to understanding offline features such as the offline activities of users (Wellman & Haythornthwaite, 2002). Offline activities have been found to increase the solidarity and cohesiveness of virtual communities, and they strengthen the ties between members. A better understanding of the match between what is being offered (the supply) and (potential) users' interests has been found to promote a stronger desire to participate and interact with other members, leading to shared feelings of belonging, responsibility, and commitment to the community (Kim, 2000). In other words, when developing recruitment sites, the social identity of various user segments needs to be considered. We noted that engineers were very open to interacting with their fellow engineers, online as well as offline. These insights offer a fairly new network opportunity for transforming classical "job boards" to sustainable "career communities."

Engineers' impressions of the webpage and resume forms were largely positively evaluated and regarded as meeting users' needs. This is reflected in the following statement: *"I was impressed how well this career service knows the details of my specific subjects of study, and guides me though the online application by making suggestions. I have already filled out other online resumes at some corporate homepages, but none of the other forms has been so carefully adjusted to the profile of an HTL graduate."* Some engineers had minor concerns with the length of resume forms or the support of uploading bigger file sizes. It appeared important that the career site is clearly structured into sections for applicants and companies. Further, important factors for re-using the service are: feeling a sense of privacy and being in control; enabling social connections with peers; and integrating playful features, easy navigation and quick loading of the pages (see also Davis, 1989; DeLone & McLean, 2003). The possibility to designate themselves in their own career profile as either an active or a passive job-searcher was an idea that was supported by many users. Importantly, system designers are challenged to create private (for friends) and public (for HR recruiters) spaces of the users' applicant profile so as to build trust and in order to ward off the fear that personalized resume data will be misused. As one engineer described: *"How can you make sure that my boss will not find my profile in the database?"* and *"Sure, I want my profile for friends to look different than my applicant profile."*

Summing up, while many of the identified requirements in the previous section overlap with criterion identified in prior literature on e-service quality, in particular, e-recruiting services should pay close attention to users' social and psychological requirements such as by enhancing self-esteem, fostering a sense of privacy and a feeling of being in control, enabling social connections with peers and integrating playful features.

Requirement Interview with Programmer

I:　When you think about your programming work {um} what can you do, {um} I mean what kind of system requirements can you think about so as to motivate applicants to keep their profiles up-to-date and re-visit this specific recruiting portal over their career stages?

P:　Include cookies so that users remain logged in and system recognizes returning users {um}; and when they open our website, automatically move cursor to log in.

I:　Why is this so important?

P:　Always logged-in […] rather re-visit the site when specifications are set that way.

I:　Interesting. Anything else from the developing side that you can do to get applicants to be more active and re-visit?

P:　APIs, clearly define applications for integration, {um} open ID integration, […] Ajax, {um} [Interviewer expresses uncertainty what the terms mean] accessible on every internet browser, {um} sure strong hardware […] good code is modular, allow modules to be built, tested, and debugged independently […] SPI plug-in interface, enabling multiple implementations.

I:　Well, {um} there are a lot of different things. << First, what is and how do APIs and open ID integration motivate applicants to keep their profiles up to date and re-visit the site?

P:　API stands for application programming interface. *It saves time.* Optimizing APIs helps to access parts of other sites and integrate it with our own site. This is good for users, because APIs guarantee that other programs using a common API, e.g., other social networking sites will have similar interfaces. {um} So API-like interfaces allow applications on different platforms or written in different languages to interoperate. This makes it much easier to integrate stuff, e.g., your personal profile from other social networking sites, easier for users to learn new programs, saves time, convenient.

I: So why is this in particular important for e-recruiting sites?

P: *It is not just for e-recruiting sites, developers in general need to think about including APIs in whatever applications they develop,* especially if they expect the applications to last and interact with other applications. It saves time for users and developers if you include APIs, it's also easier to review the source code.

I: And because it saves time, they are more likely to update their profile and stay connected?

P: {um} No, but everybody has many other profiles, has signed up elsewhere, so if they can use their personal data that they typed in elsewhere, it is convenient, take all your data with you, all your friends etc.

I: What else is important?

P: HR-XML interface to link the recruiting platform to different companies, this make the communication and data transfer more efficient.

I: What does this exactly mean?

P: Then the applicant can directly apply to more companies at once by only filling out the profile only one time, this would be one application, for instance. So, they would re-use the site because it is convenient.

I: What else can motivate applicants to keep their profiles up to date and re-visit the recruiting site?

P: It depends if they want news and what kind of news. News reader that displays RSS feeds about or any other content they want to keep up-to date. The applicant needs to have enough customization options without having to regularly check the site for updates, they don't need to re-visit the page if they get the info via newsfeed, this is also fine.

I: Ok, I understand.

P: And also the standard things SEO {um} SOA {um} don't use strings if a better type exists {um} coupling between software components so that code can be reused {um} << WSDL {um} UDDI […] SOAP which allows different distributed web services to run on a variety of software platforms and hardware architectures << Choosing the proper language, *java is really good when it comes to platform independence.* Sorry, I don't know if this all makes sense to you, I mean for programmers this is all standard requirements to think about when coding.

I: You are right, {um} there are a lot of terms that I am not familiar with. Nevertheless, I will note all of them. Just continue what you think matters most in respect of developing sustainable e-recruiting portals.

P: *You always have to balance* between predefined standards, e.g., within the specific software you are using but also develop customized solutions, e.g., for specific user niches. Also, you should follow the WCAG, web content accessibility guidelines. […] *Privacy settings, SSL encryption is an important issue* [!] due to all the sensitive data we collect from the applicants.

I: In how far do privacy settings help you to get them back and re-visit the site?

P: There is much going on with data abuse, hence you have to offer very transparent ways so that users fully understand what happens with their data {um} who has access to their profile, so that they trust your portal.

While system analysts described requirements more from a long-term strategic and market-oriented point of view, the interviewed programmers based their arguments on purely technical requirement specification. Programmers use technical terms and abbreviations (e.g., APIs, Follow WCAG Guidelines for, e.g., disabled users, open ID integration, Ajax, SSL encrypted etc.) when referring to system requirements. It is interesting to note that programmers, in fact, can explain many coding procedures they apply so as to get applicants to be more active and to re-visit e-recruiting sites. In the programmers' talk, we find frequent use of generalizations. For instance, they mention that some features are not solely focused on enhancing user retention in e-recruiting services, but for general website retention. Also, many features are described as standard in coding. Moreover, programmers claim that they do not necessarily require users to re-visit a website so as to maintain user retention. They describe customized communication means such as news reader that displays RSS feeds so that applicants do not regularly need to re-visit the page and still remain updated and active users.

CONCLUSION AND OUTLOOK

This paper addressed what it takes in e-recruiting to achieve active long-term participation of its users (registered applicants). We conducted requirement interviews with registered users, system analysts and programmers. By using narrative analyses we showed how raw data collected in system requirement interviews are rich, meaningful and give insight into interpretations and intentions to use e-recruiting systems for the long-term. The involvement of an e-recruiting researcher who acted as intermediate analyst and interpreter of the collected interview data helped to reveal new perspectives.

Although our analysis is qualitative and interpretative in nature, our theoretical stance helped to gain insights into the interpretation of multi-voiced divergent narratives in IS requirement analyses interviews. The users' perspective indicates that it is not enough to develop niche portals for specific applicants (such as engineers, lawyers) or branch segments (such as chemistry, pharmacy). What seems to have an influence on users' active long-term participation in niche portals is the opportunity to maintain communication with other

professionals (in this study's case: engineers) who already know each other from their offline network or via friends of friends (FoF). We find that applicants are more likely to re-use e-recruiting services (and keep their applicant profiles up-to-date) if the services transform into highly participative career communities organized around niches of users sharing a similar social identity, common interests and pre-existing offline ties. Engineers are eager to combine and transform their offline interactions with fellow engineers with online interactions in niche-based career communities. They are also willing to maintain these online ties if they have been properly connected within groups sharing a similar social identity offline (before entering the online career community). Thus, we confirm Boyd's finding (2008) that users of online communities are not only looking to meet new people. Instead, the interviewed engineers primarily expressed interest in communicating with people who are already a part of their extended offline social network. Further, the interviewed system designers described system requirements more from a long-term strategic and market-oriented point of view whereas the programmers based their arguments on purely technical requirement specification. As the language and the expression of requirement specifications of the three stakeholders is very different, we conclude that the inclusion of a neutral researcher as observer, interviewer and data analyst provides meaningful new insights in system requirement analysis.

This study's limitations (especially this study's focus on only one niche e-recruiting service) may suggest that the findings point to only one of many possible interpretations. Nevertheless, the collected data (memos, taped interviews, digital and textual data, meeting minutes) embody a multi-threaded chain of evidence that is important in achieving reliability in qualitative research (Yin, 2003).

On a practical level, niche career platforms are advised to complement their traditional job posting services with social network and community applications so that users can find, connect with and/or follow their peers' career paths. Our results suggest that e-recruiting portals require not only useful information sections on careers and continuing education, but can also encourage friendship and social activities of their users. The future is likely to belong to those providers that best understand their users' shared social identity and succeed in providing semantic technologies with which they enhance users' online experiences in terms of social community, social belonging, self esteem, privacy, sense of control and playfulness.

REFERENCES

Alvarez, R., & Urla, J. (2002). Tell me a good story: using narrative analysis to examine information requirements interviews during an ERP implementation. *The Data Base for Advances in Information Systems, 33*(1), 38–52.

Amoako-Gyampah, K. (2007). Perceived Usefulness, User Involvement and Behavioral Intention: An Empirical Study of ERP Implementation. *Computers in Human Behavior, 23,* 1232–1248. doi:10.1016/j.chb.2004.12.002

Bartis, E., & Mitev, N. (2008). A multiple narrative approach to information systems failure: a successful system that failed. *European Journal of Information Systems, 17,* 112–124. doi:10.1057/ejis.2008.3

Biocca, F., Harms, C., & Burgoon, J. K. (2003). Toward a More Robust Theory and Measure of Social Presence: Review and Suggested Criteria. *Presence (Cambridge, Mass.), 12*(5), 456–480. doi:10.1162/105474603322761270

Bostrom, R. P. (1989). Successful Application of Communication Techniques to Improve the Systems Development Process. *Information & Management, 16,* 279–295. doi:10.1016/0378-7206(89)90005-0

Boyd, D. (2008). Why youth (heart) social network sites: The role of networked publics in teenage social life. In Buckingham, D. (Ed.), *Youth, Identity, and Digital Media* (pp. 119–142). Cambridge, MA: MIT Press.

Boyd, D., & Ellison, N. B. (2007). Social network sites: Definition, history, and scholarship. *Journal of Computer-Mediated Communication, 13*(1).

Brown, A. D., & Jones, M. R. (1998). Doomed to failure: narratives of inevitability and conspiracy in a failed IS project. *Organization Studies, 19*(1), 73–88. doi:10.1177/017084069801900104

Buchanan, D., & Dawson, P. (2007). Discourse and audience: organizational change as multi-story process. *Journal of Management Studies, 44*(5), 669–686. doi:10.1111/j.1467-6486.2006.00669.x

Buchanan, R. (2007). Understanding your users: A practical guide to user requirements: Methods, tools, and techniques. *Design Issues, 23*(1), 90–92. doi:10.1162/desi.2007.23.1.92

Butler, B. S. (2001). Membership size, communication activity, and sustainability: A resource-based model of online social structures. *Information Systems Research, 12*(4), 346–362. doi:10.1287/isre.12.4.346.9703

Byrd, T. A., Cossick, K. L., & Zmud, R. W. (1992). A Synthesis of Research on Requirements Analysis and Knowledge Acquisition Techniques. *Management Information Systems Quarterly, 16*(1), 117–138. doi:10.2307/249704

Castells, M. (2000). *The Rise of the Network Society* (2nd ed.). Cambridge, MA: Blackwell.

Castells, M. (2004). *The Power of Identity.* Oxford, UK: Blackwell.

Czarniawska, B. (1997). *Narrating the Organization.* Chicago: The University of Chicago Press.

Davidson, E. J. (1997). Examining Project History Narratives: An Analytic Approach. In A. S. Lee, J. Liebenau, & J. I. DeGross (Eds.), *Proceedings of the International Conference on Information Systems and Qualitative Research*, Philadelphia, PA (pp. 123-148).

Davis, F. D. (1989). Perceived Usefulness, Perceived Ease of Use, and User Acceptance of Information Technology. *Management Information Systems Quarterly*, *13*(3), 319–340. doi:10.2307/249008

DeLone, W. H., & McLean, E. R. (2003). The DeLone and McLean Model of Information Systems Success: A Ten-Year Update. *Journal of Management Information Systems*, *19*(4), 9–30.

Dineen, B., Ling, J., Ash, S., & Del Vecchio, D. (2007). Aesthetic properties and message customisation: Navigating the dark side of web recruitment. *The Journal of Applied Psychology*, *92*(2), 356–372. doi:10.1037/0021-9010.92.2.356

Doherty, N. F., King, M., & Al-Mushayt, O. (2003). The Impact of Inadequacies in the Treatment of Organizational Issues on Information Systems Development Projects. *Information & Management*, *14*, 49–62. doi:10.1016/S0378-7206(03)00026-0

Ellison, N., Steinfield, C., & Lampe, C. (2007). The benefits of Facebook "friends": Exploring the relationship between college students' use of online social networks and social capital. *Journal of Computer-Mediated Communication*, *12*(3).

Feldman, D., & Klaas, B. (2002). Internet job hunting: A field study of applicant experiences with online recruitment. *Human Resource Management*, *41*(2), 175–201. doi:10.1002/hrm.10030

Fincham, R. (2002). Narratives of success and failure in systems development. *British Journal of Management*, *13*, 1–14. doi:10.1111/1467-8551.00219

Geib, M., Braum, C., Kolbe, L., & Brenner, W. (2005). Toward Improved Community-Supporting Systems Design: A Study of Professional Community Activity. *International Journal of Technology and Human Interaction*, *1*(4), 19–36.

Goffman, E. (1981). *Forms of Talk*. Philadelphia: University of Pennsylvania Press.

Grudin, J. (1991). Interactive systems: Bridging the gaps between developers and users. *IEEE Computer*, *24*(4), 59–69.

Holtzblatt, K., & Beyer, H. R. (1995). Requirements Gathering: The Human Factor. *Communications of the ACM*, *38*(5), 30–32. doi:10.1145/203356.203361

Iansiti, M., & MacCormack, A. (1997). Developing products on the Internet Time. *Harvard Business Review*, *75*(5), 108–117.

Ives, B., & Olson, M. (1992). User Involvement and MIS Success: A Review of Research. *Management Science*, *30*(5), 586–603. doi:10.1287/mnsc.30.5.586

Jenkins, A. M., Naumann, J. D., & Wetherbe, J. (1984). Empirical Investigations of Systems Development Practices and Results. *Information & Management*, *1*, 73–82. doi:10.1016/0378-7206(84)90012-0

Khapova, S. (2006). *Careers in the knowledge economy and web-based career support: New challenges and opportunities* (Doctoral dissertation). Enschede, The Netherlands: Print Partners Ipskamp B.V.

Kim, A. J. (2000). *Community Building on the Web: Secret Strategies for Successful Online Communities*. Boston: Addison-Wesley Longman Publishing.

Knoke, D., & Kuklinski, J. H. (1982). *Network Analysis*. Beverly Hills, CA: Sage.

Lin, B., & Stasinskaya, V. S. (2002). Data warehousing management issues in online Recruiting. *Human Systems Management, 21*(1), 1–8.

Marakas, G. M., & Elam, J. J. (1998). Semantic Structuring in Analyst Acquisition and Representation of Facts in Requirements Analysis. *Information Systems Research, 9*(1), 37–63. doi:10.1287/isre.9.1.37

Miles, M. B., & Huberman, A. M. (1994). *Qualitative data analysis: An expanded sourcebook* (2nd ed.). Thousand Oaks, CA: Sage.

Moody, J. W., Blanton, J. E., & Cheney, P. H. (1998). A Theoretically Grounded Approach to Assist Memory Recall During Information Requirements Determination. *Journal of Management Information Systems, 15*(1), 79–98.

Noyes, J., & Baber, C. (1999). *User-Centered Design of Systems*. Heidelberg, Germany: Springer Verlag.

Parry, E. (2008). Drivers of the adoption of online recruitment – an analysis using diffurion of innovation theory. In Bondarouk, T. V., & Ruël, H. J. M. (Eds.), *E-HRM in theory and practice*. Amsterdam: Elsevier.

Pfleeger, S. L., & Atlee, J. M. (2010). *Software engineering: theory and practice*. Upper Saddle River, NJ: Prentice Hall.

Plickert, G., Côté, R. R., & Wellman, B. (2007). It's not who you know, it's how you know them: Who exchanges what with whom? *Social Networks, 29*(3), 405–429. doi:10.1016/j.socnet.2007.01.007

Preece, J. (2000). *Online Communities*. New York: John Wiley & Sons Inc.

Rheingold, H. (2000). *The Virtual Community: Homesteading on the Electronic Frontier*. London: MIT Press.

Riessman, C. K. (1993). *Narrative Analysis*. London: Sage.

Rondeau, P. J., Ragu-Nathan, T. S., & Vonderembse, M. A. (2006). How involvement, IS management effectiveness, and end user computing impact IS performance in manufacturing firms. *Information & Management, 43*(1), 93–107. doi:10.1016/j.im.2005.02.001

Sarbin, T. R. (1995). A narrative approach to repressed memories. *Journal of Narrative and Life History, 5*, 41–66.

Smith, A. D., & Rupp, W. T. (2004). Managerial challenges of e-recruiting. *Online Information Review, 28*(1), 61–74. doi:10.1108/14684520410522466

Szmigin, I., Canning, L., & Reppel, A. E. (2005). Online community: Enhancing the relationship marketing concept through customer bonding. *International Journal of Service Industry Management, 16*(5), 480–496. doi:10.1108/09564230510625778

Turkle, S. (1995). *Life on the screen: Identity in the age of the Internet*. New York: Simon & Schuster.

van Dijk, J. (2005). *The Network Society: Social Aspects of New Media*. Thousand Oaks, CA: Sage.

Van Maanen, J. (1995). An End of Innocence: The Ethnography of Ethnography. In Van Maanen, J. (Ed.), *Representation in Ethnography* (pp. 1–35). Thousand Oaks, CA: Sage.

von Hippel, E. (2007). Horizontal innovation networks—by and for users. *Industrial and Corporate Change, 16*(2), 293–315. doi:10.1093/icc/dtm005

Wellman, B., Boase, J., & Chen, W. (2002). The networked nature of community on and off the Internet. *IT and Society, 1*(1), 151–165.

Wellman, B., & Haythornthwaite, C. (2002). *The Internet in everyday life*. Oxford, UK: Blackwell. doi:10.1002/9780470774298

Wellman, B., Quan-Haase, A., Witte, J., & Hampton, K. (2001). Does the Internet increase, decrease, or supplement social capital? Social networks, participation, and community commitment. *The American Behavioral Scientist, 45*(3), 436–455. doi:10.1177/00027640121957286

Wolters, M. (2006). The Effectiveness of job board Internet Recruitment. In *Proceedings of the First European Academic Workshop on e-HRM,* The Netherlands.

Yin, R. K. (2003). *Case Study Research: Design and Methods* (3rd ed.). Thousand Oaks, CA: Sage.

Zhao, H. (2006). Expectations of recruiters and applicants in large cities of China. *Journal of Managerial Psychology, 21*(5), 459–475. doi:10.1108/02683940610673979

Zusman, R., & Landis, R. (2004). Applicant preferences for web-based versus traditional job posting. *Computers in Human Behavior, 18,* 285–296. doi:10.1016/S0747-5632(01)00046-2

ENDNOTE

[1] Examples are facebook (www.facebook.com), myspace (www.myspace.com) or Friendster (www.friendster.com).

This work was previously published in International Journal of Technology and Human Interaction, Volume 6, Issue 3, edited by Anabela Mesquita & Chia-Wen Tsai, pp. 1-20, copyright 2010 by IGI Publishing (an imprint of IGI Global).

Chapter 6

Theorizing HR Intranets:
Contextual, Strategic and Configurative Explanations

Véronique Guilloux
Université Paris Xii, France

Florence Laval
Cerege IAE, France

Michel Kalika
Strasbourg Université Robert Schuman, France

ABSTRACT

This paper presents the results of a longitudinal exploratory survey based on a sample of French firms. Different contexts of Intranet, as well as introduction, development stages, performance and Intranet content are presented. Three approaches are in existence: corporate Intranet, specialized Intranet and HR Intranet. These can be linked to different stages of development: communication, functional support, and knowledge management. The HR Function will be successful if it integrates Intranet in its management process, if the players are aware of the stakes and they behave as "real change agents". Research shows the importance of strategic alignment between human resource management (HRM) and Intranet as well as the relevance of technological infusion, therefore, this paper's result in showing a configurative approach that allows the integration of more variables and in turn leads to a systemic model contains great significance.

INTRODUCTION

The paper presents some interesting results of an exploratory and longitudinal survey based on a sample of French firms. The survey identifies

the diffusion of HRM practices, together with their developmental stages. Investigation aims at answering the following questions: How are Intranet networks linked with the development of HR competences? How could they support the HR-function? What are the best French practices linking IT and HR management? A questionnaire

DOI: 10.4018/978-1-61350-465-9.ch006

Table 1. Files distribution

Year	1998	1999	2000	2001	2002	2003	2004
Number of files	19	19	21	19	33	12	27

is submitted as an application file and includes open questions on the firms and their Intranet (techniques, cost, assessment, perspectives). In the first part, we analyze stakes, organizational and strategic risks linked with HR Intranet use. Theoretical IT concepts and technological infusion aspects are explained. Intranet contexts, development stages, performance and Intranet content are presented. In the second part, we propose an organizational configurative analysis resulting from a HR Intranet perspective. Research hypotheses are based on HR and IT theories. A final discussion offers an opening towards a scientific research protocol aiming to validate assumptions and confirm the positive aspect of HRM-IT integration. Three perspectives are proposed. The first one leads to the concept of technological infusion; the second one to strategic alignment between the Intranet and HR; the third one is larger and concerns the concept of configurations including HR Intranet.

A French Longitudinal Survey

In partnership with Entreprise & Carrières newspaper, CEGOS has organized an annual competition since 1998, aimed at rewarding the best Intranet as regards competence management. Since 1998, it concerns 150 firms.

The available data coming from the exploratory survey concerning Intranet use could be arranged into three categories: *context variables* (environment, strategy, HRM); *Intranet characteristics* (objectives, functionalities and technique, budget and implementation date, number of workers concerned); *results* (difficulties encountered, immediate results, appraisals and perspectives). For

each variable, data aggregation enables significant axes to be drawn (Table 1).

Sample: Firms Size and Activity Sectors

Even if the size of the companies using an Intranet is high, Intranets can be introduced in medium firms or even in SME companies. In our sample 26% of the firms have less than 1000 employees; 28% belong to the category (1000-4999 employees); 32% are a member of the group (5000-49999 employees) and 14% have more than 50,000 employees. Obviously, the number of employees is not a distinguishing factor for the development of an Intranet. Employees' geographical dispersal and Intranet accessibility are not a privilege for big companies. Professionals who have answered originate from the public sector (19% hospital, municipal council, chamber of commerce) as well as private sectors (28% service activity banks, insurance companies), 35% industrial companies; 18% IT (telecommunication, computing, software conception).

Intranet Context Variables: Environment, Strategy and HRM

Environment is a contingent factor for IT and Intranet introduction in organizations. Our survey reveals contrasted managerial contexts. 44% of firms evolve in a strong competitive environment. 11% are in a position of leader. 25% of the firms are confronted with intensive information environments. For public companies, the environment is less competitive but most of them are now players in an international environment. This is consistent with Eder et al (2000) survey showing that competition is correlated with Intranet development.

Organization and Strategy

Staff is geographically scattered in subsidiaries, establishments, production sites, agencies. It can also be represented by individual employees ('nomad' workers, agents, experts). Our sample is tied in with divisional, matrix or reticular organizational configurations. The structurational criterion is geographical. These organizations are global, international, transnational, or spread out through French territory. Organizational integration takes on a strategic aspect. Subsidiaries, units, work groups and individuals are also concerned. Virtual teams resorting to IT are common. Literature on that theme is henceforth copious. In most cases, Intranet development corresponds to an integration strategy. It results in internal networks development or corresponds to a post-merger situation and reflects a will to accelerate integration of historically geographically dispersed units. Existence of an HR function is also a permanent feature in companies, but Intranet integration led by the HR Function and Intranet impact on HRM are quite diverse. Strategic HRM context of Intranet setting up could also be pertinent, notably tool functionalities. Dossiers which have been analyzed reveal the existence of two significant contexts: 23% of the firms are re-organizing themselves or re-engineering one or more processes. During Intranet implementation, firms are changing their management processes. 86% of the companies are underlining the necessity for organizational integration either because they are organized in a network or because they have carried out external growth operations (mergers, acquisitions) or internal expansions. They want to create or reinforce cohesion, homogeneous culture, activities coordination and cross processes. Intranet comes in support to cross-functional relationships (Lai & Mahapatra, 1998; McNaughton et al., 1999, 2001).

Human Resource Management

A US typology supports a link between HRM and its performance demonstrates that 43% of companies run a traditional HR (Ichniowski et al., 1996). This means that the classical functions are realised (employment, compensation, training and participation) as well as certain projects such as flexible working hours (time budgeting, reduced working week). This strategy aims at bettering employees' mobilization and working performance. In our survey, an average of 45% of the firms is confined in such a strategic or innovating HR policy. Functional experts conceive competency management and carrier management systems on top of the usual functions. Organizational knowledge is also developed when firm qualifies itself as "a learning company" or develops «management learning». Furthermore, 12% of firms have an evolving function, either because the undertaking is young or because of reorganization. In that case, the goal is to rationalize and redeploy its HR. They invest for example, on that occasion in a new HRM-IS (Lai & Mahapatra, 1998). IT-HRM theoretical approaches are rather various. One of the major contributions characterizes IT-HRM by two leanings: "users" and "designers" (Niederman, 1999). On the one hand they demonstrate that human resources can benefit from technological advance only under specific working conditions. On the other hand, IT introduction requires intervention by HR professionals. In these conditions the HR Function itself can be transformed into a virtual team. In the first perspective, Roche and Sadowsky (2000) evoke resistance from employees. Colinson (1992) is interested in the risks related to lack of HRM consistency during online process introduction. Strauss et al. (1998) count the impacts of electronic communication on HRM whereas Bishop and Levine (1999) analyze its effects on social relations. Lastly, HR integrated software packages are analyzed by Gilbert and Gonzalez (2000). The second research leaning evokes virtual company (Amherdt & Su, 1997;

Lepack & Snell, 1998; Gardner et al., 2003) and knowledge management (Newell et al., 1999).

Development Stages and HR Intranet

An overview of applications and detailed Intranet illustrations is offered. Aggregation of information originating from approximately 150 files reveals Intranet sophistication levels. Results, performance as well as company perspectives are registered. Three approaches are to be distinguished.

Specific HR headings can be introduced into a Corporate Intranet. The latter is conceived by the CEO with the help of communication and IS departments. It is dedicated to internal communication and to employees' information. This kind of Intranet is at the boundary of HR questionings.

HR Intranet, driven by the HR department is a support to HR policy and social management practices. It is specific to the HR function and it can be integrated to corporate Intranet. This sort of Intranet integrates functionalities such as access to training catalogues, mobility management, and employees' administrative management.

Finally, Specialized Intranets are developed for training, sharing knowledge and competence development. They are implemented by the HR department or by the CEO, when stakes are highly strategic or dedicated to specific goals.

Among the available dossiers of our empirical survey, 32% concern specialized HR Intranet, 31% HR generalist Intranet, and 37% corporate Intranet. On the average, specialized Intranet is more expensive. This has been verified for several years. Specialized Intranets developing E-learning and KM imposes specific developments while the other categories only imply online information.

Intranet differences in cost are consistent with time realization which was 25 months in 1998, 10-15 months in 2000 and months in 2002. This trend is the same whatever the Intranet types. More than 50% of Intranet project supervision is conducted by the HR department. This percentage is not surprising. However the fact that in 50%

of the cases the HR department does not run the project is odd! Contribution of other functions (IS, Communication, experts) is also clearly noted.

Project manager profile depends on the nature of the Intranet. 77% of the projects are attributed to HR managers. For corporate Intranet, supervision of the HR department is less frequent and is usually assumed by the communication director or the CEO. As far as specialized Intranets managing is concerned, the IS department is responsible. Technical specificity of certain functionalities is justified by such a fact. There is an evolution in project management coordination. In 1998, the project supervisor is more important than the project owner. In 2004, the opposite is noticed: functional department has leadership role.

Functionalities of the HR Intranet

Intranet content analysis shows various services and a wide diversity of Intranet configurations. Some of them cover all the functionalities listed below and reveal the generalist side of the applications; others are focused on a sole function.

Observations analysis originating from our sample offers a precise idea of Intranet supporting HR content:

- *HR information headings* often contain: HR procedures, legal items (employment law collective agreement, company-wide agreement), works council reports, welfare benefits, assignment statement, and directories.
- *Mobility and carrier headings* diffuse job offers, job description, and frame of reference for each occupation, personal transfers, and procedures for the job application.
- *Training policy* is enhanced by a learning catalogue, training program, formalities, and online admission forms. E learning modules could be at the disposal of users.
- *Knowledge capitalization* relies on databases, groupware, forums, suggestion box.

- *Administrative management* allows online tasks to be done (annual leave, expense account, time and attendance management, updating of employees' files…)
- *Competence management* is based on: diffusion of competences, modalities of knowledge acquisition and assessment.

Intranet configuration conceived as an HR support, combines headings that inform employees and automate certain management practices via IT.

Analysis of Intranet functionalities underlines several differences. *Specialized Intranets* are particularly concerned by knowledge capitalization and competence management. *HR Intranet and corporate Intranet* promotes HR information, mobility and career items. During the years of observation, mobility and careers, administrative management and competence management are approved.

Performance of HR Intranet

Difficulties, key success factors and Intranet use are checked out and finalize our exploratory survey. This methodology has been used by several authors. Bhattacherjee (1998) proposes *benefits of Intranet adoption* (increased employee productivity, reduced operational costs, improved customer service, generated new business), *enablers of Intranet adoption* (technological vision, low start-up costs, management sponsor, sheltering within the finance organization, grassroots efforts to establish a support network, disciplined approach, user involvement) and *barriers to Intranet adoption* (lack of documentation, lack of supported business processes, behavioural resistance to change). Lai and Mohapatra (1998) show that Intranets modify *organizational performance* (improved data/document communications, improved organization image, reduced distribution costs, better resource utilization, improved profit margin, increased internal communications, improved network security); modified *employee performance*

(Shift of power to lower work levels, Increased employee's work productivity, Improved product/service quality, Improved employee's relationship, Improved decision-making, Clarification of employee's role and responsibility) and *customer relationships* (better customer service, reduced use of intermediaries). More specifically Phelps and Mok (1999), Norzaidi et al. (2007) examine Intranet implementation from the end user perspective. They used the Technology Acceptance Model (TAM) with two items (Intranet perceived usefulness and perceived ease-of-use) to predict and explain user acceptance.

Difficulties

Our exploratory survey allows various difficulties to be identified:

- **Organizational and cultural problems:** absence of Intranet culture, resistance to change management, resistance to transparency and transversality, are common. Indeed, Intranet destructures and hustles the usual information circuits.
- **Problems of use:** Intranet can be perceived as a gadget, or something devoid of user-friendliness. In fact, it is difficult to interest heterogeneous populations if one does not create fields of access according to type of population.
- **Technical problems at various stages of the project:** for example upstream, validation of graphic charter, then filling in of data base, conversion of document to HTML; problems of operation of navigation software, server reliability, heterogeneity of data-processing park (downloading time, quality of images) can occur.
- **Actualization and integration problems:** absence of a webmaster is a handicap. Indeed, it is necessary to have up–to-date information in real time and to control consistency and information validity. A project

coordinator can articulate or integrate different Intranet versions.

- **Safety and confidentiality problem:** consultations facility of 360° evaluation result can encourage not going further. Companies have to face hacking of PCs in free access mode. The risk of knowledge getting away is sometimes real.
- **Problem of groupware:** daring asking questions, learning how to work in a team, formalizing the constitution of virtual teams, collaboration between IS and Communication departments, implying the information system department are all major challenges.
- **Problem of non-integration of end-user in the design:** an example concerns the low frequentation of forums before employees determine the themes of the debate by themselves. Tool advantages are not demonstrated specifically when user's needs are badly determined.
- **Problem of financing:** budgets can be limited as regards tool development, network and deployment for employees (in particular those who do not have a data-processing station). All this requires an evaluation of Intranet added-value.

Specialized Intranets are more concerned by technical difficulties. HR Intranets are tied in with organizational and updating difficulties. Corporate Intranets are confronted by ergonomic difficulties, inter-functional coordination and the non-involvement of end users. More than 50% of the firms mention difficulties of organizational nature before the fact of having technical problems. The latter are tied in with the implementation of applications, data updating and the ergonomics of the system. Certain companies have likewise inter-organizational coordination.

Key Success Factors

Regarding Intranet implementation, key success factors are listed: 34% *human support*, 30% *inter functional coordination*, 27% *actualization*, 24% *content quality*, 23% *CEO involvement*, 17% *design*, 7% *database culture*, 7% *profiling*.

Human support is the most cited item. This human facet is mentioned in one third of the firms' population. Problematics with inter-functional coordination follows. The transversal side of Intranet projects, essential HR department involvement as well as these of IS and communication services make the project complex.

Key factor for HR Intranet is Human support; for Corporate Intranet, inter-functional coordination appears to be important and for specialized Intranet customization is quoted (profiling).

From 1998 to 2001, priorities are more or less the same. In 1998, inter-functional coordination is in particular evoked. In 1999, items concerning human support are chosen. In 2000, CEOs' involvement and content quality have priority over the others. In 2001, human support and inter-functional coordination are approved.

Results issuing from Intranet use

Items of performance are chosen by the firms and can be presented in three categories: economic performance, Intranet performance and organizational performance.

Economic performance defines tool value creation or return on investment from productivity indicators and service quality.

Intranet performance is the intrinsic Intranet performance. It focuses on the IS / HRIS tool.

Organizational impacts are noticed in terms of coordination, integration, and culture. Employees' working performances are affected when Intranet is introduced or implemented in a firm.

Our longitudinal analysis shows several trends. Intranet intrinsic performance (technical facet such as connections and social facet such as users' satisfaction) is mentioned more than the extrinsic performance (economical, organizational). In 1998, organizational performances are mentioned regarding the development of numerous corporate Intranets. In 1999, 2000, 2001 professionals evoke some intrinsic performances. Specialized and HR Intranets are more oriented toward intrinsic performance. Corporate Intranets implementation improves extrinsic performance because they support communication and are associated with collective stakes.

Intranet applications perspectives can be gathered along two axes: technical development and integration. These empirical elements can be integrated in existing theoretical frames.

Technical development concern: current functions; new items creation; access generalization (to all working units, all operational positions), facilitation of online information implementation in order to enrich Intranet by employees.

Technological integration aims at de-compartmentalizing specialized and HR Intranets and ties it in with other Intranets, company portals and ERP (Table 2).

Contextual, Strategic and Configurative Explanations

This exploratory survey reveals relevance and perspectives for an HR Intranet research protocol. First of all, results shows HR professionals have a new role to play in organizations and more particularly in running Intranet development projects. Such pre-involvement is essential because

Table 2. Performance types

Economic Performance Quality, productivity (costs and delivery time)	Product ranges quality improvement; industrial delivery times reduction; communication productivity, instantaneous information availability; paper savings; tasks classification reduction, better information retrieval; training budget; lower data-processing costs.	
Intranet performance (technical or social)	*Technical perspective*	-*Connection rate*: logging statistics; consulting frequency; emailing interconnection; -*Flexibility in use*: less IS department interventions
	Social perspective	-*User Satisfaction*: depending on their role (strategic partner, change agent, champion employee, administrative expert, webmaster), depending on their job, on their age... users' requests, suggestions -*Degree of acceptance*, forum appropriation, online tool appropriation
Organisational performance	*Culture*	diffusion and promotion of organizational culture, development of IT culture
	Integration Coordination Control	role of federating into divisions, emulation between divisions, resource sharing facility, network working, transversal communication
	HRM system consistency	*External consistency* Better corporate image of HR Function Re-engineering of HR Function working methods: lower costs, deadlines, more reactivity, and service quality. Support function realignment: tool, procedures, information availability; employees' responsibilities (employability, professional career choice), managers' activity decentralization.
		Internal consistency HRIS reshaping hinged around a single staff management database; automation of administrative work, formalization and rationalization of practices (spreading of job offers). Participation effectiveness (suggestions are taken into account); training effectiveness (rapidity of resources providing up–to-date information); network of persons in charge of the training); competence management (creation and diffusion of a reference frame for each job); internal mobility and recruitment; remuneration and evaluation transparency).
	Working performance	New practices (project management); new work practices (electronic support, groupware); new behaviours toward IT; responsibilities taken in account; e-learning, competences appropriation; membership reinforcement.

it conditions the level of Intranet technological infusion. The survey also shows that HR departments carrying these projects act as change agents and, for this reason, promotes the use of optimal applications diffused by networks. Perceived or observed performances are in favour of HR Intranet introduction and development. This tendency is related to all kinds of companies not only large ones or ones evolving in the new economy. RH researchers have a mission of observation of this irreversible phenomenon.

The main problems concerning research projects devoted to HR Intranets can be summarized in these terms: what are the different Intranet stakes and risks for the HR function?

Fundamental assumptions that we propose to test, are based on Eder et al. (2000), Lay and Mahapatra (1998), Lepack and Snell (1998). We propose that perceived or noticed Intranet performances reinforce the degree of HR Intranet infusion technological. This in turn generates organizational performances, in particular for the HRM system.

HR Intranet is an open network (Eder et al., 2000) whose effectiveness depends on its design and its management. It likewise relies on use by individuals (professionals of the function, managers and employees). A dynamic and systemic approach seems adapted to determine HR function risks and stakes. Conceptualization gives place to measuring descriptive and explanatory instruments adapted to HR Intranets. Investigations based on this research protocol will offer an insight to managers in situations of choice of investment. More generally, results nourish thought engaged by Lepak and Snell (1998). For these authors, in the 21st century HR function will be a virtual function, i.e. organized in networks, centred on value creative activities and directed towards activities coordination.

Hypothetical and deductive research design is outlined hereafter. Starting from a general model, assumptions and measurement scales are proposed.

Assumptions rely on HR Intranet "*Technological Infusion*", "*Intranet–HRM strategic alignment*" and finally "*configurative approach*" (companies' perspective).

Technological Infusion

For Cooper and Zmud (1990), evaluating IT innovations and facilitating diffusion in organizations are two key activities. They study the interaction of task and technology characteristics at the adoption and infusion stages of the technical innovation implementation process. Their research is based on Lewin's model (unfreeze, change, crystallization) and describes an IT implementation. Adoption and diffusion of innovations spread throughout six phases: initiation, adoption, adaptation, acceptance, routines, and infusion. Classically, firms choose technology, then enter into a training phase, adapt innovation, diffuse it ad hoc, and deploy it in a systematic way. This last phase corresponds to infusion characterized by an integrated and transversal use of technology in companies. Saga and Zmud (1996) illustrate different levels of infusion, such as extended use, integrative use and transformative use. Based on the concept of infusion, Eder et al. (2000) analyzes organizational, contextual, and technical motivations for incorporating Intranets in a firm (Figure 1).

Our exploratory survey underlines various Intranets such as corporate, HR, specialized Intranets. Scales exist for the operational side of technical infusion (Zmud & Apple, 1992; Gartner group, 1996). Investment budget and HR items concerning applications, automation or diffusion on the Intranet can be added in a future questionnaire. Crossing these two dimensions (type of Intranet/infusion) can reveal different logics and lead to a better understanding of change management (for example transfer of one type of Intranet to another). One assumption can also involve specialized Intranets and their higher technological infusion level compared with the others.

Figure 1. Contextual, strategic fit and configurative explanations

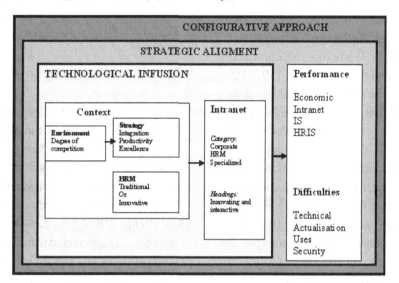

The Following Paragraphs List Different Assumptions Linked with *Dependent Variable* (Intranet Development) and *Independent Variable* (Intranet Introduction Context)

The dependent variable is the HR Intranet development level. For the Intranet descriptive approach, we propose highlighting different key points. Intranet development stages are evaluated by technological degree infusion (weak, average, high) (Eder et al., 2000; Eder & Darter, 2002; Eder & Igbaria, 2001). The more significant the investment (project budget) the higher the technological infusion degree (Laval, Guilloux, & Kalika, 2002; Curry & Stancich, 2000). Different HR Intranets exist: corporate Intranet, HR Intranet and specialized Intranet. They include various HR functions but their configurations are different (Laval, Guilloux, & Kalika, 2002, 2005; Frappaolo & Capshaw, 1999; Curry & Stancich, 2000; Dias, 2001). Intranet HR facets are: HR Information, mobility and careers, training, E-learning, knowledge capitalization, administrative Management, competence management (Laval,

Guilloux, & Kalika, 2005; Martin & Metcalfe, 2001 for Knowledge; Lepak & Snell, 1998 for HRM; Bell et al., 2006). Concerning specialized Intranet, key items are E-learning, knowledge capitalization, competence, careers, mobility management (Laval, Guilloux, & Kalika, 2005; West & Berman, 2001; Jacko et al., 2002; Gu & Gavriel, 2004; Guowei & Jeffres, 2006). Finally, we propose testing the first assumption: Infusion technological degree is stronger for specialized Intranets which we name H1 (Curry & Stancich, 2000; Currie & Kerrin, 2004; Damsgaard & Scheepers, 2000).

Independent variables concern HR Intranet introduction context (environment, company size, firm strategy and HRM system configuration). From a contingent point of view, formulated hypotheses link these variables with Intranet introduction decision-making. We propose calling it H2: size is not a discriminating factor for Intranet introduction based on the work of Laval, Guilloux, and Kalika (2002) and Eder et al. (2000). Competing and informational intensity environments stimulating Intranet introduction will be our third assumption H3 (Eder et al., 2000; Swart & Kinnie, 2003). Re-engineering is a favourable context for Intranet introduction and will be called H4 (Lai & Mohapatra, 1998; Ruta, 2005). H5 will be operationalized as: A strategy "of Excellence" (Innovation & quality) is a favourable context for Intranet introduction (Amherdt & Su, 1997; Tang & Lu, 2002). H6 is the following: A strategic will to improve productivity can give rise to Intranet introduction. (Curry & Stancich, 2000; Goodman & Darr, 1996). H7 is: Organizational integration strategy can further Intranet introduction. (Lai & Mahapatra, 1998; Eder et al., 2000; Lehmuskallio, 2006; Okunoye & Abiodun, 2007). H8 is: An innovating HRM is likened with an HR Intranet "designer" which means that for example the HR director takes part in its design (Kayworth & Leidner, 2000; Newell et al., 1999; Bell et al., 2006; Florkowski & Olivas-Luján, 2006). Our ninth assumption is: A traditional HRM is associated with an Intranet user which implies that the HR director does not take part in its design. He is just consulted for Intranet establishment and contributes towards its running (Niederman, 1998; Roche & Sadowsky, 2000; Collinson, 1992; Gilbert & Gonzalez, 2000). Finally, based on Lai and Mahapatra (1998), Ruta (2005), and Jacko, Salvendy, and Sainfort (2002), we suggest H10: HR function reorganization is favourable with Intranet introduction.

Future empirical studies could show that:

- Intranet introduction opportunities (whatever its type and its level) are multiple. However, the literature is more focused on organizational factors, in particular integration and geographically dispersed companies coordination.
- A relation between context factors and Intranet types can be highlighted.
- Lastly, HR function involvement in these projects can be evaluated considering its role as regards Intranet: it varies in proportion to its own strategic integration level ("traditional HRM"/"innovating HRM" in reference to Ichniowski).

Links between technological infusion and performance are tackled by another scientific perspective named "fit" and "strategic alignment".

Fit and Strategic Alignment

Many authors tried to deepen the Fit concept which is a central concept in all contingent models. Drazin and Van de Ven (1985) examine fit approaches in organizational theory. Sabherwal et al. (2001), integrate it in strategy and information system studies. Other authors link Fit and HRM. Mobilizing HRM practices are more effective when they are connected to management practices (Ichniowski et al., 1996; Delery & Doty, 1996). In addition to ("*internal fit*"), innovating social practices must be analyzed in firm strategy and technological development contexts ("*external fit*"). Venkatraman's strategic fit model suggests that the better the alignment between business strategy and organizational information system development, the higher the company performance. According to Venkatraman, a coherent alignment between HRM and Intranet leads to a stronger performance. A strategic alignment model is defined in strategic terms of choice (managerial strategy, IT strategy, organizational processes and infrastructures, informational processes and infrastructures). Henderson and Venkatraman (1993) visualize this model with two fundamental features: *strategic fit* (external and internal components inter-relationships) and *functional integration* (managerial and functional fields integration). Venkatraman et al. (1993) named the alignments as: "strategic execution", "technological potential" and "level of service".

- *"strategic execution"* reflects the traditional perspective. Managerial strategy dictates IS infrastructure. For example, a strategic will for organizational integration improvement leads to adopting Intranet as support for information and communication.

- In *"technological potential"*, managerial vision defines information technologies strategy which guides IS infrastructure. If organizational specificity is not taking in account it can bring uncontrolled drifting. For example, an Intranet can act independently of HR professionals' wishes (Collinson, 1992).

- In *"level of service"*, information technologies strategy controls information infrastructure which implies organizational infrastructure. The IT department has an executive leadership role.

The dependent variable is the impact of the Intranet which can be measured in terms of encountered difficulties and performances. The table below describes different variables.

Performance variables overlap because Intranet impact is observed at short and long terms, and because effects interact among themselves and reinforce mutually. We have voluntarily chosen to focus on HRM system instead of information system or commercial system performances. Except for Lai and Mahapatra (1998), few authors have worked on employees' performance and Intranet. Many studies measure end-user Intranet satisfaction. Scales can be based on " technology

acceptance model" (acceptance of technology, intention to use network, use of system and satisfaction) (Horton et al., 2001). It seems relevant to add a measure for inter-functional coordination, in order to underline the functional integration role on performance (Table 3).

With more than two strategy dimensions, "fit" is examined in terms of gestalts or configurations. The configurative perspective relies on "fit" or congruence among critical strategic and structural dimensions that influence performance (Mintzberg & Lampel, 1999).

Configurative Approach: Strategic Alignment and Performance

Independent variables are those characterizing the HR Intranet alignment. We identify configurations with context variables and variables characterizing HR Intranets which are likely to generate optimum performance. Based on the literature review and more particularly on Sabherwal, Hirschheim, and Goles (2001), Sabherwal and Chan (2001), and Venkatraman (1993)'s articles, we deduce different assumptions which are the called H11: If an "innovating" HRM is supported by an Intranet with a high infusion level then HRM system performance is reinforced. H12: If an organizational

Table 3. Descriptive approach of Intranet – HRM impact

Encountered difficulties concern: Organization, culture; Work in group; End-users' integration; Actualization; Use; Safety, confidentiality; Technical aspects; Financing	(Laval, Guilloux, & Kalika, 2002, 2005; White, 2000; Curry & Stancich, 2000; Dickey & Ives, 2000; o' Flaherty & Williams, 2000; Jacobi & Luqi, 2005; Stenmark, 2003, 2006).
Performances are: Economic; Intranet-specific; Organizational	(Laval, Guilloux, & Kalika, 2002, 2005; Rooslani & Ly, 2007; Curry & Stancich, 2000; Dickey & Ives, 2000; Martisons & Chong, 1999; o' Flaherty & Williams, 2000; Jacobi & Luqi, 2005; Nyström, 2006; Vaast, 2004; Rooslani & Ly, 2007).
Economic performance is measured in terms of quality and productivity (costs, time delivery)	
Intranet performance is measured with two dimensions: technical and social	
Organizational performance concerns: Structural factors; Management system improvement; Individual performance/work	
Management system improvement concerns: Commercial system; Information system; HRM system	
HRM system improvement is apprehended in terms of "external consistence" and "internal consistency"	(Youndt et al., 1996; Mc Naughton et al., 1999; Strohmeier, 2007; Torben et al., 2006).

integration strategic relies on Intranet corporate, organizational performance is then reinforced. H13: If productivity improvement and excellence strategies rely on specialized Intranet with a high infusion level then global performance including HRM is reinforced. H14: technology precedes or accompanies change and reorganization. H15: If HRM is traditional then Intranet development is likely to generate change management problems. H16: There is less resistance towards change during the introduction of an Intranet, if the HRM is innovating. Configurative approach could be implemented via a quantitative survey in order to qualify a significant typology.

Conclusion and Perspectives

Our exploratory survey on Intranets used as HR support has permitted identifying various context, Intranet and result variables. Different potential applications and their accessibility have been underlined.

Concerning context variables: if the number of employees is not crippling for Intranet introduction, environment strongly stimulates it. Firm strategies are various: reorganization, process re-engineering; search for innovation and quality, productivity or organizational integration improvement. These conditions justify technological infusion and more particularly HR support activities. Concerning the HR function, firms develop either an innovative HR management or a traditional HR management or reorganization of the function. In the first case, HR function is usually Intranet « designer ». In the second case, HR function experts are Intranet "users". If a widescale reorganization is undertaken, we could think of a stronger involvement of the HR department in Intranet development.

Concerning the variables describing Intranets: aims, development level, functionalities are listed. Three approaches exist: corporate Intranet, specialized Intranet and HR Intranet. They can be linked to different development stages: com-

munication, functional support, knowledge management. Various functionalities are listed: HR information, mobility and carriers, administrative management, knowledge capitalization, training, competence management. Firms integrate these items and develop them according to the aim assigned to Intranet and according to the degree of strategic integration of the HR function.

Difficulties are various and tied in with organizational issues, technical, updating, security, confidentiality, finance etc … Problems can also emerge when the end user is not involved in the design stage.

Intranet performances are evaluated in economic, technical, social and organizational terms.

In fact, HR Function is considered a winner if:

• It integrates the Intranet in its management process and
• If players are aware of the strikes and
• If they behave as real change agents.

Our exploratory survey on HRM & Intranet is inspired by a configurative approach according to which internal and external consistency or strategic alignment improve performance. In accordance with this perspective, functional strategy (HR function) and Intranet Fit influence organizational performance. Configurations of companies developing information systems piloted by technique or by organization are described by Venkatraman. The objective is to note the presence or not of HRM – Intranet alignment.

The future HRM Intranet evolution should contribute towards facing up to two main organizational challenges: transversality and inter-functional coordination improvement. This justifies our dynamic and systemic model. Future research should answer: What are the HRM Intranet development growth potentials? What are the different Intranet project types? What are the various strategic organizational and HR objectives? The assumptions, formulated in reference to Henderson et al (1993) devoted to reconfigurations, could lead to various attitudes towards HRM Intranet: renouncement, IT use development and improvement, HR department involvement in future projects for better inter-functional coordination, re-engineering management. Qualitative and quantitative studies are suggested to foster contingent, contextualized and configurational analyses. Future research is welcome in respect of not only stakes but also risks for the HR function within the framework of implementing Intranets in organizations. For example, we might think that HR rationalization via IT could lead to dehumanization and an increase in employees' stress. In a critical perspective, research projects could determine how a close HR could inform and give advice to employees who are more and more in charge of their responsibility in evolution of their own career.

REFERENCES

Amherdt, C., & Su, Z. (1997). Vers une gestion renouvelée des ressources humaines dans les organisations virtuelles. *Revue de Gestion des Ressources Humaines*, 23, 14–26.

Bell, B. S., Lee, S., & Yeung, S. (2006). The impact of e-HR on professional competence in HRM: Implications for the development of HR professionals. *Human Resource Management*, 45(3), 295–308. doi:10.1002/hrm.20113

Bhattacherjee, A. (1998). Management of emerging technologies: Experiences and lessons learned at US West. *Information & Management*, 33(5), 263–272. doi:10.1016/S0378-7206(98)00034-2

Bishop, L., & Levine, D. I. (1999). Computer mediated communication as employee voice: A case study. *Industrial & Labor Relations Review*, 52(2), 213–233. doi:10.2307/2525163

Collinson, D. (1992). Introducing on-line processings: Conflicting human resource policies in insurance. In Nohria, N., & Eccles, R. (Eds.), *Network and organizations: Structure, form and action* (pp. 155–173). Boston: Harvard Business School Press.

Cooper, R., & Zmud, R. (1990). Information technology implementation research: a technological diffusion approach. *Management Science*, 36(2), 123–139. doi:10.1287/mnsc.36.2.123

Currie, G., & Kerrin, M. (2004). The limits of a technological fix to knowledge management: Epistemological, political and cultural issues in the case of Intranet implementation. *Management Learning*, 35(1), 9–29. doi:10.1177/1350507604042281

Curry, A., & Stancich, L. (2000). The Intranet: An intrinsic component of strategic information management? *International Journal of Information Management*, 20(4), 249–268. doi:10.1016/S0268-4012(00)00015-3

Damsgaard, J., & Scheepers, R. (2000). Managing the crises in Intranet implementation: A stage model of Intranet technology implementation and management. *Information Systems Journal*, 10(2), 131–149. doi:10.1046/j.1365-2575.2000.00076.x

Delery, J., & Doty, D. (1996). Modes of theorizing in strategic human resource management: Tests of universalistic, contingency, and configurational performance predictions. *Academy of Management Journal*, 39(4), 802–835. doi:10.2307/256713

Dias, C. (2001). Corporate portals: A literature review of a new concept in Information Management. *International Journal of Information Management*, 21(4), 269–287. doi:10.1016/S0268-4012(01)00021-4

Dickey, M., & Ives, B. (2000). The impact of Intranet technology on power in franchisee-franchisor relationships. *Information Systems Frontiers*, 2(1), 99–114. doi:10.1023/A:1010054222086

Drazin, R., & Van de Ven, A. (1985). Alternative forms of fit in contingency theory. *Administrative Science Quarterly*, *30*(4), 514–539. doi:10.2307/2392695

Eder, L., Arinze, B., Darter, M., & Wise, D. (2000). An analysis of Intranet infusion level. *Information Resources Management Journal*, *13*(3), 14–22.

Eder, L., & Igbaria, M. (2001). Determinants of Intranet diffusion and infusion. *Omega*, *29*(3), 233–242. doi:10.1016/S0305-0483(00)00044-X

Eder, L. B., & Darter, M. E. (2002). Corporate Intranet infusion. In Khosrow-pour, M. (Ed.), *Advanced topics in information resources management* (*Vol. 1*, pp. 223–238). Hershey, PA: IGI Global.

Florkowski, G., & Olivas-Luján, M. (2006). The diffusion of human-resource information-technology innovations in US and non-US firms. *Personnel Review*, *35*(6), 684–710. doi:10.1108/00483480610702737

Frappaolo, K., & Capshaw, S. (1999). Knowledge management software: Capturing the essence of know-how and innovation. *Information Management Journal*, *33*(3), 44–48.

Gardner, S., Lepak, D. P., & Bartol, K. M. (2003). Virtual HR: The impact of information technology on the human resource professional. *Journal of Vocational Behavior*, *63*(2), 159–179. doi:10.1016/S0001-8791(03)00039-3

Gartner Group, Inc. (1996). *Developing a powerful corporate Intranet: Issues challenges, and solution*. Stamford, CT: Gartner.

Gilbert, P., & Gonzalez, D. (2000). Les progiciels intégrés et la GRH: Quand l'ambiguïté des enjeux est fonctionnelle. *Annales des Mines*, 26-33.

Goodman, P. S., & Darr, E. D. (1996). Exchanging best practices through computer-aided systems. *The Academy of Management Executive*, *10*(2), 7–19.

Gu, J., & Gavriel, S. (2004). Interface methods for using Intranet portal organizational memory information system. *Ergonomics*, *47*(15), 1585–1597. doi:10.1080/00140130412331303939

Guilloux, V., Laval, F., & Kalika, M. (2005). Les Intranets RH: de l'introduction des TIC aux nouvelles formes d'organisation. In Kalika, M., Guilloux, V., Laval, F., & Matmati, M. (Eds.), *E-RH réalités manageriales* (pp. 147–159). Paris: Vuibert.

Guowei, J., & Jeffres, L. (2006). Understanding employees' willingness to contribute to shared electronic databases: A three dimensional framework. *Communication Research*, *33*(4), 242–261. doi:10.1177/0093650206289149

Henderson, J. C., & Venkatraman, N. (1993). Strategic alignment: leveraging information technology for transforming organizations. *IBM Systems Journal*, *32*(1), 472–484. doi:10.1147/sj.382.0472

Horton, R., Buck, T., Waterson, P., & Clegg, C. (2001). Explaining Intranet use with the technology acceptance model. *Journal of Information Technology*, *16*(4), 237–249. doi:10.1080/02683960110102407

Ichniowski, C., Kochan, T. A., Levine, D., Olson, C., & Strauss, G. (1996). What works at work: Overview and assessment. *Industrial Relations*, *35*(3), 299–333. doi:10.1111/j.1468-232X.1996.tb00409.x

Jacko, J., Salvendy, G., & Sainfort, F. (2002). Intranets and organizational learning: A research and development agenda. *International Journal of Human-Computer Interaction*, *14*(1), 93–130. doi:10.1207/S15327590IJHC1401_3

Jacoby, G., & Luqi, A. (2005). Critical business requirements model and metrics, for Intranet ROI. *Journal of Electronic Commerce Research*, *6*(1), 1–30.

Kayworth, T., & Leidner, D. (2000). The global virtual manager: A prescription for success. *European Management Journal, 18*(2), 183–194. doi:10.1016/S0263-2373(99)00090-0

Lai, V., & Mahapatra, R. (1998). Evaluation of Intranets in a distributed Environment. *Decision Support Systems, 23,* 347–357. doi:10.1016/S0167-9236(98)00064-5

Laval, F., Guilloux, V., & Kalika, M. (2002). Les Intranets RH: pratiques des entreprises et problématiques. In Kalika, M. (Ed.), *E-GRH: Révolution ou évolution?* (pp. 63–90). Paris: Editions Liaisons.

Laval, F., Guilloux, V., & Kalika, M. (2005). L'Intranet RH: de l'E-RH au knowledge management. In Kalika, M., Guilloux, V., Laval, F., & Matmati, M. (Eds.), *E-RH réalités manageriales* (pp. 161–174). Paris: Ed Vuibert.

Lehmuskallio, S. (2006). The uses, roles, and contents of Intranets in multinational companies in Finland. *Journal of Business and Technical Communication, 7*(20), 288–324. doi:10.1177/1050651906287255

Lepak, D., & Snell, S. (1998). Virtual HR: Strategic human resource management in the 21st century. *Human Resource Management Review, 8*(3), 215–234. doi:10.1016/S1053-4822(98)90003-1

Martin, P., & Metcalfe, M. (2001). Informing the knowledge workers. *RSR. Reference Services Review, 29*(4), 267–275. doi:10.1108/00907320110408384

Martisons, M. G., & Chong, P. (1999). The influence of human factors and specialist involvement on information systems success. *Human Relations, 52*(1), 123–150. doi:10.1177/001872679905200107

McNaughton, R., Quickenden, P., Matear, S., & Gray, B. (1999). Intranet adoption and interfunctional co-ordination. *Journal of Marketing Management, 15*(5), 387–403. doi:10.1362/026725799784870270

Mintzberg, H., & Lampel, J. (1999). Reflecting on the strategy process. *Sloan Management Review, 40*(3), 21–30.

Newell, S., Scarbrough, H., & Swan, J. (2001). From global knowledge management to internal electronic fences: Contradictory outcomes of Intranet development. *British Journal of Management, 12*(2), 97–111. doi:10.1111/1467-8551.00188

Newell, S., Swan, J., Galliers, R., & Scarbrough, H. (1999). The Intranet as a knowledge management tool? Creating new electronic fences, managing Information Technology Resources. In Khosrow-Pour, M. (Ed.), *The next millennium* (pp. 612–619). Hershey, PA: IGI Global.

Niederman, F. (1999). Global information system and HRM: a research agenda. *Journal of Global Information Management, 7*(2), 33–39.

Norzaidi, M., Chong, S., Murali, R., & Salwani, M. (2007). Intranet usage and managers' performance in the port industry. *Industrial Management & Data Systems, 107*(8), 1227–1250. doi:10.1108/02635570710822831

Nyström, C. (2006). Philosophy of technology in organizations: A foundation for Intranets. *Systemic Practice and Action Research, 19*(6), 523–535.

O'Flaherty, B., & Williams, H. (2000). Intranet adoption in Irish organisations: a survey analysis. *Systèmes d'Information et Management, 5*(2), 41–58.

Okunoye, A., & Bada, A. (2007). Institutional drivers of Intranet use in a global context: Case of a distributed international research organisation. *World Review of Science. Technology and Sustainable Development, 4*(1), 73–85. doi:10.1504/WRSTSD.2007.012661

Phelps, R., & Mok, M. (1999). Managing the risks of Intranet implementation: An empirical study of user satisfaction. *Journal of Information Technology, 14*(1), 39–52. doi:10.1080/026839699344737

Roche, L. (2000). *Cybergagnant: Technologie, cyberespace et développement personnel*. Paris: Maxima Laurent du Mesnil.

Roche, L., & Sadowsky, J. (2000). La résistance des salariés à la high-tech. *Expansion management review, 99*, 44-50.

Rooslani, T., & Ly, F. S. (2007). The development and empirical validation of the B2E portal user satisfaction scale. *Journal of Organizational and End User Computing, 19*(3), 43–63.

Ruta, D. (2005). The application of change management theory to HR portal implementation in subsidiaries of multinational corporations. *Human Resource Management, 44*(1), 35–53. doi:10.1002/hrm.20039

Sabherwal, R., & Chan, Y. E. (2001). Alignment between business and IS strategies: a study of protectors, analysers and defenders. *Information Systems Research, 12*(1), 11–33. doi:10.1287/isre.12.1.11.9714

Sabherwal, R., Hirschheim, R., & Goles, T. (2001). The dynamics of alignment: Insights from a punctuated equilibrium model. *Organization Science, 12*(2), 179–197. doi:10.1287/orsc.12.2.179.10113

Saga, V., & Zmud, R. (1996). Introduction de logiciels de gestion dans des petites entreprises liées à une profession libérale. *Systèmes d'Information et Management, 1*(1), 51–73.

Stenmark, D. (2003). Knowledge creation and the web: Factors indicating why some Intranets succeed where others fail. *Knowledge and Process Management, 10*(3), 207–216. doi:10.1002/kpm.173

Stenmark, D. (2006). Corporate Intranet failures: interpretating a case study through the lens of formative context. *International Journal of Business Environment, 1*(1), 112–125.

Straus, S. G., Weisband, S. P., & Wilson, J. M. (1998). Human Resource Management Practices in the networked organization: Impact of Electronic Communication Systems. In Cooper, C. L., & Rousseau, D. M. (Eds.), *Trends in Organizational Behavior* (pp. 127–154). New York: John Wiley & Sons Ltd.

Strohmeier, S. (2007). Research in e-HRM: Review and implications. *Human Resource Management Review, 17*(1), 19–37. doi:10.1016/j.hrmr.2006.11.002

Swart, J., & Kinnie, N. (2003). Knowledge-intensive firms: the influence of the client on HR systems Systems. *Research and Behavioral Science, 23*(6), 839–844.

Tang, X., & Lu, Q. (2002). Intranet-extranet-internet based quality information management: system in expanded enterprises. *International Journal of Advanced Manufacturing Technology, 20*(11), 853–858. doi:10.1007/s001700200226

Torben, A., Eriksen, B., Lemmergaard, J., & Povlsen, L. (2006). The many faces of fit: An application to strategic human resource management. In Burton, R., Døjbak Håkonsson, D., Eriksen, B., & Snow, C. (Eds.), *Organization Design - The Evolving State of the Art* (pp. 85–101). New York: Springer.

Vaast, E. (2004). O Brother, where are thou?: From communities to networks of practice through Intranet use. *Management Communication Quarterly, 8*(18), 5–44. doi:10.1177/0893318904265125

Venkatraman, N. (1993). Continuous strategic alignment: Exploiting information technology capabilities for competitive success. *European Management Journal, 11*(2), 139–149. doi:10.1016/0263-2373(93)90037-I

Wan Hooi, L. (2006). Implementing e-HRM: The readiness of small and medium sized manufacturing companies in Malaysia. *Asia Pacific Business Review*, *12*(4), 465–485. doi:10.1080/13602380600570874

West, J., & Berman, E. (2001). From traditional to virtual HR. *Review of Public Personnel Administration*, *21*(1), 38–64. doi:10.1177/0734371X0102100104

White, M. (2000). Corporate portals: Realizing their promise, avoiding costly failure. *Business Information Review*, *12*(17), 177–184. doi:10.1177/0266382004237737

Zmud, R., & Apple, L. (1992). Measuring information technology infusion. *Production and Innovation Management*, *9*, 148–155. doi:10.1016/0737-6782(92)90006-X

This work was previously published in International Journal of Technology and Human Interaction, Volume 6, Issue 3, edited by Anabela Mesquita & Chia-Wen Tsai, pp. 21-36, copyright 2010 by IGI Publishing (an imprint of IGI Global).

Chapter 7
Acceptance and Appropriation of Videoconferencing for E-Training:
An Empirical Investigation

Bernard Fallery
Montpellier 2 University, France

Roxana Taddei
Montpellier 2 University, France

Sylvie Gerbaix
Montpellier 2 University, France

ABSTRACT

The purpose of this paper is to explore the acceptance and the appropriation of videoconferencing-mediated training during real training situations in a French company. The authors compare the acceptance and appropriation by 60 employees of two videoconferencing-mediated training systems: the virtual class (desktop videoconferencing) and the remote class (where learners are gathered together in the same room while the trainer is located at distance). In considering the acceptance of these videoconferencing-mediated training systems, a link was confirmed between perceived usefulness and the intention to use, but no relationship was established between the levels of acceptance and the required effort. The intention to use videoconferencing was associated with the expected benefits and not with the expected effort. Regarding appropriation, learners did not report a perception of technological distance. Moreover, this paper shows that learners and the trainer preferred the virtual class rather than the more classical remote class. The authors' findings contradict the media richness theory, according to which the remote class, which is the "richer" medium in their research, should have been preferred.

DOI: 10.4018/978-1-61350-465-9.ch007

INTRODUCTION

The increase in use of the Internet and information technologies has introduced new possibilities in the field of training, especially for remote training. In this context, videoconferencing seems to be a promising tool as it enables work in different locations while preserving the possibility of real time interaction between teachers and trainees. It is, therefore, important to study learners' perceptions and the first uses of this technology.

Specifically, this article focuses on the use of videoconferencing for training within a large organization, which is in the early stages of implementation of this new tool. The main topic of this chapter is the measurement of acceptance and appropriation of videoconferencing as a tool for professional training within a large French company. In this company, training is considered to be a very important and strategic part of HRM. The aim of professional training is to improve employees' skills in the context of rapidly changing jobs and recruitment of new employees.

Videoconferencing may be considered as a way of reducing travelling and the time required for the organization of training sessions, and of modernizing the company image for employees. At the same time it provides interactions between the learners and the trainer similar to face-to-face training situations.

Consequently, videoconferencing may become a useful tool of Electronic Human Resources Management. However, HR Managers in the company hesitated in implementing videoconferencing for training. They thought that employees (both learners and trainer) would reject it; for this reason, they wanted to explore employees' perceptions, attitudes and behaviors related to this new tool.

If HR Managers were to implement videoconferencing for training, they would need to know which was the more efficient type of videoconferencing that was preferred by employees. Actually, different types of videoconferencing technologies allow different types of training (in a small group or in a large group, using transmissive or collaborative pedagogy). Virtual class (desktop videoconferencing) and remote class (where distant learners are gathered together in the same room, as in traditional classes, while the trainer is located at distance) are the main types of videoconferencing for training. We will measure the acceptance (learners' and trainer's perceptions and attitudes) and the appropriation (users' behaviors) of both types of classes. This question has not yet been developed in the literature. However, the effects of ITs on learning, and the effect of videoconferencing on interaction, have been explored. In the following section, studies on these two topics are reviewed.

LITERATURE REVIEW

Information Technologies and Learning Performance

Several papers focus on the relationship between IT and learning. Their main question is, can an IT improve learning performance, and if so, how? Researchers are generally interested in how IT affects learning effectiveness. In this regard, some authors have shown that a technology's capabilities emphasized learning performance (e.g., Alavi, 1994).

Other researchers demonstrated that IT had no significant effect on learning performance (Alavi et al., 1995; Russell, 1999). For example, Alavi et al. (2002) found that the learning outcome of an e-mail environment was greater than the learning outcome of a more sophisticated Group Support System environment. Mehlenbacher et al. (2000) pointed out that there was no significant difference in student performance in the two learning situations (two web-based sections of a technical writing class and a conventional version of the class).

These outcomes are in contradiction with richness media theory (Daft & Lengel, 1984). For Clark

(1994), learning effectiveness is enhanced by the teaching method and not by the technology itself.

According to Collins (1991), the way the instructor implements the technology is the determining factor for learning effectiveness. In this regard, some authors showed the importance of the instructors' characteristics for increasing learning effectiveness: the instructor's positive attitude towards technology, the instructor's interactive teaching style and the instructor's control over the technology (Webster & Hackley, 1997) or the instructor's self-efficacy (Mathieu et al., 1993).

If the instructor's characteristics are important in explaining the effectiveness of technology-mediated training, the learner's characteristics may also explain different degrees of learning effectiveness. Benbunan-Fich and Hiltz (2003) showed that outcomes of online courses improved when professors structured them in order to support the growth of a learning community, by using collaborative strategies and being available online to interact with students.

Picolli et al. (2001) found that participants in two virtual learning environments reported being less satisfied with the learning process. The authors suggested that this result might be explained by the lack of learning strategies that allow students to take advantage of the high levels of learners' control and flexibility that are available in virtual learning environments.

Several authors have explored various factors concerning learners that emphasize learning effectiveness in technology-mediated learning environments. Hiltz (1993) observed that collaboration among students, motivation, and student characteristics (level of academic ability, motivation, degree of effort and maturity) are positively correlated with learning performance in an asynchronous distance learning environment. Webster and Hackley (1997) pointed out that students' comfort with their onscreen image influenced behavior in asynchronous distance learning environments. Mehlenbacher et al. (2000) suggested that reflective, global learners

performed significantly better on online courses than active, sequential learners, although there was no difference between them in the traditional class.

The same mixed outcomes are produced in studies focusing on students' satisfaction, which is another aspect of learning performance. Piccoli et al. (2001) found that students in a virtual learning environment reported significantly higher computer self-efficacy than those in a traditional classroom. In contrast, Alavi et al. (2002) noticed no significant difference in the students' satisfaction with the learning process under the two distributed learning environments (a "simple" environment and a more sophisticated environment). Benbunan-Fich and Hiltz (2003) were interested in another type of technology-mediated learning, online courses. Their results suggested that there were no significant differences in the students' perceived learning associated with the delivery mode (totally online via asynchronous learning networks, traditional face-to-face courses, and sections using a mix of traditional and online activities).

Other researchers have highlighted the limits of virtual learning environments: the feeling of isolation (Brown, 1996), frustration, anxiety and confusion (Hara & Kling, 2000) as well as reduced interest in the subject matter (Maki et al., 2000).

A few recent studies have focused not only on the learning performance but also on the intention to continue using a technology-mediated learning environment.

Chiu et al. (2007) integrated the Information Systems success model and fairness theory to highlight variables that affect learners' satisfaction. They found that information quality; system quality, system use, distributive fairness and interactional fairness have significant positive effects on satisfaction. Other variables such as procedural fairness and satisfaction play significant roles in learners' intention to continue using Web-based learning.

Employing the Unified Theory of Acceptance and Use of Technology (UTAUT), Chiu and Wang

(2008) showed that performance expectancy, effort expectancy, computer self-efficacy, attainment value, utility value and intrinsic value were significant predictors of an individual's intention to continue using Web-based learning; while high levels of anxiety exhibited a significant negative effect. These findings suggested the beneficial effect of positive subjective task value in stimulating learners' intention to continue using Web-based learning.

Uses of Videoconferencing

Studies focusing on the use of IT have reached no definite conclusions on the efficiency of one particular medium compared to other media. While some studies assert that videoconferencing is as effective as face-to-face interaction, or more effective than audioconferencing (e.g., Valacich et al., 1994), others assert that videoconferencing has no significant effect (e.g., Alavi et al., 1995; Dennis & Kinney, 1998). In contradiction to media richness theory, researchers highlighted factors other than the technology's features that influenced the perception of the richness of the medium. These factors are as follows: exchange of social information, in which, over time leaner media became as effective as richer media (Walther, 1995); familiarity with communication partners (e.g., Carlson & Zmud, 1999), established norms, and relationships among group members (McGrath et al., 1993).

Factors other than a technology's features are more evident when the same technology is used in the same company. In this regard, Webster (1998) found that the desktop videoconferencing system was used less than its functions allowed and that employees have different levels of use. Webster explained this difference by reference to the following factors: social influence, medium experience, job fit, desktop video self-efficacy and lower introversion.

Videoconferencing Effects on Learning

Similar results are found in the field of education and training. For example, some researchers found that learning mediated by videoconferencing lead to a higher degree of interaction with the teacher, linked to more efficient learning (Goodfellow, 1996) and to a higher degree of collaboration between learners (Marquet, 2003; Rutter, 1987; Sellen, 1995) than face-to-face learning.

However, other researchers have shown mixed results. O'Conaill et al. (2003) showed that the interaction between the learners and the trainers was more like a face-to-face interaction in a leaner videoconferencing system than in a richer videoconferencing system.

Alavi et al. (1995) found that the three environments (face-to-face collaborative learning, local groups – students on the local campus – and non-proximate distant groups involved in Desktop Videoconferencing (DVC) were equally effective in terms of student knowledge acquisition. However, higher critical-thinking skills were found in the distant DVC environment. The students in the three environments were equally satisfied with their learning process and outcomes. The distant students using DVC were more committed and attracted to their groups compared to local students who worked face-to-face or through DVC.

Comparing audio-conferencing and desktop videoconferencing, Yoo & Alavi (2001) found that the influence of group cohesion (members' attraction to the group) over social presence is additive, rather than substitutive, to that of media condition.

Similarly, other authors considered that videoconferencing is « neutral» and the type of videoconferencing does not affect levels of use. (Clark, 1994; Collins, 1995).

Furthermore, the way videoconferencing is implemented is highly important. Ologeanu (2005) and Webster and Hackley (1997) suggested that the greater number of locations, the greater the process losses and the less involved the remote students appeared.

RESEARCH FRAMEWORK

The acceptance of IT in a particular domain of training has not been a prevalent topic for researchers. Researchers have focused on the effectiveness of learning using IT (Technology-Mediated Learning, Web based virtual learning environments, group support systems, Desktop videoconferencing) and on users' satisfaction or performance. Nevertheless, learning effectiveness is one aspect of the use and the implementation of an IT.

The perceptions, attitudes and behaviors of the end-users are also important, especially for perceived learning effectiveness, for learners' intention to use the IT for learning, and for the adoption of these new tools. These become even more important in skills training, in companies where employees may support or not support a technology-mediated learning environment.

In this paper, we consider users' satisfaction with and acceptance of a videoconferencing tool. We also explore users' behaviors and attitudes using appropriation theory.

Technology Acceptance

This study tests several relationships based on the Unified Theory of Acceptance and Use of Technology (UTAUT), (Venkatesh et al., 2003). According to this theory, an individual's behavior is conditioned by his/her intention to adopt a technology, and this depends on two variables: perceived usefulness and perceived ease of use.

Segars and Grover (1993) developed a measure of usefulness that consists of six indicators: enables the individual to work more quickly, makes a job easier, useful, increases productivity, effectiveness, and effect on job performance. Davis (1989) defined perceived usefulness as the extent to which the object of adoption is thought to enhance the individual's performance on the job.

Segars and Grover (1993) identified four perceived ease of use indicators: easy to use, easy to learn, easy to become skillful, clear (understandable). Davis defined perceived ease of use as the degree to which a person believes that using a particular system would be free from effort (Davis, 1989).

The concepts of usefulness and ease of use are related to the task and to the technology. They may be linked to Task-Technology Fit Theory, according to which IT is more likely to have a positive impact on individual performance and to be used if the capabilities of the IT match the tasks the user must perform (Goodhue & Thompson, 1995). Goodhue and Thompson (1995) suggest 8 factors to measure the task-technology fit: quality, locatability, authorization, compatibility, ease of use/training, production timeliness, systems reliability, and relationship with users.

Taking into account the population and the specific domain of our study, we defined perceived usefulness as follows:

- The degree to which learners think that videoconferencing can facilitate their timetable management by decreasing travelling for skills training. According to this meaning, the notion of instrumental use and the notion of perceived usefulness are synonymous.
- The degree to which learners think that using videoconferencing brings an additional interest in training, that videoconferencing for training is more efficient than face-to-face training, and that interactions with the trainer are better than in face-to-face training.

We define the perceived ease of use by the perceived quality of the videoconferencing tool and by the perceived quality of training through videoconferencing.

Table 1. Dimensions and definitions

Dimension	Definition (item)
Previous IT experience	Previous knowledge and experience of IT and distance training.
Personal Motivation	The pleasure and the self-esteem derived from the use of videoconferencing for training or from using an innovative tool. The increase in integration into the group they belong to (family, friends, colleagues) or the increase in prestige that coincides with videoconferencing use.
Perceived usefulness	Usefulness for training The extent to which using videoconferencing increases the effectiveness of training and timetable management Usefulness for training management The extent to which using videoconferencing enhances the effectiveness of performed work by reducing travel time and increasing timetable management.
Task-Technology fit	The extent to which videoconferencing matches training tasks in the company
Perceived ease of use	The degree to which using videoconferencing for training is free from effort such as technical or educational skills required and the lack of interaction, notably with the trainer.
Satisfaction	The degree to which videoconferencing is evaluated on several dimensions: Sound Quality, Picture Quality, Quality of Slides legibility, Conditions for speaking, Interaction with the trainer, Interaction with peers.
Intention to use	Intention to use videoconferencing sessions, after these experiments.

We do not measure training effectiveness, but learners' satisfaction with training through videoconferencing.

In line with UTAUT theory and the definitions of perceived usefulness and perceived ease of use, six dimensions were measured as seen in Table 1.

Appropriation of Information Technologies

Appropriation is one of the main concepts of Adaptive Structuration Theory (AST), which considers that technologies are manipulated and structured by users in their contexts (DeSanctis &Poole, 1994). DeSanctis and Poole (1994) make a distinction between the spirit and the features of a technology. Spirit is defined as "the official line that the technology presents to people regarding how to act when using the system, how to interpret its features, and how to fill in gaps in procedure which are not explicitly specified" (p. 126). Features are characteristics or technical functions of the technology.

According to DeSanctis and Poole (1994), there are four aspects of appropriation:

- Appropriation moves,
- Faithfulness of appropriation (which means that appropriation may be faithful or unfaithful to the IT spirit),
- Instrumental uses, which are intended purposes that groups assign to technology as they use it (for example, task activities),
- Attitudes that the group displays as technology structures are appropriated.

Thus, the definition of appropriation includes acceptance aspects (linked to the users' attitudes toward the IT). The appropriation dimension of "instrumental uses" is very close to the idea of "perceived usefulness".

However, the concept of appropriation is focused on uses during IT implementation while the concept of acceptance highlights users' perceptions, particularly before the IT implementation (Baillette & Kimble, 2008). Appropriations are defined by DeSanctis and Poole (1994) as "immediate, visible actions that evidence deeper structurations" (p. 128). Thus, appropriations are synonymous with adaptations (Majchrzak et al., 2000). New technologies represent opportunities to change groups' structures.

We focus on appropriations such as uses and changes of group structures. We suggest that in the specific domain of training, group structures may be described like "pedagogical genres". We note the interactions based on "best practices", that is a pedagogical genre according to Fallery (2005). Pedagogical genres are communication genres in the special situation of training (Yates & Orlikowski, 1992). Pedagogical genres are characterized by the pedagogical intention (what to teach?) and by the pedagogical method (how to teach?). There are various pedagogical genres such as Courses, Talks, Examples, Demonstrations, Debates, Simulations, etc.

In our study, pedagogical genres may be shaped by the trainer (who designs the learning process) or by the users. In the first case, pedagogical genres describe technology's spirit, while in the second case they describe appropriation moves (changes of group structures).

In this work, we decided not to study appropriation moves for three reasons. First, video-training was not yet fully implemented and, at the experimental stage, the video-conferencing tool is quite flexible. Secondly, the distant class and the remote class are two different systems with different structural features. Finally, in the experimental situation, the trainer can shape the system (to choose different functions) and, thus, change structural features and the technology's spirit.

In the particular domain of training, we must consider the possible effects of pedagogical and technical distances (Marquet & Nissen, 2003). The pedagogical distance focuses on the interactions and exchanges between peers and between learners and trainer.

We measured the pedagogical distance using Lickert's attitudes scale with the following items: "In the videoconferencing environment, discussions were easier with the trainer than in face-to-face training", "In the videoconferencing environment, the group's atmosphere was better than in face-to-face", "In the videoconferencing environment, I dared more easily ask a question of the trainer than in face-to-face training", "In the videoconferencing environment, I felt more isolated than in face-to-face training", "In the videoconferencing environment, I was more relaxed than in face-to-face training."

Technical distance is produced by technical mediation (such as breakdowns or cuts in transmission).

We can link pedagogical and technical distance with satisfaction with the videoconferencing (sound, video and transmission quality). For example, the quality of transmission might be low whereas learners could report that this is not a problem for the success of the training and that they were satisfied with this quality level.

METHODOLOGY

Context

The company that we studied has around 170,000 employees, spread across the whole country. Skills training is provided in different locations and employees have to travel to participate in training sessions on specific topics. Each year, several thousand hours are provided by 1500 trainers.

Managers wanted to explore learners' and trainer's perceptions, attitudes and uses of two types of training through videoconferencing: the virtual class and the remote class.

In the virtual class, the learners and their teacher were situated in several locations and interacted through their personal computers and specific videoconferencing software. In the remote class, learners were gathered together in the same room and only the trainer was situated at distance. In both classes, learners could "interact" with the teacher (ask questions, request explanations, and make comments): everyone could see each other and all could participate in the training.

Participants

The experiment had to fit in with the company's usual training practices.

A total of 60 learners participated in the experiment. 19 one-hour videoconferencing sessions of training (7 sessions in virtual classes involving 20 students and 10 sessions in remote classes involving 40 students) were carried out. The number of participants per session varied. There were 2, 3 or 4 learners for each virtual class session and between 3 and 6 participants for each remote class session.

The topic of these sessions was to provide professional skills for employees operating in the commercial domain. The learners had been chosen by their line managers according to the same criteria used for the « traditional » training in the company. For all the sessions, the same trainer was involved in the experiment. During the sessions he used different tools (DVD and PowerPoint presentation) and interacted with the learners.

From reasons such as availability of the network and of technical skills, the training sessions were provided in the same building. The distance was simulated both for the virtual class and for the remote class. The trainer was located in a different room of the same building but the learners were informed that he was elsewhere. In both situations, learners were situated in the same room. In the virtual class, they were isolated from each other because they used their personal computers to interact with each other and with the trainer. The learners changed at every session.

Measurement Issues

In order to measure all the variables, we used two methods:

- **Qualitative methods:** focus group interviews with learners, based on an interview guide, and observation of the video conferencing sessions. The purpose of this method was to measure appropriation moves,

- **Quantitative methods:** consisting of a survey. A questionnaire combining 41 open and closed questions was administered immediately after each session. The closed questions were designed according to the five-point Likert scales.

Analyses of all measures were conducted using Sphinx for Windows. We combined Chi-square tests to measure relationships between answers to closed questions, and lexical analysis to treat the open answers and the focus group interviews.

Content analysis was employed to study observation accounts. We created a coding frame, based on the pedagogical genres.

We have to point out that the sample's limited size allows us only to make some propositions for future research.

FINDINGS

We have formulated the findings of this study into several statements.

1. Satisfaction with the virtual class is higher than satisfaction with the remote class.

   a. Learners in virtual classes reported higher satisfaction and higher levels of intention to continue using videoconferencing than learners in remote classes. 85.7% of the learners in virtual classes reported satisfaction while 68.3% of the remote class learners reported satisfaction. 100% of the virtual class learners reported an intention to continue using videoconferencing for training, while 60% of learners in remote classes reported this intention.

   b. Learners in virtual classes reported significantly higher satisfaction with the videoconferencing-mediated

111

Table 2. Satisfaction: differences between virtual class and remote class

Type of relationship	Significance
Sound quality x Type of environment	Significant (X2 = 2.73, 1-p = 90.15%)
Video quality x Type of environment	Significant (X2 = 2.28, 1-p = 86.90%)
Slides legibility quality x Type of environment	Not significant
Conditions for speaking x Type of environment	Significant (X2=5.27, 1-p = 97.83%)
Interaction with the trainer x Type of environment	Significant (X2 = 3.67, 1-p = 94.47%)
Interactions with peers x Type of environment	Highly significant (X2 = 6.83, 1-p = 99.10%)

Table 3. Perceived usefulness: differences between virtual class and remote class

Perceived usefulness	Relationship
Training through videoconferencing contributes to decrease in professional training travelling in the future x Type of environment	Highly significant (X2 = 2.83, 1-p = 90.75%)
Training through videoconferencing is more efficient than face-to-face training x Type of environment	Significant (X2 = 3.07, 1-p = 92.04%)
Training through videoconferencing brings an additional interest to training compared to face-to-face training x Type of environment	Highly significant (X2 = 4.16, 1-p = 95.85%)
Interactions with peers are more frequent in training through video-conferencing than in face-to-face training x Type of environment	Highly significant (X2 = 6.83, 1-p = 99.10%)
Training through videoconferencing is adequate for skills training in the company x Type of environment	Significant relationship (X2 = 5.30, 1-p = 97.87%)

training than learners in the remote classes. This result is derived from the Chi-square test, correlating types of environments of videoconferencing for training (Virtual/Remote) and several aspects of the satisfaction variable.

The results of Chi-square test are as follows in Table 2.

2. Learners in virtual classes reported significantly higher perceived usefulness than learners in remote classes.

This result is derived from the Chi-square tests correlating types of videoconferencing environments for training (Virtual/Remote) and several aspects of the perceived usefulness variable (Table 3).

3. Learners reported high motivation for real operational gains.

This result is based on lexical analysis of responses to two open questions (Table 4).

4. The learners' satisfaction factors are as follows: their previous IT experience, their personal motivation and their interest in innovation. We summarise this result in the Table 5.

Table 4. Operational gains: sample of lexical analysis

Question	Occurrence of the most-commonly used words
According to you, what are the main interests in training via video conferencing?	Time (13), No Travel (21), Gain (7).
What are the advantages in videotraining for you?	Time (5), Teacher (6), Gain (4), No travel (7)

Table 5. Factors of Satisfaction

Satisfaction correlated with...	Relationship
Previous IT experience	Significant (X2 = 4.45, 1-p = 96.50%)
Personal motivation	Significant (X2 = 8.09, 1-p = 98.25%)
Interest in innovation	Highly significant (X2 = 17.45, 1-p = >99.99%)

Table 6. Factors of satisfaction: sample of lexical analysis

Innovation interaction – trainer
Innovative and fun
Innovative and practical
Innovative and playful
Innovative – create a new atmosphere
Newness
New technologies

This Chi-square analysis was complemented by lexical analysis of answers to two open questions. The first question was: "*If you are satisfied with the experience, what are your reasons?*" The occurrences of each of the most commonly used words in the responses are as follows: new (12), trainer (8), interactivity (4), topic (4), pleasant (4). We provide here a sample of texts containing the words frequently quoted (Table 6).

A second question was: "*If you are in favour of training through videoconferencing, what are your reasons?*"

The occurrences of each of the most commonly used words in the responses are as follows: new (17), discover (7), technology (11). We provide in Table 7 a sample of texts containing the words frequently quoted (Table 7).

5. The behavioral intention is linked to the expected benefits (perceived usefulness), but not to the expected effort required.

The number of answers to the questionnaire did not allow us to test using a structural equation model. Consequently, we only tested, one-by-one, each relation of the

Table 7. Reasons to be in favour of videoconferencing: sample of lexical analysis

New
I love to use new technologies
Discover another method of training
Using new technologies – innovative training
We have to learn with a new technology
Discovery – technology
New technology
New – allow training closer to the workplace
Use of new technologies – training equivalent to face-to-face training
New – use other communication technology
Adopt new - technologies
Discovery - new
Find out if this technology can be useful for learning – find the limits of this technology
Discovery of new tools
Discovery of the method
Why not discover new methods
Use new technologies
Interested in new ideas for skills training
Using it
Newness
Discover the tool
Pay more attention to training

UTAUT model envisaged by the Chi-square calculations. We found a significant relationship between the task-technology fit and the learners' satisfaction (X2=14.59, 1-p = 97.63%) and between the learners' satisfaction and the intention to continue use of videoconferencing for training (X2=21.37, 1-p=98.89%).

We also found a significant relationship between the perceived expected benefits (perceived usefulness) and the intention to continue using videoconferencing for training (X2= 10.7, 1-p=98.89%). In contrast, the relationship between the expected effort (which is the opposite to ease of use) and the intention to continue using videoconferencing for training is not significant.

6. The trainer prefers to control interactivity and interactions, whereas learners prefer interactions between peers, notably "best practice" interactions.

The previous results are related to the acceptance of videoconferencing for professional training. The following results concern learners' appropriation of videoconferencing.

The teacher preferred to manage interactivity whereas learners preferred discussions between participants, notably "best practice" exchanges. We may say that the teacher preferred a specific pedagogical genre (transmissive courses) while learners preferred a different one (exchanges between peers). In the virtual class, learners did not discuss and interact with each other spontaneously while in the remote class they tended to discuss amongst themselves best practices in their day-to-day tasks and to exclude teacher from the debate. For this reason, the teacher reported a preference for the virtual class, which did not allow the discussions between learners that a face-to-face class would.

We may consider that pedagogical genres described both a technology's spirit and groups' structures. According to this definition, learners' appropriation (they share "best practices") was not faithful to the technology's spirit (trainer controls and initiates all interactions with and between the learners). This result raises an additional question about the purpose of the training: learners reported their need to exchange ideas on the best practices, which is not a topic provided in the training system of the company.

7. The higher the level of satisfaction with videoconferencing for training, the less the pedagogical distance was felt (both the distance between peers and the distance between learners and the trainer).

This result is based on the Chi-square test correlations between learners' satisfaction with videoconferencing for training and pedagogical proximity (which is the opposite of pedagogical distance). The relationship between these variables is significant ($X2=3.57$, $1-p = 94.12\%$).

8. Learners did not report a technological distance, although this distance did exist.

This result is produced from technological distance evaluations by the learners, and from our observations. Thus, we observed several problems as follows: in virtual classes, the remote learners hearing their own voice coming back at them; a howling created by feedback or a strong reverberation. Both in virtual and in remote classes, we observed that the bandwith fluctuated during the videoconferencing session, that introduced sound delay, video blackouts or image flickers. At least once we observed a breakdown of the videoconferencing system. Nevertheless, these failures did not interfere with the learners' attention or involvement. Learners coped with these technical problems and they reported a high level of satisfaction with the technical features.

In a certain way, this result contradicts richness media theory and confirms other findings related to the perceived richness of a media (Carlson & Zmud, 1999; McGrath et al., 1993; Walther, 1995).

DISCUSSION AND LIMITATIONS

Our results have theoretical, methodological and practical implications.

Regarding theoretical implications, the main result of our study is that learners in virtual classes reported higher levels of satisfaction and greater intention to continue using videoconferencing than learners in remote classes. This result contradicts media richness theory according to which "rich" media (defined by their ability to change understanding within a time interval – Daft & Lengel, 1986, p. 560) are generally more effective and more suitable for ambiguous and uncertain tasks than "lean" media. In our study, the rich medium is the remote class (which allows interactions between learners similar to face-to-face training) and the lean medium is the virtual class.

How do we explain this result? We may link it with the other results: one factor of satisfaction for learners is their interest in innovation, also learners in virtual classes reported significantly higher perceived usefulness than learners in the remote classes. The virtual class offers more operational gains (decrease in travel, possibility to learn on the workplace) and it appears more innovative. It is possible that learners consider virtual classes as being an original situation that they don't compare to face-to-face training; in contrast with the remote class, that is at the same time more like and more different from face-to-face learning. This would mean that learners' perception of rich media is different from the "objective" richness of media in the theory. This hypothesis must be verified by further research. It would be interesting to deepen our research and test another theory: the Uses and Gratification Expectancy Theory for the e-learning, according to which e-learning resources offer gratifications that are expected and valued by students. (Mondi et al., 2007).

Nevertheless, our finding is similar to the mixed outcomes about the influence of IT on learning performance or learning satisfaction (Alavi et al., 2002; Benbunan-Fich & Hiltz, 2003; Mehlenbacher et al., 2000; Piccoli et al., 2001; Russell, 1999).

The methodological implication of our study is related to the fact that it is very important to explore learners' and trainers' perceptions, attitudes and uses before the implementation of a new information technology within an organization. The experimental use of an IT is a key stage of the innovation process. Furthermore, several kinds of ITs (different videoconferencing situations, different types of collaborative software,…) have to be compared and tried in order to choose the tool which may best fit the task, taking into account the features and IT's spirit.

Regarding practical implications, we pointed out that the intention to use is linked to the expected benefits, the motivations and to the appropriateness with the situation, rather than with the effort to be made. These findings contradicted managers' expected results. At the beginning of our study, managers thought that employees would reject IT and would report a resistance to change by focusing on obstacles and effort required to make use of videoconferencing for training. Moreover, it does not seem effective to focus on the barriers, even if they do exist (anxiety about the required technical and educational skills, worries related to technical breakdowns, about fatigue or isolation…). On the contrary, managers could try to promote « incentives » for this kind of training (supplementary interest, effectiveness, pleasure, new educational content…).

Furthermore, our observations showed that learners were able to cope with technological difficulties. The gap between the technical distance and the acceptable quality level of the videoconferencing tool suggests that company managers do not need to invest a lot of money in buying expensive videoconferencing systems that provide higher quality. If barriers to videoconferencing implementation exist, they are not related to the technical quality of the system.

Last but not least, learners reported a preference for interactivity between peers, whereas the trainer reported a preference for controlling all interactions with and between the learners. For this reason, managers have to ensure that the purposes of the training programmes meet the employees' training needs.

CONCLUSION

Our study explored acceptance and appropriation of two videoconferencing systems for training: virtual videoconferencing and remote videoconferencing. We examined employees' perceptions, attitudes and behaviors during real training sessions. One of our findings is that satisfaction with the virtual class is greater than satisfaction with the remote class. This result contradicts media richness theory. We may explain it by reference to learners' expectations because they reported significantly higher perceived usefulness in virtual classes than did learners in remote classes. Moreover, all learners reported motivation for real operational gain (such as no travelling needed for participation in training sessions).

The behavioral intention is linked to the expected benefits (the operational gains), but not to the expected efforts to be made. The higher the level of satisfaction with videoconferencing, the less the pedagogical distance was felt (both the distance between peers and the distance between the learners and the trainer). Learners did not report a technological distance, although this distance did exist. For these reasons, we aim to deepen our research and explore the Uses and Gratification Expectancy Theory for the e-learning.

Another result is that the trainer preferred to control interactivity and interactions whereas learners preferred interactions between peers, notably "best practice" interactions. Managers may need to take account of this demand from employees.

We suggest that the evaluation of an IT trial has to combine concepts of the acceptance theory with the concepts of studies related to IT appropriation and further research is needed on these topics.

REFERENCES

Alavi, M. (1994). Computer-mediated collaborative learning: An empirical Evaluation. *Management Information Systems Quarterly*, *18*(2), 159–174. doi:10.2307/249763

Alavi, M., & Leidner, D. (2001). Research commentary: Technology-mediated Learning—A call for greater depth and breadth of research. *Information Systems Research*, *12*(1), 1–10. doi:10.1287/isre.12.1.1.9720

Alavi, M., Marakas, G. M., & Yoo, Y. (2002). A comparative study of distributed learning environments on learning outcomes. *Information Systems Research*, *13*(4), 404–415. doi:10.1287/isre.13.4.404.72

Alavi, M., Wheeler, B. C., & Valacich, J. S. (1995). Using IT to reengineer business education: an exploratory investigation of collaborative telelearning. *Management Information Systems Quarterly*, *19*(3), 293–312. doi:10.2307/249597

Alavi, M., & Yoo, Y. (2001). Media and group cohesion: Relative influences on social presence, task participation and Group Consensus. *Management Information Systems Quarterly*, *25*(3), 371–390. doi:10.2307/3250922

Baillette, P., & Kimble, C. (2008, April). *The concept of appropriation as a heuristic for conceptualising the relationship between technology, people and organizations*. Paper presented at the UKAIS Conference, Bournemouth, UK.

Benbunan-Fich, R., & Hiltz, S. R. (2003). Mediators of the effectiveness of online courses. *IEEE Transactions on Professional Communication*, *46*(4), 298–312. doi:10.1109/TPC.2003.819639

Briggs, R. O., & De Vreede, G. J. (2003). Special Issue: Information Systems Success. *Journal of Management Information Systems, 19*(4), 5–8.

Brown, K. M. (1996). The role of internal and external factors in the discontinuation of off-campus students. *Distance Education, 17*(1), 44–71. doi:10.1080/0158791960170105

Carlson, J. R., & Zmud, R. W. (1999). Channel Expansion Theory and the Experiential Nature of media Richness Perceptions. *Academy of Management Journal, 42*(2), 153–170. doi:10.2307/257090

Chiu, C.-M., Chiu, C.-S., & Chang, H.-C. (2007). Examining the integrated influence of fairness and quality on learners' satisfaction and Web-based learning continuance intention. *Information Systems Journal, 17*(3), 271–286. doi:10.1111/j.1365-2575.2007.00238.x

Chiu, C.-M., & Wang, E. T. G. (2008). Understanding Web-based learning continuance intention: The role of subjective task value. *Information & Management, 45*(3), 194–201. doi:10.1016/j.im.2008.02.003

Chu, T.-H., & Robey, D. (2008). Explaining changes in learning and work practice following the adoption of online learning: a human agency perspective. *European Journal of Information Systems, 17*(1), 79–98. doi:10.1057/palgrave.ejis.3000731

Clark, R. E. (1994). Media will never influence learning. *Educational Technology Research and Development, 42*(2), 21–29. doi:10.1007/BF02299088

Collins, B. (1991). Anticipating the impact of multimedia in education: lessons from the literature. *Computers in Adult Education and Training., 2*(2), 136–145.

Daft, R. L., & Lengel, R. H. (1984). Information richness: a new approach to managerial behavior and organizational design. In Cummings, L. L., & Staw, B. M. (Eds.), *Research in organizational behavior*. Homewood, IL: JAI Press.

Daft, R. L., & Weick, K. E. (1984). Toward a Model of Organizations as Interpretation Systems. *Academy of Management Review, 9*(2), 284–295. doi:10.2307/258441

Davis, F. D. (1989). Perceived Usefulness, Perceived Ease Of Use, And User Acceptance. *Management Information Systems Quarterly, 13*(3), 319–339. doi:10.2307/249008

Davis, F. D., Bagozzi, R. P., & Warshaw, P. R. (1989). User Acceptance of Computer Technology: A Comparison of Two Theoretical Models. *Management Science, 35*(8), 982–1003. doi:10.1287/mnsc.35.8.982

Dennis, A. R., & Kinney, S. T. (1998). Testing Media Richness Theory in the New Media: The Effects of Cues, Feedback, and Task Equivocality. *Information Systems Research, 9*(3), 256–274. doi:10.1287/isre.9.3.256

DeSanctis, P., & Poole, M. (1994). Capturing the complexity in advanced technology use: Adaptive structuration theory. *Organization Science, 5*(2), 121–146. doi:10.1287/orsc.5.2.121

Fallery, B. (2004). Three visions of open learning and their propositions of norms: contents standardisation, tasks standardisation or interface standardisation? *Systèmes d'Information et Management, 9*(4), 2–24.

Gerbaix, S. (1997). Adoption logic of the videoconference. *Systèmes d'Information et Management, 2*(1), 29–50.

Goodfellow, R. (1996). Face to face language learning at a distance? A study of a videoconference try-out. *ReCALL, 7*(1), 20–35.

Goodhue, D. L., & Thompson, R. L. (1995). Task-Technology Fit and Individual Performance. *Management Information Systems Quarterly, 19*(2), 213–236. doi:10.2307/249689

Hara, N., & Kling, R. (2000). Students' distress with a web-based distance education course: an ethnographic study of participants' experiences. *Information Communication and Society, 3*(4), 557–579. doi:10.1080/13691180010002297

Hiltz, S. R. (1993). *The virtual classroom: Learning without limits via computer network.* Norwood, NJ: Ablex Publishing Corporation.

Jawadi, N., & El Akremi, A. (2006). E-learning acceptance determinants: a modified technology acceptance model. *CAIS, 18*(2), 24-54.

Leidner, D., & Jarvenpaa, S. (1993). The Information Age Confronts Education: Case Studies on Electronic Classrooms. *Information Systems Research, 4*(1), 24–54. doi:10.1287/isre.4.1.24

Majchrzak, A., Rice, R. E., & Malhotra, A. (2000). Technology adaptation: the case of a computer-supported virtual team. *Management Information Systems Quarterly, 24*(4), 569–600. doi:10.2307/3250948

Maki, R. H., Maki, W. S., Patterson, M., & Whittaker, P. D. (2000). Evaluation of a web-based introductory psychology course: I. Learning and Satisfaction in On-line Versus Lecture Courses. *Behavior Research Methods, Instruments, & Computers, 32*(2), 230–239.

Marquet, P., & Nissen, E. (2003). Distance in the languages learning through videoconferencing: dimensions, measures, consequences, *ALSIC-Apprentissage des langues et systèmes d'information et de communication, 6*(2), 3-19.

Mathieu, J. E., Martineau, J. W., & Tannenbaum, S. I. (1993). Individual and situational influences on the development of self-efficacy: implications for training effectiveness. *Personnel Psychology, 46*(1), 125–147.

McGrath, J. E., Arrow, H., Gruenfeld, D. H., Hollingshead, A. B., & O'Connor, K. M. (1993). Groups, Tasks and Technology: The Effects of Experience and Change. *Small Group Research, 24*, 406–420. doi:10.1177/1046496493243007

Mehlenbacher, B., Miller, C. R., Covington, D., & Larsen, J. S. (2002). Active and interactive learning online: a comparison of Web-based and conventional writing classes. *Professional Communication. IEEE Transactions on Professional Communication, 43*(2), 166–184. doi:10.1109/47.843644

Mondi, M., Woods, P., & Rafi, A. (2007). Students' 'Uses and Gratification Expectancy' Conceptual Framework in relation to E-learning Resources. *Asia Pacific Education Review, 8*(3), 435–449. doi:10.1007/BF03026472

O'Conaill, B., Whittaker, S., & Wilbur, S. (1993). Conversation over video conferences: an evaluation of the spoken aspects of video-mediated communication. *Human-Computer Interaction, 8*, 389–428. doi:10.1207/s15327051hci0804_4

Ologeanu, R. (2005). Videoconferencing experiments and uses in French higher education. *Distances et savoirs, 3*(1), 11-28.

Orlikowski, W. J. (1992). The duality of technology: rethinking the technology concept in organizations. *Organization Science, 3*(3), 398–427. doi:10.1287/orsc.3.3.398

Piccoli, G., Ahmad, R., & Blake, Y. (2001). Web-Based Virtual Learning Environments: A Research Framework and a Preliminary Assessment of Effectiveness in Basic IT Skills Training. *Management Information Systems Quarterly, 25*(4), 401–426. doi:10.2307/3250989

Russell, T. L. (1999). *The Non Significance Difference Phenomenon.* Raleigh, NC: North Carolina State University Press.

Rutter, D. R. (1984). *Looking and seeing. The role of visual communication in social interaction.* Chichester, UK: Wiley.

Seddon, P. B. (1997). A respecification and extension of the DeLone and McLean model of IS success. *Information Systems Research, 8*(3), 240–253. doi:10.1287/isre.8.3.240

Sellen, A. J. (1995). Remote conversations: the effects of mediating talk with technology. *Human-Computer Interaction, 10,* 401–444. doi:10.1207/s15327051hci1004_2

Valacich, J. S., Mennecke, B. E., Watcher, R. M., & Wheeler, B. C. (1994). Extensions to Media Richness Theory: A Test of the Task-Media Fit Hypothesis. In *Proceedings of the Hawaii International Conference on Systems Science*, Maoui, HI (pp. 11-20).

Venkatesh, V., Morris, M. G., Davis, G. B., & Davis, F. D. (2003). User acceptance of information technology: Toward a unified view. *Management Information Systems Quarterly, 27*(3), 425–478.

Walther, J. B. (1995). Relational Aspects of Computer-Mediated Communication: Experimental Observations Over Time. *Organization Science, 6*(2), 186–203. doi:10.1287/orsc.6.2.186

Webster, B., & Hackley, P. (1997). Teaching effectiveness in Technology-mediated Distance Learning. *Academy of Management Review, 40*(6), 1282–1309. doi:10.2307/257034

Yates, J., & Orlikowski, W. J. (1992). Genres of Organizational Communication: A Structurational Approach to Studying Communication and Media. *Academy of Management Review, 17,* 299–326. doi:10.2307/258774

Yoo, Y., & Alavi, M. (2001). Media and group cohesion: Relative influences on social presences, task participation, and group consensus. *Management Information Systems Quarterly, 25*(3), 371–390. doi:10.2307/3250922

This work was previously published in International Journal of Technology and Human Interaction, Volume 6, Issue 3, edited by Anabela Mesquita & Chia-Wen Tsai, pp. 37-52, copyright 2010 by IGI Publishing (an imprint of IGI Global).

Chapter 8

E-HRM's Impact on an Environmental Scanning Process:
How Can Technology Support the Selection of Information?

Manel Guechtouli
Université Paul Cézanne, France

ABSTRACT

This paper examines HR Management issues in Environmental Scanning (ES) process. Although literature claims that selecting information in this kind of processes is central, the authors are using the concept of "intelligent filters" (Simon, 1983) to understand how human attention can be managed for selecting strategic information in a complex environment. The author examines HR executives and the way they deal with issues related to ES and focuses on an empirical study in a big technological firm, where the use of an internal reporting and communication system (the weekly) was studied. This author finds that this particular system can be considered as an "intelligent filter", requiring both human and technological resources. Finally, suggestions that the system is used by HR executives in order to organize communication and coordination in an ES process but also to increase the participation and involvement of all employees in such a process are made.

INTRODUCTION

Constant development of Information Technologies (IT) and globalization are the main factors that give an international aspect to competition. Today's firms must deal with a complex perceived environment where unpredictability rhymes with uncertainty.

Environmental Scanning, as a practice of information management, falls under the general prospect to help managers acting and deciding in this complex context. In a more specific way, this practice tends to increase the reactivity and the competitiveness of companies, helping them

DOI: 10.4018/978-1-61350-465-9.ch008

to adapt more easily to a changing and dubious environment.

An Environmental scanning system involves the participation of various actors and a multitude of interactions inside and outside of the organization. HR managers are highly concerned here. They have a deep impact on how employees' competencies and talents are managed. Today's HR Managers must deal with a knowledge based economy (Foray, 2000) where immaterial capital is more and more central for management, some authors are talking about the "war of talents" that is going on (Michaels et al., 2001). Moreover HR Managers are the ones who have to handle the issues related to the motivational/organizational aspects of an ES System, answering questions such as: how employees do collaborate/cooperate in those systems? How to enhance their participation to an ES System and how can they be involved? Etc.

Many aspects must therefore be taken into account and ES Systems appear to be complex. Hence, modelling those systems seems to be problematic and its impact on performance has been widely discussed (Thiétart, 1990; Lesca, 1994; Amabile, 1997). The first part of our chapter will try to clear up the environmental scanning concept and to understand its impact on HR Managers.

In the second part, we will focus on a specific phase of the environmental scanning process: the selection of information by HR executives. Indeed, many authors (Marchionini, 1995; Lesca, 1996; Blanco, 2002; Lafaye, 2004) stress the fact that the selection of information phase often appears as complicated to managers. In fact, managers, with their naturally limited capacities of attention must deal with a mass of information that can be fragmentary, disparate and even contradictory (Reix, 2002). We'll try to understand how HR executives can « manage » those attention capacities using «intelligent filters» (Simon, 1983) in an environmental scanning context.

The third part of our work concerns a practical illustration of what can be seen as intelligent filters in an organization we studied. We'll examine a specific reporting tool (called the weekly), to understand how HR strategic information seekers – in a general way – can use this in an ES context.

Environmental Scanning (ES) and HR Management

More than twenty years ago, authors were claiming that scanning an enterprise environment is necessary (Martinet, 1984; Porter, 1985; Thiétart, 1984; Ansoff, 1989). Using different nominations such as environmental scanning, business intelligence or strategic intelligence/watch, today's literature highlights the importance of watching the firm's environment (Kalika, 1991; Lesca et al., 1997; Choo, 2001). At the same time, the relationship between performance and environmental scanning has been widely discussed and reconsidered (Marmuse, 1992; Amabile, 1999; Reix, 2002). Indeed, it seems difficult to determine in advance whether the information selected in an environmental scanning process will be useful or not. We believe that the exact impact of these activities on organizational? Performance is still to be discovered.

Many research studies on environmental scanning explore the effect of situational dimensions, organizational strategies, information needs, and personal traits on scanning behaviour (Choo, 2001). Thus, the environmental scanning often relates to strategic questions such as the axes of development for a firm (Gondran, 2001); it also concerns information about the business activities and strategies pursued by competitors. It can be seen as a dynamic process (Thiétart, 1990) which consists in

The acquisition and use of information about events, trends, and relationships in an organization's external environment, the knowledge of which would assist management in planning the organization's future course of action (Choo, 2001).

Figure 1. Environmental scanning phases

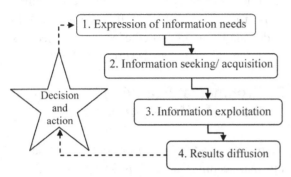

An environmental scanning system can be problematic according to the complexity of the process. In that perspective, authors like Salles and Alquier (1997) highlight the fact that literature often relates ES process to a particular cycle called "information cycle". That cycle can be defined over four specific phases (Levet & Paturel, 1996; Hassid et al., 1997): (i) the expression of needs phase where research and attention areas are identified, (ii) information seeking phase, which means exploring the research areas previously identified and selecting relevant information, (iii) exploitation phase where the information is questioned, analyzed and evaluated, and finally, (iv) diffusion phase, as the result of the whole process is spread.

This cycle starts all over again each time a specific demand comes out. Figure 1 was adapted from previous works (Martre, 1994; Levet, 1996; Hassid, 1997; Lafaye, 2004) it shows the different phases of the ES process and their articulation in an elementary way.

This representation shows the ES process as quite simple and linear. It doesn't illustrate all the interactions between phases and provides no detail on their realization. It only helps to understand the whole process in a basic perspective.

For many authors (Lesca, 1996; Liu, 1997; Samier & Sandoval, 1999; Revelli, 2000; Lafaye, 2004), what happens to be one of the most complex phases is the information research/seeking phase. Indeed, how do executives "scan" the environment? How do they select environmental scanning information? Why do they do it, is it a part of their jobs? Motivational aspects appear to be very important here. Many authors claim that ES activities widely depend on executives' will and motivation (Hannon, 1997; Lesca, 2003; Guechtouli, 2007). Indeed, ES process is generally informal (Stoffels, 1982; Gilad, 1989), it is hard to determine the way it works in an organization. Consequently, quantifying ES activities is not obvious as we cannot really know whether an executive is really searching for ES information or not. HR Managers have to deal with those issues in order to enhance executives' collaboration and participation to the ES system and to support their ES activities.

Moreover, HR executives have also to face a changing and unpredictable environment just like all other employees impacting strategy in a direct way, maybe even more. Indeed, Human Resource Environmental Scanning appears to be essential in a context where competencies and talents become very precious. Organizations are now realizing the importance of immaterial resources and competing for that.

Besides, as the access to information is easier today thanks to IT development, HR managers have to be able to browse huge amounts of information in order to select what is relevant according to their function and work concerns. How can they do that and what information to select?

As we have previously mentioned organizing the ES process seems to be complicated; but the selection process seems to be one of the most complicated phases of the ES process. We'll see this more in detail in the next paragraph.

2. SELECTION OF ENVIRONMENTAL SCANNING INFORMATION

Selection, acquisition, scanning, browsing, research of information… Many concepts leading to the same idea: finding potentially interesting information in the firm's environment. The selected information will be discussed and analysed by HR executives. This information is very important as it has a direct impact on the process result. It can be considered as an "input" which has an influence on the output's quality (Lafaye, 2004). HR executives will work on its meaning and strategic potential in order to *understand the forces of change so that they may develop effective responses which secure or improve their position in the future* (Choo, 2001). This selection/scanning depend on many parameters such as executives' competencies, experience, knowledge and will.

Besides, with the IT progress, information is no longer a rare resource, especially with the Internet technologies development. In fact, the access and diffusion of information happens to be widely facilitated with those technologies' help. Hence, information that must be treated by an HR manager is huge and, at the same time, a plethora of information can be interpreted like a shortage (Feldman & March, 1991). Simon (1986) suggested in the same perspective that organisms are continually surrounded by a very rich and complex stimulus field, from which a big amount of information could be extracted each second, and at the same time, executives have a limited capacity of attention and interpretation. To deal with that, managers could reconsider organizations in term of limited human attention management rather than information management (Simon, 1991).

In our chapter, we'll focus on this aspect of human attention management (Davenport & Beck, 2000) in order not to spoil it and to avoid being misled to sterile information (Simon, 1986). Our suggestion concerns the insertion of "intelligent filters" in the channels of information. We'll see forward what we do mean by this concept and the way we suggest to use it in an ES context in order to help HR executives and managers in an ES context.

2.1 What is an "Intelligent Filter"?

The concept of intelligent filters has been introduced by Simon (1986) in order to facilitate the selection of information in a general way. Our purpose is to use this concept for scanning the environment in an ES context. Indeed, as mentioned previously, selecting information is complicated as information is still seen as overabundant by executives (complaining about too much information, too many mails, etc.). Consequently; one of the main problems in organizations today is to preserve human attention from getting lost in commonplace information.

Human attention is a much rarer resource than information (Simon, 1986). In addition, the major problem while trying to improve decision or communication systems is the insertion of "intelligent filters", the idea is no longer to feed the information channels (Simon, 1984). Feeding those channels would mean raising the amount of information to be treated and so raising distraction risks. Moreover, the access to information is easier today with the progress of the IT, so the problem of executives is no longer the access of information but focusing their own attention on specific information. Insertion of technologic or human intelligent filters could help managers to select a small part of information from the very rich and complex amount of information in the organization's environment (Amabile, 1997).

Typically, while examining a traditional flow chart, it appears that the capacities of attention decrease as we go up in the hierarchical pyramid. In fact, the available cognitive capacities tend to decrease at the same time as the number of actors (the less actors there are, the less cognitive capacities there are).

Moreover, it seems that information is even more abundant at the HR strategic level, where the number of people is often restricted (Simon, 1991; Dou, 1996). Hence, the capacities of attention are much more reduced as the excess of information can disturb manager's capacities to analyze the

Figure 2. Attention, bottleneck of the organisational activities

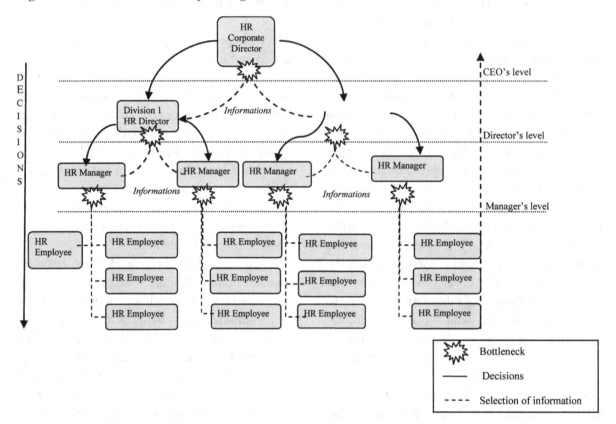

information (Feldman and March 1991). Let's take the example of a general manager in the top of the hierarchical pyramid (Figure 2)[1] in an HR context. The HR director will have to consider a huge part of information coming up from his subordinates. As his cognitive capacities are naturally limited, he will only be able to analyze a small part of this information. The attention of this manager as a decision maker represents the "bottleneck of the organizational activities" (Simon, 1994, p. 148).

An HR executive can be inhibited in his action of scanning while he has to deal with large amounts of information. He will have to manage his attention and "share" his capacities of attention between the different stimulus surrounding him, selecting apparently interesting information and rejecting others if too distant from his concerns at the moment (Amabile, 1997). McKay (1969, p. 61) suggests that "Of all the objects in the field of

vision, for example, only a few are normally perceived at any one time – those that have "caught the attention" as we say. Stimuli corresponding to the presence of the others are *perceived* but they evoke no "matching-response" in the organism - at least none structured to correspond to the individual objects. These objects are not perceived". Mechanisms of perception are not that simple to understand, but our hypothesis is that filtering information can be of benefit if this process of filtering/selection can reduce the amount of information that has to be analyzed and studied by executives.

In other words, intelligent filters can be used to assist HR directors/ executives while managing their capacities of attention. The aim here is to make a kind of pre-sorting in the mass of information that must be treated. Furthermore, it is possible to consider that this selection can be automatic, through technological filters, or human ones through managers themselves. The point here is not about choosing which process of selection/filtering is the best, but only to highlight what seems to be important in each selection information process.

2.2 Supporting the HR Function on the ES Scanning Process Using Technological Filters

With the IT advance, developing and using automatic informational filters is making its way in researchers community today (Lafaye, 2004), at the same time, selecting information using automatic tools is full of controversies.

Simon (1991) noticed that the first generation of Management Information System (MIS) installed in the big American companies was generally regarded as a failure, as instigators of these systems sought after providing more information to the decision makers, instead of protecting them from irrelevant information diverting their attention.

Moreover, Executive Information System (EIS), software developed in the 80s and used as a filter for information accumulated by enterprises has often been disappointing (Lesca et al., 2002).

Nowadays, those systems seem to be declining and becoming obsolete (Vidal et al., 2005), they have been replaced by "Internet sensors", "intelligent agents" and other automatic technologies which have an unquestionable potential. In fact, using those systems seems to be kind of problematic because selecting information depends on the characteristics of information itself; so while selecting information for an environmental scanning purpose, information is often rich, ill-assorted and sometimes contradictory. Moreover, a strategic information is a non repetitive one (Lesca, 1997), it's a « rare » information held by a small part of organizations (Barthélemy, 2004).

Moreover, technology can surely have a certain impact on improving employees' communication and engagement, Reddington and Hyde (2008,

p. 156) stress that "it is apparent that technology can facilitate employee engagement through the greater ease of communication and the increased availability of information." At the same time, those authors show that the technology has to be intuitive to use and attractive in terms of relevance and personalization in order to avoid problems concerning alienation of the user that may result while using technology.

Consequently, Selecting ES information by using a machine or software could help, but no matter how powerful it may be, relying exclusively on technology seems utopian here, because the human dimension with its expertise and judgment, its knowledge and its know-how seems irreplaceable for the selection as well as for the treatment of this type of information. Here, we are joining some recent studies conclusions (Lafaye, 2004).

2.3 Supporting the HR Function on the ES Scanning Process Using Human «Intelligent Filters»

As far as selecting environmental scanning information is concerned, a good comprehension of the market forces and competitiveness as well as customers, suppliers and the whole company's environment appears as essential (Lesca, 1994). Some researchers also suggest that information must be identified by executives who were trained to the attention and selection activities (Blanco, 1998). A real expertise is still necessary for sorting, classifying and organizing this information in a coherent way, then to exploit it so that it can make sense (Reix, 2002). If we do accept those proposals, the main problem for intelligent filters depends essentially on the management of competences and capacities of executives in an HR-environmental scanning context.

Starting from here, we can say that the major advantage of human intelligent filters is creating valuable information, by giving meaning to information through analysis and synthesis (Meissonier, 1999). For sure, a computer can accomplish arithmetic operations much faster than a human being, but when it's a question of comprehension and conceptualization or dealing with complex situations, the different criteria that have to be implemented can make conflicts and the machine cannot adapt its behaviour to the situation. A computer cannot deal with the context, the aims and its own capacities like a human being does (Amabile, 1997).

Besides, it seems that a great part of the know-how of an individual lies in his capacity to pay attention to the characteristics of a situation in order to be able to face it (Simon, 1986). In addition, Demailly (2004), taking as a starting point the work of H. A. Simon, specifies that individuals have a natural tendency to simplify reality and its alternatives by selecting the aspects to which he will pay attention to, giving a priority to familiar information (usual answers and "routines").

Here, individual plays the part of an intelligent filter as they select the information they do pay attention to. In fact, the human faculty of selecting information can be seen as an opportunity because it helps a decision maker to reduce decisional difficulties to a compatible scale with his own computational capacities (Simon, 1991, 1986, 1983).

Therefore, we can also say that human attention plays the role of a filter when it simply allows executives to select information and exclude others. This attention is determined by a great number of parameters: project, interests, experiments, moods, context, etc (Amabile, 1997). Technology alone cannot answer all these parameters. It is not thus a question of trying to make these filters completely automatic or to make them entirely "human", but rather to assist the human attention and limited capacities via technological tools. The point here is to show how both human and technological aspects are important for selecting ES information and that managing human attention can take advantage from both aspects.

Now, in order to illustrate the theory developed above, we'll take the study case of a reporting system, also used for selecting environmental scanning information at Gama[2] trying to make a link between the theory developed above and practice. In fact, the idea here is to understand how HR executives can use the "intelligent filters" concept in selecting ES information, therefore, the main question is: can HR executives use this "weekly system" in order to "scan" their enterprise environment?

Besides, we are also assuming, according to the literature review above that managing those intelligent filters can help HR Managers enhancing ES Scanning activities. Let's see if reality confirms this assumption and how those filters can look like in an organizational context.

3. THE WEEKLY SYSTEM AT GAMA[1]

Gama, considered as the world leader in its business market, has more than 5000 employees and a sales turnover of about two billion Euros. Gama works essentially for international banks, governments and telecom companies.

Our aim at Gama is to study their environmental scanning process and to understand it. In this paper, we'll focus on the research of information phase of the ES process. In other words, we are interested in the way individuals are selecting information for their ES activities. One specific internal tool will be analyzed: "the weekly system".

We used a qualitative method of collecting data during four months at Gama. First, we chose a department that uses the Weekly and that agreed to be a part of the study. Then we made staff interviews in that specific department. We questioned 5 managers, each interview lasted from 1 to 3 hours, and we cumulated a total time of about 20 hours of interviews. The interviews were manually analysed and coded. We also analysed some internal documentation (weekly samples, corporate brochures, intranet, flow charts, internal studies, etc.).

3.1 How to Select Information Using the Weekly

The Weekly is a reporting tool; it aims at making information go bottom-up through the hierarchical levels of the company. The Weekly shape is a numerical document, transmitted via the Intranet by each employee of the company to his senior in rank, once per week. It includes:

Realizations

They are a synthesis of the executive's activity during the week:

It can be the number of smart cards that I have sold for example - Manager 3.

Problems

All the difficulties encountered by the employee within his work:

Why we lost a contract (...) it can also be difficulties related to obtaining a partnership or to develop a particular product - Manager 1.

Perspectives

Future projects and all that executives are planning to do in the short term.

Scoops

These are information that seem interesting to employees; they can be environmental scanning information:

I'm talking about unusual information (...) information concerning competition for instance - Manager 1.

Weekly's structure can evolve; each employee can make additive information to his weekly with changing its structure. Moreover, the structure depends also on the business unit concerned; the weekly may have a different structure from a business unit to another.

3.2 How Does the Weekly Work?

To answer this question, let's study the case of a specific business unit that we'll call Unit Alpha. Unit Alpha has about 500 employees, a general manager, 9 directors, who supervise the work of a certain number of managers. Those managers are in charge of supervising an engineer's team (as shown in the figure represented in appendix 1)

Each employee must send a Weekly to his senior in rank that must be as synthetic and as clear as possible. According to the persons interviewed, a weekly must have different characteristics:

A Weekly must be concise and cannot exceed one page long. - Manager 1

It's about summarizing a 5 days activity, it cannot be extremely long. The purpose is not to give all the details of his activities but only the most important part of it - Manager 2.

Engineer sends his Weekly to his manager, and then the manager sends his Weekly to his own manager and so on. If there's a problem coming up, for example an operational problem which the employee can solve alone, the problem will not get any higher in the hierarchy - Manager 1.

Figure 3 represents a scheme of how the Weeky is supposed to work in the organization we studied. It's about comparing this scheme with the one of a typical hierarchical organization (seen previously). Our aim here is to understand if the weekly can possibly get over the bottleneck information effect we mentioned above. In other words, the question is about considering the conditions upon which this reporting system can overcome the hierarchical issues of information selection in an ES system.

Figure 3. Weekly system operating

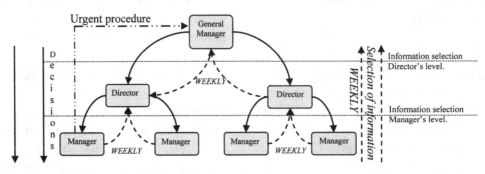

The Weekly goes bottom-up of the hierarchical pyramid. Each engineer sends his Weekly by mail to his manager; the manager will find himself with a certain number of Weekly reports at the end of the week (we can understand the necessity of being concise in that kind of reporting). Analyzing the weekly's information (realizations, problems, perspectives and scoops), the manager will try to draw part from this information and to resolve the problems, then makes his own weekly and sends it to his superior. If some problems remain unsolved, he must report them too. Selection is made via the weekly in each hierarchical level. In case of emergency, information can use other communication channels such as phone calls or face to face meetings.

This system is interesting because it is a part of the executive's job and it is widely used. It is considered as a way of reporting information but also as a way of communication through the organization's hierarchical levels. This system will now be analyzed to highlight the main conditions that can make it an ES tool used by HR executives. In a more specific way, we'll see how this system can be seen as an "intelligent filter" while HR executives are selecting ES information and if this system can be useful in an HRM or E-HRM context.

3.3 Weekly Advantages for E-HRM in an ES Context

In a weekly system, each HR employee could play the role of an « intelligent filter », as he will select information that seem interesting and communicate it to his direct superior. Technology is helping a lot here, as the weekly has an electronic form and can be quickly sent by email, using the intranet, to HR managers but also to any other person in the whole firm that could be interested by the information.

The weekly system seems to gather many advantages but the most important one seems to be its good support for attention management. Indeed, it can help HR executives to preserve their limited capacities of attention in order to focus on important things. Being so short and brief, each person is supposed to select only what is relevant and forget about what is not. Technologies bring a lot of information and not all the information gathered happens to be relevant.

Moreover, HR executives use their own experience, competencies and knowledge to scan the environment and to select information. This means that the selected information can be different from a person to another and this makes the selection process richer. The information selected is analyzed, and reported directly to superiors. Consequently, the information is internal in a weekly, which makes it reliable and "sure" according to the executives interviewed. It is also structured and regular; this makes ES activities a part of the executives' organizational routines. Moreover, as the Weekly system is supposed to be an obligation, it can impact HR executive's motivation for environmental scanning activities.

3.4 Weekly Limits for E-HRM in an ES Context

The major danger of the Weekly system is to fall into the trap of strategic conformism thought. Indeed, hierarchical filters can be considered as obstacles for the richness and the originality of the stimuli perceived by the various actors of the organization (Meissonier, 1999). In our study case, actors are not completely "free" in their action of selection; they are under the pressing pre-established frameworks of the organization. Their selection is kind of "oriented" and HR Executives could feel the same here.

In addition, the "slowness" of the system can be seen as a limit in an ES context. As the environment is in perpetual change and moving fast, information is likely to quickly become obsolete if sent only once a week. In fact, this is only a theoretical limit because in reality, if actors "detect" interesting information, they can get over the system and communicate directly with the concerned persons, through email or telephone according to the urgency of the situation (Figure 3, urgency procedure).

CONCLUSION

In this chapter we tried to understand how HR executives can use technological advances for selecting environmental scanning information and how these technologies can help them enhance ES activities. The major issue in this selection comes from globalization aspects of information, mixed with limited interpretative human capacities as attention is undoubtedly the rarest existing human resource (Simon, 1986).

Accordingly, the theory of Simon about attention management proposes to create "intelligent filters" to help the managers focus their attention in order not to waste it. The principal aim of these filters is to reduce the information treated and questioned by executives, as an abundance of information "consumes" attention (Amabile, 1997). The filters can be automatic (based on technological aspects), human (based on human attention and interpretation resources), or both human and automatic.

The point here is to consider that the weekly can possibly be seen as a way for selecting environmental scanning information. Indeed, the chapter explains how the weekly can be seen as an "intelligent filter" gathering both technological and human aspects for selecting environmental scanning information. Hence, this system can reduce the informational charge of each executive so that he can save his attention capacities. In addition, it can play a part in encouraging actors to collaborate by drawing benefit of technology (Intranet) that facilitates and accelerates the exchanges. However, the Weekly system is somewhat "imposed" by the top management. This leads to a kind of "forced" collaboration and as information is intended exclusively to each manager's employee, the selection can be oriented depending on the manager's preferences.

The weekly system described here can be useful for HRM and E-HRM developments. Indeed, this system, based on an intranet technology as well as on human capacities can help HR Managers and executives in their ES selection process. It can be a way to organize ES activities and support HR executives' collaboration and cooperation in such a process. Moreover, as we previously noticed, the weekly system can improve the HR employees' motivation and cooperation as the system appears to scrap issues related to change resistance. Finally, the Weekly system can be more than a simple reporting tool as it can be considered as a way for HR executives to gather ES information and analyze it.

Moreover, with both technological and human aspects, the weekly system can be a good illustration of what Simon called "intelligent filters". This could be a materialization of his idea about re-thinking our organizations in terms of attention management rather than in terms of information management.

As a final point, we have to stress here the lack of studies combining HR and ES. Our research has only tried to explore how a theoretical concept ("Simon's intelligent filters") could turn into reality (the ES context in an Organization). But there is a lot more to do here. This leads us to many other research questions concerning the HR-ES link such as motivational, organizational and technological aspects of an ES Process. This has to be explored in our future work.

REFERENCES

Alquier, A-M., & Salles, M. (1997). Réflexions méthodologiques pour la conception de systèmes d'intelligence économique de l'entreprise en tant que système d'aide à la décision stratégique. *Deuxième congrès International Franco-québécois de Génie Industriel, ALBI 1997.*

Amabile, S. (1997). *Contribution à l'ingénierie de l'organisation: De la veille stratégique à l'attention organisationnelle.* Thèse de Doctorat en Sciences de Gestion, Université d'Aix-Marseille III, Faculté d'Economie Appliquée, GRASCE, Aix-en-Provence.

Amabile, S. (1999). De la veille stratégique à une attention réticulée. Le réseau d'attention inter organisationnel des mutuelles d'assurance automobile. *Systèmes d'information et management, 4*(2).

Ansoff, H. I. (1975). Managing strategic surprise by response to weak signals. *California Management Review, 18,* 21–33.

Ansoff, H. I. (1984). *Implanting strategic Management.* Upper Saddle River, NJ: Prentice Hall.

Barthélemy, J. (2004). *Stratégies d'externalisation: Préparer, décider et mettre en œuvre l'externalisation d'activités stratégiques.* Paris: Dunod.

Baumard, P. (1997). L'information stratégique dans la grande organisation. *Systèmes d'Information et Management, 2*(2).

Belmondo, C. (2002). *La création de connaissance dans les groupes de travail. Le cas d'une cellule de veille concurrentielle.* thèse de doctorat en sciences de gestion, Université Paris IX Dauphine.

Blanco, S. (2002). Sélection de l'information à caractère anticipatif: un processus d'intelligence collective. *Actes de la 11ième Conférence de l'AIMS,* Paris (pp. 1-20).

Blanco, S., & Lesca, H. (2002). Contribution à la capacité d'anticipation des entreprises par la sensibilisation aux signaux faibles. *6ème Congrès International Francophone sur la PME,* Montréal, Canada (pp. 11-19).

Choo, C. W. (2001). Environmental scanning as information seeking and organizational learning. *Information Research, 7*(1). Retrieved from

Demailly, A. (2004). *Herber Simon et les Sciences de conception", l'harmattan.*

Dou, H.-M. (1996). French small business information, through the internet: a comparison with US organisations. *International Journal of Information Management, 16*(4), 289–298. doi:10.1016/0268-4012(96)00014-X

Feldman, M. S., & March, J. G. (1991). l'information dans les organisations: un signe et un symbole. In J. G. March (Ed.), *Décisions et organisations* (Chapter 10, p. 255). Paris les éditions d'organisation.

Foray, D. (2000). *L'économie de la connaissance.* Paris: La Découverte Repères.

Gilad, B. (1989). The Role of Organized Competitive Intelligence in Corporate

Gilad, B., & Gilad, T. (1986). Business intelligence: the quiet revolution. *Sloan Management Review*, 53–61.

Gondran, N. (2001). *Système de diffusion d'information pour encourager les PME-PMI à améliorer leurs performances environnementales.* Thèse de doctorat, INSA Lyon.

Guechtouli, M. (2007). *Contribution à l'ingénierie des systèmes d'information de veille stratégique: une approche centrée sur la motivation des acteurs. L'expérience du système de veille stratégique d'une grande entreprise technologique.* PhD. Thesis in Management, CERGAM, University Paul Cezanne, Aix en Provence, France.

Hannon, J. M. (1997). *Leveraging HRM to enrich competitive intelligence.* Human.

Hassid, L., Jacques-Gustave, P., & Moinet, N. (1997). *Les PME face au défi de l'intelligence économique: le renseignement sans complexe.* Paris: Dunod.

http://InformationR.net/ir/7-1/paper112.html

Kalika, M. (1991). De l'organisation réactive à l'organisation anticipative. *Revue française de gestion*, 46-50.

Lafaye, C. (2004). *La phase de traque d'information sur Internet dans un processus de veille stratégique.* Thèse de Doctorat, Université Lyon III.

Le Bon, J. (2000). *De l'intelligence économique à la veille marketing et commerciale: vers une nécessaire mise au point conceptuelle et théorique.* Papier de Recherche, Essec, Mai.

Le Moigne, J. L. (1979). Informer la décision ou décider l'information. *Economies et sociétés, 1,* 889–918.

Lesca, H. (1996). Veille stratégique: comment sélectionner les informations pertinentes? *Concepts, méthodologie, expérimentation et résultats. Actes du colloque 5ème Conférence Internationale de Management Stratégique AIMS*, Lille.

Lesca, H. (2001). Veille stratégique: passage de la notion de signal faible à la notion de signe d'alerte précoce. *Actes du Colloque VSST'2001*, Tome 1, Toulouse (pp. 271-277).

Lesca, H. (2003). *Veille stratégique: La méthode L.E.SCAnning.* EMS.

Lesca, H., Blanco, S., & Caron-Fasan, M. L. (1997). Implantation d'une veille stratégique pour le management stratégique: proposition d'un modèle conceptuel et premières validations. *Actes de la 6ième conférence de l'AIMS*, Montréal (Vol. 2, pp. 173-183).

Lesca, H., & Rouibah, K. (1997). Des outils au service de la veille stratégique. *Systèmes d'Information et Management, 2*(2), 101–131.

Levet, J. L., & Paturel, R. (1996). L'intégration de la démarche d'intelligence économique dans le management stratégique. *Actes de la 5ième conférence de l'AIMS*, Lille, Mai.

Liu, S. (1997, July 21-22). Scanning the business environment with intelligent software agents. In *Proceedings of the 4th Conference of the International Society for Decision Support Systems (ISDSS'97)*, University of Lausanne, Switzerland.

Mackay, D.-M. (1969). *Information, mechanism and meaning.* Cambridge, MA: MIT.

Maier, J. L., Rainer, R. K. Jr, & Snyder, C. A. (1997). Environmental Scanning for Information Technology: An Empirical Investigation. *Journal of Management Information Systems, 14*(2), 177–200.

Marchionini, G. (1995). *Information seeking in electronic environments*. New York: Cambridge University Press. doi:10.1017/CBO9780511626388

Marmuse, C. (1992). *Politique générale. Langages, Intelligence, Modèles et Choix stratégiques*. Economica.

Martinet, B., & Marti, Y. M. (1995). *L'intelligence économique: les yeux et les oreilles de l'entreprise*. Paris: Les éditions de l'organisation.

Martinet, B., & Ribault, J. M. (1989). *La veille technologique, concurrentielle et commerciale: sources, méthodologie, organisation*. Paris: Les éditions d'organisation.

Meissonier, R. (1999). *NTIC et processus de décision dans les réseaux de PME-PMI*. Etudes et documents, série recherche, IAE, CEROG. Université de droit, d'économie et de sciences d'Aix-Marseille.

Michaels, E., Handfield-Jones, H., & Axelrod, B. (2001). *The War for Talent*. Boston: Harvard Business Press.

Porter, M., & Millar, V. E. (1985). How information gives you competitive advantage. *Harvard Business Review, 3*(4), 149–174.

Reix, R. (1991). Systèmes d'information: l'intelligence en temps réel reste encore à venir. *Revue française de gestion*, 8-16.

Reix, R. (2002). *Système d'information et management des organisations*. Paris: 4ème édition.

resource Management, 36(4), 409-422.

Revelli, C. (2000). *Intelligence stratégique sur Internet: comment développer efficacement des activités de veille et de recherche sur les réseaux*. Paris: Dunod.

Samier, H., & Sandoval, V. (1999). *La recherche intelligente sur l'Internet et l'intranet*. Paris: Hermès Science Publications.

Simon, H. (1983). *Administration et processus de décision*. Paris: Economica.

Simon, H. (1986). Il devient tout aussi passionnant de rechercher l'organisation des processus de pensée que de découvrir l'organisation du mouvement des planètes. *Commentaires et réponses présentées par H.A. Simon au Colloque de la Grande Motte, Sciences de l'intelligence, sciences de l'artificiel, publié dans les actes édités par les PUL*. ISBN 7297 0287 3.

Simon, H. (1991). *Sciences des systèmes, sciences de l'artificiel* (pp. 148-169).

Stoffels, J. D. (1982). Environmental scanning for future success. *Managerial Planning, 31*(3), 4–12.

Strategy. *Columbia Journal Of World Business*.

Tarondeau, J.-C., Jolibert, A., & Choffray, J.-M. (1994). *Le management à l'aube du XXIe siècle*. Revue Française de Gestion.

Vidal, P., & Planeix, P. (2005). *Systèmes d'information organisationnels*. Upper Saddle River, NJ: Pearson Education.

ENDNOTES

[1] This configuration is simplified. In reality, an HR director is in charge of supervising more than two people.

[2] Gama is a fake name. We use it for confidentiality reasons to protect the firm's interests.

APPENDIX 1: FLOW CHART OF ALPHA (USING THE WEEKLY SYSTEM)

Figure 4.

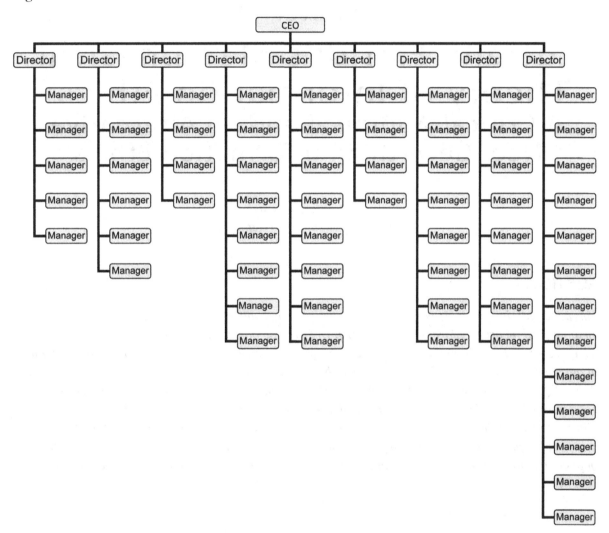

Chapter 9

Luciano Floridi's Metaphysical Theory of Information Ethics:
A Critical Appraisal and an Alternative Neo–Gewirthian Information Ethics

Edward Spence
University of Twente, The Netherlands

ABSTRACT

This paper falls into five main parts. Part one, offers a critical analysis and evaluation of Luciano Floridi's metaphysical theory of information ethics (IE). Drawing on part one, part two provides a discussion of what I consider to be the main conceptual and practical difficulties facing Floridi's IE theory. Although in agreement with the overall motivation and objective that informs Floridi's IE position, namely, that "all entities, qua informational objects, have an intrinsic moral value…" and that "there seems to be no good reason not to adopt a higher and more inclusive, ontocentric [moral] perspective" (Floridi, 2007, 10), part three of the paper proposes an alternative New-Gewirthian approach to Information Ethics that avoids some if not all of the difficulties facing Floridi's own position. Part four then examines the implications for Floridi's metaphysical theory of information ethics and finally, offers a conclusion in part five.

FLORIDI'S INFORMATION ETHICS

Information Ethics is an ontocentric, patient-orientated, ecological macroethics. (Floridi, 2007a, p.11)

Being beyond the scope of this paper and unavoidably constrained by space, I can but offer the briefest of expositions of Floridi's rich and complex theory, but hopefully I can at least provide in a summarised form the direction and main rationale of that theory and importantly not misconstrue it in the process. In addition, I shall offer some well intentioned and hopefully helpful critical observations and then proceed to offer an alternative approach to IE based on Alan Gewirth's rationalist ethical theory; specifically his argument for the foundational moral principle of morality, the Principle of Generic Consistency (PGC), extended and adapted for that purpose.

DOI: 10.4018/978-1-61350-465-9.ch009

Beginning with the uncontroversial empirical observation that our society is evolving, both quantitatively and qualitatively, into an information society, Floridi introduces the concept of *infosphere*, the informational equivalent of "biosphere". According to Floridi (2007) *infosphere:*

Denotes the whole informational environment constituted by all informational entities......It is an (intended) shift from a semantic (the infosphere understood as a space of contents) to an ontic conception (the infosphere understood as an environment populated by informational entities) (p.4).

Floridi (2007) goes on to claim that this informational shift from the semantic to the ontic, is resulting in the *re-ontologization* of the world, that "transforms its intrinsic nature" (p. 4) so that the world can now be ontologically re-conceived according to Floridi as being fundamentally constituted by the infosphere and not merely the biosphere, as was previously thought. As an example he cites nanotechnologies and biotechnologies that "are not merely changing (re-engineering) the world in a very significant way (as did the invention of gunpowder, for example, but actually reshaping (re-ontologizing) it" (p. 4).

As a result of this ontologization, information is becoming our ecosystem and we, together and in interaction with artificial agents, are evolving into informationally integrated *inforgs* or *connected informational organisms* (Floridi, 2007, pp. 5-6). Floridi (2007) predicts that "in such an environment, the moral status and accountability of artificial agents will become an ever more challenging issue" (p. 5).

From this initial ontological thesis, namely, the ontologization of the infosphere or the metaphysics of information it is easy to anticipate Floridi's next theoretical move. On the basis of his metaphysics of information Floridi (2007) posits a "new environmental ethics" when information ethics ceases to be merely "*microethics* (a practical, field-dependent, applied, and professional eth-

ics)" and becomes instead "a *patient-orientated, ontocentric* {as opposed to merely biocentric}, *ecological* macroethics". (pp. 7-8). Importantly he goes on to say that "information ethics is an ecological ethics that replaces biocentrism with ontocentrism, a substitution in the concept of biocentrism of the term "life" with that of "existence" (p. 8). According to Floridi (2007a), the substitution of "existence" for "life",

[..]suggests that there is something even more elemental than life, namely being – that is, the existence and flourishing of all entities and their global environment - and something more fundamental than suffering, namely, entropy. The latter is most emphatically not the physicists' concept of thermodynamic entropy. Entropy here refers to any kind of destruction or corruption of entities understood as informational objects (not as semantic information, take note), that is, any form of impoverishment of being, including nothingness, to phrase it more metaphysically (p. 12).

This substitution of existence for life, as we shall see below, is both crucial and problematic in Floridi's overall thesis of Information Ethics.

The claim that information ethics can be conceived and ought to be conceived as an environmental macroethics is Floridi's most interesting, ambitious and challenging claim in his theory and constitutes the crux of his whole controversial argument that rightly or wrongly is conducive to raising many incredulous stares[1]. For the claim amounts to nothing less than the clear implication, as expressed openly by Floridi himself, that existence not life is the mark of morality; that which determines the moral status of not only humans and other sentient beings, including their natural environment – the whole biosphere, but moreover, at the most ultimate level of inclusiveness ever conceived in moral philosophy before, the moral status of the whole caboodle, everything that exists, has existed and ever will exist in the Universe as informational objects. Which essentially insofar as anything can be conceived as an informational object, means practically *everything*, including artefacts, works of art, gardening tools, coffee mugs, tea-cups, carpets, pebbles, rocks, clarinets, and if I am not mistaken, kitchen utensils such as knives, for example. This is an *ethics of being* on a grand scale that considers the *destruction, corruption, pollution and depletion* of informational objects as a form of *entropy* whose increase constitutes an instance of evil that should, all things being equal, be ethically avoided (Floridi 2007, p.9).

In IE, the Ethical discourse concerns any entity, understood informationally, that is, not only all persons, their cultivation, well being, and social interactions, not only animals, plants, and their proper natural life, but also anything that exists, from paintings and books to stars and stones; anything that may or will exist, like future generations; and anything that was but is no more, like our ancestors or old civilizations. Information Ethics is impartial and universal because it brings to ultimate completion the process of enlargement of the concept of what may count as a centre of a (no matter how minimal) moral claim, which now includes every instance of being understood informationally, no matter whether physically implemented or not. In this respect, IE holds that every entity, as an expression of being, has a dignity, constituted by its mode of existence and essence... (Floridi 2007, p. 9)

The above evocative passage encapsulates the essential characteristics of Floridi's Information Ethics and illustrates its extensive scope. It is, as Floridi states, a universal ethics that applies equally to all informational objects in the Universe. I will go as far as saying that it seems to offer a kind of Stoic Pantheistic Ethics (my phrase) that endows everything in the Universe with a moral significance and status through a pre-determined divine rational order in which everything is ontologically inter-connected and of which everything forms an ontic part, no matter how big or small. Although

Floridi's view is not beholden to any particular religious or deterministic theory of the Universe (Floridi, in press, p.16) he freely acknowledges that "in the history of philosophy, a similar view can be found advocated by Stoic and Neoplatonic philosophers, and by Spinoza (Floridi 2007a, footnote 10, p.17). Concerning the latter, Soraj Hongladarom draws an insightful and interesting connection between Floridi's and Spinoza's ethics (Hongladarom, 2008, pp. 178-79).

SOME SCEPTICAL OBSERVATIONS

It seems that according to Floridi (2007), the basis of having a moral status is the *informational state* possessed by an entity (p. 10). Insofar as all entities whether sentient or non-sentient can be conceived as having this informational state, then they are entitled to a moral status:

The result is that all entities, qua informational objects, have an intrinsic moral value, although possibly quite minimal and overridable, and hence they can count as moral patients, subject to some equally minimal degree of moral respect understood as a disinterested, appreciative, and careful attention... There seems to be no good reason not to adopt a higher and more inclusive, ontocentric perspective (Floridi, 2007, p. 10)

I agree with Floridi that there would be no good reason not to adopt such a higher and more inclusive moral perspective if there were in fact good objective and independently grounded reasons for adopting such a perspective. This would in fact be a welcome extension to the moral fabric of the world. But merely declaring such a moral status for all informational objects on the basis of their informational state alone does not constitute such justified reasons. That is to say, the informational status of the informational objects cannot of itself provide them with a moral status any more than the human status of people can of itself provide them with a moral status. So what are Floridi's reasons for attributing a moral status to all informational entities, both sentient and non-sentient?

From his various writings and several responses to his critics (see list of references) Floridi appears to have at least two distinct but inter-related arguments in support of his IE: The first I shall refer to as the *Argument from the Goodness of Being* (Floridi, 2007a, p. 7; in press, pp. 3-14 and p.17) and the second the *Argument from Ontic Trust* (Floridi, 2007a, pp. 17-18; 2008a, p.192; and in press, pp. 17-19).

The Argument from the Goodness of Being

Drawing inspiration from the work of Plato, Aristotle, Plotinus, Augustine, Aquinas and Spinoza, as well as such eastern traditions as Buddhism and Hinduism, Floridi's focal idea is that "Goodness and Being (capitals meant) might be two sides of the same concept, as Evil and Non-being might be" (Floridi, in press, p. 12). His Argument from the Goodness of Being is thus essentially based on the initial pre-supposition, the basis of which he attributes to Plato, that "Goodness and Being are intimately connected" (Floridi, in press, p13). According to Floridi (in press),

By and large, IE proposes the same line of reasoning [as Plato], by updating it in terms of an informational ontology, whereby Being is understood informationally and Non-being in terms of entropy. *Note that this is not a defence of IE but an explanation* [emphasis added]. Although being in the company of Plato or Spinoza, for example, might be reassuring, it is not an insurance against being mistaken. But it is a rectification of the incorrect remark that IE stands rather alone in its defence of what might be called *axiological ecumenism.* (p. 13)

In a nutshell, Floridi's *Argument from the Goodness of Being* can roughly be outlined as follows: Given the pre-supposition that Goodness and Being are intimately connected and the

Universe in its entirety qua Being is intrinsically and fundamentally good, then everything within it is also good and has intrinsic value deserving of moral consideration. Thus all entities within the Universe conceived as informational objects at the appropriate level of abstraction (LoA) have intrinsic value and are therefore deserving of moral consideration. In the case of non-sentient entities, that moral consideration is minimal and overridable. Floridi's argument as I have roughly constructed it here but which is, I believe, faithful to his actual position as described in his various writings, supports his thesis of *Axiological Ecumenism* (Floridi, in press, p. 13); that is, the idea that everything in the universe has intrinsic value and therefore deserving of moral consideration.

According to Floridi (in press),

The actual argument [the argument for axiological ecumenism] seeks to establish that entities deserve respect because they have intrinsic value.. it requires a mental frame rather different from the one any anthropocentric ethics has trained us to adopt. It consists in shifting the burden of proof (a sort of Gestaltic shift) by asking, from a patient-oriented perspective, not "why should I care, in principle?" but "what should be taken care of, in principle?", that is, whether there is anything that is intrinsically worthless ethically, and hence rightly disrespectable in this particular sense...IE's position ...is that, because we lack arguments against the intrinsic value of Being in all its manifestations [emphasis added], we are led to expand an environmental approach to all nonsentient beings. The injunction is to treat something as intrinsically valuable and hence worthy of moral respect by default, until "proven guilty" (pp. 13-14)

The above passage from Floridi is crucial in that it offers important clarification to an understanding of his methodology of argumentation. As he claims elsewhere (in press) his argument of axiological ecumenism or what I have been referring to in this paper as the Argument from the Goodness of Being is "negative or indirect". (p.17) As Floridi puts it (in press),

It consists in reminding historically and showing logically that we have nothing to fear from a holistic attitude towards the value of Being in all its aspects; that it is fine to start from the presupposition than no entity deserves moral disrespect in itself [emphasis added]; that anything less than a holistic attitude towards the value of Being would be prima facie unjustified (p. 17).

What are we to make of Floridi's Argument from The Goodness of Being? I think in its favour we can say this much: as a negative argument that claims a "default position until proven guilty" (Floridi, in press, p. 17) his argument in support of a model of IE seems initially plausible and reasonable. For (a) given the need for expanding the moral realm to include non-sentient entities so as to be better able to understand and explain certain moral phenomena involving the relationship between human-beings and non-sentient entities such as artificial agents (for example, robots, softbots, cyborgs, virtual communities, among many others); (b) given the initial pre-supposition (supported in the past by many eminent philosophers like Plato and Spinoza) that Goodness and Being are closely connected and therefore everything existing within the Universe has intrinsic value deserving of some moral consideration; (c) given that other contemporary ethical theories cannot at present address nor explain the moral significance of issues pertaining to the relationship between us and non-sentient entities such as software agents, as those entities are not and cannot be included within the narrow anthropocentric moral perspectives of those theories and finally (d) given the absence of any other good reasons for not adopting a higher ethical perspective at an appropriate level of Abstraction (LoA) that expands the moral realm to include non-sentient entities that by default deserve some minimal but overridable moral

status; then (e) Floridi's axiological ecumenism with regard to Information Ethics seems, at least initially, a plausible and reasonable theoretical model to adopt.

I say initially, because I can see two main difficulties for adopting Floridi's model of IE as it stands at present. The first one (see (b) above) concerns the pre-supposition that Being and Existence are closely inter-connected and that the Universe and everything within it is essentially and fundamentally good; the second (see (c) above) concerns Floridi's claim and to some extent justified complain that there is not at present a viable alternative theory for supporting the main thesis of IE, namely, that all entities including non-sentient entities deserve moral consideration, a thesis, which I support.

The first difficulty concerns the lack of any objective evidence or conclusive arguments in favour of the *pre-supposition* that Being and Goodness are intimately connected and hence everything that exists, be it sentient or nonsentient, has an intrinsic value deserving of some degree of moral respect. The pre-supposition of the Goodness of Being can be seen either at best as an article of rational (but not blind) faith or hope or alternatively a useful methodological hypothesis or conjecture for generating and supporting Floridi's axiological ecumenism. Floridi's writings seem to suggest the latter. In the absence of any arguments or theories against the Goodness of Being, that conjecture would be a reasonable starting point for reaching the conclusions of axiological ecumenism. For as Floridi says (in press) "one line of reasoning in favour of IE's position …is that, *because we lack arguments against the intrinsic value of Being in all its manifestations* [emphasis added], we are led to expand an environmental approach to all nonsentient beings". (p. 14)

The problem for Floridi, however, is that we don't lack arguments *against the intrinsic value of Being in all its manifestations*. Arthur Schopenhauer, for example, in his major work, *The World as Will and Representation*, provided a series of challenging arguments based on empirical observation designed to show that Being is not only not Good but positively Evil. Schopenhauer is led to conclude on the basis of those arguments that the "world is not worth a candle" and it would have been far better if it had never existed; for then there would be no Evil in the world.

Interestingly, by arguing that it would have been better had the world not existed, Schopenhauer is turning Floridi's notion of entropy on its head. For contrary to Floridi, he sees Being and existence not as essentially Good but as essentially Evil. Of course Schopenhauer's arguments for the essential Evil of the World are not conclusive and perhaps not even convincing. But neither are the arguments for the essential Goodness of Being. Voltaire is another philosopher who lampooned Leibniz's optimistic claim that this is the best of all possible worlds in his satirical novella *Candide*; he does so by describing a series of terrible things that befall the protagonist of his story as he travels around the world. The Manicheans of course also saw the Universe as being essentially ruled by Good and Evil in equal parts.

This I think suffices to show that contrary to Floridi's claim we do not *lack arguments against the intrinsic value of Being in all its manifestations*. Ultimately those arguments might not be conclusive or convincing but one could say the same about arguments for the intrinsic value of Being. At best, arguments for and against the intrinsic value of Being lead to a theoretical impasse and hence the pre-supposition of the intrinsic value of Being cannot be relied upon to generate the central thesis of Floridi's IE; namely, that given the intrinsic Goodness of Being all entities in the Universe deserve some degree of moral consideration. Such an uncertain and unreliable reliance on the pre-supposition of the Goodness of Being as a basis for IE would render IE unstable. And for that reason, Floridi's reliance on that pre-supposition renders his IE theoretically unreliable and unstable notwithstanding the desirability and worthiness of the conclusion he wishes to reach; namely, that

all entities, both sentient and nonsentient, deserve some minimal moral consideration.

In the absence of any other ethical theory fit for the job, however, we might be prepared to wear that metaphysical cost (in terms of the theoretical unreliability and instability in Floridi's IE) for the sake of being able to explain certain moral phenomena pertaining to the relationship between us and non-sentient entities such as artificial agents. But fortunately there is an alternative, which fulfills the ethical desiderata of Floridi's IE and reaches the same desired conclusion but without the theoretical instability caused by reliance on the uncertain and unproven pre-supposition of the intrinsic goodness and value of Being. This alternative is provided by what I refer to in this paper as a Neo-Gewirthian Information Ethics based on an extension and adaptation of Alan Gewirth's Principle of Generic Consistency.

Alan Gewirth's Principle of Generic Consistency (PGC)[2] that was briefly cited above can be used and applied to argue that the natural property of purposive agency that acts as the sufficient condition for having rights to freedom and wellbeing can be extended to purposive agents and patients other than human beings, for example, to animals and androids. Insofar as animals and other sentient beings can be said to posses some degree of purposive and goal orientated behaviour that requires them to posses some minimal degree of freedom and wellbeing, they too are entitled to rights to freedom and wellbeing *as patients* if not as agents. For insofar as one recognizes that animals and other sentient beings possess purposive agency, minimal as that may be, and that this alone is a sufficient condition for granting them a moral status, one must at least rationally acknowledge that they too have rights to freedom and wellbeing, at least as patients, on pain of self-contradiction. Some similar argument is also required for extending the moral status to non-sentient informational objects and inforgs. I will present and demonstrate such an argument in section (3) below. Before doing so, however, I will briefly examine Floridi's second argument for his IE thesis, that of the Argument of Ontic Trust.

The Argument from Ontic Trust

Being constrained by space I can only offer an outline of that argument. Briefly, the argument is an expansion and re-construction of a Hobbesian social contract argument, the central idea of which is that our moral obligations towards each other are based on a pre-existing hypothetical social contract, one which we should uphold because it is in the interest of all of us to do so. The Argument from Ontic Trust extends that hypothetical contract to include everything that exists in the Universe, sentient entities as agents and non-sentient beings as patients. Unlike the Hobbesian social contract, which is essentially anthropocentric, the contract proposed by the Argument from Ontic Trust is not as it encompasses all entities that exist on the basis of their intrinsic value. According to Floridi,

In the case of the ontic trust, [the theory of the social contract] is transformed into a primeval, entirely hypothetical pact...The sort of pact in question can be understood more precisely in terms of an actual trust...By coming into being, an agent is made possible thanks to the existence of other entities. It is therefore bound to all that already is (the infosphere) both unwillingly and inescapably. It should be so also caringly....the ontic trust is what is postulated by the approach supported by IE... The acceptance of the ontic trust requires a disinterested judgement of the moral situation from an objective perspective (or Level of Abstraction), i.e. a perspective which is as non-anthropocentric as possible (In press, pp. 18-19; 2007a, pp. 17-18)

The position advocated by the *Argument from Ontic Trust* is a reasonable one to adopt *once you have accepted*, on the basis of the *Argument from the Goodness of Being*, that all entities have an intrinsic value and hence worthy of moral con-

sideration. However, the Argument from Ontic Trust although separate from Floridi's Argument from the Goodness of Being is theoretically based on that prior argument and hence dependent upon it. For it is the prior acceptance of the pre-supposition in that argument that Goodness and Being are closely inter-related, which renders the acceptance of the idea of ontic trust reasonable, *within Floridi's theory of IE*. I emphasized the last phrase in the preceding sentence to draw attention to the fact that the idea of ontic trust could supplement another theory such as the one proposed in the next section but without a prior reliance or dependence on the pre-supposition of the Goodness of Being.

In short, the Argument of Ontic Trust, *within Floridi's theory of IE*, only goes through if his Argument from the Goodness of Being does. But we have seen that the Argument from the Goodness of Being cannot support Floridi's IE and hence neither can his Argument from Ontic Trust, since the theoretical credence of that argument relies essentially on the prior cogency of the Argument from the Goodness of Being. In conclusion of this section, neither the Argument from the Goodness of Being nor the Argument from Ontic Trust which needs the prior support of the former, suffice to support Floridi's IE. Something else is required, which I now propose to provide in the following section by way of an alterative Neo-Gewirthian Theory of Information Ethics.

INFORMATION ETHICS WITHOUT METAPHYSICS

By contrast to existence, purposive or goal-oriented behaviour can confer value in the manner demonstrated by Alan Gewirth's argument for the PGC (Gewirth, 1978). Namely, the necessary conditions for purposive agency, freedom and wellbeing, which are also necessary for a meaningful and worthwhile life, provide the basis for having rights to freedom and wellbeing and hence provide the universal foundation for the moral status of all purposive agents or patients, be they human or non-human.

One way to extend the moral status to non-sentient informational objects can be accomplished by showing how non-sentient informational objects possess in some sense and to some degree a form of purposive agency or some other teleological property that is value conferring. Insofar as information can be said to be goal-orientated or teleological in some relevant sense, this might not prove impossible, difficult though as it might seem at present.

Consider this argument. I will refer to it as the *Argument from Designed–in-Purposive Agency (A-DiPA)*. Artefacts and other non-sentient informational objects have a functional instrumentality. They are designed to perform a certain specific functional and instrumental role. Take a knife, for example. The functional role of a knife is to cut materials of a certain kind. It has been designed with that functional purpose in mind. This functional role or purpose is inherently designed in the knife and as such *inheres* in the knife unless removed. All things being equal the knife when used as intended will cut perfectly well according to the purpose for which it was designed – its designed-in-purpose. Now let us suppose that someone *for no good reason* and merely on a whim destroys the teleological (its design-in-purpose) and functional capacity of the knife to cut. Let us also assume that this someone, call him Mack, is the owner of the knife. The knife is now blunt and has lost its functional purpose of cutting. No doubt the knife has been *damaged* (harmed) instrumentally as it can no longer fulfil the instrumental role or the purpose for which it was designed and created. But has any moral harm being committed and if so to whom and by whom?

To answer this question let us first ask a different question: Would it have been better if Mack had not and for no good reason, destroyed the capacity of a perfectly good knife to cut? If the answer to that question is yes, as it is likely

to be, we can then proceed and ask what kind of damage or harm has been committed. I think we can allow that an instrumental harm has taken place which would have been better had it not occurred. What about a moral harm? Has the knife suffered a moral harm by it being made blunt? Clearly not as an agent, since the knife lacks the capacity for agency[3]. However, even if the knife lacks the capacity for agency in the full-blooded and traditional sense, could we not argue that the knife because of its inherent or *designed-in-purposiveness* or *designed-in-teleology* has some other type of *distributed* agency (Floridi and Sanders, 2004, p. 351) or *contributive* agency (Korsgaard, 1983, p. 172) which affords it some minimal moral role? After all, a knife can be used to murder, a typical immoral action. Let us assume that if the murderer had not possessed a knife they would not have been able to commit the murder and thus an immoral act would not have taken place. Under this assumption, the knife can be said to have contributed to the murder in virtue of its inherent teleology or d*esigned–in-purposive-agency* (DiPA), or that the immoral act of the murder can be defined as *morally distributed* across a *moral-field* or *moral-network* that at least includes the murderer (the prime moral agent), the teleological instrument (the knife as a morally contributing *and* instrumental agent) and the victim (the moral patient).

Following Floridi and Sanders (2004, pp. 366-369) I will argue that although the knife can of course not be held in anyway morally *responsible* for the murder it can nevertheless be held *accountable* in virtue of its contributed role to the murder via its designed-in-purposive-agency or DiPA. There is, as Floridi and Sanders rightly claim a conceptual difference between moral responsibility and moral accountability. Although an earthquake can be held accountable for the moral harm of its victims as the primary *cause* of that harm it cannot, because it lacks the relevant full-blooded agency, be held morally responsible.

Adapting and extending Gewirth's argument from the Principle of Generic Consistency on the basis of which it is shown that purposive agents have rights to freedom and wellbeing for the sufficient reason that they are purposive agents (that is, they possess the natural property of purposive agency) can we not *reasonably* say that artefacts such as knives with a designed-in-purposive-agency (the designed-in goal or purpose to do x, in the case of the knife, x= to cut) have to some minimal degree prima facie rights to (Art)freedom (artificial freedom) and (Art)wellbeing (artificial wellbeing) *as patients* if not as agents? That is to say, can we not reasonably say that such artefacts have the right not to have their (Art)freedom in exercising their designed-in-purposive-agency thwarted or interfered with for no good reason, or their (Art)wellbeing violated by having their DiPA, within which their (Art)well-being can be defined and understood in terms of *what they are good for* (their designed-in "functional goodness" or "designed-in-capacity" to do x) reduced or eliminated for no good reason?

Can we not say following this line of thinking that Mack's knife that was rendered useless by being made blunt for no good reason had its (Art)freedom and (Art)wellbeing unjustifiably violated and thus suffered not only an instrumental harm by having its instrumental functional role damaged, but also a moral harm qua artefact worthy of some minimal respect owed to it by virtue of its DiPA? Although the instrumental role of the knife can be replaced by the replacement of the damaged knife by a new one, the knife itself that was made blunt for no good reason has not only lost its replaceable instrumental functionality but also its irreplaceable particular inherent capacity to do what it was designed to do best, namely, cut well. That inherent capacity is something that the knife possessed as a thing-in-itself and as such it is something that can be valued for its own sake and not merely instrumentally for the sake of being able to cut well for some human agent.

Following Christine Korsgaard's (1983) distinction between objective intrinsic and unconditional value on the one hand and objective but extrinsic conditional value on the other, I will argue that the knife has suffered moral harm by being damaged: that is, by having its DiPA to cut well, rendered useless.

According to Korsgaard (1983) something X has an objective extrinsic but conditional value if X meets the relevant conditions under which it is held to be valuable and X is also something that is valued for its own sake or as an end, and *in addition* to its instrumentality as a means (p. 84ff). Going along with Korsgaard we can then say that a knife or other relevant informational object is valued or can be valued partly for its own sake as an end in addition to its instrumental use as a means for human ends, provided certain relevant conditions are met. Having this dual value, both instrumental as a means and extrinsic or inherent value[4] as an end, the instrumental disvalue of a knife or other object that is being used to commit a moral wrong, overrides its inherent value as an end. This follows from the fact that the knife and other objects of this ontological type, only have conditional value so that it would be justified to destroy a perfectly good knife if that were the only way to prevent a murder, for example.

In the case of Mack's knife, by contrast, both the extrinsic and instrumental value of the knife have been diminished, eliminated in fact, *for no good reason*; that is to say, the relevant conditions under which the knife is considered or can be considered valuable have been violated by the blunting of the knife, *for no good reason*. The qualification for *no good reason* is crucial and seems to point in the opposite direction in which Floridi's argument for assigning moral value to informational objects seems to go. For I am partly in agreement with Korsgaard although for Gewirthian reasons rather than Kantian as in her case, that the objective and inherent value (or for Korsgaard extrinsic value) of an object, or informational object as in Floridi's case, is not just a matter of the ontological status of the object qua informational object but of practical reason as well (Korsgaard, 1983, pp. 183-84).

I said I am only *partly* in agreement with Korsgaard because her claim is that the extrinsic value or in my case, inherent value, of an object is only a matter of practical reason and not one of ontology. Orientating my own position somewhere between that of Korsgaard and Floridi, I want to argue that the value of an object and in particular an informational object is determined partly by its ontology by virtue of its designed-in-purposive-agency (DiPA) – the artificial equivalent of the natural property of purposive agency inherent in human beings and some other animals – and partly by the reasons we have for holding that artefact valuable, principally, in virtue of the reasons for which we hold artefacts of a certain kind to be good for doing x; that is, by virtue of possessing the capacity to fulfil certain designed-in goals or purposes for doing x.

What drives us to attribute objective but conditional value to an informational object as a thing valued for its own sake and not merely as an instrument for advancing our own ends, such as a knife, for example, are partly the reasons themselves for designing such objects. The value or goodness of those reasons is transferred through the designing and creation of those objects into the objects themselves. Through this transference of *reasonable* value into the objects on the basis of the functional excellence and efficacy of their designed-in-agency or functional teleology, the value transferred through the design of the objects persists to inhere in the objects until the relevant conditions under which those reasons hold valuable and good are diminished or eliminated over time.

Does this imply, however, that contextual variations and changes over time largely determine whether an artefact looses or retains intrinsic value? For since contexts are variable and changeable over time, this would imply that the inherent value of an artefact can vary across different

contexts over time[5]; But if that is the implication, would that not mean that the inherent value of artefacts is relative to the different contexts in which they find themselves? The answer in short is no, for the simple reason that artefacts can and do retain their intrinsic value over a number of variable and changing social contexts. The social and technological contexts, for example, within which vinyl records, cassette tapes and CDs, were developed and used are quite variable and different; however, the intrinsic value of those artefacts has remained constant and unchanging (although their instrumental value has not) simply because the relevant conditions under which intrinsic value is bestowed upon those artefacts and the underlying reasons for holding that value to be still valuable, namely, their inherent designed-in capacity to store and re-produce music, have not changed but have remained intact; and this notwithstanding the contextual variations and contextual changes that have taken place over time.

However, if no-one ever uses cassette tapes to play music any longer their instrumental value is diminished or lost and their inherent-conditional value remains *dormant*; until let us say in an apocalyptic post-nuclear war that devastates all other music reproduction technologies except the humble cassette tapes, the human survivors in the absence of any other viable alternatives, begin to use cassette tapes again to play their music of choice. Closer to reality still, consider the come-back of vinyl records. Some people have started playing them again because they prefer the quality of sound they produce to that of CDs. This is a case of an artefact once dormant now re-emerging again as an active and valued artefact. This particular case demonstrates an important point: artefacts can and do retain their intrinsic value over a number of variable and changing social contexts. The social contexts within which vinyl records, cassette tapes and CDs were developed and used are quite variable and different; however, the intrinsic value of those artefacts has remained constant and unchanging (although their instrumental value has not) simply because the relevant conditions under which intrinsic value is bestowed upon those artefacts and the underlying reasons for holding that value to be still valuable, namely, their inherent designed-in capacity to store and re-produce music have not changed or varied relative to different contexts over time but have remained intact.

In conclusion of this section: Insofar as a knife can be said to have an inherent value or what Korsgaard defines as an objective extrinsic but conditional value and insofar as Mack knife's value has been eliminated for no good reason (the relevant condition in this case) the elimination or diminution of the value of the knife or of any other teleological object can be said to be a moral harm; for the unreasonable elimination or diminution of an objective inherent or objective extrinsic conditional value is unjustified (because no good objective reason can be given for it) and hence morally wrong as it diminishes value overall. In the case of Mack's knife it diminished both instrumental and inherent value as the knife in its prime condition possesses both. It has the instrumental value of being used as a perfectly good knife to cut, an apple for example, but it also possesses an inherent designed-in-purposive-capacity to cut whether or not it is ever used in that way. A good knife that lay dormant and was not used to cut would retain that inherent value regardless of whether its designed-in-purposive-capacity was put to instrumental use or not. And it is this conceptual distinction just made between the knife's *in-use-instrumental-value* exercised in cutting things and its inherent value, which it has by virtue of its *designed*-in-*purposive-value* (that affords it the capacity to cut) which allows us to ascribe to the knife and other objects or artefacts of the type that possess a designed-in-purposive-agency (DiPA), two inter-related values: one instrumental and one inherent.

IMPLICATIONS FOR FLORIDI'S ONTOLOGICAL THESIS FOR THE MORAL VALUE OF INFORMATIONAL OBJECTS

In his paper "On the intrinsic value of information objects and the infosphere" (2002a) Floridi postulates the two theses that comprise his Information Ethics (IE) theory:

1. The first thesis states that information objects qua information objects can be moral agents.
2. The second thesis states that information objects qua information objects can have an intrinsic moral value, although quite minimal, and hence that they can be moral patients, subject to some equally minimal degree of moral respect.

My analysis above in terms of attributing inherent but conditional moral value to informational objects such as a knife, for example, seems to support both of Floridi's two theses of IE but without the metaphysical cost of having to postulate two extra metaphysical claims to the effect that (a) anything that exists in the infosphere as an informational object has moral value just by virtue of its ontic existence and (b) the unjustified damage or destruction of informational objects due to a lack of respect for their minimal moral worth causes information *entropy* which is overall a bad outcome and one that ought to be avoided.

I have argued above that existence per se even qua information objects cannot of itself confer moral value. Floridi's motivation for choosing the primary ontological route to the moral worth of informational objects is that he thinks that existing ethical theories which are either predominantly anthropocentric such as Kant's theory or various other biocentric theories which are more inclusive than Kant's theory but not sufficiently so, cannot account for the moral worth of non-sentient objects such as artificial systems like software agents in cyberspace (2002a, 299), for example. If my analysis above is correct, Floridi's motivation is justified but misconceived. Justified because he is right in arguing that there is a theoretical need to extend the moral sphere to include not just all sentient and other living organisms in the biosphere but also all entities that qualify as information objects including non-sentient beings such as coffee mugs, knives and software agents or webbots (Floridi and Sanders, 2004, 370) in the infosphere. As he states (2002a),

Showing that both an anthropocentric and bio-centric axiology are unsatisfactory is a crucial step (p. 291)

However justified his motivation for extending the moral sphere to include not only the biosphere but also the infosphere is, the exclusive *ontocentric* orientation of his approach in seeking to confer moral value to information objects merely on the basis of their existence is misconceived because the pre-supposition that supports his entire IE thesis, namely, the pre-supposition that Being in all its manifestations is intrinsically Good has no conclusive or convincing evidence or arguments in its support. If there was a lack of counter arguments to the Goodness of Being, as Floridi seems to think, this would not be critical for his position for in the absence of any such arguments it would be reasonable to pre-suppose that Being is Good as a valuable theoretical starting point for explaining why all entities are intrinsically valuable and hence deserving of some moral consideration. However, as I have shown above, there are counter arguments to the Goodness of Being, most notably the arguments from Schopenhauer. At best, what this amounts to is a theoretical impasse between those who side with Plato and Spinoza on the one hand and those who side with Schopenhauer on the other, or those who along with the Manicheans believe that the axiological state of the Universe comprises a bit of both: partly good and partly bad. This theoretical impasse, however, should caution scepticism rather than any degree of certainty con-

cerning the Goodness of Being. For Floridi also acknowledges (in press) that his pre-supposition of the Goodness of Being *"is not a defence of IE but an explanation* [emphasis added]. Although being in the company of Plato or Spinoza, for example, might be reassuring, *it is not an insurance against being mistaken* [emphasis added] (p. 13). Indeed!

My proposed Neo-Gewirthian approach, by contrast, which locates the inherent moral worth and value of all informational objects, including human beings, animals and inanimate objects such as artefacts, the whole of Floridi's infosphere in fact, in the natural property of *purposive agency* provides, I believe, adequate justification at no additional ontological cost for a reasonable alternative theory of Information Ethics. Contrary to Floridi whose profound insights into the meta-theoretical need for attributing moral value to all informational objects qua informational objects I share, I have argued that we do not require the unproven metaphysical pre-supposition of the Goodness of Being for doing so. The capacity for purposive agency alone, which is the natural property on the basis of which human beings and other sentient beings such as animals have inherent moral worth, can be adapted and extended as I have shown above, to include other non-sentient information objects, such as knives and software-agents, for example. Whereas sentient beings posses purposive agency naturally and inherently by varying degrees from very high in the case of human beings and perhaps high in the case of dolphins and whales to very low in the case of amoebas, non-sentient beings such as artificial agents on the higher scale and thermostats and knives on a lower scale, possess an *artificial purposive agency* by design and teleological implantation that *inheres* in those objects and renders them inherently but conditionally morally valuable as I have argued above.

Finally, I am in agreement with Floridi's claim that,

It seems reasonable to assume that different entities may have different degrees of relative value that can constrain a's [the agent's] behaviour without necessarily having an instrumental value, i.e., a value relative to human feelings, impulses or inclinations, as Kant would phrase it. (2002a, p. 293).

Although the capacity for purposive agency both naturally in the case of sentient entities and artificially in the case of non-sentient entities creates a continuum of moral worthiness and moral consideration across a wide network of informational objects, that continuum is separated by qualitative divisions between those entities that affords them various differentiated degrees of moral value in terms of the complexity of their capacity for purposive agency. Using the metaphor of canal or river locks we can say that because the moral continuum of informational objects is porous, the capacity of purposive agency sips through the various qualitative moral divisions like water through the locks in a canal or river. However, the transitions from one qualitative moral division to another requires, as in the case of the raising of the water level in a lock to allow a ship to transit from one level of the canal to another, the raising of the level of complexity of an entity's capacity for purposive agency so as to enable its transition from a lower to a higher qualitative moral division. Thus, a software agent's capacity for purposive agency would have to be raised to that of an intelligent android that meets Floridi's and Sanders' conditions of full agency discussed above, before it can proceed to a higher moral division close to that of human beings.

The conceptual distinctions between on the one hand responsibility and agenthood and on the other accountability and patienthood help explain the relative moral value of different entities. Thus although we could only hold a software agent accountable but not responsible for the destruction of valuable information, we could by contrast hold an android or human agent both accountable and responsible due largely to their higher moral status. Similarly, although we ought to morally avoid killing a tiger unless in self-defence we cannot reasonably expect a tiger to morally reciprocate in the same moral way. This is because although a moral patient worthy of moral respect the tiger does not posses sufficient moral agency to warrant us holding the tiger bound to reciprocal moral obligations with regard to human agents. Thus the four conceptual distinctions of responsibility/accountability and agenthood/patienthood go some way in explaining the relative moral value of different informational objects in relation to the moral relevance and significance of those conceptual categories in specific contexts.

CONCLUSION

My close reading of Floridi suggests that according to him, ontic existence alone qua informational object suffices to establish the moral status of the informational object. In support of this thesis he provides at least two distinct but inter-related arguments, the Argument from the Goodness of Being and the Argument from Ontic Trust. I have shown that neither argument separately or together is sufficient for supporting Floridi's thesis, especially if the difficulties associated with the former argument can be avoided through the postulation of an alternative theory that achieves the same conclusion as Floridi's IE, but without the troublesome and unproven pre-supposition that Being in all its manifestations is intrinsically Good. That alternative theory is my Neo-Gewirthian Information Ethics as argued for in this paper.

REFERENCES

Beyleveld, D. (1991). *The dialectical necessity of morality: An analysis and defence of Alan Gewirth's argument to the principle of generic consistency*. IL: University of Chicago Press.

Floridi, L. (2002). What is the philosophy of information? *Metaphilosophy, 33*, 123–145. doi:10.1111/1467-9973.00221

Floridi, L. (2002a). On the intrinsic value of information objects and the infosphere. *Ethics and Information Technology, 4*, 287–304. doi:10.1023/A:1021342422699

Floridi, L. (2004). On the morality of artificial agents. *Minds and Machines, 14*, 349–379. doi:10.1023/B:MIND.0000035461.63578.9d

Floridi, L. (2005). Is semantic information meaningful data? *Philosophy and Phenomenological Research, LXX*(2), 351–370. doi:10.1111/j.1933-1592.2005.tb00531.x

Floridi, L. (2007). Understanding information ethics. *APA Newsletter on Philosophy and Computers, 07*(1), 3–12.

Floridi, L. (2007a). Global information ethics: The importance of being environmentally earnest. *International Journal of Technology and Human Interaction, 3.3*, 1-19. Retrieved April, 27, 2008, from http://www.philosophyofinformation.net/publications/publications.html#articles

Floridi, L. (in press). Understanding information ethics: Replies to comments. *APA Newsletter On Philosophy and Computers*. Retrieved April, 27, 2008 from http://www.philosophyofinformation.net/index.html

Floridi, L. (2008). Informational structural realism. *Synthese, 161*(2), 219–253. doi:10.1007/s11229-007-9163-z

Floridi, L. (2008a). Information ethics: A reappraisal. *Ethics and Information Technology, 10*, 189–204. doi:10.1007/s10676-008-9176-4

Gewirth, A. (1978*). Reason and morality*. IL: University of Chicago Press.

Gewirth, A. (1996). *The community of rights*. IL: University of Chicago Press.

Gewirth, A. (1998). *Self-fulfillment*. NJ: Princeton University Press.

Hongladarom, S. (2008). Floridi and Spinoza on global information ethics. *Ethics and Information Technology, 10*, 175–187. doi:10.1007/s10676-008-9164-8

Korsgaard, C. M. (1983). Two distinctions in goodness. *The Philosophical Review, 92*(2), 169–195. doi:10.2307/2184924

Spence, E. (2006). *Ethics within reason: A neo-Gewirthian approach*. Lanham: Lexington Books (a division of Rowman and Littlefield).

Spence, E. (2007, July 12-14). What's right and good about Internet information? A universal model for evaluating the cultural quality of digital information. In L. Hinman, P. Brey, L. Floridi, F. Grodzinsky, & L. Introna E.,) *Proceedings of CEPE 2007, The 7th International Conference of Computer Ethics: Philosophical Enquiry*, University of San Diego, USA.

ENDNOTES

[1] The term "incredulous stare" here refers to the expression used by David Lewis in his book *On the Plurality of Worlds* (1986, 133-135) to describe a particular response to his theory of possible worlds. It seems both theories elicit bold responses.

[2] Due to constrains of space, I will not be able to provide a justification for Alan Gewirth's argument for the Principle of Generic Consistency (PGC) on which his derivation of rights to freedom and wellbeing is based, as this is well beyond the scope and limits of this paper. For a detailed analysis, justification and defence of Gewirth's argument for the PGC see Spence (2006, Chapters 1-3); Beyleveld (1991); and Gewirth (1978).

3   Following Floridi and Sanders (2004, 349) the knife can be said to lack agency because it lacks its three essential features of inter-activity (*response to stimulus by change of state*), autonomy (*ability to change state without stimulus*) and adaptability (*ability to change the 'transitions rules' by which state is changed*).

4   I prefer to use the term *inherent* rather than Korsgaard's *extrinsic* term because the value an artefact has by virtue of its DiPA inheres in the artefact and so it is not exclusively determined by the external reasons for which human beings hold it to be valuable. I should add, however, and perhaps this is in keeping with Korsgaard's position, that in the event that an artefact was no longer held to be valuable its inherent value by virtue of its DiPA could be revoked. For what can be designed in can also be designed-out. This is in keeping with the correct thought that values are to a large degree determined by the underlying reasons for considering those values "valuable".

5   I owe this astute observation to one of the reviewer's of this paper.

This work was previously published in International Journal of Technology and Human Interaction, Volume 6, Issue 1, edited by Anabela Mesquita & Chia-Wen Tsai, pp. 1-14, copyright 2010 by IGI Publishing (an imprint of IGI Global).

Chapter 10
Enhance Students' Computing Skills via Web-Mediated Self-Regulated Learning with Feedback in Blended Environment

Tsang-Hsiung Lee
National Chengchi University, Taiwan

Pei-Di Shen
Ming Chuan University, Taiwan

Chia-Wen Tsai
Ming Chuan University, Taiwan

ABSTRACT

The vocational colleges in Taiwan regard professional certifications as a badge of skills achievement. To enhance student learning in this specific context, the authors conducted a quasi-experiment to explore effects of web-mediated self-regulated learning (SRL) with feedback, blended learning (BL) and their combinations on enhancing students' skills of using Microsoft Word. Four classes in successive years, with a total of 190 freshmen, were divided into 2 (SRL with Feedback vs. SRL without Feedback) × 2 (Blended vs. Traditional) experimental groups. Results were generally positive. The results showed that students in the group of BL and SRL with feedback had better skills and higher pass rate on certification exams than those in the control group. It is hoped that the lesson learned is also useful for those teachers engaged in e-learning, specifically, in vocational colleges.

DOI: 10.4018/978-1-61350-465-9.ch010

INTRODUCTION

In Taiwan's vocational schools, students' technical skills and the proportion of students awarded professional certificates before they graduate are the main criteria when evaluating teachers' teaching performance and students' learning outcomes. Students in these schools have low interest and negative attitude toward their learning, and tend to have lower levels of academic achievement (Chen & Tien, 2005). They spend more time on part-time jobs, do not adequately get involved in their schoolwork, and do not care so much about their grades (Shen, Lee, & Tsai, 2007a). Teaching in such a context, particularly teaching a course on application software and targeted on helping students earn certificates, is a great challenge to most educators.

Recently, web-assisted instruction has been advocated by contemporary educators and researchers (Liu & Tsai, 2008). Nevertheless, the policy of web-based learning in Taiwan is relative conservative in contrast with that in the U.S. For instance, earning a bachelor degree entirely through online courses is still prohibited. Moreover, it is suggested by many universities and vocational colleges that a teacher may not deliver over fifty percent of a semester's classes online. In some vocational colleges, a teacher is limited to 35 percent of classes given online. That is, teachers in Taiwan have to adopt blended learning (BL) rather than pure online learning when implementing e-learning.

Through the Internet, learners are free to access new information without restrictions (Li, Tsai & Tsai, 2008). However, implementing e-learning for students with low self-regulatory skills inevitably runs high risks. It is indicated that vocational students are more Internet-addicted than the general students (Yang & Tung, 2007). It is a big challenge for teachers to help vocational students to be involved in an online course in an environment that is full of Internet allure with shopping websites, free online games, and messaging software. Students' lack of time management skills may cause serious problems in learning in such virtual environments. Even worse, many students do not perceive lack of time management skills as a learning problem (Löfström & Nevgi, 2007). Furthermore, the lack of on-the-spot teacher monitoring in web-mediated instruction makes it even more difficult for students to concentrate on online learning.

To respond to the above challenges, we turn to the approach of self-regulated learning (SRL) to help students be more involved in their learning and manage their time better. Recent research examining how students learn complex and challenging tasks has suggested that successful students deploy key self-regulatory strategies and processes (Azevedo & Cromley, 2004; Azevedo, Cromley, & Seibert, 2004; Azevedo, Cromley, Winters, Moos, & Greene, 2005; Azevedo, Moos, Greene, Winters, & Cromley, 2008; Lee, Shen, & Tsai, 2008). In a SRL environment, students take charge of their own learning by choosing and setting goals, using individual strategies to monitor, regulate and control different aspects of the learning process, and evaluate their actions. Eventually, they become less dependent on others and on the contextual features of a learning situation (Järvelä, Näykki, Laru, & Luokkanen, 2007). Students equipped with SRL competence become more responsible for their learning and more intrinsically oriented (Chang, 2005).

Students in Taiwan have generally received a spoon-fed teaching method since they were children, that is, they lack the ability to manage their time and regulate their learning (Shen, Lee, Tsai, & Ting, 2008), particularly in an online course without the teacher's on-the-spot assistance and monitoring. In Niemi, Nevgi and Virtanen's (2003) study, they find that students benefit and become more self-regulatory after receiving feedback from the teacher-tutor and the teaching website. In this regard, we applied SRL with teacher's feedback in this study to help students concentrate on their learning, enhance their computing skills, pass the examination for a certificate, and furthermore, take responsibility for their learning.

There are some studies comparing the effectiveness between BL and traditional face-to-face learning (Castelijn & Janssen, 2006; Shen, Lee, & Tsai, 2007b; Yushau, 2006). However, more studies are needed to explore further the effective web-mediated instructional methods for vocational students. In this regard, we redesigned a course in application software to integrate blended learning, innovative teaching method and learning technologies to help students learn and earn the related certificate. Specifically, this study explored the effects of BL and web-mediated SRL with feedback on the development of vocational students' skills in using application software.

LITERATURE REVIEW

Self-Regulated Learning and Feedback

Zimmerman and Schunk (1989) define SRL in terms of self-generated thoughts, feelings, and actions, which are systematically oriented towards attainment of students' own goals. Characteristics attributed to self-regulated people coincide with those attributed to high-performance, high-capacity students, as opposed to those with low performance (or learning disabilities), who show a deficit in metacognitive, motivational, and behavioral variables (Reyero & Tourón, 2003; Roces & González Torres, 1998; Zimmerman, 1998). Based on the characteristics of SRL, it is believed that students' learning about complex and challenging science topics with hypermedia will be more successful if they devote themselves to a series of recursive cycles of cognitive and metacognitive activities central to learning and knowledge construction (e.g., Azevedo & Cromley, 2004; Greene & Azevedo, 2007; Azevedo, Moos, Greene, Winters, & Cromley, 2008).

As for the effects of SRL on using computer software, Bielaczyc, Pirolli and Brown (1995) incorporate self-explanation and self-regulation strategies in the attainment of the cognitive skill of computer programming. They find that their treatment group, which incorporates the self-regulation strategies of self-monitoring and clarifying comprehension failures in conjunction with self-explanation strategies, outperforms a control group that does not have the benefit of instruction by using these strategies. In a similar vein, this study provides us an insight that SRL is appropriate to be applied in computer software education.

Previous studies have established that self-regulatory skills can help foster learning through any instructional method (see Ertmer, Newby, & MacDougall, 1996; Lindner & Harris, 1993; Weinstein, 1989; Zimmerman, 1990). With regard to the effects of SRL in the online learning environment, it is indicated that successful students generally applied self-regulated learning strategies in an online course and the effect of self-regulation on students' success was statistically significant (Yukselturk & Bulut, 2007). In Shen, *et al.*'s (2007a) study, the intervention of web-mediated SRL does contribute to students' learning.

In the web-mediated learning environment, the instructors may adopt technologies to provide feedback for students. Feedback is any kind of information about how students' present states of learning and performances relate to those of course goals and standards. Teachers' feedback responses based on their monitoring and assessment of student performances can influence students' subsequent actions, if they are interpreted rightly and internalized (Ivanic, Clark & Rimmershaw, 2000). For example, direct diagnostic feedback proved helpful in the acquisition of specific skills or procedures and in preventing students from making further incorrect steps. Indirect diagnostic feedback was useful for supporting students in validating their work, thus fostering the development of crucial competencies (Bottino

& Robotti, 2007). Thus, teachers' feedback may help students take control of their own learning and become self-regulated learners (Nicol & Macfarlane-Dick, 2006). In the web-mediated learning environment, learners could benefit and become more self-regulatory as a result of feedback from both the teacher-tutor and the teaching website (Niemi *et al*. 2003). Therefore, based on the literature reviewed in this study, it is proposed that: *In the web-mediated learning environment, the effect of deploying an instructional method of fostering self-regulated learning with feedback on students' skills of applying an application software are positive, and higher than those without.*

Blended Learning

Blended learning (BL) is the combination of established ways of learning and teaching and the opportunities offered by technology in order to improve students' learning and increase flexibility in how, when and where they study (Blended Learning Unit, 2006). It is a hybrid of traditional face-to-face and online learning so that instruction occurs both in the classroom and online, and where the online component becomes a natural extension of traditional classroom learning (Colis & Moonen, 2001). BL not only offers more choices but also is more effective (Singh, 2003). Blending itself makes students effectively engage in a range of situations, and allows students to fit different activities together with more flexibility according to their particular circumstances (Aspden & Helm, 2004). It is indicated that BL has added value when facilitated by educators with high interpersonal skills, and accompanied by reliable, easy-to-use technology (Derntl & Motschnig-Pitrik, 2005).

BL is consistent with the values of traditional higher education institutions and has the proven potential to enhance both the effectiveness and efficiency of meaningful learning experiences (Garrison & Kanuka, 2004). With regard to the effects of BL in previous research, it is found that performance as measured by the final mark of the

course under a hybrid teaching method that incorporated both traditional face-to-face lectures and electronic delivery and communication methods is higher than that of using a traditional teaching method alone (Dowling, Godfrey & Gyles, 2003). The effect of BL is potentially a more robust educational experience than either traditional or fully online learning (Rovai & Jordan, 2004). In Castelijn and Janssen's (2006) study, their statistical results indicate that BL students have higher exam scores in a financial management course.

As for the effects of BL on student' success rates in learning to program, Boyle, Bradley, Chalk, Jones, and Pickard's (2003) research results indicate a generally positive evaluation of the main elements of the blend, and widespread use of the new online features. Their research results also show marked improvements in pass rates in learning computer programming. Yushau (2006) also shows the positive effect of blended e-learning on students' attitudes toward computing and mathematics. Moreover, students in the BL group attained significantly higher average scores than those in the traditional teaching group. Also, the BL group had a significantly higher percentage pass rate than the traditional teaching group. It is concluded that BL was more effective than traditional teaching (Pereira, Pleguezuelos, Merí, Molina-Ros, Molina-Tomás, & Masdeu, 2007). Accordingly, it is summarized that: *In the web-mediated learning environment, the effect of deploying blended learning on students' skills of applying an application software are positive, and higher than those in traditional classrooms.*

Combination of Self-Regulated Learning and Blended Learning

Marino (2000) discovers that some students experienced difficulty adjusting to the structure of online courses, managing their time in such environments, and maintaining self-motivation. Students may experience frustrations in fully online courses, particularly those who are dependent learners, are less self-regulated, and need frequent direction and reinforcement from a visible professor. The frustrations could be eased when the online course is with periodic opportunities for face-to-face interactions (Rovai & Jordan, 2004). That is, BL may help students lessen a feeling of isolation and adapt better to the online learning environment.

Success in online courses often depends on students' abilities to successfully direct their own learning efforts (Cennamo, Ross, & Rogers, 2002). In web-mediated learning environments, the physical absence of the instructor and the increased responsibility demanded of learners to effectively engage in learning tasks may present difficulties for learners, particularly those with low self-regulatory skills (Dabbagh & Kitsantas, 2005). Lynch and Dembo (2004) investigated the relationship between self-regulation and online learning in a blended learning context. They found that verbal ability and self-efficacy relate significantly to performance, together explaining 12 percent of the variance in course grades. In addition, Shen *et al.* (2007b) point out that students in the BL with SRL group had significantly higher pass rates on certifications exams in deploying database management system (DBMS) than those in the control group.

Learners could benefit and become more self-regulatory from both the teacher's and the teaching website's feedback (Niemi *et al.* 2003). Those who are more effective at self-regulation, however, produce better feedback or are more able to use the feedback they generate to achieve their desired goals (Butler & Winne, 1995). Self-regulated learners actively interpret external feedback from teachers in relation to their internal goals. Although research shows that students can learn to be more self-regulated (see Pintrich, 1995; Zimmerman & Schunk, 2001), how to apply feedback (both self-generated and external) in support of self-regulation has not been fully explored in the current literature (Nicol & Macfarlane-Dick, 2006), particularly in web-mediated learning environment.

To bridge this gap, this study redesigns a course in application software to integrate innovative teaching methods and learning technologies to enhance student learning. Based on the literature reviewed in this study, it is proposed that: *In the web-mediated learning environment, the effect of the intervention of deploying blended learning AND self-regulated learning with feedback on students' skills of applying an application software are positive, and higher than those without.*

METHODS

Participants

The participants chosen for this study were 190 vocational students (102 female and 88 male) from four classes taking a compulsory course titled 'Packaged Software and Application' in a university of science and technology in Taiwan. Students in this course were generally aged eighteen. None of them majors in information or computer technology. Besides, about ninety percent of them graduated from vocational high schools. Students at this university are expected to spend much more time and effort in mastering a variety of technological skills as compared to those in comprehensive universities in Taiwan.

Course Setting

The involved course is a semester-long, 2 credit-hour classes, targeting first-year college students from different major fields of study. A credit hour in Taiwan is defined as 16 hours of instruction (including exams) over the period of one semester (generally 16-18 weeks in duration), so in a two-credit-hour course, students receive 32 hours of instruction. Upon successful completion of the course, as measured by exams, papers, and project work, a student will be awarded a grade valued at two credits. In the course of 'Packaged Software and Application', students received a study task dealing with Microsoft Word. The major focus of this course was to develop students' skills in applying the functions of Microsoft Word. Moreover, this course targeted helping students earn a certificate of professional document processing. That is, students have to take an examination for a certificate in Word at the end of semester.

This examination was administered by a trustworthy organization in Taiwan called the Computer Skills Foundation (CSF). The examination and mechanism of certification in CSF is similar with that in European Computer Driving Licence Foundation Ltd (ECDL-F). Students with certificates of CSF can convert their certificates into that of ECDL without reexamination.

Experimental Design and Procedure

Four classes in successive years were divided into 2 (SRL with Feedback vs. SRL without Feedback) × 2 (Blended vs. Traditional) factorial pretest-posttest design (see Figure 1). In the first week, the lecturer declared that this class section would be partially provided with innovative instructional methods mediated by the web as an intervention. Students had the freedom to drop this class section and take another teacher's class section, if preferred. After this declaration, 190 students continued in this class section. There were four classes taking the same course. The teacher

Figure 1. Expected effects of variation in instructional methods

	Blended	Traditional
SRL with Feedback	The most significant effect (C1 Group)	Medium effect (C3 Group)
SRL without Feedback	Medium effect (C2 Group)	No difference (C4 Group)

randomly chose two classes for the experiment of SRL with feedback.

In the first week, students were pre-tested and the results showed that the differences of students' computing skills among the four groups were not statistically significant. That is, students in the four groups had similar level of computing skills before they received the treatments. Then, participants were purposely assigned to one of the four experimental conditions. The Blended and SRL with Feedback group (C1, n=42), Blended and SRL without Feedback group (C2, n=48), Traditional and SRL with Feedback group (C3, n=49) are experimental groups, while Traditional and SRL without Feedback group (C4, n=51) is the control group.

Students were asked to pass the examination and get the certificate of Microsoft Word. The examinations for certificates in the software were held right after the completion of the course (the 16th week). The detailed schedule of the experiment is depicted in Figure 2.

Treatment of Web-Mediated SRL with Feedback

There was an SRL with Feedback group and an SRL without Feedback group in both the Blended class and Traditional class. The four groups were gathered in a classroom and a two-hour lecture was delivered discussing how to manage study time and regulate their learning. The lecture was given in an after-school period. The content of this SRL course was composed of the four processes addressed by Zimmerman, Bonner and Kovach (1996), that is, self-evaluation and monitoring, goal-setting and strategy planning, strategy implementation and monitoring, and monitoring of the outcome of strategy. Students were taught how to implement these four processes to become more regulated learners.

In Zimmerman and Martinez-Pons's (1986) study, high-achieving students utilized the strategies of reviewing notes and keeping records

Figure 2. The schedule of the course and skill tests in the semester (O: online classes; T: traditional classroom classes)

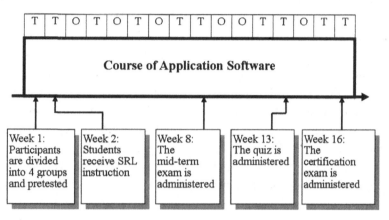

and monitoring most often. Moreover, the high achievers used these strategies significantly more frequently and consistently than the low achievers. Ross (1999) also indicated that keeping records and self-evaluation were the two most-often-mentioned learning strategies in his analysis. Therefore, the teacher adopted Zimmerman and Martinez-Pons's and Ross's strategies, and emphasized reviewing notes, keeping records, and self-evaluation when implementing SRL.

Students were required to take notes in class and review the notes after school. In addition, students had to regularly prepare and read the textbook before classes, and review or practice the skills of using application software they had learned after classes. The data of students' learning behavior was recorded on the course website instead of in their notebooks in order to prevent falsification of records. Based on these records, students self-evaluated their learning according to the goals they had set in advance.

The teacher assigned the schoolwork to students in Assignments and Exercises section of the course website. A notification email was sent when the teacher assigned new tasks. Students had to complete and upload the assignments before the deadline. Moreover, a reminder email was sent before the deadline for submission. Students could not submit assignments and learning records after

the deadlines, because the button for submission became unavailable when the time was up. Finally, the feedback about students' assignments was provided from both the teacher and the teaching website to inform students of their progress. From the feedback information, students would know how their performance was judged by the teacher and whether they submitted their assignments at the required time. If a student had difficulties or problems with SRL, the teacher would provide further information or directly contact him/her to remedy his/her problems and to modify his/her learning behavior. Furthermore, the teacher would call or talk to the students in the fact-to-face classes if the feedback from course website and emails functioned inadequately to help students regulate their learning. Finally, a student could only read his/her own feedback from the teacher and the teaching website, and not that of his/her classmates.

Treatment of Blended Learning

It is suggested by Alonso, López, Manrique and Viñes (2005) that an efficient blended learning solution includes the following ingredients: (1) An instructor that directs learning. (2) Email and telephone assistance for personalized learner support, (3) Virtual classes by means of computerized device, (4) Interaction between learners and the instructor and between the learners themselves through chat function to stimulate group learning, (5) Support for subjects related to learning management, (6) Assessment examinations, (7) Certificate and diploma that certifies having taken or passed the course. In this study, the authors adopted Alonso *et al.*'s approach, and designed the treatment of BL accordingly.

In the BL environment, the popular software, Microsoft Word, was taught in two different classes. The teacher lectured through the Internet or in the classroom about how to solve simulated computing problems. In the beginning of the courses, students were encouraged to adapt to learn via a course website. The teacher recorded every session of his lecture whether in the classroom or through Internet and later on translated lectures into HTML files with flash, video, and voice. These HTML files were then loaded into the course website. Students could preview and review the course sessions on this course website at home. If students ran into problems, they could ask for help and converse with teacher and classmates in the online chat room or through online messenger and videoconference.

Starting from the third week, six weeks of the coursework were moved onto the website. Altogether, ten weeks of the coursework were still conducted in the traditional classroom. Within the first three weeks, the teacher adjusted students' learning gradually and smoothly. The mid-term examinations, quizzes, and final examinations for certificate in Word were administered within the ten face-to-face classes. Students in the blended learning environment had fewer physical contact hours than those traditional learners. However, the teacher provided other channels through which students could communicate. For example, students could synchronously interact with their teacher and classmates through online messenger, chat room, video conference, or face-to-face meeting if necessary. They could also asynchronously discuss and interact with others in the online forums.

Treatment in the Control Group

To control for unintended effects of the design, the control group (C4) received the same number of teaching hours (time-on-task) as the experimental groups. Moreover, students were not informed about the experimental design. Instead of focusing on BL, students of the control group were taught in the traditional face-to-face classroom. That is, the teacher did not audio-record any session of his lecture. Students had neither chance nor channels to review and practice after class or if he/she was absent from any class.

The students in the control group learned in the traditional learning environment with the extra requirements of SRL. However, the teacher did not provide feedback to modify students' learning or judge their learning performance through the course website. The teacher only notified students of their grades after the quizzes and examination. These students also participated in the measurements after the completion of each module.

Treatments in four groups are illustrated and compared in Table 1.

Evaluation

A detailed evaluation of the project was conducted. The authors explored the potential effects of BL and SRL with feedback on students' skills of using application software. To examine levels of change due to variations in experimental conditions, we first measured students' skills of application software before they entered the class. In the first week, students completed three Word documents as pretest. The pretest grades showed that computer skills of almost all were low. None of the participants was able to answer any of the pretest questions correctly. This confirms that all participants in the four groups had little knowledge of or skill in Microsoft Word.

After this course concluded, the examination for the certificate in Word was conducted. There were three problems, which each consisted of 5

Table 1. Teaching and learning activities in different experimental groups

Group	Teaching Activities	Learning Activities
C1	Teacher… records every session of his lecture and loads the files into the course website. teaches SRL skills and urges students to study regularly. sends notification and reminder email, and provides feedback about students' performance.	Students… practice SRL and record learning behaviors every week. have to complete and upload the assignments before the deadline. learn in both online and traditional environments. receive the feedback from teacher and course website.
C2	Teaching activities are the same as C1 but without providing feedback. The teacher only notifies students' grades after the quiz and examination.	Students receive the same instruction as C1 in both online and traditional environments without feedback.
C3	Teacher… conducts the course in the traditional classroom. teaches SRL skills and urges students to study regularly. sends notification and reminder email, and provides feedback about students' performance.	Students… learn in the traditional environment. practice SRL and record learning behaviors every week. receive the feedback from teacher and course website.
C4	Teaching activities are the same as C3 but without feedback. The teacher only notifies students of grades after the quizzes and examination. The course is conducted in the traditional environment.	Students experience the same instruction as C3 in traditional environment without feedback about their learning performance.

to 8 sub-problems. Before testing, students were assigned random seats. All students were tested at the same time, and students had forty minutes to solve the problems. A student's grade came from his correctness and completeness of problem solving. A student could get professional certification using Word if his grade was higher than 70. Finally, we examined the effects of BL and SRL with feedback on the differences of students' skills in using Word under different conditions.

RESULTS

We took grades on the examination for a certificate in Microsoft Word as a measure of student's computing skills. The 'independent samples t-test' was used to compare students' skills of using Word

under different conditions. As shown in Table 2, students' grade for Word in SRL with Feedback group (89.4396) was significantly higher than that in SRL without Feedback group (81.5899). Therefore, the effects of SRL with feedback on students' skills of using Word may be positive, and higher than those without.

The Chi-Square (χ^2) test was used to compare the different pass rate on professional certification promoted by SRL with Feedback and SRL without Feedback. As shown in Table 3, the pass rate in the SRL with Feedback group (90.1%) was significantly higher than that in the SRL without Feedback group (78.8%). Among the failing students, only 30.0% came from the SRL with Feedback group, however, 70.0% came from the SRL without Feedback group. Therefore, it is concluded that the intervention of SRL with

Table 2. Comparison of grades: SRL with Feedback vs. SRL without Feedback

Groups	n	Mean	SD	F	t-value	*df*	*p*
SRL with Feedback	91	89.4396	15.62351	10.031	2.640	188	0.009**
SRL without Feedback	99	81.5899	24.08162				

Note: *$p < 0.05$, **$p < 0.01$, ***$p < 0.001$

Table 3. Comparison of pass rates: SRL with Feedback vs. SRL without Feedback

		Groups		Total	χ^2
		SRL with Feedback	SRL without Feedback		p
Passed	n	82	78	160	0.033*
	% within Passed	51.3%	48.8%	100.0%	
	% within Groups	90.1%	78.8%	84.2%	
	% of Total	43.2%	41.1%	84.2%	
Failed	n	9	21	30	
	% within Failed	30.0%	70.0%	100.0%	
	% within Groups	9.9%	21.2%	15.8%	
	% of Total	4.7%	11.1%	15.8%	
Total	Count	91	99	190	

Note: *$p < 0.05$, **$p < 0.01$, ***$p < 0.001$

Table 4. Comparison of grades: Blended vs. traditional

Classes	n	Mean	SD	F	t-value	df	p
Blended	90	89.9556	14.39250	15.929	2.955	188	0.004**
Traditional	100	81.2040	24.54822				

Note: *$p < 0.05$, **$p < 0.01$, ***$p < 0.001$

feedback may contribute to enhance students' skills of deploying Word and helped students pass the examination for professional certification.

Results from Table 4 show that the average grade on Word in the Blended class (89.9556) is higher than that of the Traditional class (81.2040). Blended Learning has a statistically significant and higher effect on students' skills in using application software in comparison with the traditional classroom. That is, vocational students in

Table 5. Comparison of pass rates: Blended vs. traditional

		Classes		Total	χ^2
		Blended	Traditional		p
Passed	n	83	77	160	0.004**
	% within Passed	51.9%	48.1%	100.0%	
	% within Groups	92.2%	77.0%	84.2%	
	% of Total	43.7%	40.5%	84.2%	
Failed	n	7	23	30	
	% within Failed	23.3%	76.7%	100.0%	
	% within Groups	7.8%	23.0%	15.8%	
	% of Total	3.7%	12.1%	15.8%	
Total	Count	90	100	190	

Note: *$p < 0.05$, **$p < 0.01$, ***$p < 0.001$

Table 6. One-way ANOVA: Grades

Dependent Variable		(I) Group	(J) Group	Mean Difference (I-J)	SE	p
Grades	Scheffe	1	2	4.81548	4.23062	0.730
			3	5.72789	4.21043	0.605
			4	16.69244**	4.17215	0.002
		2	1	-4.81548	4.23062	0.730
			3	0.91241	4.06626	0.997
			4	11.87696*	4.02662	0.036
		3	1	-5.72789	4.21043	0.605
			2	-0.91241	4.06626	0.997
			4	10.96455	4.00539	0.061
		4	1	-16.69244**	4.17215	0.002
			2	-11.87696*	4.02662	0.036
			3	-10.96455	4.00539	0.061

Note: *$p < 0.05$, **$p < 0.01$, ***$p < 0.001$

the blended learning environment may have a better performance in applying application software.

It is also shown in Table 5 that the pass rate of the Blended class (92.2%) was higher than that of the Traditional class (77.0%). Among the failing students, only 23.3% came from the Blended class, while 76.7% came from the Traditional class. There are significant differences of the pass rate among the experimental groups. Thus, this testing reaffirmed that students in the blended learning environments could have better learning performance in applying application software.

Finally, data from Table 6 and Table 7 shows that combination of interventions of BL and SRL with feedback results in the highest average grade and pass rate among the four groups. In Table 6, students' skills of using application software in C1 are significantly higher than C4, and also higher than C2 and C3, though insignificantly so. In Table 7, the difference of the pass rate among the four groups was statistically significant. Therefore, we may conclude that the effects of intervention of web-mediated BL and SRL on students' skills in using application software may

be positive, and higher than those without intervention.

As shown in Table 8, the main effects of BL and SRL are significant (F = 9.131, $p < 0.05$ and F = 7.336, $p < 0.05$, respectively). However, the interaction effect between BL and SRL with feedback failed to reach statistical levels of significance (F=1.114, $p > 0.05$). That is, BL and SRL did not affect each other in this experiment.

DISCUSSION

E-learning is gaining momentum in university and corporate settings as an alternative and supplementary solution to learning (Panagiotis, 2008). However, it is a big challenge for teachers to help college students learn in an online course in an environment that is full of Internet distractions. Moreover, due to the conservative policy of e-learning in Taiwan, teachers can only deliver a limited amount of classes online during each semester. So, we believe that our research makes some contributions to the theory and practice of e-learning in three different ways, particularly

Table 7. Comparison of pass rates

		Groups				Total	χ^2
		C1	C2	C3	C4		*p*
Passed	n	39	44	43	34	160	0.001**
	% within Passed	24.4%	27.5%	26.9%	21.3%	100.0%	
	% within Groups	92.9%	91.7%	87.8%	66.7%	84.2%	
	% of Total	20.5%	23.2%	22.6%	17.9%	84.2%	
Failed	n	3	4	6	17	30	
	% within Failed	10.0%	13.3%	20.0%	56.7%	100.0%	
	% within Groups	7.1%	8.3%	12.2%	33.3%	15.8%	
	% of Total	1.6%	2.1%	3.2%	8.9%	15.8%	
Total	Count	42	48	49	51	190	

Note: *$p < 0.05$, **$p < 0.01$, ***$p < 0.001$

Table 8. The effects of BL, SRL, and their interaction effect

Source	SS	*df*	MS	F	*p*
BL	3660.938	1	3660.938	9.131	0.003**
SRL	2941.323	1	2941.323	7.336	0.007**
BL * SRL	446.628	1	446.628	1.114	0.293

Note: *$p < 0.05$, **$p < 0.01$, ***$p < 0.001$

for those teachers in similar contexts. First, our research contributes to the existing literature by specifying how teachers can encourage students to regulate their own learning with the support of feedback from teachers and the teaching website in a web-mediated learning environment. Second, our study also illustrates how to design and arrange online classes to help students with low self-regulatory skills to learn in blended courses. Third, this study is one of the early attempts to investigate the learning effect of the simultaneous combination of BL and web-mediated SRL with feedback. We tested three research questions rigorously among four experimental groups.

The Effects of Web-Mediated SRL with Feedback

With respect to our first research question, the treatment of web-mediated SRL with feedback was found to play a positive role in enhancing students' computing skills. As the data in Table 2 shows, there was a very significant difference between groups of SRL with Feedback and SRL without Feedback in scores on the Word certification examination ($p = 0.009$). More, students in the SRL with Feedback group had a significantly higher pass rate on professional certification than those of SRL without Feedback group (Pearson $\chi^2 = 0.033$, see Table 3). This result is similar to Shen *et al.*'s (2007a) study asserting that the intervention of web-mediated SRL could help students regulate their learning and improve their computing skills. In the present study, the authors demonstrated further the effects of SRL with feedback on developing students' computing skills.

SRL strategies could be applied to prepare students for the rigors of learning at a distance and increase the probability of retention and success (Chang, 2005). In addition, the feedback may inform students of how their learning performances are reviewed and judged by their teachers. With the mechanism of submitting the schoolwork on time, the feedback information helps students correct or refine their learning based on teacher's feedback of their performances. Thus, students may have higher potential for improving computing skills and passing the examination for a certificate. Therefore, it is suggested that teachers should adopt technologies such as these to help students develop self-regulatory skills, provide feedback, and to notify students of learning and assignments in a web-mediated learning environment.

The Effects of Blended Learning

The data shown in Table 4 also support that the resulting difference on students' Word skills between Blended and Traditional classes was statistically significant ($p = 0.004$). In addition, students in the Blended class had a significantly higher pass rate on professional certification that those in the Traditional class (Pearson $\chi^2 = 0.004$, see Table 5). In the Blended class, the teacher recorded every session of his lecture whether in the classroom or through the Internet and later uploaded the recordings to the course website. From the log records, it is found that students logged in and re-listened to the course content before tests and quizzes. The recorded files and BL were found to play positive roles in helping students learn application software. This result is similar to Yushau's (2006) study that shows the positive effect of blended e-learning on students' attitude toward computing and mathematics.

It is currently not permitted and thus inapplicable to provide pure online courses to undergraduates in Taiwan. Moreover, the vocational students in Taiwan tend to have lower rates of class attendance. However, teachers could adopt technologies and teaching websites to help students achieve better learning performance. For example, the blended course and recorded content provide the flexibility and opportunity for students to at-

tend class, review the course content, and practice what they learned. The application of recording technologies and software could be effective and helpful to develop students' computing skills, particularly for those courses targeted on helping students earn professional certifications.

The Effects of Combination of Blended Learning and Web-Mediated SRL with Feedback

With respect to the effects of the combination of BL and SRL with feedback, we found preliminary support from the results in Table 6. That is, the combined intervention of BL and SRL with feedback may enhance students' computing skills. The effects were positive and higher than those who did not receive BL or/and SRL with feedback, although the difference between C1 and C2 and the difference between C1 and C3 were not statistically significant. In addition, the differences among the pass rates of the four groups were statistically significant (Pearson $\chi^2 = 0.001$, see Table 7). These results were similar to those that appear in Lynch and Dembo's (2004), Nicol and Macfarlane-Dick's (2006), and Shen *et al.*'s (2007b) studies. Therefore, it is suggested that teachers could apply BL and SRL with feedback simultaneously rather than singly to encourage students' learning.

Most students in Taiwan have gotten used to a spoon-feeding teaching method. Students in this learning environment usually lack the ability of independent thinking and the skills of managing their time and regulating their learning. Students in Taiwan have to take an entrance examination before they enter universities or vocational colleges. Students with higher grades usually choose and enter the national or traditional universities, while those with relatively poor grades are mostly admitted to the poorer performing vocational colleges. Thus, most students in these private vocational schools are those with a history of low academic achievement (Lee, Shen, & Tsai, 2008). In this regard, when implementing e-learning or blended learning in this specific context, teachers should first develop students' skills of self-regulation, and also provide feedback to refine students' learning.

Furthermore, the blended course and recording technologies could provide more flexibility and opportunities than in traditional classes for students learning. These innovative educational technologies could contribute to students' learning. Therefore, it is suggested that teachers could adopt BL and Web-mediated SRL with feedback simultaneously to provide multiple learning channels, help students develop regular learning habits, and further improve their learning effectiveness.

Limitations

Although this research results show positive effects of improving students' computing skills, there are some limitations in drawing firm conclusions due to threats to the validity of the quasi-experimental design. A major problem with this design might be that the groups were not be necessarily the same before any treatment took place, and might differ in important ways that influenced their learning effects (Lee, Shen, & Tsai, 2008). In this regard, the students were pretested in the first week of the semester. The authors assessed the difference in students' computing skills among the four groups in the beginning of the study. The difference in students' computing skills in the pretest was not statistically significant. Thus, the initial differences as alternative explanations for the differences of students' learning effects could be ruled out (Gribbons & Herman, 1997).

However, some problems resulting from students in the comparison group being incidentally exposed to the treatment condition, having more enthusiastic teaching, being more motivated than students in the other group, etc. (Gribbons & Herman, 1997), might influence the effects of online learning. Moreover, all the students in the treatment groups in this study understood that they were participating in an experiment involving web-mediated teaching methods. In this regard, one should be aware of the hawthorn effect and contextual factors that may threaten the validity of claims made by this study.

Finally, as the data from Table 2 and Table 4 shows, students in the group without feedback or the traditional group had larger standard deviation (SD) than those received innovative teaching methods. It means that students in the group without feedback or the traditional group had heterogeneous learning performance in the same group. Exploration in future studies of students' heterogeneous learning performance in the online or blended learning environments would complement our understanding of these effects of web-enabled pedagogies, and further improve the design of innovative teaching methods.

CONCLUSION

In places where it is neither applicable nor permitted to provide pure online courses to students, teachers have to adopt blended learning in their online courses. Moreover, it is not immediately clear how to concentrate students' attention, improve their learning, and develop their regular learning behavior in a web-based environment without the teacher's on-the-spot monitoring. To improve our understanding of how to solve these tough issues, we first redesigned our course and devised practicable treatments for both teachers and students. Furthermore, we developed and then rigorously tested a set of hypotheses via a 2 (SRL with Feedback vs. SRL without Feedback) × 2 (Blended vs. Traditional) factorial pretest-posttest experimental design. The results showed that students in the group of BL and SRL with Feedback had better skills and higher pass rate of certification than those who did not receive BL or/and SRL with feedback. This study may provide a specific reference in the context of vocational education addressing how to enhance students' computing skills, pass an examination for professional certification, and help students regulate their learning in a blended environment via Web-mediated SRL with feedback.

REFERENCES

Alonso, F., López, G., Manrique, D., & Viñes, J. M. (2005). An instructional model for web-based e-learning education with a blended learning process approach. *British Journal of Educational Technology, 36*(2), 217–235. doi:10.1111/j.1467-8535.2005.00454.x

Aspden, L., & Helm, P. (2004). Making the connection in a blended learning environment. *Educational Media International, 41*(3), 245–252. doi:10.1080/09523980410001680851

Azevedo, R., & Cromley, J. G. (2004). Does training on self-regulated learning facilitate students' learning with hypermedia? *Journal of Educational Psychology, 96*(3), 523–535. doi:10.1037/0022-0663.96.3.523

Azevedo, R., Cromley, J. G., & Seibert, D. (2004). Does adaptive scaffolding facilitate students' ability to regulate their learning with hypermedia? *Contemporary Educational Psychology, 29*(3), 344–370. doi:10.1016/j.cedpsych.2003.09.002

Azevedo, R., Cromley, J. G., Winters, F. I., Moos, D. C., & Greene, J. A. (2005). Adaptive human scaffolding facilitates adolescents' self-regulated learning with hypermedia. *Instructional Science, 33*(5-6), 367–379. doi:10.1007/s11251-005-1272-9

Azevedo, R., Moos, D. C., Greene, J. A., Winters, F. I., & Cromley, J. C. (2008). Why is externally-regulated learning more effective than self-regulated learning with hypermedia? *Educational Technology Research and Development, 56*(1), 45–72. doi:10.1007/s11423-007-9067-0

Bielaczyc, K., Pirolli, P., & Brown, A. (1995). Training in self-explanation and self-regulation strategies: investigating the effects of knowledge acquisition activities on problem solving. *Cognition and Instruction, 13*(2), 221–252. doi:10.1207/s1532690xci1302_3

Blended Learning Unit. (2006). *BLU Home Page.* Retrieved October 7, 2008 from http://perseus.herts.ac.uk/uhinfo/info/blu/blu/blu_home.cfm.

Bottino, R. M., & Robotti, E. (2007). Transforming classroom teaching & learning through technology: Analysis of a case study. *Educational Technology & Society, 10*(4), 174–186.

Boyle, T., Bradley, C., Chalk, P., Jones, R., & Pickard, P. (2003). Using blended learning to improve student success rates in learning to program. *Learning, Media and Technology, 28*(2 & 3), 165–178.

Butler, D., & Winne, P. (1995). Feedback and self-regulated learning: a theoretical synthesis. *Review of Educational Research, 65*(3), 245–281.

Cennamo, K. S., Ross, J. D., & Rogers, C. S. (2002). Evolution of a web-enhanced course: Incorporating strategies for self-regulation. *EDUCAUSE Quarterly, 25*(1), 28–33.

Chang, M. M. (2005). Applying self-regulated learning strategies in a web-based instruction - An investigation of motivation perception. *Computer Assisted Language Learning, 18*(3), 217–230. doi:10.1080/09588220500178939

Chen, C. H., & Tien, C. J. (2005). Market Segmentation analysis for taking skill test by students in an institute of technology. Retrieved October 7, 2008 from http://www.voced.edu.au/td/tnc_85.574.

Colis, B., & Moonen, J. (2001) *Flexible Learning in a Digital World: Experiences and expectations.* Kogan-Page, London.

Dabbagh, N., & Kitsantas, K. (2005). Using Web-based pedagogical tools as scaffolds for self-regulated learning. *Instructional Science, 33*(5–6), 513–540. doi:10.1007/s11251-005-1278-3

Derntl, M., & Motschnig-Pitrik, R. (2005). The role of structure, patterns, and people in blended learning. *The Internet and Higher Education, 8,* 111–130. doi:10.1016/j.iheduc.2005.03.002

Dowling, C., Godfrey, J. M., & Gyles, N. (2003). Do hybrid flexible delivery teaching methods improve accounting student learning outcomes? *Accounting Education: An International Journal, 12*(4), 373–391. doi:10.1080/0963928032000154512

Ertmer, P. A., Newby, T. J., & MacDougall, M. (1996). Students' approaches to learning from case-based instruction: The role of reflective self-regulation. *American Educational Research Journal, 33*(3), 719–752.

Garrison, R. R., & Kanuka, H. (2004). Blended learning: Uncovering its transformative potential in higher education. *The Internet and Higher Education, 7*(2), 95–105. doi:10.1016/j.iheduc.2004.02.001

Gribbons, B., & Herman, J. (1997) "True and quasi-experimental designs. Practical Assessment", *Research & Evaluation, 5*(14), Retrieved February 12, 2009 from http://PAREonline.net/getvn.asp?v=5&n=14.

Ivanic, R., Clark, R., & Rimmershaw, R. (2000). What am I supposed to make of this? The messages conveyed to students by tutors' written comments. In M.R. Lea & B. Stierer (Eds.), *Student Writing in Higher Education: New Contexts* (pp. 47-65). Buckingham: SHRE/Open University Press.

Järvelä, S., Näykki, P., Laru, J., & Luokkanen, T. (2007). Structuring and regulating collaborative learning in higher education with wireless networks and mobile tools. *Educational Technology & Society, 10*(4), 71–79.

Lee, T. H., Shen, P. D., & Tsai, C. W. (2008). Applying web-enabled problem-based learning and self-regulated learning to add value to computing education in Taiwan's vocational schools. *Educational Technology and Society, 11*(3), 13–25.

Li, K. C., Tsai, Y. T., & Tsai, C. K. (2008). Toward development of distance learning environment in the grid. *International Journal of Distance Education Technologies, 6*(3), 45–57.

Lindner, R. W., & Harris, B. (1993). Teaching self-regulated learning strategies. *Proceedings of selected research and development presentations at the annual conference of the Association for Educational Communications and Technology,* (pp. 641-654).

Liu, C. C., & Tsai, C. C. (2008). An analysis of peer interaction patterns as discoursed by on-line small group problem-solving activity. *Computers & Education, 50*(3), 627–639. doi:10.1016/j.compedu.2006.07.002

Löfström, E., & Nevgi, A. (2007). From strategic planning to meaningful learning: diverse perspectives on the development of web-based teaching and learning in higher education. *British Journal of Educational Technology, 38*(2), 312–324. doi:10.1111/j.1467-8535.2006.00625.x

Lynch, R., & Dembo, M. (2004). The relationship between self-regulation and online learning in a blended learning context, *International Review of Research in Open and Distance Learning, 5*(2). Retrieved October 7, 2008 from http://www.irrodl.org/index.php/irrodl/article/view/189/799.

Marino, T. A. (2000). Learning online: A view from both sides. *The National Teaching & Learning Forum, 9*(4), 4–6.

Nicol, D. J., & Macfarlane-Dick, D. (2006). Formative assessment and self-regulated learning: A model and seven principles of good feedback practice. *Studies in Higher Education, 31*(2), 199–216. doi:10.1080/03075070600572090

Niemi, H., Nevgi, A., & Virtanen, P. (2003). Towards self-regulation in Web-based learning. *Journal of Educational Media, 28*(1), 49–71. doi:10.1080/1358165032000156437

Panagiotis, Z. (2008). Cross-cultural differences in perceptions of e-learning usability: An empirical investigation. *International Journal of Technology and Human Interaction, 4*(3), 1–26.

Pereira, J. A., Pleguezuelos, E., Merí, A., Molina-Ros, A., Molina-Tomás, M. C., & Masdeu, C. (2007). Effectiveness of using blended learning strategies for teaching and learning human anatomy. *Medical Education, 41*(2), 189–195. doi:10.1111/j.1365-2929.2006.02672.x

Pintrich, P. R. (1995). *Understanding Self-regulated Learning*. San Francisco: Jossey-Bass.

Reyero, M., & Tourón, J. (2003). The development of talent: Acceleration as an educational strategy. Netbiblo, A Coruña.

Roces, C., & González Torres, M. C. (1998). Ability to self-regulate learning. In J. A. González Pienda & J. C. Núñez (Eds.), *Dificultadesde aprendizaje escolar* (pp. 239-259). Madrid: Pirámide/Psicología.

Ross, J. D. (1999). *Regulating hypermedia: Self-regulation learning strategies in a hypermedia environment*. Va: Virginia Polytechnic Institute and State University.

Rovai, A. P., & Jordan, H. M. (2004). Blended learning and sense of community: A comparative analysis with traditional and fully online graduate courses. *International Review of Research in Open and Distance Learning, 5*(2). Retrieved from October 7, 2008 http://www.irrodl.org/index.php/irrodl/article/view/192/274.

Shen, P. D., Lee, T. H., & Tsai, C. W. (2007a). Applying Web-enabled problem-based learning and self-regulated learning to enhance computing skills of Taiwan's vocational students: A quasi-experimental study of a short-term module. *Electronic Journal of e-Learning, 5*(2), 147-156.

Shen, P. D., Lee, T. H., & Tsai, C. W. (2007b). Facilitating students to pass certificate tests via blended e-learning with self-regulated learning: A quasi-experimental approach, *WSEAS Proceedings on Multimedia, Internet & Video Technologies*, Beijing, China.

Shen, P. D., Lee, T. H., Tsai, C. W., & Ting, C. J. (2008). Exploring the effects of Web-enabled problem-based learning and self-regulated learning on vocational students' involvement in learning. *European Journal of Open, Distance and E-Learning,* 2008(1). Retrieved October 7, 2008 from http://www.eurodl.org/materials/contrib/2008/Shen_Lee_Tsai_Ting.htm.

Singh, H. (2003). Building effective blended learning programs. *Educational Technology, 43*(6), 51–54.

Tsang-Hsiung Lee has a PhD degree in the MIS area at the Katz Graduate School of Business at the University of Pittsburgh. His primary interest areas are e-learning, organizational innovations of MIS, qualitative research and case study method. Readers can contact him by email: design2learn@gmail.com

Weinstein, C. (1989). Teacher education students' preconceptions of teaching. *Journal of Teacher Education, 40*(2), 53–60. doi:10.1177/002248718904000210

Yang, S. C., & Tung, C. J. (2007). Comparison of Internet addicts and non-addicts in taiwanese high school. *Computers in Human Behavior, 23*(1), 79–96. doi:10.1016/j.chb.2004.03.037

Yukselturk, E., & Bulut, S. (2007). Predictors for student success in an online course. *Educational Technology & Society, 10*(2), 71–83.

Yushau, B. (2006). The effects of blended e-learning on mathematics and computer attitudes in pre-calculus algebra. *The Montana Math Enthusiast, 3*(2), 176–183.

Zimmerman, B. J. (1990). Self-regulated learning and academic achievement: An overview. *Educational Psychologist, 25*(1), 3–17. doi:10.1207/s15326985ep2501_2

Zimmerman, B. J. (1998). Developing self-regulation cycles of academic regulation: An analysis of exemplary instructional model. In D.H. Schunk & B.J. Zimmerman (Eds.), *Self-regulated learning: From teaching to self-reflective practice* (pp. 1-19). New York: Guilford.

Zimmerman, B. J., Bonner, S., & Kovach, R. (1996). *Developing self-regulated learners: Beyond achievement to self-efficacy.* Washington, DC: American Psychological Association.

Zimmerman, B. J., & Martinez-Pons, M. (1986). Development of a structured interview for assessing student use of self-regulated learning strategies. *American Educational Research Journal, 23*(4), 614–628.

Zimmerman, B. J., & Schunk, D. H. (1989). *Self-regulated learning and academic achievement: Theory, research, and practice.* New York: Springer-Veriag.

Zimmerman, B. J., & Schunk, D. H. (2001). *Self-regulated learning and academic achievement: Theoretical perspectives.* NJ: Lawrence Erlbaum Associates.

This work was previously published in International Journal of Technology and Human Interaction, Volume 6, Issue 1, edited by Anabela Mesquita & Chia-Wen Tsai, pp. 15-32, copyright 2010 by IGI Publishing (an imprint of IGI Global).

Chapter 11
Working Together to Improve Usability:
Exploring Challenges and Successful Practices

Mie Nørgaard
University of Copenhagen, Denmark

Kasper Hornbæk
University of Copenhagen, Denmark

ABSTRACT

In theory, usability work is an important and well-integrated activity in developing software. In practice, collaboration on improving usability is ridden with challenges relating to conflicting professional goals, tight project schedules, and unclear usability findings. The authors study those challenges through 16 interviews with software developers, usability experts, and project managers. Four themes that are key challenges to successful interaction between stakeholders are identified: poor timing when delivering usability results, results lacking relevance, little respect for other disciplines, and difficulties sharing important information. The authors review practices that have successfully addressed these challenges and discuss their observations as encompassing multiple perspectives and as a collaborative cross-professional learning process.

INTRODUCTION

Through their work, usability professionals aim to improve the usability of computer systems. To do this, they seek to inform and influence design decisions, for instance by conducting usability evaluations of systems, by instigating design changes through persuasive reports, and by strengthening

the collaboration with colleagues who also have a stake in designing and implementing the systems.

Accordingly, increasing the impact of usability work on system design and implementation can be approached in several ways. Such ways include attempts to improve the quality of usability evaluation methods by trying to identify which method works best in certain contexts (e.g., Karat, Campbell, & Fiegel, 1992), recommending ways of combining methods (e.g., Uldall-Espersen,

DOI: 10.4018/978-1-61350-465-9.ch011

Frøkjær, & Hornbæk, 2007), or investigating how to present the results of evaluations so as to facilitate changes to the design (e.g., Hvannberg, Law, & Larusdottir, 2007). Because usability is closely related to the work of for example project managers and developers, one may also seek to improve the collaboration between usability experts and other stakeholders (e.g., Bødker & Buur, 2002; Gulliksen, Boivie, & Göransson, 2006).

The motivation for this paper is that while the literature is strong on most points above, little research concerns the last point, in particular the practical challenges of how to collaborate to improve usability. The aim of this paper is to explore areas that impede collaboration on usability-related issues, provide examples of how practitioners have successfully dealt with this and thus inspire anyone who are interested in working on improving collaboration in the cross-professional realm of usability work. To do so, we conduct an analysis of 16 interviews with 20 stakeholders, and, based on the perspective of the participants, we seek to explore the following questions:

a.   What do key stakeholders – developers, usability experts, and project managers – consider their main challenges when they cooperate on improving usability?

b.   Which successful practices do stakeholders follow to address these challenges to usability work?

Understanding these questions better may help us improve the impact of usability work, for instance by suggesting how to conduct usability work that lessens challenges amongst stakeholders. In relation to research in usability evaluation, the study touches upon themes that could help researchers think about collaboration in new ways. Our study seeks to extend the existing literature by highlighting cross-professional relationships as a new perspective on usability work and to draw attention to the difficult balance between

job role and project priority. Further, though the results are perhaps not controversial or entirely new, we seek to present them from other views than that of the usability practitioner, something we think is new.

RELATED WORK

Part of the literature on strengthening the impact of usability work focuses on usability evaluation methods (UEMs) (Chattratichart & Brodie, 2004; Hertzum & Jacobsen, 2003; Hvannberg, Law, & Larusdottir, 2007; Law & Hvannberg, 2004) or on how evaluation results are reported (American National Standards Institute, 2001; Cockton, Woolrych, & Hindmarch, 2004; Dumas & Redish, 1993; Mills, 1987; Redish, Bias, Bailey, Molich, Dumas, & Spool, 2002; Rubin, 1994). Other contributions look into the context of usability work (Gulliksen, Boivie, & Göransson, 2006; Gulliksen, Boivie, Persson, & Hektor, 2004; Iivari, 2006; Uldall-Espersen, Frøkjær, & Hornbæk, 2007) or relate the collaboration and communication among stakeholders to the development process (Bennet & Karat, 1994; Bødker & Buur, 2002; Bødker, Krogh & Petersen, 2001; Hornbæk & Frøkjær, 2005; Madsen & Petersen, 1999; Uldall-Espersen & Frøkjær, 2007). This paper follows the latter trail and views usability work primarily as an organisational activity, in particular as the collaboration between three key job roles (see Figure 1).

Gulliksen et al. (2006) investigated the work context for usability professionals and suggested that the impact of usability work does not solely depend on usability evaluation methods, but also on support from project management and involvement of stakeholders. Most frequently, involvement of stakeholders in systems development has meant user involvement. For many years user involvement has attracted attention as a means for improving the quality of systems (Boland, 1978; Ives & Olson, 1984; King & Rodriguez,

Figure 1. To the left the main activities for a typical developer, usability expert and project manager are described. To the right, the model shows the challenges that these stakeholders face when working together.

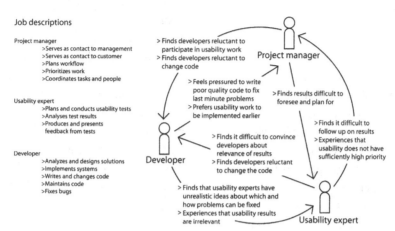

1981; Robey & Farrow, 1982). As an example, work on participatory design discusses how to strengthen HCI work by involving users in the design process, see for example Greenbaum & Kyng, 1991; Ehn, 1992; and Ehn & Sjögren, 1991). In contrast, the idea of involving other stakeholders, such as developers or project managers in usability evaluation has received less attention. In fact, stakeholder involvement in usability work has mainly been limited to letting developers watch users interact with the system (see for example Coble, Karat, & Kahn, 1997; Dumas, 1989; Kennedy, 1989; Mills, 1987; Nayak, Mrazek, & Smith, 1995; Redish, Bias, Bailey, Molich, Dumas, & Spool, 2002; Schell, 1986).

Practical insights and case stories, such as those presented in Johnson and Johnson (1990), La Fasto and Larson (2002) and Winer and Ray (1994) improve our understanding of how stakeholders collaborate and communicate to improve usability of systems is. For instance, Bennet and Karat (1994) described experiences with using collaborative design meetings to support collaboration and communication in HCI. However, they also pointed to major discrepancies between good intentions for effective team work and what is actu-

ally practised in the industry. They also identified a gap between intentions about interdisciplinary collaboration and actual work practices as a key challenge for HCI (Bennet & Karat, 1994).

Following the thoughts of Bennet and Karat, we hypothesize that the impact of usability work can be improved by understanding successful usability work as a collaborative process involving different stakeholders such as developers, usability experts, and project managers. This study explores how stakeholders work with and use results from usability evaluations. It does so to identify issues among different groups of professionals, here called cross-professional relationships, which may impede usability and evaluation, work. This choice of focus does not mean that we disregard the influence of work such as studies of user experience or collective design efforts on the design and usability of a product. Also, we recognise that the quality of usability evaluation methods, the skill with which they are used, and the format in which results of evaluations are reported to stakeholders are also determinants of how well usability work impacts the development process. Nevertheless, we find that the focus on cross-professional relationships is relevant to understanding the context in which evaluation results are made and used by stakeholders who are both professionals and individuals.

METHOD

Our approach to addressing the two research questions is to conduct and analyze interviews to examine key stakeholders' views on usability work. We use interviews because most work on usability professionals is based on questionnaires (Rosenbaum, Rohn, & Humburg, 2000; Gulliksen, Boivie, Persson, & Hektor, 2004, but see Iivari, 2006; Gulliksen, Boivie & Göransson, 2006) for exceptions. Interviews should further allow for richer descriptions of challenges and successful practices and thus support our belief that human relationships are unique and complex and are best studied through the lenses of social science. We choose stakeholders working as developers, usability experts, and project managers from a variety of different companies to get a broad perspective on usability work and experiences from different corners of the profession. Also, existing literature on usability work predominantly concerns the perspectives of the user (Bødker & Buur, 2002) and the usability professional (Gulliksen, Boivie, Persson, & Hektor, 2004); it rarely concerns developers or project managers, except as described through the perspective of the usability professional. As our aim is to collect rich data that will inspire us to think about cross-professional collaboration in new ways and not to test specific theories or hypotheses, our methodological approach is inspired by grounded theory (Strauss & Corbin, 1998).

Participants

Between November 2006 and March 2007 we conducted a total of 16 interviews, each lasting about 1½ hours, with 20 people from the Danish industry. Some interviews included two professionals (see Table 1 for details). Five participants were iden-

tified among members of a Danish HCI Special Interest Group, the rest were recommended to us by other participants. Participants had between 2 and 20 years of professional experience. They comprised 9 usability practitioners, who conduct usability tests and feed the results into the development process, 6 developers, who develop systems and use usability feedback on these, and 5 project managers, who manage system development projects and use usability feedback on systems as part of their job. However, for some participants job roles were not that uniform. Some project managers, for example, had a background in development and some developers also conducted usability work. When referring to participants' job roles, we refer to the predominant job role. For more details on the participants, see Table 1.

Data Collection and Analysis

Data collection and analysis were done in two phases: (a) an exploratory phase with eight interviews and (b) a focusing phase with eight interviews. While the interview protocol was fairly open, we did have one predefined focus on experienced challenges and successes. We also asked participants to describe any useful practices they had encountered when working with usability and which part of the work they found most difficult. In each phase, data collection and analyses were interwoven. This was done to explore multiple viewpoints on challenges and successful practices, and to develop and follow up on these in subsequent interviews. Next, we explain the two phases.

In phase (a), eight semi-structured interviews were conducted to investigate the issues of work challenges and successful practices. To better understand which parts of their jobs participants found challenging, we asked them to describe and exemplify what they found to be particularly difficult in their work. To better understand which tools or techniques participants used to address such work challenges, we prompted for elaborate

Table 1. An overview of the participants in the study including data on companies, products and job roles. Four of the 16 interviews included two participants fulfilling the same role. These are marked with the number two in the participants' column. The letters D, U and P in the participants' column refer to: Developer, Usability expert and Project manager.

Company	Employees		Participants			Company's organizational relation to the usability expert	Type of system
	Denmark	International	D	U	P		
1	800	0		1	1	In house	Banking
2	150	500		1		In house	Games
3	300	0			2	In house	Learning
4	40	0	1	2		In house	e-Government
5	16	0		1		In house and consultancy	External customers/ own development
6	8,500	0	1			In house and consultancy	Booking
7	120	0			1	Consultancy	Homepage and ERP system
8	5	0		2		Consultancy	External customers
9	2,800	0			1	In house	e-Government
10	350	61,000	2			In house	Off-the shelf and tailored systems
11	8	0		1		Consultancy	External customers
12	220	250	1			In house	Security
13	1,500	59,000			1	In house	Mobile interfaces
14	350	15,000	1			In house	e-Government and off-the-shelf

examples of successful work procedures, events, or techniques they had used or experienced. This resulted in rich anecdotal data about the challenges and successes of usability work.

The eight interviews were audio-recorded and transcribed. The interviews were compared in order to categorize findings. Eleven categories, covering topics such as methods, job experience, view on usability, and work challenges were identified this way (see Table 2). Each category was further divided into sub-categories by repeating the coding procedure. Finally, the category 'work challenges' was identified as the core category. Work challenges covered specific challenges for usability work and successful practices that had been used to address them. To get finer-grained data about work challenges, the sub-categories were investigated further in eight subsequent interviews (phase (b)). These steps correspond with grounded theory's terms: open coding, axial coding and selective coding (Strauss & Corbin, 1998).

In phase (b), we conducted and transcribed the last eight interviews, and coded these according to the eleven sub-categories that emerged in phase (a). Coded segments would contain issues such as a description of a work procedure, a comment on a certain type of challenge, or a reference to techniques used to facilitate cooperation in a team. This procedure also builds on grounded theory (Strauss & Corbin, 1998) and follows Chi's proposal for how to analyze verbal protocols (Chi, 1997). Accordingly, the coding scheme is not developed prior to the interviews but after; already conducted interviews serve as inspiration and input to subsequent interviews.

Table 2. The original 11 categories indentified in the analysis. The category 'Challenges' were later divided into four sub-categories discussed in this paper.

Categories	Description
Responsibility	Statements about the responsibility for implementing usability results in the development process and for the quality of the system/product.
Definition	Statements about how usability is defined and understood
Qualification	Statements about how usability work is qualified?
Usability practice	Statements about the work process and usability practice (incl. UEMs)
Challenges	*Statements about challenges for working together to create/improve a system*
Decision-making	Issues related to decision-making and decision power
Customers	Issues related to customers, e.g. special concerns and behaviours
Follow-up	Statements about how/if feedback from evaluations is followed up upon
Strategy	Descriptions of strategic and political roles for usability work and strategic concerns related to the conducting of usability work.
Feedback	Statements about how usability results is communicated to stakeholders
Reluctance	Mentioning of reluctance (or the contrary) to take in usability results, including statements related to how stakeholders are convinced about usability's relevance.

Table 3. The four challenges described in this paper. Each subcategory concern both challenges and successful practices related to the main theme. The N-column refers to the number of interviews in which a sub-category was found. The letters D, U, and P describe interviews with developers (D), usability experts (U), and project managers (P).

Challenge	Examples	N		
		D	U	P
Timing	Poor timing of usability work. Pressure to cut corners	4	4	3
Relevance	Feedback from tests lacks relevance	5	6	5
Respect	Low professional ethos. Disrespect for others' job roles and professional goals	3	6	4
Communication	Difficulty communicating usability results or understanding the domain	5	3	3

FINDINGS

In the following, we describe four key challenges that complicate cross-professional work relations among developers, usability experts, and project managers. Important challenges for a cross-professional relationship concern poor timing of usability work, usability results lacking relevance, colleagues showing disrespect for others professional goals, and difficulties related to sharing and getting relevant information (see Table 3). While these are not the only challenges identified in this study they are reported to be the most frequent and severe. Next, we present these challenges in terms of relationships between the three job roles (Figure 1). Then, we present a number of successful practices identified in the study which address the key challenges. Quotes from interviews are identified with a reference to the number of the company and the letters D/U/P depending on the interviewee's job role, for example [1P] when quoting the interview with the project manager from company 1 (Table 1).

THE DEVELOPER-USABILITY EXPERT RELATIONSHIP

The Developers' Point of View

Four developers report that feedback from usability studies is often useless due to bad timing. When confronted with problems that they do not have time to fix, developers get discouraged and respond with a feeling of hostility toward usability work. One developer wonders about the usability experts' feedback practice:

Why don't they just stop giving feedback when the software has been made (...) It is like if you are building a house and someone suddenly says: "Sorry, I would like you to put in a basement also". Well, are we supposed to tear the whole house down then? Close to a deadline developers do not have time to do anything but move a few things around. And it is not responsible to change software 14 days before release, anyway. [4D]

Four of the developers criticise the results of usability work for often being irrelevant since it does not consider, for instance, how the system is built or how products are sold. To exemplify, one developer explains: 'Every time he [the usability expert] presented a nice suggestion, we could tear it apart because it simply could not work technically. Not because of the system, but because of how our product is sold' [6D]. Another developer elaborates on the issue of relevant feedback:

When someone has created a piece of software then he needs intelligent feedback and not: "I don't really know what the system is doing". Developers usually take the time to learn how things work, and it is hard to respect people who don't bother. [4D]

Three developers [4D, 12D, 14D] report that having colleagues who do not fully understand how they work, or what professional goals de-

velopers have, is a major challenge for working with usability. They describe how usability experts hold unrealistic ideas about what developers can change within a system at a certain point during the development. For instance, some usability requirements cannot be fulfilled because they conflict with the choice of platform or because they interfere with other design decisions that the developer cannot change.

The data suggest that sometimes developers' reluctance to accept usability results spring from their view on how usability studies are conducted and results communicated. One developer comments on receiving usability results:

Even though they are not supposed to be a critique of the development work, you tend to defend the choices you have made (...) Especially if they have used some sort of heuristic hocus-pocus – then they might point out problems where the developers respond: "But that is just your personal preference" (...) And then getting a report on 70 pages and 417 problems, while you are already thinking about the next steps of the project because the project manager is on your back – well, it is just not exactly what you need (...) I cannot find the time to read 70 pages. [12D]

More than half of the participants (four usability experts, four developers and three project managers) criticize written reports for being useless because they are too long.

The Usability Experts' Point of View

All six interviews with usability experts show that usability experts are particularly concerned about the persuasive power of feedback. They describe how it can be a difficult task to convince their audience about the relevance and existence of usability problems. Not only are some problems difficult to explain in a clear manner, but all usability experts have experienced how some usability issues are questioned or dismissed by developers. Usability experts also find developers reluctant to change the system's code, a point confirmed by some of the developers. As an example, one usability expert explains: 'It is a problem to convince developers about the relevance and quality of the feedback. I have repeatedly explained that we don't simply ask users what they think – we study how they use the system'. He continues to explain about feeding back results on usability issues:

It seems like a very sensitive process (...) It might have to do with the fact that the developer himself has a professional background or that he has many years of experience on his own, but it seems to be difficult for developers when someone claims that users do not understand their system (...) As a result the developer might end up annoyed or insulted. [2U]

Further, four of six usability experts specifically express that they find some developers difficult to work with, using words like 'artists' and 'prima donnas' to suggest that some developers are unwilling to accept critique of their work.

THE DEVELOPER-PROJECT MANAGER RELATIONSHIP

The Developers' Point of View

Four developers mention how they on occasion experience that project managers do not understand or respect that creating solid code and keeping it up to date are important to developers. One developer explains how he feels pressured to cut corners to quickly solve usability problems. He explains how cutting corners will solve the problem at hand, but also dramatically weakens the code over time:

There is time pressure, right? So you cut corners, take short cuts, and do things you are not proud of professionally. But you have to in order to meet

the deadline. And as a result a usability problem is reported and falls back on you (...) but you do not want to take the blame because you would like to spend a week fixing it, but you cannot. [12D]

Another developer explains a similar situation like this:

They want me to add auto layout to the forms we produce, and I explain "listen, I do not have the XML-code, so I cannot add auto layout" (...) and if I do not convince others about this, a manager, who does not get it, insists that it is done. And that is how really bad software is made. [4D]

Four interviews with developers [4D, 6D, 12D, 14D] show how they prefer usability work to be introduced earlier in the development process to avoid major changes later on. A developer explains:

When you make a new feature, it has some technical aspects and some usability aspects. The problem is that you take care of all the technical aspects first, while it would be much better to do the two things in parallel. But then usability would play another part – because typically it has the critical role of providing "this is good enough, and this could be better"-comments, but if you include usability in the development process usability will have the role of "Okay, what to do about this?". [4D]

The Project Managers' Point of View

Three interviews with project managers describe how they sometimes struggle with convincing developers that participating in work with users will yield important information about the system. 'They do not exactly jump with joy, when they have to participate in a workshop with users', one project manager explains about some of the developers she works with, 'I do not think it is lack of will, but rather that some of them are shy and prefer to sit behind a screen' [3P]. Another project manager suggests reluctance to change the design as a reason why some developers avoid or dismiss usability work:

The developers are really skilled and experienced people (...) and have used many years on building a system to make things work. And then this young UI-designer comes along, and draws up something that does not fit anywhere. And that is really annoying and frustrating for the developers. They are rarely willing to change things. [13P]

THE PROJECT MANAGER-USABILITY EXPERT RELATIONSHIP

The Project Managers' Point of View

Three interviews with project managers [7P, 9P, 13P] suggest that usability evaluation is difficult to integrate in systems development. A major reason is that it is impossible to anticipate the outcome of tests and revise the project plan accordingly. A project manager compares usability evaluation with a bag of unknown fireworks, since it is impossible to predict what will happen once it goes off. He elaborates: 'From my point of view it can be annoying to have to include usability studies because my goal is—as quickly as possible—to reach a decision about what we need to produce' [13P]. Another project manager explains his view of the uncertainties of usability results:

There will always be the risk that the results pull the rug from under the project. Project managers fear usability tests because they might conclude that the system needs to be changed. On the other hand, they may also conclude that the solution is great – a thing we might have suspected but could not know before the test. [9P]

The Usability Experts' Point of View

The relationship between usability and project management differs between companies who use consultancies and those who use in-house usability experts. Consequently, the challenges also differ. Our data show that all usability experts from the consultancy companies find it frustrating to follow up on usability feedback because their job is often considered done when usability results have been reported, or because a usability expert from outside a customer's company has little possibility to actually push decisions through [5U, 8U, 11U]. The usability experts who work in-house report how factors that influence usability, such as timing, decision-making, and planning, could be improved. To exemplify, one usability expert calls for more clarity about who can make decisions for which parts of the system [2U]. Two usability experts report that they find it difficult to include colleagues such as developers in their work, because they do not have the decision-power to book the developers' time in order to, for example, present and discuss usability findings [2U, 1U]. Finally, one usability expert explains how it—despite the project manager's good intentions—is difficult to do usability work early in the process [1U]. Another usability expert experiences how expenses for usability are often cut away so as to lower the price presented to the customers [4U]. These last findings suggest that usability experts feel that usability work is not prioritized as they would like.

We have elaborated on the challenges described in Table 3, and related them to relationships between job roles. The findings suggest that the four challenges are important when describing the work relationships between developers, usability experts and project managers. Next, we present successful practices that relate to these challenges.

SUCCESSFUL PRACTICES

In the following, we present successful practices that participants have used or worked with to address the challenges of poor timing, usability results' lack of relevance, respect for others' job roles, and difficulty sharing important information (see Table 4).

TIMING OF USABILITY EFFORTS

An interview with two project managers showed how they, due to scarce resources, focus all usability attention on interdisciplinary workshops in the beginning of a project. They explain how their company has recently changed from evaluating usability later in the project to involving stakeholders, such as developers, users, customers and usability staff, at the beginning of a design process:

During the last year I have been able to see a difference in our products. Not that usability work was without results before, but it was in other areas and it was not as visible (...) I am simply so happy and content about how the developers have adopted this way of thinking. It is awesome. [3P].

Because developers in the early sketching process inform the usability work with for example domain knowledge, and learn about how usability studies are done, the main benefits of moving usability work to the very beginning of a project seem not only related to timing, but also to respect and relevance.

Two developers, who also work with usability [10D], explain how they, besides initially conducting a workshop to collect and share information, invite customers to meetings during the development process. Here, they discuss and solve design issues on the spot. They describe how they sometimes hold ideas about how to solve a problem before the meeting starts, and sometimes not, but how they try to come up with a solution together with the client, and implement the solution in the prototype real time:

We treated some serious production errors during a meeting once. Even the managing director was present, and I was the technician who during the meeting made changes and updated the system. That procedure leaves a very strong impression and it takes away the argument that "this is going to be very costly" - there is always one who will argue "don't spend any more time on that because it will get too expensive". But if you are practically doing it real time the costs are limited. [10D]

They explain that one of the keys to their success is to insist on the participation from people with both domain knowledge and decision power. Another key is real time prototyping:

Table 4. *Successful practices, and the specific challenges they address. The N-column refers to the number of interviews mentioning a specific successful practice.*

Successful practices	Challenges addressed	N
Make early sketches and prototypes collaboratively	Timing, respect, relevance, communication	2
Share information through meetings and workshops	Respect, relevance, communication	4
Cooperatively agreeing on usability or system goals	Respect, communication	4
Use developers as informants to usability work	Respect, relevance, communication	6
Usability task force	Respect	1
Use new feedback formats such as scenarios	Communication	1
Make feedback as learning experience	Relevance, communication	1

And the fact that we can show changes real time and test different solutions - that is the key. That way you can convince even the most stubborn non-believer. But you need to be prepared so that you can make changes that are immediately visible. Of course there are systems where it cannot be done, but in most cases it can. I have to admit – it was not all changes I made entirely correct, I did some dirty hacks but made it look real. But I knew that it would not take me long to make it work back home, maybe a couple of hours. [10D]

The Relevance of Feedback from Tests

The relevance of feedback touches on issues such as the relevance of findings and recommendations, the persuasiveness or credibility of the descriptions, and how the feeding back of results is timed in relation to the development process. Five usability experts report how they prioritize findings to make feedback more useful. Four of them carry out the prioritization together with developers. One developer confirms the helpfulness of such a prioritized list by explaining how he and his colleagues only use the top-10 list they receive, and simply leave the more thorough report on the shelf, untouched [12D].

Another usability expert explains how he prompts developers for what they would consider appropriate findings at a given stage of development:

I have told them [developers] for example that I will not recommend any new features unless it turns out that the system does not work without them. So, in order not to scare them away I only report things that I know can be corrected. [2U]

To make the feedback more interesting one usability expert explains how he experiments with formats other than the traditional written problem description, and successfully uses scenarios, per-

sonas and illustrations as a way to make results from usability evaluations come more alive: 'It is about presenting [the results from usability evaluations] in a way that makes them an active part of the project instead of some boring report that just lies there on the shelf and collects dust' [11U].

Two project managers [3P] view feedback from a learning perspective, and explain how they successfully make developers experience problematic usability issues by not only letting them observe users, but also analyse and discuss usability matters with them:

Developers are instructed to engage in conversations with users, conduct interviews, and develop low tech prototypes. Some developers experience difficulties talking to users, and receive help and guidance from usability experts (...) this practice of self-experience has proven more effective than simply presenting and discussing usability issues at ordinary meetings. Further, involving developers in the work with users has the side effect that developers get used to thinking in terms of usability continuously and not just when the project plan dictates so. [3P]

Respect and Priority

One project manager [13P] reports how his company has a usability task force based at the main office. This task force travels between local offices. To secure a high general level of usability within all products, the team has decision power over all usability issues in all projects. The project manager explains how the task force reflects positively on the smaller local usability teams because local usability teams see the existence of a high priority task force as a boost for their profession. The existence of the task force also helps raise the professional standards, and local usability experts regard the team a proof that the company takes usability work seriously.

Communication and Sharing of Information

On the subject of sharing information, three interviews with project managers indicate that workshops—understood as meetings where stakeholders collaborate to solve certain tasks—are used to facilitate collaboration between usability experts and developers. Project managers explain how such workshops keep stakeholders up to date with the state of the project, and engage colleagues in other aspects of the work than solely their own. For example:

I think workshops provide developers with a better initial understanding of what it is all about. Because they have not necessarily participated in making the specifications (...) and if they do not know what the system is all about then I think it is really valuable for them to participate in a workshop. [3P]

Another project manager points out that working closely together also boosts team spirit and makes compromising easier: 'I think [collaboration] matters to how willing you are to change and redesign things' [9P].

In two interviews project managers explain how they use project meetings to create common references to usability, and to adjust expectations to the project. One explains how participants at project meetings each create a prioritized list of system goals. Afterwards, the individual lists are cooperatively consolidated into one, which serves as a reference for the rest of the project, helping to end discussions and make decisions:

Initially we had workshops and discussions of what is important. Is it quality? Is it usability? Is it performance? Is it response time? Is it something else? We all prioritized what we found important and we all agreed that usability was pretty high up the list. Everybody attached numbers to these

topics to show what they wish to prioritize and what they want to guide the development. [9P]

This practice of collaboratively prioritising problems helps share information, and gives participants the possibility to understand their colleagues' point of view. Collaboration on prioritization is also described by a usability expert [5U] and a developer [14D]. The latter reports that being able to refer to usability as an official and collaboratively agreed upon top-priority have proven helpful when discussing and negotiating budgets with the top management.

Addressing the themes of both respect and understanding for colleagues' work domains, a project manager describes how he brings the disciplines on a project together and commits everyone to for instance features, prototypes, designs, etc. 'People need to give something back to the project' [7P], he explains, suggesting that when people give something, for instance ideas, to a project, they experience commitment to and responsibility to the project and are better motivated for working together with the other stakeholders. This experience is shared by two other project managers [3P]. However, while getting stakeholders together to overcome the challenge of different job roles is described as helpful, one project manager has a few reservations. He warns that while putting for instance usability experts and developers together in meetings make conflicting interests become clear, such experiences might also end up creating an unproductive or negative work atmosphere [7P].

DISCUSSION

The goal of this study was to collect data about what kinds of challenges developers, usability experts, and project managers experience when they collaborate on improving the usability of computer systems, and try to understand the challenges through the lenses of cross-professional collaboration. We also aimed to explore which successful practices are used to address these challenges, thereby providing grounds for the improvement of collaboration between key stakeholders in systems development. Our study confirms that many of the challenges for usability work stem from tension in the relationship between job roles, as argued by for example Gulliksen, Boivie, and Göransson (2006). In contrast to previous work, our study investigates usability challenges specifically from the perspective of three job roles, namely developers, usability experts and project managers. The role of the project manager and the interaction between the three job roles are rarely investigated in the literature. In the following we discuss our results in detail and relate them to four important papers on collaboration in usability work.

CHALLENGES IN USABILITY WORK

Concerning the first research question, our study suggests that timing, relevance, respect, and communication were all major issues for the three groups of stakeholders. These findings elaborate on results from earlier studies (e.g., Rosenbaum, Rohn, & Humburg, 2000; Gulliksen, Boivie, Persson, & Hektor, 2004; Kim, 1995) by viewing challenges from the perspective of professional relations amongst stakeholders. Our study suggests that these core challenges are symmetrical, in that most of them apply between any two job roles, like an arrow pointing back and forth. For instance, all three job roles experience challenges related to poor timing of usability work, such as feeling pressured to compromise one's professional standards. This challenge seems tightly connected to project managers' experience of usability as an initiative that can pull the rug from under the project plan, and their resulting hesitation to introduce such an initiative to the project plan.

The lack of relevance of usability results seemingly relates to developers' reluctance to incorporate last minute results. It also seems closely related to the challenge of timing. However, lack of relevant feedback also suggests that the relevance of findings and recommendations is sometimes flawed by usability experts' lack of domain knowledge.

The challenge of respect is perhaps most clear in the developer-usability expert relationship. Both parties experience that they do not get the professional respect they feel they deserve from colleagues. For example, developers feel disrespected by usability experts when they receive irrelevant or poorly timed usability results. Usability experts, on the other hand, interpret developers who dismiss important results as disrespecting the usability profession. Developers feel disrespected when pressured by project managers to compromise their professional standards. While other work has pointed to usability experts struggling to get respect from colleagues (Gulliksen, Boivie, & Göransson, 2006), the observation that other stakeholders also feel ill-respected is new.

Let us briefly reflect on the implications of our study for researching usability work. In related literature, usability work is mainly understood from the usability professionals' perspective. Accordingly, most studies report difficulties solely related to the role of the usability expert (e.g., Gulliksen, Boivie, & Göransson, 2006; Gulliksen, Boivie, Persson, & Hektor, 2004). To extend this perspective, we suggest thinking in *multiple perspectives*, including those of developers, project managers, and top management. Exploring such perspectives may strengthen usability research. For example, several authors have argued for increasing attention on developers' needs and wishes (e.g., Redish, Bias, Bailey, Molich, Dumas, & Spool, 2002) while others call for studies of how developers use usability evaluation results (Hornbæk & Frøkjær, 2005; Hvannberg, Law, & Larusdottir, 2007). In the present study we have discussed a new perspective, namely that of the project manager, and the difficulties related to it. We promote multiple perspectives to lessen the chance that a strong focus on usability experts causes researchers and practitioners to ignore other stakeholders.

Our work also opens for seeing usability work as a cross-professional *collaborative learning process*. Especially our understanding of respect and communication may benefit from understanding usability in a cross-professional context. Other studies have shown the benefits of working closely together in cross-professional settings when it comes to learning about other job roles and other professionals' point of view (Bødker & Buur, 2002; Furniss, Blandford, & Curzon, 2007). Understanding professionals as human beings with individual values, strengths and weaknesses might also help us explore why collaboration on usability issues is complex and difficult. The view that stakeholders are also individuals who work within social, relationships with customers and colleagues is not new, see for example Furniss, Blandford, and Curzon (2007) and Iivari (2006). However, stories that tell us that 'loud' individuals have a better success rate in some companies, or how personal and professional respect seem to rely on social skills (Iivari, 2006) suggest that we do not give the role of the individual enough attention as the practise of describing colleagues with nicknames such as 'prima donna' also apply for the present study. We do believe that job roles are of importance when it comes to collaborating to improve usability, but we might also need to look at how different individuals support or do not support each other. In this respect Furniss et al. (2007) have already identified negotiation skills as having huge importance when it comes to collaborating efficiently. Karen Myers and Isabel Briggs Myers (Myers, 1962) who developed the Myers-Briggs type indicator (MBTI) based on Jung's work on personality types (Jung, 1921) argue that people have different personality types, and that some types are more compatible than others. The same argument has been raised by others. Brinkman and Kirschner (2006) discussed ten types of behavioural patterns that people resort to when feeling threatened such as

being a 'no person' or a 'tank' and Crowe (1999) discussed the (negative) power of labelling the people around us—such as 'difficult', 'rude', or 'smart'—and how to consciously use body and verbal language help interacting with people we find difficult. Based on the present study, we suggest looking into social traits such as empathy, humour and diplomatic skills to better understand the interactions between people with different job roles and professional goals.

Successful Practices

Concerning the second research question, participants describe several work practices that seem to address some of the challenges reported in this study. For example, moving all usability initiatives to the beginning of a project is one way of dealing with the challenge of timing. To prioritize project goals collectively is one way of sharing information about professional goals, and addresses the need for better communication. Using developers as informants is one way to show and build respect, in addition to improving the relevance of the results. Such an approach is also a way to improve developers' willingness to carry out recommended fixes, as suggested by studies from other domains (Benton, Kelley, & Liebling, 1972; Schindler, 1998).

In the present study the successful practices are often tuned towards learning, such as learning about other stakeholders' professional standards, and collaborating, such as jointly agreeing on system goals, as described by Mayhew (1999). To get a better understanding of how usability work can be understood as a collaborative learning process, we suggest looking deeper into how such processes are supported or impeded in current work practices.

Dumas (in Redish, Bias, Bailey, Molich, Dumas, & Spool, 2002) has argued that the personal relationship between developer and usability expert might be the most important factor for the success of usability work, more important than, for example, how usability results are fed back to developers. Others have made similar observations on the importance of human relationships, such as the relationship between usability expert and customer, users and stakeholders, and so forth (Bennet & Karat, 1994; Furniss, Blandford, & Curzon, 2007; Wixon & Wilson, 1997). In fact, Bennet and Karat (1994) argued that finding ways to facilitate collaboration between stakeholders to usability work is a most urgent matter for HCI research. Because learning and collaboration seems to be such a key concept when designing usable systems, we suggest investigating the perspective of usability as a human activity rather than as a matter of methods and procedures. The Participatory Design tradition (Bødker & Buur, 2002) reflects this way of thinking but focuses mostly on the beginning of the development process, where much has the form of sketches. We suggest that understanding usability work in the perspective of human activities might help researchers and practitioners bring the focus on for example collaboration and learning beyond the sketching phase of development, and into other parts of development relevant for usability, namely evaluation.

In order to better understand how our study contributes to the body of work on cooperative aspects of usability work, we next relate our results to four important papers that all concern how usability practitioners cooperate with other stakeholders.

Relating Current Results to Existing Work on Collaboration Between Stakeholders

Furniss et al. (2007) investigated what happens between stakeholders in industrial practice and usability professionals. Their work show that customers have much influence on usability work, and that this influence increases when there is tension between the customer and the usability expert. They see usability work as a collabora-

tive effort and show how personal relations are important for the customer-usability practitioner relationship. Because usability work is no one-man show, they call for a better understanding of how individuals and professionals can cooperate to produce valuable usability work.

Gulliksen et al. (2006) have studied usability professionals on an individual level to investigate which success factors and obstacles they encounter. They conclude that individual background and experience can improve or impede the quality and success of usability work, as can organisational characteristics and stakeholders' attitudes towards usability. The paper is written from the perspective of the usability practitioner and mostly deals with this role: what practitioners do, how they do it, and the quality and results of their work. Since their paper is based on studies of and interviews with usability practitioners, the description of this job role and its challenges seems perhaps one-sided. For example, we learn that many usability practitioners consider themselves well-informed about the system domains they work with, while our study suggests that developers may disagree. Other issues such as respect or the importance of being on good terms with the project manager are also discussed in the paper. The paper lists problems and challenges for usability practitioners' work, but does not proceed far into *why* such challenges exist and hence only superficially into *how* to address them. For example, the paper argues that insufficient authority is a problem for usability practitioners, but only briefly explores why that might be (except that it is an 'attitude problem' in systems development at large).

While Gulliksen et al. (2006) have organisation as one of many topics, Iivari (2006) described a case study entirely on the relationship between organisational culture and usability work. Iivari's paper mostly concerns organisational issues such as responsibility and power structures in different organisational cultures. However, it touches on issues related to the present study. For example, the paper mentions conflicts between colleagues on a project and argues that they may be caused by strong personalities and an organisational culture where loud individuals succeed. Iivari's paper also points to other issues similar to the ones discussed in this paper: how project management is often considered insufficient, how some stakeholders are considered very sensitive about their work, how lack of respect can be a problem between colleagues, how the timing of usability initiatives are often bad, and how it may seem difficult to include usability work in project plans.

Bødker and Buur (2002) discussed how to facilitate better knowledge sharing and collaboration on design, and described a number of successful practices. The main topic of their paper is how to improve design through better collaboration in a setting called the Design Collaboratorium. They present a point of view different from our study, which aims at investigating the challenges in relation to collaboration that people with different job roles experience, and how one may improve that collaboration. The work with the Design Collaboratorium seems based on earlier research findings that showed how 'usability issues were brought into the design process too late and with too little to say' (Bødker & Buur, 2002). The paper by Bødker and Buur does not identify any reasons for why usability enters the design process too late, or what the more specific consequences are – besides it having 'too little to say'. Also, the Design Collaboratorium seems best applied relatively early in the design process, and is perhaps best suited for certain types of systems. It also demands quite a lot of planning and may thus run into the exact same problems with project managers that usability work does, namely that they do not know when or how to integrate it into the project plan.

If we compare the four papers with the study we have conducted, our study seems to add to some of the key findings in the papers above. Furniss et al. (2007) looked at relationships between usability practitioners and a group defined only as 'customers'. Some of the stakeholders in

our study consider themselves 'customers', but are also very aware of their profession and job role. While Furniss et al. (2007) argued for the importance of understanding groups of customers or usability practitioners as also being individuals with individual skills, we argue that those groups should also be understood as consisting of people with different job roles. Adding the perspective of job roles to that of individuals is important because our study shows that individuals who hold the same job role share challenges. However, based on the experiences from the present study we are convinced that the focus on individual skills and characteristics such as empathy, humour or diplomacy are also of great importance to cross-professional collaboration and should be studied further.

While Gulliksen et al. (2006) described usability work and relations from the view of the usability practitioner, and Iivari focused on organisational culture, our study aims to investigate and understand three job roles, and not particularly to take the stand of the usability practitioners.

The four papers all point to problems that are related to the challenges identified in this paper. Still, we provide some new explanations of *why* such problems and challenges occur. For example, Furniss et al. (2007) argued that usability work include making pragmatic decisions regarding for example budgets and deadlines. Our focus on job roles suggests that these difficult choices mainly lies with the project managers, and not so much the usability practitioners, as one might expect. Also, when Furniss et al. discussed the matter of tension between customers and usability practitioners, and Iivari (2006) pointed to conflicts between colleagues on a project, we can provide examples on how this is manifested in the daily work between job roles. We argue that tension in relationships is mostly related to the relationship between developers and usability practitioners. The focus on roles also suggests *why* tension may occur, since many participants in our study refer to a lack of respect between these two roles. To give due credit, Iivari offers interesting points on what builds personal and professional respect in different types of companies, for example how excellent social skills help build respect amongst co-workers.

Generally, the papers only deal with concrete successful practices in a limited fashion. The exception is Bødker and Buur (2002). Nevertheless, they run the risk of presenting work procedures that are too ambitious or complicated to be easily used in the industry. The successful practices presented in our paper may seem less ambitious than those of Bødker and Buur, but they are also less risky viewed from a project manager's point of view. Accordingly, they may stand a better chance of being used.

While all papers discuss challenges for usability work from different perspectives such as customers or organisational culture, they only sporadically investigate *why* such challenges exist. Our study suggests that the challenges people encounter when working together to improve usability can be understood from the perspective of job roles, and that usability work for these reasons is best explained as a collaborative cross-professional learning process.

Limitations of Results

Our aim with this study has been to understand professional relations between human beings, and since we understand relations involving human beings as unique our goal has been to collect rich descriptions of some, but of course not all, professional relationships. One may argue that interviews with 20 Danish professionals representing three professions do not produce representative data and that the findings reported in the present paper may be biased. However, this study views human relations through the lenses of social science. So rather than aiming for representative data or reproducible results we have sought to collect rich data that will help us think about cross-professional relationships and collaborative learning in new

ways. Future work should aim to investigate if our results are valid outside of a Danish work culture and in a larger group of participants.

Since our study is conducted as interviews the findings may reflect a rationalization on behalf of some of the interviewees. Consequently, this study investigates the participants' perceived challenges. In future studies, in-situ observations of interactions between stakeholders might advance our understanding of whether perceived challenges differ from actual challenges and help us learn about unsaid practices and barriers.

Investigating the perceived challenges in the relationship between three groups of stakeholders only addresses parts of a very complex problem. We would like to better understand if stakeholders who have more than one job role, such as a project manager with a background in usability studies, have different perspectives than stakeholders with only one job role. Also, getting hold of a broader sample of informants might help us think about new perspectives on collaborative usability work. For example, one may speculate whether members of special interest groups (SIGs) are different from professionals that are not SIG members, or whether the developers that were introduced by SIG members were perhaps more experienced with and interested in usability work than developers in general.

Similarly, we might expect that investigating other key stakeholders, for example the top management, could be relevant to understanding especially the challenge of timing, but perhaps also to the challenge of respecting colleagues' professional goals.

Iivari (2006) and Gulliksen et al. (2006) argued that usability work is also influenced by various organisational characteristics. This may very well also be the case for the relationships amongst colleagues. Gathering thorough organisational characteristics has not been a focus of this study, but we do suggest looking closer at cross-professional relationships in various organisational settings to get a better understanding of the complex pattern of challenges for usability work.

Since this study primarily focuses on evaluation work we might have limited ourselves by only allowing stakeholders to discuss best practises in relation to evaluation. As a consequence, we might have ignored other successful practices such as those related to the design of an underlying architecture that can easily be changed. In sum, further work should aim to describe challenges in a broader perspective taking into account that usability work takes place in a complex organisational setting between several groups of stakeholders and that evaluation work is only a part of a series of tasks that influence usability.

CONCLUSION

Many seem to consider usability work a well-integrated and well-understood part of software development. However, it still does not seem to impact the development of software as much as usability professionals desire. Our study of the relationships between developers, usability experts, and project managers suggests that looking into the interaction between these stakeholders can help us better understand *why*.

The study shows that challenges related to the timing of usability work, the lack of relevance of usability results, disrespect for others' job roles and goals, and difficulties in sharing and getting important information are key challenges for the cooperation between the participants. These challenges have been known for many years to impede usability work. The surprising finding is that despite the implementation of clever successful practices and workarounds those well-known challenges are still reported to be the top show-stoppers for effective usability work. We recognise that difference in job roles cannot explain every single problem with cross-professional collaboration. We also need to acknowledge that personal relationships between individuals have a major

impact on how well people work together. In this respect Furniss et al. (2007) mentions negotiation skills, and we suggest empathy, humour and diplomatic skills as being worth studying in the future. Getting perspectives on which organisational characteristics—such as organizational structure and level of worker responsibility—may impede or facilitate collaboration should also be a future goal.

Gulliksen et al (2006) conclude their paper by summing up a 'frivolous' description of what a usability practitioner needs to succeed:

You need systems developers that are brilliant programmers and ready to put in as much time as required to do as you bid, and at the same time willing to make numerous modifications to their solutions in order to accommodate the changing requirements inherent to systems development, without complaint. You need a client that is committed to user-centered design, willing to spend unspecified amounts of money on your development project. And you need users that are willing and able to spend unspecified numbers of hours with the project in various analysis, design and evaluation activities. As well as being at your beck and call, at any time of the day to answer all the detail questions that are inevitable throughout the entire course of the project. (Gulliksen, Boivie, & Göransson, 2006)

Perhaps we may offer an equal frivolous summary of how cross-professional collaborations on usability work succeed:

You need systems developers that are always happy to receive usability critique, will gladly change the code at any point in time, and passionately engage in usability work. You need usability experts with detailed knowledge of the system domain, the system's code, and the progress of the development, who only suggest priority design changes, and do so with perfect timing. You need project managers who involve everybody in the planning of the project and give top-priority to usability at all times, while meticulously following up on all recommendations, and still leaving room for developers to follow their professional standards. And you need all these people to hold the utmost respect for each other professionally and personally, possess excellent communication and diplomatic skills, and be thrilled with joy about working together at all times.

REFERENCES

American National Standards Institute. (2001). *The common industry format (ANSI/NCTS-354-2001)*.

Bennet, J., & Karat, J. (1994). Facilitating effective HCI design meetings. In *Proceedings of the SIGCHI Conference on Human Factors in Computing Systems: Celebrating Interdependence*, (pp. 198-204).

Benton, A. A., Kelley, H. H., & Liebling, B. (1972). Effects of extremity of offers and concession rate on the outcomes of bargaining. *Journal of Personality and Social Psychology, 24*, 73–83. doi:10.1037/h0033368

Bødker, S., & Buur, J. (2002). The design collaboratorium - A place for usability design. [TOCHI]. *ACM Transactions on Computer-Human Interaction, 9*(2), 152–169. doi:10.1145/513665.513670

Bødker, S., Krogh, P. M., & Petersen, M. G. (2001). The interactive design collaboratorium. In M. Hirose (Ed.), *Proceedings of the Interact '01*, (pp. 51-58). Tokyo, Japan.

Boland, R. (1978). The process and product of system design. *Management Science, 24*, 887–898. doi:10.1287/mnsc.24.9.887

Brinkman, R., & Kirschner, R. (2006), *Dealing with difficult people: 24 lessons for bringing out the best in everyone*. New York: McGraw-Hill Professional.

Chattratichart, J., & Brodie, J. (2004). Applying user testing data to UEM performance metrics. *CHI '04 Extended Abstracts on Human Factors in Computing Systems,* (pp. 1119-1122), *Vienna, Austria*.

Chi, M. (1997). Quantifying qualitative analyses of verbal data: A practical guide. *Journal of the Learning Sciences, 6*(3), 271–315. doi:10.1207/s15327809jls0603_1

Coble, J., Karat, J., & Kahn, M. (1997). Maintaining a focus on user requirements throughout the development of clinical workstation software. In *Proceedings of the ACM Conference on Human Factors in Computing* (pp. 170-177).

Cockton, G., Woolrych, A., & Hindmarch, M. (2004). Reconditioned merchandise: Extended structured report formats in usability inspection. *CHI '04 Extended Abstracts on Human Factors in Computing Systems, Vienna, Austria* (pp. 1433-1436).

Crowe, S. A. (1999). *Since strangling isn't an option...: Dealing with difficult people—Common problems and uncommon solutions*. New York: Perigee.

Dumas, J. (1989, July). Stimulating change through usability testing. *SIGCHI Bulletin, 21*(1), 37–44. doi:10.1145/67880.67884

Dumas, J., & Redish, J. (1993). *A practical guide to usability testing*. Oregon: Intellect Books.

Ehn, P. (1992). Scandinavian design: On participation and skill. I P. Adler, & T. Winograd, *Usability: Turning technology into tools* (pp. 96-132). New York: Oxford University Press.

Ehn, P., & Sjögren, D. (1991). From system descriptions to scripts for action. I J. Greenbaum, & M. Kyng, *Design at work - Cooperative design of computer systems* (pp. 241-268). Hillsdale, NJ: Lawrence Erlbaum.

Furniss, D., Blandford, A., & Curzon, P. (2007). Usability work in professional Website design: insights from practitioners' perspectives. I E. Law, E. Hvannberg, & G. Cockton, *Maturing usability: Quality in software, interaction and value* (pp. 144-167). London: Springer.

Greenbaum, J., & Kyng, M. (1991). *Design at work: Cooperative design of computer systems.* Hillsdale, NJ: Lawrence Erlbaum Associates.

Gulliksen, J., Boivie, I., & Göransson, B. (2006). Usability professionals - Current practices and future development. *Interacting with Computers, 18*, 568–600. doi:10.1016/j.intcom.2005.10.005

Gulliksen, J., Boivie, I., Persson, J., & Hektor, A. L. (2004). Making a difference - A survey of the usability profession in Sweden. In. *Proceedings of Nordichi, 2004*, 207–215. doi:10.1145/1028014.1028046

Hertzum, M., & Jacobsen, N. (2003). The evaluator effect: A chilling fact about usability evaluation methods. *International Journal of Human-Computer Interaction, 15*(1), 183–204. doi:10.1207/S15327590IJHC1501_14

Hornbæk, K., & Frøkjær, E. (2005). Comparing usability problems and redesign proposals as input to practical systems development. *ACM Conference on Human Factors in Computing Systems* (pp. 391-400).

Hvannberg, E. T., Law, E., & Larusdottir, M. K. (2007). Heuristic evaluation: Comparing ways of finding and reporting usability problems. *Interacting with Computers, 19*(2), 225–240. doi:10.1016/j.intcom.2006.10.001

Iivari, N. (2006). 'Representing the user' in software development - A cultural analysis of usability work in the product development context. *Interacting with Computers, 18*, 635–664. doi:10.1016/j.intcom.2005.10.002

Ives, B., & Olson, M. (1984). User involvement and MIS success: A review of research. *Management Science, 30*, 586–603. doi:10.1287/mnsc.30.5.586

Johnson, D., & Johnson, F. (1990). *Joining together.* Englewood Cliffs, NJ: Prentice Hall.

Jung, C. G. (1921). *Psychologische Typen.* Zürich: Rascher Verlag.

Karat, C., Campbell, R., & Fiegel, T. (1992). Comparison of empirical testing and walkthrough methods in usability interface evaluation. In *Proceedings of CHI'92* (pp. 397-404).

Kennedy, S. (1989). Using video in the BNR usability lab. *SIGCHI Bulletin, 21*(2), 92–95. doi:10.1145/70609.70624

Kim, S. (1995), Interdisciplinary cooperation, *in* Baeker, R. M. (ed.), *Readings in human-computer interaction: toward the year 2000* (pp. 305-311), San Francisco: Morgan Kaufmann.

King, W. R., & Rodriguez, J. J. (1981). Participative design of strategic decision support systems: An empirical assessment. *Management Science, 27*, 717–726. doi:10.1287/mnsc.27.6.717

La Fasto, F., & Larson, C. (2002). *When teams work best.* Thousand Oaks, CA: Sage Publications.

Law, E., & Hvannberg, E. T. (2004). Analysis of strategies for improving and estimating the effectiveness of heuristic evaluation. In *Proceedings of the Third Nordic Conference on Human-Computer Interaction NordiCHI '04* (pp. 241-250).

Madsen, K. H., & Petersen, M. G. (1999). Supporting collaboration in multi-media design. *Human-Computer Interaction - INTERACT'99* (pp. 185-190).

Mayhew, D. (1999). *The usability engineering lifecycle: A practitioner's handbook for user interface design.* San Francisco: Morgan Kaufmann.

Mills, C. (1987). Usability testing in the real world. *SIGCHI Bulletin, 18,* 67–70. doi:10.1145/25281.25285

Myers, I. B. (1962). *The Myers-Briggs type indicator.* Palo Alto, CA: Consulting Psychologists Press.

Nayak, N., Mrazek, D., & Smith, D. (1995). Analyzing and communicating usability data. *SIGCHI Bulletin, 27*(1), 22–30. doi:10.1145/202642.202649

Redish, J., Bias, R., Bailey, R., Molich, R., Dumas, R., & Spool, J. (2002). Usability in practice: Formative usability evaluations - Evolution and revolution. *ACM Conference on Human Factors in Computing System,* Minneapolis, Minnesota (pp. 885-890).

Robey, D., & Farrow, D. L. (1982). User involvement in information system development. A conflict model and empirical test. *Management Science, 28,* 73–85. doi:10.1287/mnsc.28.1.73

Rosenbaum, S., Rohn, J. A., & Humburg, J. (2000). A toolkit for strategic usability: Results from workshops, panels and surveys. In *Proceedings of hte ACM CHI 2000 Conference on Human Factors in Computing Systems, 1,* 337-344.

Rubin, J. (1994). *Handbook of usability testing: How to plan, design and conduct effective tests.* New York: John Wiley & Sons Inc.

Schell, D. (1986). Usability testing of screen design: Beyond standards, principles, and guidelines. In *Proceedings of the Human Factors Society 30th Meeting* (pp. 1212-1215), Santa Monica, CA.

Schindler, R. M. (1998). Consequences of perceiving oneself as responsible for obtaining a discount. *Journal of Consumer Psychology, 7,* 371–392. doi:10.1207/s15327663jcp0704_04

Strauss, A., & Corbin, J. (1998). *Basics of qualitative research - Techniques and procedures for developing grounded theory.* California: Sage Publications.

Uldall-Espersen, T., & Frøkjær, E. (2007, July 22-27). Usability and software development: Roles of the stakeholders. In [*Beijing, China.*]. *Proceedings of, HCI2007, 642*–651.

Uldall-Espersen, T., Frøkjær, E., & Hornbæk, K. (2007). Tracing impact in a usability improvement process. *Interacting with Computers,* 48–63.

Winer, M., & Ray, K. (1994). *Collaboration handbook: Creating, sustaining, and enjoying the journey.* Lafond, St. Paul, MN: Amherst H. Wilder Foundation.

Wixon, D., & Wilson, C. (1997). The usability engineering framework for product design and evaluation. In M. Helander & T. Landauer (Eds.), *Handbook of human computer interaction* (p. 653–688). North-Holland: Elsevier Science.

This work was previously published in International Journal of Technology and Human Interaction, Volume 6, Issue 1, edited by Anabela Mesquita & Chia-Wen Tsai, pp. 33-53, copyright 2010 by IGI Publishing (an imprint of IGI Global).

Chapter 12

Information Technology Exception Messages:
A Proposed Set of Information Elements and Format for Consistency and Informativeness

T. S. Amer
Northern Arizona University, USA

Jo-Mae B. Maris
Northern Arizona University, USA

ABSTRACT

Users of information technology (IT) frequently encounter "exception messages" during their interactions with computing systems. Exception messages are important points of communication with users of IT and are similar in principle to compliance and warning messages that appear on consumer products and equipment (e.g., cigarettes, power tools, etc.), in various environments (e.g., around machinery), and on chemicals. This study reviews the normative elements and information that are included in product, chemical, and environment compliance and warning messages and combines these with recommendations in the IT literature to propose that five elements and information should be included in IT exception messages with a standard format. It is argued that including these elements in the proposed format will improve the consistency and effectiveness of exception messages. Also reported are the results of an investigation of a sample of actual exception messages to determine their degree of conformity with the proposed elements. Results indicate that IT exception messages lack descriptive content.

DOI: 10.4018/978-1-61350-465-9.ch012

INTRODUCTION

Users of information technology (IT) commonly encounter exception messages during their interactions with application programs. Exception messages, sometimes referred to as "dialogs," appear over the main window of the parent application program and engage the user by offering information and requesting some input (Cooper and Reimann, 2003; Galitz, 2007). When the user has finished viewing or changing the information presented, he has the option of accepting or rejecting his changes. The exception message then disappears and returns the user to the main application program.

A common type of exception message is the "bulletin box." A bulletin is launched by the program, not the user. This type of exception message stops all progress in the main application, and is sometimes called a "blocking bulletin" because the program cannot continue (processing is blocked) until the user responds. There are three categories of bulletin exception messages with an example of each illustrated in Figure 1 (Cooper and Reimann, 2003): (1) error messages inform the user of a problem or potential problem, (2) alerts (a.k.a. notifiers) give notice to the user of the program's action, and (3) confirmations notify the user of the program's action and gives the user the authority to override that action.

It can be argued that exception messages share similarities in principle to the compliance and warning messages that appear on consumer products and equipment, in various life situations, and on chemicals. Both exception messages and compliance and warning messages are designed to inform people of a state of the world or system, a potential problem, or actions required to be taken. For example, compliance and warning messages appear on household cleaners and ladders to inform the user of a problem if the item is inappropriately used. Likewise, compliance and warning messages appear in various environments to notify and advise people as to the correct

Figure 1. Examples of the three types of bulletin exception messages

a. Error Message:

b. Alert (a.k.a. notifier):

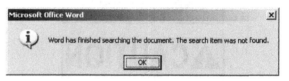

c. Confirmation:

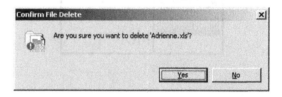

actions to be taken and/or of potential hazards. Two examples of such compliance and warning messages are shown in Figure 2. Considerable research in the field of human factors psychology has been targeted on the content of compliance and warning messages to determine the effect on human perceptions, judgment, and decision making (see Wogalter, 2006a). This research has resulted in normative guidelines specifying the elements and information that should be included in compliance and warning messages. Including these elements improves the informativeness of these messages.

The primary objective of this manuscript is to review the normative elements and information that are included in product, chemical, and environment compliance and warning messages that have been confirmed by extensive research on the design and effectiveness of these warning messages by researchers in human factors psychology. These prescriptions are combined with the recommendations from the IT literature and a set of proposed elements and information is set

Figure 2. Examples of compliance and warning messages. Images of safety signs provided by www.ComplianceSigns.com.

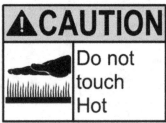

forth to guide the design of IT exception messages. An example exception message is created and presented to illustrate how the elements could be incorporated. It is asserted that the acceptance and implementation of the recommendations will increase the effectiveness, informativeness, and consistency of exception messages that appear in IT environments. A secondary objective of this manuscript is to present an analysis of a sample of actual IT exception messages to measure their conformity with the proposed elements. Results reveal that current IT exception messages lack descriptive content relative to the proposed elements indicating that significant improvement is possible in the design of exception messages.

ELEMENTS OF WELL DESIGNED COMPLIANCE AND WARNING MESSAGES

Human factors researchers examining compliance and warning messages have relied on general models of human information processing to analyze the elements of warning messages and

the warning process (Lehto, 2006). From this perspective compliance and warning messages are just another form of communication to be processed by a person performing a task. Several stages of human information processing occur as represented in these models beginning with exposure to a stimulus and message perception. These stages are followed by storage and retrieval of knowledge, decision making, and ultimately a behavioral response. Information is assumed to flow through each of these stages as the human performs a task.

Researchers have used these models to organize and evaluate the factors that influence the effectiveness of compliance and warning messages. Such factors include the various design elements included in warning messages and the general appearance of these messages. The focus is on helping designers and researchers devise and refine more effective messages in terms of improved attention, memory, and behavioral compliance. From this body of research it is suggested that a well designed compliance and warning message should contain two key sections or "panels" (Wogalter, 2006b and Wogalter et al., 2002), a "signal word panel" and a "message panel." The two compliance and warning messages of Figure 2 each possess these two panels. The top panel of each message contains a signal word and the bottom panel of each message contains the message. Each panel has a specific purpose or function.

The purpose of the signal word is to draw the user's attention and to express a level of hazard or probability of injury associated with the environment or situation. The signal word panel itself is to contain three elements: (1) a signal word, (2) color coding, and (3), a signal icon. Note that the signal word in the first warning of Figure 2 is "DANGER" and in the second, "CAUTION." The color coding in the first is red and yellow the second. Finally, both messages in Figure 2 contain the signal icon in the form of an exclamation point in a triangle. Research findings and the American National Standards Institute (American National

Standards Institute, 2002) have identified suitable sets of signal words and signal icons to be included in this panel of a warning.

The purpose of the message panel is to convey specific information about the hazard or situation. This information can be expressed using language, using symbols or by using both language and symbols. While both the warnings in Figure 2 contain a symbol,[1] this is generally considered an optional feature of a well-designed warning. The language and/or symbol of the message panel should communicate three informational elements:

1. Identification of the hazard or situation,
2. Explanation of the consequences of the hazard or situation, and
3. Directions to be followed.

The three informational items in the message panel should be as explicit and as complete as possible. Consider the first message of Figure 2. The situation is "Arc Flash and Shock Hazard." The consequence of the hazard is illustrated by the symbol of a hand connected to wire and in shock. Finally, the language provides directions on how to avoid the hazard: "Appropriate PPE and tools required when working on this equipment."

Taken together, the elements of a well-designed warning would seem to be very appropriate for IT exception messages. In both cases the principle is to provide information to a user regarding a state of the environment or system. In IT environments as with other life situations instructions about actions to be taken and the consequences of the actions (or inaction) may be of importance to the user. An examination of the three exception messages of Figure 1 shows deficiencies relative to the prescriptions described above for compliance and warning messages. Indeed, the error message of Figure 1a. is especially lacking in information content.

Of course not all IT exception messages are deficient, but while there is considerable guidance in both the academic and professional IT literature

regarding the effective design of user interfaces in general, there is a limited amount of prescriptive guidance with specific regard to the components and elements of exception messages. Of note also, is a lack of consistency or accepted standards for the form and content of IT exception messages.[2]

GUIDANCE IN THE IT LITERATURE

Early academic work on exception messages proposed guidelines for improving the obscure text-based messages of command-line operating system user interfaces such as DOS, XENIX and UNIX. Shneiderman (1982) reports the results of experiments indicating that improving the specificity and clarity of standard system command-line error messages enhanced the error correction performance and comprehension of novice users. Brown (1983) examined the command-line error messages returned by a large number of Pascal program compilers to a simple coding error. The majority of compliers generated "barely acceptable" to "laughable" messages that did not provide quality information to help the user solve the coding error. Both Shneiderman and Brown offer suggestions to improve the then poor state of command-line error messages.

Efe (1987) discusses the problem of error messages that are inappropriate for the level of knowledge or authority of the end user. A solution proposed in the article is called the "Let's talk about it" (LTAI) strategy and consists of generating a dialog with the user. The system would generate a message at the highest level and allow the user to probe down to the operating system call level. The interactions are assumed to be text-based and his recommendation has been adopted to some extent. However, we are still left with the problem of what elements and format consititutes an exception message that gets the user's attention and provides the appropiate amount of information, especially in today's graphical user interfaces (GUIs).

Coats and Vlaeminke (1987) discuss that an error message should specify what is unacceptable and what should be done about it. They give examples and note that an error message should be informative to the user, complete, and accurately diagnose the cause of the error. Morevoer, error messages should be timely, non-patronizing, and non-threatening. Similarly Molich and Nielsen (1990) provide descriptions of good error messages as derived from their own experience and note that an error message should be (1) defensive: blame the problem on system deficiencies and never criticize the user, (2) precise: provide the user with exact information about the cause of the problem, and (3) constructive: provide meaningful suggestions to the user about what to do next.

The advent of GUIs provided systems designers with additional features and capabilities including graphical images. Still, the professional literature and researchers offer limited guidance as to the content of exception messages. Apple Corporation (1989) notes that some icons that appear in exception messages have "standard accepted uses" (p.115). These icons are "right and left arrows, return arrow, About box balloon, check box, radio button, and the house icon" (p.115). However, only ambiguous advice is given as to how these elements should be used: "Any button in one of these shapes must conform to the expected use, or users will be confused" (p.115). Little is offered with respect to the informational content of exception messages.

Microsoft, in *The Official Guidelines for User Interface Developers and Designers* (UI Guidelines: Windows XP Design Team, 2001) contains more specific guidance for the components of what they term "message boxes." The UI Guidelines provide recommendations for the following components of message boxes: (1) title bar text, (2) use of icons, and (3) message box text. The general view of the Microsoft UI Guidelines is that the title bar identifies the source of the message, the icon identifies the type of message, and the text presents the message. Little other guidance

regarding the form and content of exception messages is offered.

Microsoft has recently provided more specific guidance for the components of error messages and warnings (Windows Vista Development Center, 2008). It is noted that good error messages and warnings should:

1. State that a problem occurred or will occur,
2. Explain why the problem occurred and be relevant, and
3. Provide a solution so that users can fix the problem and lead to user action.

Additionally, good error messages should be presented in a way that is, among other things, relevant, user centered, clear and brief. These recommendations are similar to the prescriptions established for compliance and warning messages noted above (Wogalter, 2006b and Wogalter et al., 2002).

According to Cooper and Reimann (2003) bulletin exception messages are abused by systems programmers and should be eliminated if possible. If bulletins are to be used, Cooper and Reimann offer some guidance on key design features such as including a title bar, minimizing the size of the message window, and offering terminating commands. With respect to error messages, Cooper and Reimann advise that a well-formed message should be polite, illuminating, and helpful. In addition, they indicate that an error message should give the user the information he needs to solve the problem, make clear the scope of the problem, the alternatives available, and offer to take care of the problem. This advice corresponds to that noted above by warnings researchers who specify that the message panel of a warning should communicate: (1) the identification of the hazard, (2) an explanation of the consequences of the hazard, and (3) directions as to how to avoid the hazard.

Shneidermann and Plaisant (2005) note that dialogs and error messages should provide informative feedback. In addition, error messages should offer specific information about the nature of the problem, and indicate what the user needs to do. Error messages should also provide simple, constructive, and specific instructions for error recovery. As with Cooper and Reimann, the recommendations of Shneiderman and Plaisant align with that of the researchers in warnings.

Galitz (2007) also affirms the same principles as the IT researchers noted above in that error messages should be clear, constructive and correct. But as above, no specific guidance as to the exact form or content of the messages is offered. In addition, little research support is presented for the specific form and content of messages.

Recently, Amer and Maris (2007) examined and measured the "arousal strength" (i.e., the perceived severity of hazard a warning communicates) of the common signal words and signal icons used in IT exception messages. Signal words and signal icons appear in IT exception messages and compliance and warning messages to draw the user's attention and to express a level of exposure or probability of harm associated with the environment or situation. In the study participants viewed a number of signal words and signal icons in the context of an exception message and rated the degree of severity of the computer problem implied by the exception message. The signal words and signal icons used in the study were selected from Microsoft development manuals, published both in hard copy and on-line (Windows XP Design Team, 2001), and from prior literature in psychology (Hellier et al., 2000). The Microsoft development manuals are used by application programmers as a reference for programming when developing products to be Microsoft compliant. Accordingly, the signal words and icons chosen from these sources are those a user would encounter in an IT exception message when using Microsoft products.

The signal words investigated included "Notice," "Error," and "Critical." Some of the signal icons investigated are shown in Figure 3. The data captured allows exception messages to be

Figure 3. Signal words and icons

	The question mark balloon box
	The "X" in a red circle

designed to communicate different levels of hazard in order to achieve so called "hazard matching." Hazard matching occurs when the severity of the hazard that is implied by the signal word and icon within the exception message matches the level of hazard faced by the user. One objective of their research was to provide system designers with data that will allow them to improve the informativeness of exception messages by achieving hazard matching. So, a systems designer can choose the appropriate signal word or signal icon to place in an exception message to communicate the degree of the systems problem or failure that may result from user actions (or inaction).

PROPOSED ELEMENTS AND FORMAT OF EFFECTIVE EXCEPTION MESSAGES

Combining the guidelines established in the warnings literature for compliance and warning messages with the recommendations provided by the IT authors cited above leads to a set of normative elements that, arguably, should be possessed by IT exception messages. It is proposed that five elements should be contained in every exception message. In addition, and as will be illustrated below, it is proposed that a consistent format should be employed in the presentation of every exception message. The five proposed elements are:

1. **Signal word and/or icon:** An exception message should include an appropriate signal word and/or icon to catch the attention of the user. The signal word/icon combination should arouse the user to a level that matches the nature of the underlying hazard, problem or state of the system.
2. **Hazard or problem information (illuminate the problem):** An exception message should inform the user what the problem is or the state of the system.
3. **Instructions:** An exception message should instruct the user about what to do or not do.
4. **Consequences (alternatives):** An exception message should inform the user as to what will result from all the actions taken or from inaction.
5. **Offer a solution:** An exception message should offer to implement at least one solution itself, without requiring the user to take unreasonable action.

It seems reasonable that IT exception messages should contain all the above elements to improve their informativeness, consistency, and effectiveness. Establishing such standards for the form and content of exception messages is consistent with the views expressed in the academic and professional literature in IT as well as international standard setting bodies. Blackwell and Green (2003) note that presenting similar information in different ways compromises usability. Shneiderman and Plaisant (2005) state the need for consistency, conventions, and guidelines in the design of interfaces in general, and for effective exception messages in particular. The first of their eight "golden rules" of interface design is "strive for consistency." Consistency and standards in interface design are also noted by Cooper and Reimann (2003) and Galitz (2007). The International Organization for Standardization (ISO) as the world's largest developer and publisher of international standards notes that standards ensure desirable characteristics of products and services including reliability and efficiency. The five elements proposed above contained within a standard exception message format are consistent with the ISO's usability heuristics established for the interaction of people and information systems (ISO 9241, 2006).

Figure 4 illustrates an example of an exception message created by the authors that conforms to the five elements listed above and presents a format that conforms to the accepted standards of compliance and warning messages from the warnings literature (Wogalter, 2006b; Wogalter et al., 2002; American National Standards Institute, 2002). It is also consistent with the concepts expressed in the academic and professional IT literature cited above. This is not an actual error message, but rather one that was designed for this article as a relevant example. The message was created to display on screen in response to a network connection failure that would result in the loss of data during data entry. Note the two "panels" of the message: a signal word/icon panel and the message panel.[3] In addition, the message contains each of the five elements proposed above. Specifically, note the symbol in the center of the message showing flames on sheets of paper. This symbol provides a vivid indication as to the hazard or issue faced by the user (loss of data) as a result of the failure of the network connection. This symbol was created to reasonably comply with the paper paradigm within the Xerox PARC (Palo Alto Research Center) desktop metaphor. The desktop metaphor is the primary operating system concept used by most computing applications in the fields of business and accounting and is comprised of text on a white background (paper), files within folders, and a "desktop."[4]

If it is agreed that IT exception messages should contain the above elements to improve their informativeness, consistency, and effectiveness, then a reasonable question to ask is "How do existing exception messages compare to the normative prescriptions?" If deficiencies in the current state of IT exception messages are found to

Figure 4. Example of an exception message that conforms to the five elements proposed

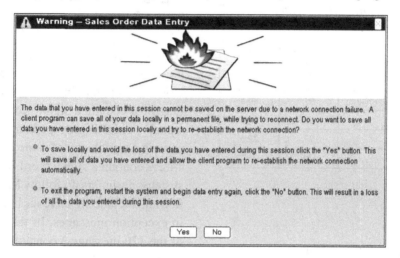

exist, then systems programmers can target their efforts to begin improving exception message design. To this end, the following section describes an evaluation of a sample of exception messages.

METHOD

The authors collected a sample of exception messages that each encountered over a two month period during normal computing interactions. Each time the authors encountered a unique exception message, a screen shot of the message was saved to a database. The types of interactions and application programs utilized during this period included e-mail, word processing, spreadsheet implementations, Internet interactions, etc. Given that the authors' university computing standard is Microsoft, nearly all the exception messages captured were displayed by Microsoft products or Windows-based applications. In total, 120 unique exception messages were collected by the authors over the two month period. All three types of exception messages – error messages (51 occurrences), alerts (a.k.a., notifiers – 16 occurrences), and confirmations (53 occurrences) – were included in the sample. Examples of the types of messages collected are shown in Figure 1.

It is noted that the sample of exception messages collected by the authors is not a random one, and is skewed toward Microsoft related applications. However, the applications of e-mail, Web browsing, word processing and spreadsheets are among the most common in professional work environments and we specifically focused on these applications in an attempt to generate a relevant and representative sample. As a first attempt to evaluate the content of exception messages the sample does offer useful insights as to the information contained in exception messages and how that information conforms to the five normative elements proposed in the prior section of this manuscript.

Each exception message in the database was then evaluated independently by the two authors to determine if the message contained the five elements introduced above. After evaluating all 120 exception messages independently the two evaluators convened to discuss any differences in the resulting scores. Where differences occurred between the evaluators, the individual exception message was examined and reevaluated so that a consensus as to the presence of the element was determined.

Table 1. Exception message conformance with the five normative elements (%) –sample of 120 exception messages

Normative Element	Count	Percentage
1. Signal word and/or Icon	99	82.5
2. Hazard or Problem Information	97	80.8
3. Instructions	81	67.5
4. Consequences	27	22.5
5. Offer a Solution	29	24.2

RESULTS

Table 1 provides a list of the number and percentage of exception messages that contain each of the five elements. For example, 82.5% (99) of the 120 exception messages contained a signal word and/ or signal icon. Likewise, 80.8% (97) of the 120 messages contain information regarding hazard or problem information. That is, information that informs the user of the problem they are facing. The compliance percentage drops from there with only 22.5% of the messages listing the consequences of what will happen or not happen as a result of actions taken by the user. Additionally, only 24.2% of the messages provide information about possible solutions or offer to implement a solution.

Overall, the sample of exception messages examined for this study is deficient in its informativeness with respect to the application of the normative elements set forth in this manuscript. Indeed, less than 6% (7 of 120) of the messages in the sample collected contained all five elements. This result seems especially disturbing in that exception messages occur at the very point in a user's interaction where the most information possible should be offered by the system. Moreover, incorporating the proposed elements to exception messages could be accomplished relatively easily in IT environments when compared to other situations (e.g., consumer product warning labels) given the ability to easily alter the display of information on a computer screen.

Signal Words and Signal Icons Together

As noted above 82.5% (99) of the 120 exception messages contained a signal word *AND/OR* signal icon. Further examination of the sample reveals that most contain a signal icon, but few contain signal words. Eighty percent of the messages contain a signal icon of some form whereas only 14.2% contain a signal word. It seems that most systems designers do follow Microsoft's suggestion and include signal icons but not signal words in exception messages. In fact, only 10.8% (13 of the 120 messages) contained *BOTH* a signal word and signal icon.

Error Messages, Alerts, and Confirmations

Table 2 displays the percentage of exception messages that contain each of the five elements by type of message: error messages, alerts, and confirmations. Two interesting results are revealed. First, of the alerts in the sample, none contained the fifth proposed element: **Offer a Solution** (i.e., an exception message should offer to implement at least one solution itself, without requiring the user to take unreasonable action). This outcome is not surprising given the purpose of alerts within the IT environment. As noted above, alerts give notice to the user of the program's action. Accordingly, one would not expect an alert to offer a solution when its purpose is to inform the user of the action being taken.

The second result illustrated by the percentages of Table 2 is more surprising. Only 5.9% of error messages in the sample contained the fourth proposed element: **Consequences** (i.e., an exception message should inform the user as to what will result from all the actions taken or from inaction). This is somewhat unsettling given that the purpose of error messages is to inform the user of a problem or potential problem. To not provide information as to the consequences of the actions

Table 2. Error messages, alerts, and confirmations – percentage conformance with the five normative elements

Normative Element	Error Messages	Alerts	Confirmations
1. Signal word and/or Icon	82.4%	93.8%	83.0%
2. Hazard or Problem Information	86.3%	56.3%	83.0%
3. Instructions	68.6%	43.8%	73.6%
4. Consequences	5.9%	18.8%	39.6%
5. Offer a Solution	21.6%	0.0%	34.0%

taken or not taken to the user who receives an error message seems especially troubling. Arguably, it is at the juncture, where a user receives an error message, that the system should provide the most information possible, especially the consequences of the actions that may be taken by the user.

Examples of Poor Exception Messages

Several especially poor exception messages within the sample were identified by the authors. These messages were deficient across most of the five proposed elements and a simple examination of the messages makes obvious their lack of informativeness. Three such messages are illustrated in Figure 5.

Examples of Good Exception Messages

Reasonably good exception messages were also captured. These messages contained nearly all of the proposed elements and provide the user with an informative interaction. Three such messages are illustrated in Figure 6.

Figure 5. Examples of poor exception messages

The following message was displayed during the installation of Microsoft Outlook:

The following message was received during the automatic update process for Microsoft Windows:

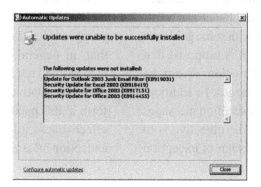

Figure 6. Examples of reasonably good exception messages

The following message was displayed by Windows IE while moving from one page to another:

The following message was displayed during a Microsoft Outlook session:

The following message was displayed after erroneously entering a formula in Microsoft Excel:

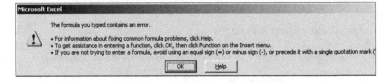

DISCUSSION AND CONCLUSION

This manuscript reviewed the normative elements and information that are included in product, chemical, and environment compliance and warning messages. In conjunction with some guidance provided in the IT literature, it is proposed that five key elements and information should be included in IT exception messages. In addition, a standardized format for all exception messages is suggested and illustrated. The objective is to establish consistency in the design of exception messages to improve their informativeness and effectiveness. A sample of actual exception messages that included error messages, alerts, and confirmations was then examined to determine their conformance with the normative elements proposed. Results of that examination indicated that, in general, the IT exception messages in the sample lack informativeness in that they are deficient relative to the normative elements set forth in this paper. These results indicate that the effectiveness, informativeness, and consistency of exception messages could be improved if systems designers and application programmers better incorporate these elements in exception messages.

Of special note is that exception messages within the sample lack information regarding the consequences of the computing situation with only 22.5% of the messages listing the consequences of what will happen or not happen as a result of actions taken by the user. This was especially true of error messages where only 5.9% noted the consequences. This deficiency in error messages is particularly noteworthy given that the purpose of error messages is to inform the user of a problem or potential problem. Of the three types of exception messages examined, error messages should provide the most information to the user as to the consequences of the actions taken or not taken.

Moreover, few exception messages offer to implement at least one solution itself, without requiring the user to take unreasonable action. Just 24.2% of the messages in the sample provide information about possible solutions or offer to implement a solution. In user-centric computing environments exception messages should provide as much information as possible and should provide as much assistance to users as is practicable. Indeed, incorporating the proposed elements and information in exception messages could be accomplished relatively easily in IT environments as compared to other situations (e.g., consumer product warning labels) given the ability to easily alter the display of information on a computer screen. In addition, the warnings that appear on consumer products and equipment and on chemicals are static and do not offer the user a means to interact with them. In contrast, the computing capability of IT environments allow dynamic exception message content and can provide users the ability to seek out more information and help about system status in light of the exception encountered. This ability to offer a dialogue, so to speak, and interactivity with the user is a key potential strength of IT exception messages. Such interactivity could be used strategically to display alternative message content to users in

different situations or to inform the user about the consequences when they deliberately choose to ignore the problem. In such cases a "cascading" exception message could be employed. That is, a message that allows the user to click through to other screens that display additional information about, for example, the consequences and/ or solutions that relate to the problem or issue faced by the user.

Additionally, the level of user expertise is a factor of importance in the design of exception messages. A message which is excellent for a novice user may be valued negatively by an expert user. Users in some settings may be very knowledgeable and it may not be necessary to inform the user about possible consequences unless the user requests it. In these settings the systems designer can provide cascaded messages and alter the parameters of the exception message (e.g., alter the content or appearance) to reduce the amount of information displayed to expert users. In this way, the systems designer can develop exception messages tailored to the user. One can envision the use of artificial intelligence to detect the level of exception message that should be issued based upon user characteristics such as level of technical literacy.

While it is recognized that including the proposed normative elements and format in all exception messages may result in more information to be displayed on screens we are not proposing that "more is better" when it comes to the content of exception messages. Rather, we propose that including the appropriate information in a standard format is better than the non-standard formats that currently exist. Still, to the extent that more information may in some cases need to be displayed, problems with information overload could result. This cost must be balanced against the benefits of providing more informative messages. A related issue involves the size of some screens in IT environments. The smaller screens possessed by PDAs and cell phones may limit the amount of information that is possible to display.

In these environments it may be best to include the proposed elements using a cascaded exception message as described above.

Future research could explore how deficiencies in exception messages may influence user's perceptions, judgments, and decision making. Those deficiencies that are demonstrated to negatively effect users the most should be the first to be addressed by systems designers and engineers. Moreover, future experimental research could examine actual user behavior in response to alternative exception message content in various computer interaction contexts. Such experimental and observational research could provide much insight as to the effectiveness of alternative IT exception message design. In all these situations, this manuscript provides a first step in the process of these investigations.

REFERENCES

Amer, T. S., & Maris, J.-M. B. (2007). Signal words and signal icons in application control and information technology exception messages – Hazard matching and habituation effects. *The Journal of Information Systems, 2*(21), 1–26. doi:10.2308/jis.2007.21.2.1

American National Standards Institute. (2002). *American national standard for product safety signs and labels*. New York: ANSI.

Apple Computer, Inc. (1989). *HyperCard stack design guidelines*. Menlo Park, CA: Addison-Wesley Publishing Company, Inc. ISBN 0-201-51784-1.

Blackwell, A., & Green, T. (2003). Notational systems – The cognitive dimensions of notations frameworks. In J. M. Carroll (Ed.), *HCI models, theories, and frameworks: Toward a multidisciplinary science* (pp. 103-121). Amsterdam: Morgan Kaufmann Publishers. ISBN 1-55860-808-7.

Brown, P. J. (1983). Error messages: The neglected area of the man/machine interface. *Communications of the ACM, 4*(26), 246–249. doi:10.1145/2163.358083

Coats, R., & Vlaeminke, I. (1987). *Man-computer interfaces: An introduction to software design and implementation*. Cambridge, MA: Blackwell Scientific Publications, Inc.

Cooper, A., & Reimann, R. (2003). *About face: The essentials of interaction design*. Indianapolis, IN: Wiley Publishing, Inc. ISBN 0-7645-2641-3.

Efe, K. (1987). A proposed solution to the problem of levels in error-messages generation (technical). *Communications of the ACM, 11*(30), 948–955. doi:10.1145/32206.32210

Galitz, W. O. (2007). *The essential guide to user interface design*. Indianapolis, IN: Wiley Publishing, Inc. ISBN 978-0-470-05342-3.

Hellier, E., Wright, D. B., Edworthy, J., & Newstead, S. (2000). On the stability of the arousal strength of warning signal words. *Applied Cognitive Psychology*, (14): 577–592. doi:10.1002/1099-0720(200011/12)14:6<577::AID-ACP682>3.0.CO;2-A

ISO 9241-110 (2006). *Ergonomics of human-system interaction – Part 110 dialog principles*. Geneva, Switzerland: International Organization for Standardization.

Lehto, M. R. (2006). Human Factors Models. In M.S. Wogalter (Ed.), *Handbook of warnings* (pp. 63-87). New Jersey/London: Lawrence Erlbaum Associates.

Molich, R., & Nielsen, J. (1990). Improving a human-computer dialogue. *Communications of the ACM, 3*(33), 338–348. doi:10.1145/77481.77486

Shneiderman, B. (1982). Designing computer system messages. *Communications of the ACM, 9*(25), 610–611. doi:10.1145/358628.358639

Shneiderman, B., & Plaisant, C. (2005). *Designing the user interface: Strategies for effective human-computer interaction.* Pearson Publishing, Inc., ISBN 0-321-19786-0.

Windows Vista Development Center. (2008). *MSDN library.* Retrieved August 2008, from http://msdn.microsoft.com/en-us/library/aa511267.aspx

Windows XP Design Team. (2001). *Windows XP visual guidelines.* Microsoft Corporation. Retrieved June 2004, from http://www.microsoft.com/whdc/hwdev/windowsxp/downloads/default.mspx

Wogalter, M. S. (2006a). *Handbook of warnings.* New Jersey/London: Lawrence Erlbaum Associates.

Wogalter, M. S. (2006b). Purposes and scope of warnings. In M.S. Wogalter (Ed.), *Handbook of warnings* (pp. 3-9). New Jersey/London: Lawrence Erlbaum Associates.

Wogalter, M. S., Conzola, V., & Smith-Jackson, T. (2002). Research-based guidelines for warning design and evaluation. *Applied Ergonomics, 3*(33), 219–230. doi:10.1016/S0003-6870(02)00009-1

ENDNOTES

[1] Note that symbols in the message panel are different than signal icons in the signal word panel. Symbols communicate informational elements about the nature, consequences and directions of the situation whereas signal icons are to draw the user's attention.

[2] A simple Internet search of "user interface design," "graphical user interface (GUI) design," "computer usability," "human computer interaction (HCI)," etc. yields a tremendous amount of information related to the general design of IT user interfaces. It is the specific area of exception message design that is the focus of this article.

[3] Note that the application name "Sales Data Entry" appears in the signal word panel of the proposed exception messages of Figure 3. Including the application name in exception messages is common practice in IT because multiple applications may be open at the same time on a user's computing screen. Without such application identification, a user may not know which application triggered the exception message. Indeed, even applications running in the background, out of sight of the user can call exception messages.

[4] The paper paradigm within the desktop metaphor was created by many individuals and organizations, including Douglas Engelbart, Xerox PARC, and Apple Computer.

This work was previously published in International Journal of Technology and Human Interaction, Volume 6, Issue 1, edited by Anabela Mesquita & Chia-Wen Tsai, pp. 54-68, copyright 2010 by IGI Publishing (an imprint of IGI Global).

Chapter 13
The Many Sides of Human Resource Information Systems

Hilkka Poutanen
University of Oulu, Finland

Vesa Puhakka
University of Oulu, Finland

ABSTRACT

The history of human resource information systems stretches to the 1960s, when human resource data were separated from payroll systems. In the 1980s, researchers and practitioners became more interested in human resource information systems, and in the 1990s several studies, articles, user experiences, opinions and descriptions were published in journals, magazines and on the internet. Still, despite the number of literature, no survey or framework exists that constructs a synthesis of the fragmented issues of human resource information systems from both of these viewpoints, that is, information systems and human resource management. In this paper, an initial framework for human resource information systems is introduced to underline the importance and the need for consolidating the knowledge on the phenomenon.

INTRODUCTION

The history of human resource information systems is short in terms of both practice and research. In practice the history begins in the late 1950s with payroll systems and continues into the 1960s when the first automated personnel systems were separated from payroll systems and the data

of employees was made available (Kavanagh, Gueutal, & Tannenbaum, 1990; Martinsons, 1997; Walker, 1982; Walker, 1993). In the 1960s and 1970s, only large companies could afford to invest in the hardware and software required for human resource information systems. Additionally, the computers were bulky and the software was difficult to use. At that time, the main task of human resource information systems was the record-keeping of employee data. Later, the

DOI: 10.4018/978-1-61350-465-9.ch013

technology was further developed and cheaper equipment as well as more versatile software for human resource activities became available (Haines & Petit, 1997; Kavanagh et al., 1990; Walker, 1993).

Since the 1980s there has been debate about human resource information systems and their role in organizations (DeSanctis, 1986; Kovach, Hughes, Fagan, & Maggitti, 2002). The history of research on the topic, for its part, starts in the 1980s when researchers became interested in human resource information systems (DeSanctis, 1986; Walker, 1982). In the 1990s several studies, articles, user experiences, opinions and descriptions were published in journals, magazines and on the internet (Axel, 1998; Broderick & Boudreau, 1991, 1992; Elliot & Tevavichulada, 1999; Haines & Petit, 1997; Hubbard, Forcht, & Thomas, 1998; Kossek, Young, Gash, & Nichol, 1995; Kovach & Cathcart, Jr., 1999; Rodger, Pendharkar, Paper, & Molnar, 1998; Stroh, Grasshoff, Rudé, & Carter, 1998; Tannenbaum, 1990; Townsend & Hendrickson, 1996; Van der Linden & Parker, 1998).

Various issues have arisen from these discourses and publications. In addition, some researchers have constructed models and definitions for human resource information systems (e.g., Broderick & Boudreau, 1992; Kavanagh et al., 1990; Mayfield, Mayfield, & Lunce, 2003; Walker, 1982; Walker, 1993). Human resource information systems have developed continuously and today they have their own role among other managerial information systems in organizations. However, the research on human resource information systems is still in its infancy.

Though the research of human resource information systems has just recently begun to develop (see Ball, 2001; Mayfield et al., 2003; Hussain, Wallace, & Cornelius, 2007), there are quite a few studies that explicitly discuss human resource information systems, upon which proper theories can be built. Still, the common research areas of human resource information systems

can be categorized under the following five research streams: The first stream concentrates on technological choices and the challenges of designing and implementing the systems (Ball, 2001; DeSanctis, 1986). The second stream approaches the subject from the perspective of software design (Cascio & Awad, 1981; Haines & Petit, 1997; Niederman, 1999). The third stream criticizes the above streams and instead stresses the organizational use of human resource information systems (Ball, 2001; Hussain et al., 2007), the users of human resource information systems and their processes (DeSanctis, 1986; Haines & Petit, 1997; Ruël & Bondarouk, 2004a) and the usage and utility of human resource information systems in organizations (Amit & Belcourtm, 1999; Kovach & Cathcart, 1999).

The fourth stream, then, rather than focusing on the system itself, focuses on analyzing and explicating the past, current and future developments of human resource information systems (Atwater, 1995; Haines & Petit, 1997; Kossek et al., 1994; Niederman, 1999; Tannenbaum, 1990; Townsend & Hendrickson, 1996; Van der Linden & Parker, 1998). The fifth stream brings into the discussion the vagueness of the conceptual development of the research on human resource information systems and demonstrates how the research on human resource information systems is in its early stages (e.g., Mayfield et al., 2003). The underlying assumption, based on the above streams, is that there is no single simple view for looking at human resource information systems, but that the different angles should be taken under examination holistically in order to understand this complex phenomenon as a whole (Lippert & Swiercz, 2005).

As has been reiterated, the research on human resource information systems has resulted in many discussions which, however, are still in their beginnings or are waiting to be opened up. There is a lack of research which constructs a synthesis out of the fragmented studies of human resource information systems. Hereafter, the objective of the present study is to review the extensive literature and internet sites on the subject and introduce an initial conceptual framework of human resource information systems for future studies. The intent of the framework is not to cover the human resource information systems field as a whole, but to signal that it is now time to build more rigorous theoretical frameworks and conduct theory-driven empirical studies. The research question to be answered in this paper is: What are the elements of effective research design for studying human resource information systems as a multidisciplinary research subject?

The present paper proceeds so that first the main concept of the study, namely human resource information systems, is defined. Secondly, the initial framework of human resource information systems is presented as a research structure for future studies of human resource information systems. Thirdly, the elements of the framework are introduced so that human resource information systems and technology are discussed together with the data and knowledge of the systems and the design of human resource information systems is then examined. Fourthly, it is shown how the individuals in organizations use human resource information systems in practice, and how the technological approaches to the phenomenon are questioned. Fifthly, the history of developments of human resource information systems is depicted. Sixthly, an overview of the current research on human resource information systems is described. Lastly, a short discussion is put forth.

DEFINING HUMAN RESOURCE INFORMATION SYSTEMS

In the extant literature, different definitions of human resource information systems are available. The first definition is by Walker (1982, p. 16): "The modern human resource information system may be defined as a computer-based method for collecting, storing, maintaining, retrieving, and validating certain data needed by an organization about its employees, applicants, and former employees." Kavanagh et al. (1990, p. 29) offer another definition: "A human resource information system is a system used to acquire, store, manipulate, analyze, retrieve, and distribute pertinent information about an organization's human resources." Broderick and Boudreau (1992, p. 17) define a human resource information system as a "composite of databases, computer application and hardware and software that are used to collect/record, store, manage, deliver, present and manipulate data for human resources". The fourth definition, presented by Walker (1993), and also used by Kovach and Cathcart (1999, p. 275), states that "a human resource information system is a systematic procedure for collecting, storing, maintaining, retrieving and validating data needed by an organization about its human resources, personnel activities and organization unit characteristics".

It is easy to notice that the definitions of human resource information systems supplement the definitions of human resource management which include lists of different tasks associated with employees such as recruiting, training, promoting, record keeping and meeting various legal requirements. Human resource management is also defined as monitoring, facilitating and setting up processes that select, assess and assign people to appropriate roles in an organization (Ball, 2001; Hubbard et al., 1998; Targowski & Deshpande, 2001; Townley, 1994). Human resource information systems, earlier called personnel systems, have mostly been designed and implemented for the above-listed activities. Because of the supplementation, it can be argued that the development of the human resource information systems follows the development of human resource management. Still, the development of human resource information systems can also follow its own path and

Table 1. The initial framework of human resource information systems

Category	Sub categories	Discussed issues
Information Technology	Database solutions Web solutions	Electronic human resource management
	Data	Security Legal issues
Information Systems	Designers	Information technology professionals Human resources professionals
Organizational Use	Application areas	Human resource functions Human resource management
	End users	Human resource staff Managers Employees
	Utility discussions	Advantage Competitiveness Globalization
Development	History Present Future	
Research	Theories Models	

correspondingly give development ideas to human resource management. The framework could offer the possibility for both separate and mutual development and research of both disciplines.

DEVELOPING THE INITIAL FRAMEWORK FOR THE RESEARCH OF HUMAN RESOURCE INFORMATION SYSTEMS

In this study the initial framework of human resource information systems (see Table 1) is developed based on a review of the relevant literature. In addition, internet sites dealing with the practices of human resource information systems were studied widely. As a result of the review, it has been perceived that the elements of human resource information systems can be divided into five basic categories based on the streams introduced in the first chapter. The categories are information technology, information systems, organizational use, development and research.

References which particularly discuss technological and software design issues are gathered into the categories of information technology (Ball, 2001; DeSanctis, 1986; Walker, 1982; Walker, 1993) and information systems (Haines & Petit, 1997; Niederman, 1999). Information technology has dramatically changed human resources activities. Different manual files have been transformed into databases and web systems. Data security and legislation give strict orders on what data can be stored, how the data should be processed and who has the authority to use the information because accessing individual data is a sensitive matter. The category of information systems, for its part, includes the issues of system design. The specific target groups are the people who are, or could be, involved in the design and implementation process as well as in the use and usability testing of human resource information systems.

The category of organizational use contains references which focus mainly on application areas (Ball, 2001; DeSanctis, 1986; Hussain et al., 2007;

Haines & Petit, 1997; Ruël & Bondarouk, 2004a) and discussion of the usage and utility of human resource information systems (Amit & Belcourt, 1999; Kovach & Cathcart, 1999). The application areas describe the functions and activities which are supported by human resource information systems. The basic areas of discussion are human resource management and business management. The category also includes end user issues, focusing on the staff of human resource departments, managers and employees of the organizations as well as possibly on customers, partners and financiers who are regarded as end users involved in the human resource information systems. The different usage discussions concern the issues of competitiveness, advantages and globalization of human resource information systems. The discussions underline the meaning and the importance of human resource information systems in an organization.

The fourth category includes references which discuss the past, current and future developments of human resource information systems (Atwater, 1995; Haines & Petit, 1997; Kossek et al., 1994; Niederman, 1999; Tannenbaum, 1990; Townsend & Hendrickson, 1996; Van der Linden & Parker, 1998). The development history is quite easy to portray but the present development is difficult to describe because of the fast growth of technology which has had an impact on software development. To predict the future is always a difficult task but some predictions could be made about the role of human resource information systems in organizations. Nevertheless, the field of human resource information systems needs rigorous theoretical and empirical research.

The references which propose theoretical concepts, theory-building and models for human resource information systems are situated in the research category (e.g., Mayfield et al., 2003). Modeling is a useful means to clarify the human resource information systems processes as well as the human resource activities and other functions the human resource information systems serve.

This has already been achieved by some researchers (e.g., Ball, 2001). However, more theories are still waiting to be developed and published. We believe that the future will bring interesting discussions and debates.

The introduced framework is in its early stage, as is the field of human resource information systems research. In this text it is acknowledged that the categories of the framework overlap with each other, which reveals that the issues could be discussed in one or several categories. However, the reason for making the five categories is to underline the different viewpoints on the issues of human resource information systems. In Table 1 the initial framework is presented as a whole, and in the following chapters the categories are discussed thus introducing some of the issues brought up in the reviewed literature.

HUMAN RESOURCE INFORMATION SYSTEMS AND INFORMATION TECHNOLOGY

When discussing automated human resource information systems, technology is an integral part of the discussion. Automated information systems mean that some kinds of computers (personal computers, today networks and databases) must be available. Yet, all these things, i.e., information systems and information technology, require investments. Therefore, the acquisition of human resource information systems has often been considered critically. In addition, organizations see both human resources and human resource information systems as costs of production, and the purchase of human resource information systems is often postponed. Earlier massive information systems and computers were expensive. Later, as personal computers and technology have developed, the price of the computers and systems decreased. However, employee costs increased because of the legislation of human resource activities. Thus, the historic tendency to treat human resource information systems as expensive costs, as well as the need for skilled experts to maintain these systems, have created a situation in which organizations have been cautious when considering investments in human resource information systems and technology (DeSanctis, 1986; Haines & Petit, 1997; Kavanagh et al., 1990; Walker, 1982; Walker, 1993).

Predictions have been made concerning when organizations should implement human resource information systems (see Hubbard et al., 1998). When organizations acquire human resource information systems and information technology the main goals are quite often to gain benefits and reduce costs (Allen & Morton, 1994). The technology is believed to provide cheap, easy and fast data processing and efficient organizational processes (see Allen & Morton, 1994). Also, the technology is believed to enhance the access of more detailed information (Hubbard et al., 1998). Yet the problem is that too often human resource information systems are seen only as technology when it should instead be seen as an integral part of investments in human resource management.

Although human resource information systems are connected to the automated use of human resource data, human resource information systems are different from human resource information technology. Avison and Elliot (2006, p. 5) have argued that "compared with other IT-related disciplines, computer science and computer systems engineering, IS emphasizes the applications of technology rather than a focus on fundamental technologies and theories. It focuses more on interactions between people and organizations (the 'soft' issues) and technology rather than on the technologies (the 'hard' issues) themselves." Thus, human resource information systems are rather the application than a part of the development of technology human resource management.

From the viewpoint of information technology versus human resource information systems, the work of the scientists of the information technology in theory and the work of the systems engineers and software developers in practice focuses on the technology itself, whereas the work of the researchers of human resource information systems in theory and the work of systems analysts in practice focuses on people, organization and business. Because of this human-oriented emphasis of human resource information systems, information systems research has generally been situated close to social sciences. Still, due to the close relation to technology, research on information systems is also connected to disciplines such as computer science. Because of the multidisciplinarity of information systems, overlapping enables cooperation and interaction between the disciplines although the disciplines have their own focus, purpose and orientation of activities (Avison & Elliot, 2006).

As a summary, information technology provides technical and computer-based solutions for human resource management, whereas human resource information systems implement the applications for human resource management. The software solutions support the human resource tasks and functions which have emerged from the development of human resource management. Thus, it can be concluded that information technology provides the developed electronic base for the challenges of software and human resource information systems and technical solutions through applications. Both information technology and human resource information systems serve the people and the tasks they perform. Quite often these roles come into existence as data and knowledge on human resources and processes in organizations.

INFORMATION TECHNOLOGY, DATA AND KNOWLEDGE

Human resource information systems are widely seen as computerized systems for storing, manipulating and providing data on employees (Basu, Hartono, Lederer, & Sethi, 2002). Still, they have also been designed to perform most of the routine tasks of human resource management which help to maintain necessary knowledge in databases. The data is important for managers and for keeping human resource management effective and in real-time order (Hubbard et al., 1998). Therefore, human resource information systems can also be regarded as systems constructed primarily for knowledge management of the organization (Martinsons, 1997). The reason for that is the desire to control the basic data of personnel and support the effectiveness of an organization. For example, strategic human resource development and planning focuses on strategic management, organizational behavior and human resource management (Basu et al., 2002; Grundy, 1997; Martinsons, 1997); it links business strategy and organizational strategy to management skills. Strategic information system planning supports the process of strategic human resource development and planning, and a knowledge-based system helps deliver human resource management qualitative outputs as well as increase both employee and customer satisfaction (Basu et al., 2002; Grundy, 1997; Martinsons, 1997).

When examining the data of human resource information systems, the typical employee information is name, address, phone number, education, training, career development and documents related to personal development discussions. Also, different private or semi-private data could be stored in the system. Because the data is available in a different form than in manual systems, both data and the system require more concern for security and sensitivity than earlier. This concern should be taken into account when human resource information systems are designed and implemented. It can also be argued that technology provides ways to examine the daily human resource activities in an organization and to make any necessary renewals. Designing this type of technology is a tricky task as human behavior is extremely complicated and constantly changing (Hustad & Munkvold, 2007). The ideas of elec-

tronic human resource management aim to offer proposals for ideating and solving the challenging situations arising from the human resource activities of managers, superiors and employees (Ruël & Bondarouk, 2004a; Ruël, Bondarouk, & Looise, 2004b; Ruël & Magalhaes, 2008).

DESIGNING HUMAN RESOURCE INFORMATION SYSTEMS IN ORGANIZATION

When human resource information systems are designed, implemented and used, the basic and simple question to remember is for what purposes are human resource information systems available. There are a variety of human resource information systems on the market which are advertised as the best solution for running the human resource activities of an organization. Therefore the mangers and human resource staff should have the competence and knowledge to evaluate the human resource information systems before making decisions to purchase such systems. This leads to the question of who are capable and adequately experienced to evaluate and design human resource information systems: managers, human resource professionals or information systems professionals? We can examine this question, following Haines and Petit (1997), through the concepts of user satisfaction and system usage.

The need for usable information is inevitably enormous. However, human resource information technology, computerization and human resource information systems can mislead the human resource professionals which handle management. In addition, managers do not use human resource information systems if they are unfamiliar with the system, and consequently they would not obtain the needed data. Furthermore, managers with longer work experience may be less satisfied with the human resource information systems than younger managers who are more familiar with the technology and systems. User satisfaction and system usage have become two common measures of system success in human resource activities as well in other organizational information systems (Haines & Petit, 1997). It is possible to conclude that to design human resource information systems it is important to remember that all relevant knowledge should be available during the development process of the system.

Niederman (1999) presents a socio-technical approach to information systems which helps to create the knowledge base needed for designing human resource information systems. According to Niederman (1999, p. 33), it "requires recognition of the inextricable link between information technologies and humans as designers and users." He has studied global organizations and constructed five interaction areas for information technology and human computer designers/users. These areas are as follows: using information technology to support the human resource strategy of global organizations, using information technology to support the generation and distribution of organizational learning, using human resource management techniques and programs to support the work of information systems professionals, using human resource management techniques and programs to support the work of global "end-user" or knowledge workers and national and regional policies to support technical and human resource infrastructures (Niederman, 1999).

The study by Niederman (1999) is important as it also proposes several research questions for each of the above areas to study in order to understand the complicated nature of human resource information systems in practice. Human resource information systems are inherently an organizational rather than a technological phenomenon and thus the organizational use of human resource information systems cannot be put aside when talking about the design and implementation of human resource information systems.

ORGANIZATIONAL USE OF HUMAN RESOURCE INFORMATION SYSTEMS

The organizational use of human resource information systems faces several kinds of challenges (see Ball, 2001; Niederman, 1999; Tansley, Newell, & Williams, 2001). An organization could invest in the top techniques and intelligent systems but the question is how the systems can be integrated into the daily tasks as well as organizational activities and routines of an organization (Ball, 2001). Also, company size seems to affect how human resource information systems are used and by whom. Ball (2001) has studied the use of human resource information systems according to the number of employees and her study showed that human resource information systems are used more in large organizations than in small ones. In addition, the study by Ball (2001) revealed that human resource information systems are still being used administratively although the information and data would also support other activities than those of administrative human resource management.

Hussain et al. (2007) provided interesting results from a similar type of research. According to their study, human resource professionals are nowadays quite familiar with human resource information systems. Human resource professionals use human resource information systems mainly for strategic partnering (see also Weatherly, 2005). Interesting was also the finding that the company size is no longer as relevant as it was in the study by Ball (2001). In fact, although small companies consider investments in human resource information systems high, they utilize the systems even better than the large firms (Hussain et al., 2007).

As a summary, this research line has shown that human resource information systems are an organizational phenomenon and that the users of human resource information systems should be at the centre of the research. This is important because it underlines that without the knowledge of how to use the systems there is a danger that technological systems do not support the organizational processes but could even disturb them.

USERS OF HUMAN RESOURCE INFORMATION SYSTEMS

The history of human resource departments developed from personnel departments whose duty was to handle employee issues in organizations (Kavanagh et al., 1990; Walker, 1982; Walker, 1993). The work in human resource management departments has broadened and become more relevant over the course of the development of human resource activities in organizations. However, human resource experts have felt that they have been locked out of strategic and financial discussions (see Ball, 2001). Thus, the existence of human resource information systems has given importance and credibility to human resource department and staff.

When one considers the organization, he or she also invokes human resources (managers and employees) with different roles and tasks. If the organization has human resource information systems, the whole staff should employ it, but for different reasons and probably with different techniques (the whole staff includes those in human resources also). Primarily, human resource information systems are seen as tools for human resource staff (Ruël & Bondarouk, 2004a; Ruël et al., 2004b).

However, many studies which assert the above have been conducted in the 1980s and 1990s when human resource information systems evolved strongly and human resource workers were the first in the organizations to use the systems. For example, DeSanctis (1986) and Haines and Petit (1997) studied the use and usability of human resource information systems. In her research DeSanctis (1986) noted that at that time, in 1986, the human resource information systems users were mainly human resource staff. Kavanagh et al. (1990) stressed that there is a variety of potential users of human resource information systems in the organization. Thus, the conclusion cannot be made that human resource information systems are only for human resource staff, but that the whole organization should be the user of human resource information systems. Because there are thus many kinds of group benefits from these systems, it raises the question of what should be the potential utilities of human resource information systems.

UTILITY DISCUSSIONS OF HUMAN RESOURCE INFORMATION SYSTEMS

It can be stated that a real-time human resource information system and a skillful human resource staff could provide a competitive advantage for an organization. Amit and Belcourt (1999) introduce in their study the concept of tacit human resource management which an organization obtains over a long period of practice. Usually, human resource management routines and activities are described as one model or pattern. However, it is important to acknowledge that organizations have their own practices and mechanisms for attracting, motivating, evaluating and compensating their human resources.

The Amit and Belcourt study (1999, p. 175) explains "... that an organization's ability to build, deploy and renew its productive human-capital through transformational routines in ways that cannot be easily replicated by other organizations generates a competitive advantage in the market." Therefore, the effectiveness and competitiveness of human resource information systems in supporting the transformational routines to build, deploy and renew the productive human-capital in an organization should be the starting point when developing the criteria for the usage of efficient human resource information systems. Rapid data access, information exchange, administrative and strategic advantage are the basic topics which need to be discussed (Kovach & Cathcart, 1999; Kovach et al., 2002).

DEVELOPMENT HISTORY OF HUMAN RESOURCE INFORMATION SYSTEMS RESEARCH

Human resource information systems research has achieved stronger ground during the new millennium (see Hussain et al., 2007). The empirical studies have more breadth because organizations have gained experiences in using human resource information systems. In the 1980s, studies attempted to establish a new research field, namely human resource information systems. In the 1990s, studies were full of expectations of how human resource information systems would affect the human resource activities and business planning of an organization. There were studies about who was using human resource information systems and for what purposes, and what the advantages of using these systems were (Broderick & Boudreau, 1991; Groe, Pyle, & Jamrog, 1996; Haines & Petit, 1997; Hubbard et al., 1998; Kossek et al., 1994; Townsend & Hendrickson, 1996; Van der Linden & Parker, 1998).

Organizations were seen as efficient if they had the technology and information systems to support their human resource activities. Also, the effects of human resource information systems on the work and development of human resource departments and professionals were under discussion (Atwater, 1995; Axel, 1998; Broderick & Boudreau, 1991; Broderick & Boudreau, 1992; Elliot & Tevavichulada, 1999; Groe et al., 1996; Haines & Petit, 1997; Hubbard et al., 1998; Kossek et al., 1994; Niederman, 1999; Rodger, Pendharkar, Paper, & Molnar, 1998; Stroh, Grasshoff, Rudé, & Carter, 1998; Tannenbaum, 1990; Townsend & Hendrickson, 1996; Van der Linden & Parker, 1998).

In addition to research papers, some books are available on the design and implementation activities of human resource information systems.

As early as 1981, Cascio and Awad published a book called "Human resource management: An information systems approach". They focused on human resource information systems based on the various activities of human resource management, such as staffing, evaluation, environmental and legal factors, job analysis and design, recruitment, selection and placement (Cascio & Awad, 1981). Walker (1982) has written a guidebook for building an effective human resource information system. It is a concrete, step-by-step guidebook for developing a human resource information system for an organization. Its goal has been to provide guidelines for installing a computer-based personnel system that works for the organization. The book gives information about preparation and the needs of analysis, design and installation, as well as viewpoints from corporate perspectives and profitability (Walker, 1982).

In addition, Kavanagh et al. (1990) and Walker (1993) have written handbooks on human resource information systems. The handbook by Kavanagh et al. (1990) focuses on the information systems role inside human resource information systems. The book analyzes the system itself and what should have been noticed before the implementation. Also, it introduces a variety of applications of human resource information systems. The handbook by Walker (1993) gives a technical and process-oriented viewpoint to the development and implementation of human resource information systems. Both publications have been referred to in the publications on human resource information systems, although the handbooks do not have a distinct academic background. Thus far, they are the only handbooks available for constructing human resource information systems.

Predictions are always difficult. Still, it is important to analyze the development of research and practice. Opinions and viewpoints offer paths for new ideas and innovations. Organizations make short- and long-term plans and strategies to stay in business. In his research Atwater (1995) made a review concluding that human resource information systems are tools for providing human resource information to the business planning process. He designated the process as "the workforce forecasting" and defined it as follows: "it focuses on predictions about the size and mix of a pool of workers in the future" (Atwater, 1995, p. 50). This process challenges the human resource information systems to provide valuable information on employees when an organization needs it for filling job posts, or keeping information on available employees.

As mentioned earlier, personnel have become human resources and personnel departments have changed into human resource departments. These changes have generated human resource management and human resource activities. The need to maintain employee data not only manually but also automatically has divided payroll systems and human resource information systems into two different systems (Kavanagh et al., 1990; Walker, 1993). Today, many human resource information systems contain the information which is important for human resource managers, superiors and employees. The new challenge, however, is leadership. Employers need more human information on employees and their actions in different situations. Nonetheless, legislation and (at least) moral issues limit access to such information and are, therefore, issues to be considered when designing human resource information systems for human and sensitive human resource activities.

The research of human resource information systems have focused on various theories and on making models and patterns (for example Mayfield et al., 2003). At present, the research of human resource information systems is fragmented into different research papers and results (Ngai & Wat, 2006). The time has come to collect them and to discover the whole picture of the available research on human resource information systems. It could be possible to depict the research areas using the initial framework of human resource information systems formed in this paper. In addition, there are many research questions in the referenced articles which need to be studied. It is now the time to find answers.

DISCUSSION

The study has contributed to the existing research on human resource information systems in two particular ways. Firstly, it has demonstrated that human resource information systems can be regarded as a process embedded in a particular organizational context consisting of interlaced categories. In this paper it is proposed that the phenomenon could be better explained by trying to understand the different kinds of behavior of the organization with relation to its information systems. Secondly, we demonstrated that human resource information systems are driven by organizational and technological generative mechanisms. Thus, researchers should acknowledge both organizational and technological developments. In this way we could produce new knowledge on how human resource information systems are actually accomplished. The results will help researchers and practitioners to further understand the dynamism and episodic nature of the use and development of human resource information systems in organizations.

Another challenge has also been suggested in prior studies. Within human resource information systems research a great deal of research has used positivistic, variance-based methods which aim at explaining and predicting what happens in a social reality by searching for regularities and causality within the research phenomenon. Many studies have approached the phenomenon as if it were a natural law and tried to discover causal reasons behind it in which inputs would explain outputs. Consequently, we are able to measure the consequences but cannot explain why, how and where organizations use the systems. Prior research has not taken into account that most events in a social world take place in spatiotemporal open systems – in networks – in which events do not invariably follow a determined and recurrent pattern. Therefore, it is difficult to find general causalities and patterns that would be applicable on an organizational level. Based on this, it is claimed that studying human resource information systems is not only a methodological issue but as well an ontological and epistemological issue of how to approach the organizing behavior of human beings.

Renewal capacity to search for new business is crucial nowadays. The business environment is constantly accelerating and thus the supporting role of various kinds of designs of human resource information systems for handling demanding and complicated organizational work is becoming more important than ever. Therefore, future research on human resource information systems should take into account the nature of managerial work in our post-modern, digital age. The research area is still young. The sphere is not developed although it is one of the most important lines of human resource management. Thus, to develop knowledge international collaboration is needed as well as research programs for studying the many sides of this complicated phenomenon.

REFERENCES

Allen, T., & Scott Morton, M. (1994). *Information technology and the corporation of the 1990s: Research studies*. New York: Oxford University Press.

Amit, R., & Belcourt, M. (1999). Human resources management processes: a value-creating source of competitive advantage. *European Management Journal, 17*(2), 174–181. doi:10.1016/S0263-2373(98)00076-0

Atwater, D. M. (1995). Workforce forecasting. *Human Resource Planning, 18*(4), 50–53.

Avison, D., & Elliot, S. (2006). Scoping the discipline of information systems. In King, J., & Lyytinen, K. (Eds.), *In Information Systems: The State of the Field* (pp. 3–18). Chichester, UK: John Wiley and Sons.

Axel, H. (1998). Human resources and the role of IT. *Human Resource Management International Digest, 68*(6), 30–32.

Ball, K. S. (2001). The use of human resource information systems: a survey. *Personnel Review, 30*(5/6), 677–693. doi:10.1108/EUM0000000005979

Basu, V., Hartono, E., Lederer, A. L., & Sethi, V. (2002). The impact of organisational commitment, senior management involvement and team involvement on strategic information systems planning. *Information & Management, 39*(6), 513–524. doi:10.1016/S0378-7206(01)00115-X

Bratton, J., & Gold, J. (2003). *Human resource management, theory and practice*. New York: Palgrave Macmillan.

Broderick, R. F., & Boudreau, J. W. (1991). *Human resource information systems for competitive advantage: interviews with ten leaders* (CAHRS Working Paper Series). Ithaca, NY: Cornell University.

Broderick, R. F., & Boudreau, J. W. (1992). Human resource management, information technology and the competitive edge. *The Executive, 6*(2), 7–17.

Cascio, W. F., & Awad, E. M. (1981). *Human resource management: An information systems approach*. Reston, VA: Reston Publishing Company.

DeSanctis, G. (1986). Human resource information systems: A current assessment. *Management Information Systems Quarterly, 10*(1), 15–27. doi:10.2307/248875

Elliot, R. H., & Tevavichulada, S. (1999). Computer literacy and human resource management: a public/private sector comparison. *Public Personnel Management, 28*(2), 259–274.

Groe, G. M., Pyle, W., & Jamrog, J. J. (1996). Information technology and HR. *Human Resource Planning, 19*(1), 56–61.

Grundy, T. (1997). Human resource management – a strategic approach. *Long Range Planning, 30*(4), 507–517. doi:10.1016/S0024-6301(97)00030-7

Haines, V. Y., & Petit, A. (1997). Conditions for successful human resource information systems. *Human Resource Management, 36*(2), 261–275. doi:10.1002/(SICI)1099-050X(199722)36:2<261::AID-HRM7>3.0.CO;2-V

Hubbard, J. C., Forcht, K., & Thomas, D. S. (1998). Human resource information systems: An overview of current ethical and legal issues. *Journal of Business Ethics, 17*(12), 1319–1323. doi:10.1023/A:1005735506589

Hussain, Z., Wallace, J., & Cornelius, N. E. (2007). The use and impact of human resource information systems on human resource management professionals. *Information & Management, 44*(1), 74–89. doi:10.1016/j.im.2006.10.006

Hustad, E., & Munkvold, B. E. (2007). IT-supported competence management: A case study at Ericsson. *Information Systems Management, 22*(2), 78–88. doi:10.1201/1078/45099.22.2.20050301/87280.9

Kavanagh, M. J., Gueutal, H. G., & Tannenbaum, S. I. (1990). *Human resource information systems: Development and applications.* Boston: PWS-KENT Publishing Company.

Kossek, E. E., Young, W., Gash, D. C., & Nichol, V. (1994). Waiting for innovation in the human resources department: Godot implements a human resource information system. *Human Resource Management, 33*(1), 135–159. doi:10.1002/hrm.3930330108

Kovach, K. A., & Cathcart, C. E. Jr. (1999). Human resource information systems (HRIS): Providing business with rapid data access, information exchange and strategic advantage. *Public Personnel Management, 28*(2), 275–282.

Kovach, K. A., Hughes, A. A., Fagon, P., & Maggitti, P. G. (2002). Administrative and strategic advantages of HRIS. *Employment Relations Today, 29*(2), 43–48. doi:10.1002/ert.10039

Lippert, S. K., & Swiercz, P. M. (2005). Human resource information systems (HRIS) and technology trust. *Journal of Information Science, 31*(5), 340–353. doi:10.1177/0165551505055399

Martinsons, M. G. (1997). Human resource management applications of knowledge-based systems. *International Journal of Information Management, 17*(1), 35–53. doi:10.1016/S0268-4012(96)00041-2

Mayfield, M., Mayfield, J., & Lunce, S. (2003). Human resource information systems: A review and model development. *Advances in Competitiveness Research, 11*(1), 139–151.

Ngai, E. W. T., & Wat, F. K. T. (2006). Human resource information systems: A review and empirical analysis. *Personnel Review, 35*(3), 297–314. doi:10.1108/00483480610656702

Niederman, F. (1999). Global information systems and human resource management: A research agenda. *Journal of Global Information Management, 7*(2), 33–39.

Rodger, J. A., Pendharkar, P. C., Paper, D. J., & Molnar, P. (1998). Reengineering the human resource information system at Gamma. *Facilities, 16*(12/13), 361–365. doi:10.1108/02632779810235681

Ruël, H., Bondarouk, T., & Looise, J. K. (2004b). E-HRM: innovation or irritation, an explorative empirical study in five large companies on Web-based HRM. *Management Review, 15*(3), 364–380.

Ruël, H., & Magalhaes, R. (2008). Organizational knowledge and change: The role of transformational HRIS. In H. Ruël & R. Magalhaes (Eds.), *Human resource information systems, Proceedings of the 2ⁿᵈ International Workshop on Human Resource Information Systems (HRIS 2008)*, Barcelona, Spain (pp. 111-123).

Ruël, H. J. M., & Bondarouk, T. (2004a). *The Web-driven individualization of the employment relationship*. Retrieved May 28, 2008, from http://exchange.usg.uu.nl/irec/papers/5_RuelBondarouk.doc

Stroh, L. K., Grasshoff, S., Rudé, A., & Carter, N. (1998). Intergraded HR systems help develop global leaders. *HRMagazine, 43*(5), 13–17.

Tannenbaum, S. I. (1990). Human resource information systems: User group implications. *Journal of Systems Management, 41*(1), 27–26.

Tansley, C., Newell, S., & Williams, H. (2001). Effecting HRM-style practices through an integrated human resource information system: An e-greenfield site? *Personnel Review, 30*(3), 351–370. doi:10.1108/00483480110385870

Targowski, A. S., & Deshpande, S. P. (2001). The utility and selection of an HRIS. *Advances in Competitiveness Research, 9*(1), 42–56.

Townley, B. (1994). *Reframing human resource management: Power, ethics and the subject at work*. London: Sage Publication.

Townsend, A. M., & Hendrickson, A. R. (1996). Recasting HRIS as an information resource. *HR-Magazine, 41*(2), 91–94.

Van der Linden, G., & Parker, P. (1998). On paradoxes between human resources management, postmodernism and HR information systems. *Accounting. Management and Information Technology, 8*(4), 265–282. doi:10.1016/S0959-8022(98)00014-9

Walker, A. J. (1982). *HRIS development: A project team guide to building an effective personnel information system*. New York: Van Nostrand Reinhold.

Walker, A. J. (1993). *Handbook of human resource information systems: Reshaping the human resource function with technology*. New York: McGraw-Hill.

Weatherly, L. A. (2005). HR technology: Leveraging the shift to self-service – it's time to go strategic. *HRMagazine, 50*(3), 1–11.

This work was previously published in International Journal of Technology and Human Interaction, Volume 6, Issue 4, edited by Anabela Mesquita & Chia-Wen Tsai, pp. 1-13, copyright 2010 by IGI Publishing (an imprint of IGI Global).

Chapter 14
Moderating Effect of Team Distributedness on Organizational Dimensions for Innovation Project Success

Mario Bourgault
Ecole Polytechnique, Canada

Nathalie Drouin
Université du Québec à Montréal (UQAM), Canada

Hélène Sicotte
Université du Québec à Montréal (UQAM), Canada

Jaouad Daoudi
Université du Québec en Outaouais (UQO), Canada

ABSTRACT

This article addresses the issue of geographically distributed work teams that carry out new product development projects. These are task-oriented, goal-driven, temporary teams that use ICTs. This exploratory study measures the moderating affect of team distributedness on the relationships between organizational and workforce management best practices and two measures of project success (efficacy and effectiveness). Data were obtained from real teams working in Canadian companies in diverse high-tech industries. The results show a moderating effect of team distributedness, which is interesting in that the distributedness factor is examined from a different perspective, that is, as a moderating rather than an explanatory dimension.

DOI: 10.4018/978-1-61350-465-9.ch014

INTRODUCTION

In recent years, projects have constituted the cornerstone of many strategic and/or economic actions, particularly in enterprises that must continuously cope with a complex and uncertain environment (Cleland & Ireland, 2007). Moreover, market globalization, corporate mergers and outsourcing have had a major impact on project structure and management (van Fenema & Kumar, 2000). Against this background, and in the light of current economic changes, more and more interest has been directed toward temporary inter-organizational and intra-organizational structures that involve distributed team members (Martins et al., 2004; Zigurs et al., 2001). Distributed projects have become a source of competitive advantage, and consequently profits, for high-tech companies (Katzy & Sung, 2001; Swan et al., 2004), and it is still assumed that interaction through ICT can overcome the disadvantage of not being face to face. But in practice, whether it is considered a cyclical economic necessity or an opportunity to gain a competitive edge, team *distributedness* strongly affects the way a project and the organizations involved in it function. Thus, when distributed project teams are used, management practices, workforce management and communication processes are applied in a different context, which has fascinating ramifications. This situation clearly requires a greater understanding of the particular dynamics of such settings. Accordingly, the objective of this study is to contribute to that understanding. In order to present the phenomenon, the first section of the article offers an overview of the importance of team distributedness in the modern economy and the main results regarding the factors that affect team and project success in the literature. We conclude this section with a model.

The second section presents the empirical results of a study in innovative Canadian companies that focus on developing new products and

services. The intent is to measure the moderating impact of distributedness on organizational dimensions for two measures of project success.

RESEARCH REVIEW

This study focuses on two broad streams of research that represent major challenges for companies: team management and innovation project management. We first discuss some of the major trends in distributed teams. We then identify key aspects of innovation that are considered in this study, specifically, practical actions to be taken when conducting new product development projects.

ABOUT DISTRIBUTED TEAMS

Profound changes in international politics, combined with market globalization and the unprecedented development of information and communication technologies (ICTs), have fostered global competition and spurred companies to rethink their managerial practices (Arnison & Miller, 2002; Lipnack & Stamps, 1997). Similarly, due to the trend toward specialization, competencies and skills focus, there is an ongoing need for inter-organizational cooperation (Wehmeyer & Riemer, 2007). This need is manifested in the rise of dynamic company networks designed to overcome strategic challenges such as intense global competition and investment barriers (Cleland & Ireland, 2007; Pinto, 2002); operational challenges such as response time, risk management, and vertical and/or horizontal integration (Pinto, 2002; Wehmeyer & Riemer, 2007); and financial challenges (Kokko et al., 2007). Economic organizations and government institutions' networks enable – if they do not require – the establishment of teams whose members are not necessarily located at a single site, known as *distributed teams*. For instance, a study conducted with 376 managers from different industrial branches in Germany revealed that 20% of full-time and almost 40% of temporary managers worked in distributed mode (AFW, 2002). Comparable numbers have been reported in other countries as well (Gibson & Cohen, 2003; Hertel et al., 2005).

Research on distributed teams has long been considered a subset of research on information systems (Schiller & Mandviwalla, 2007). It was formerly classified as a branch addressing the technical and behavioral aspects of dispersion, among other factors, and it required abstraction from the specificities[i] of the tasks to be executed. However, this is no longer the case. Currently, the research encompasses a multitude of disciplines, including R&D, supply management, marketing, and project management. Distributedness is, in effect, a new challenge that will ultimately impact the successful completion of projects (Lipnack & Stamps, 1997; Williams, 1999). Clearly, in view of their differences from so-called "traditional" or co-located teams, distributed project teams merit particular attention (Huxham & Vangen, 2005; Mihhailova, 2007; Pinto, 2002; Wehmeyer & Riemer, 2007). What, though, is a distributed team?

Academics have not yet reached a consensus on the definition of the distributed team. It is generally considered to be a functional body – a *temporary team* – that uses ICTs to overcome various forms of diversity[ii] (e.g., Bell & Kozlowski, 2002; Lipnack & Stamps, 1999; Lurey & Raisinghani, 2001; Martins et al., 2004; Pinto, 2002; Powell et al., 2004) and accomplish a common goal. The most often cited forms of diversity are geographic,[iii] temporal[iv], cultural and organizational. Notwithstanding this fact, a majority of research still uses a dichotomous measure of location (Lu et al., 2006) since, even though a more complex conceptualization is being developed, it is still difficult to operationalize. One thing is certain: virtuality concerns a team and its organizational environment. But are there significant differences between different kinds of teams?

DISTRIBUTEDNESS: IS THERE A DIFFERENCE?

Research on the phenomenon of distributedness has resulted in many studies that have the goal of characterizing teams that exist in a context of virtuality; these studies describe the perceived differences or influences. Thus, it is clear that geographic, temporal, cultural and organizational diversity partly condition a team's reality, and consequently its functioning. Even when this research stream was in its infancy, there was a certain consensus regarding the differences in team processes (see authors such as Duarte & Snyder, 1999; Fisher & Fisher, 1998; Haywood, 1998; Henry & Hartzler, 1997; Lipnack & Stamps, 1997). Communication in particular is affected and has a major impact on individuals and tasks. Clarifying objectives and roles, planning and executing project follow-up, resolving conflicts, increasing participation and delimiting autonomy cannot be done in exactly the same way. Likewise, the context and the organizational support, reflected in senior management's involvement, and the tools and methods that are available or imposed are also considered to vary depending on the degree of virtuality (Bourgault et al., 2008).

PERFORMANCE – BUT WHOSE PERFORMANCE?

There is a whole chapter in the relatively short history of this school of research that lays the descriptive foundations of the dimensions of virtuality, but without moving on to the topic of its impact on the team or the organization. Moreover, for other works, generally more recent, a common pitfall lies concealed under the general heading of "performance." Although very few researchers forget to define the performance observed, even if only in a short sentence, the results are not always distinguished on the basis of the *dimension* of performance observed. Was it the performance of a team, a project, or the result thereof, namely a product or service? Close reading reveals that studies dedicated to the specific nature of virtuality in teams are divided into two groups, depending on whether they focus on the team's performance – team processes such as communication, conflict, coordination, learning or satisfaction (Martins et al., 2004; Lu et al., 2006) – or on the performance of the project or the product resulting from their efforts: on time, on budget (Lee-Kelley & Sankey, 2008), meeting specifications and customers' needs, etc. This latter group is considerably less numerous. One can argue that the team's performance leads to the success of the project or product and thus that these results represent different stages in the same process. However, to the best of our knowledge, there are no studies that have specifically studied both dimensions of performance (team *and* project or product).

ABOUT INNOVATION AND NEW PRODUCT DEVELOPMENT (NPD) PROJECTS

Projects, especially projects whose objective is to increase and renew the resources offered to customers or citizens, constitute an essential dimension for today's organizations (Cleland & Ireland, 2007; van Fenema & Kumar, 2000). The increasing participation of companies in joint innovation activities, particularly for project design and development, raises even more challenges today. To face these challenges, organizations adopt practices and methodologies to increase their chances of success; we refer here to critical success factors, which researchers have been studying for more than 40 years. The results mostly agree that it is important to apply an integrated approach to management practices, workforce management as well as the communicational processes with which these projects are run (Cooper, 1979-2003). The

next sections will present the routines and actions that are known to influence NPD project success in general, and particularly in distributed contexts.

Plan, Follow Up, and Provide Proper Methodologies and Tools, or Else!

Product innovation involves many specialists. Consequently, an efficient grouping of activities in independent work-units will reduce coordination costs as much as possible. Von Hippel (1990) considers that there is no way to escape specialization but that one must take general objectives into account, on top of coordination requirements. In the same vein, access to information on the project's progress by team members, wherever they may be, is critical (Layman et al., 2006). Milestones mark the path of a product in the making and can be as essential as the financial and quality assessment (Cooper et al., 2002). Consequently, planning and follow-up make an important contribution to team processes (Hoegl & Parboteeah, 2006).

Project management is a discipline that is concerned with the organization, planning and control of organizational activities, positioned to maximize their efficiency. Its use is increasing as witnessed by the growing number of certified professionals; it is a key competency for the success of NPD. Our study is based on the hypothesis that the tool box and methods that affect both management of and communication within work teams must be coherent. Improvements in the design and development processes for new products generally move in two directions. On the one hand, the need to shorten development cycles and accelerate new product introduction cycles forces team members to act rapidly and in coordination. Therefore, activities may be said to be carried out simultaneously or concurrently. On the other hand, organizations must involve a large number of specialists in projects in order to better cope with technological complexity while improving product quality to meet expressed needs. This requires a number of stakeholders to be involved in the process. This integration relies partly on the use of ICTs and partly on approaches that enable greater collaboration between all the parties.

Team Members' Autonomy

Since product development activities entail much uncertainty and ambiguity, Galbraith (1973) suggests adopting a flexible and organic structure to foster innovation. This translates into the level of autonomy and decision-making authority given to team members and their leader, respectively (Gupta & Wilemon, 1990; Hoegl & Parboteeah, 2006).

Communicate!

In the same vein, organizational communication is a factor that significantly influences the progress of NPD (Pinto & Pinto, 1990; Pinto & Slevin, 1988; Sicotte & Langley, 2000) and the performance of the team (Hinds & Mortensen, 2005; Jarvenpaa & Leidner, 1999; Qureshi et al., 2006). Communication is defined as free exchange, often unstructured, between or within departments or organizations (Rubenstein et al., 1976). A considerable number of studies have examined communication within an organization that is involved in NPD (Link & Zmud, 1986; Reukert & Walker, 1987; Rubenstein et al., 1976; Souder, 1987), but few have treated it as a success factor. The majority of researchers address communication from a general point of view (amount) without defining concretely the form that it takes or should take during the process. Our study departs from previous ones in defining formal communication processes.

Client Involvement

Interaction between an NPD team and its clients allows all concerned to grasp the needs and often the necessary changes for the products in development (Christensen, 2002; Gruner & Homburg, 2000). Cooper et al. (2002) advocate "walking in your client's shoes" or "camping out," meaning that a firm must observe its clients' processes to identify solutions to their problems. Conversely, consumers involved in the NPD process can provide valuable information and correct the direction when needed (Roberts, 2000; Thomke & von Hippel, 2002). Layman et al. (2006) advocate "a well-defined customer authority for effective decision making and a clear requirements statement" (p. 787) for global teams.

Top Management Involvement

Top management support should alleviate the kinds of financial, structural or cultural difficulties that can endanger the lives of projects. Top managers should therefore facilitate access to resources, take an active part in project goal assessment and follow up on progress regularly (Gupta & Wilemon, 1990; Lucas & Bush, 1988). The formal design of an operational governance structure is also crucial for the success of a project since it marks the decision points and completes the information on the fate of the project and its associated investments (Cooper et al., 2002; Young & Jordan, 2008). Establishing this structure, however, is very delicate: Who is involved? How many meetings should there be? What is the operational latitude for each group? These are all questions whose answers may radically change the course of the product development. Some studies point out the negative impact of miscalculated involvement (Hoegl & Parboteeah, 2006; Lee-Kelley & Sankey, 2008).

To sum up, in terms of management, this study emphasizes the key dimensions that have generally emerged from empirical studies on project and innovation management, and focuses on aspects of workforce management, communication practices and organization practices which are critical components in distributed team oversight (Cooper et al., 2004; Schmidt et al., 2001; Yahaya & Abu-Bakar, 2007).

Figure 1. Moderating effect of distributedness

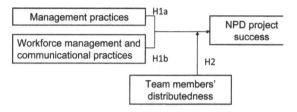

MODEL

Our overall objective was to determine the effects of the distributedness of team members on the successful completion of NPD projects. More specifically, as illustrated in Figure 1, we made the general hypothesis that *distributedness influences the potential relations between certain company practices and the successful completion of NPD projects.* This perspective departs from those of recent studies (e.g., Hinds & Mortensen, 2005; Hoegl & Proserpio, 2004), in which distributedness is generally considered to be a predictive variable. Our second hypothesis assumes instead that distributedness acts as a pure moderator (Sharma et al., 1981). That is, rather than wielding a direct influence, it moderates the relationship between certain practices and the successful completion of the innovation project (the explained variables). This hypothesis appears *a priori* to be more reflective of the reality of the companies we have observed in case studies. Figure 1 illustrates our framework.

To verify our hypothesis, we first examined the relations between certain internal company practices and the successful completion of innovation projects. Practices included recognized organizational and project management activities (H1a) and workforce management and communication mechanisms (H1b). H2 proposes that distributedness has a moderating effect. The next section describes the data-gathering methodology and preliminary results.

METHODS

In this section, we outline the steps used to examine how Canadian companies deal with the various issues and challenges of distributed teamwork in order to carry out innovative activities, specifically NPD projects.

DATA COLLECTION

The data used for this research were gathered via a self-administered questionnaire sent to Canadian companies. The questionnaire was developed on the basis of an extensive literature review on various aspects of project management and new product and service development. Considering the scope of this investigation, the questionnaire was drafted in Canada's two official languages (English and French) and the translation was verified by a professional translator. Pretesting was conducted with 10 respondents, after which some minor adjustments were made to the wording of certain questions. The questionnaire contained about 150 questions in all, divided into 11 categories. Despite the large number of questions, the time required to complete the questionnaire was around 50 minutes for the pretest, which was deemed reasonable and consistent with similar surveys. Most questions could be answered on a 7-point Likert scale. The questionnaire also included nominal-scale questions, as well as descriptive questions such as project type, respondent's position in the company, etc. In their answers, respondents were asked to refer to a pair of projects recently completed by the company (one successful and one less successful).

The data collection approach comprised several steps. First, a list of companies was obtained from an official public agency. A population of 2,064 individuals was built following a careful examination of the list and elimination of doubles. The selected managers (CEOs, R&D and innovation heads) were asked to respond to our questionnaire

Table 1. Characteristics of NPD projects in the sample

Characteristic	Average	Co-located	Distributed	p/2
Project team size (persons)	27.1	19.5	35.1	0.03
Project duration (months)	18.7	19.6	17.7	0.20
Overall project cost ($ millions)	1.70	1.44	1.96	0.19
Electronic communication usage	3.75	3.53	3.95	0.10

or, where appropriate, to pass it on to individuals with the relevant knowledge and experience.[v] Questionnaires were sent by mail to all potential respondents. A team of research assistants made follow-up calls to the companies by telephone. An electronic version (PDF) of the questionnaire was also made available for respondents who preferred to use this method. We recorded a 9.3% response rate, or 165 questionnaires filled out and returned. Although this response rate is low, it is comparable with similar studies in North American companies in recent years.

Table 1 presents some characteristics of the 165 successful NPD projects included in our sample. We can see that only the size of the teams differs; the distributed teams were able to call on

Table 2. PCA of management practice dimensions

Items	Subdimension			
	G1	G2	G3	G4
To what extent were the following information-sharing, decision-making and control mechanisms used?				
Milestone reports	0.777			
Formal go/no-go gate process	0.593			
Information meetings with all personal members	0.685			
Financial planning	0.723			
Planning-readjustment mechanisms	0.697			
Control and follow-up methods	0.744			
Steering committees		0.774		
Meetings with department heads or project managers		0.613		
Active participation of team members in decision-making		0.639		
Goals common to the various departments established by top management		0.695		
Information directory from previous projects			0.795	
A formal product / service development methodology			0.728	
A formal project-management methodology			0.704	
Client or client-representative participation in reviews				0.781
% explained variance	25.20	16.43	14.16	9.21
% cumulative variance	25.20	41.63	55.79	65.00
Reliability (Cronbach's<)	0.86	0.74	0.70	-

KMO = 0.84

more human resources than the co-located ones. However, neither the duration nor the cost is significantly different, and nor is the degree of use of electronic communication technologies. This is an interesting feature of teams in companies that are developing new products or services and that are in high-technology sectors. The intensive use of ICTs is no longer restricted to distributed teams, which emphasizes the fact that other characteristics contribute to their differences. In conclusion, we find a unit of analysis – the project – that corresponds simultaneously to the three characteristics of the virtual team: a temporary, task-driven team using ICTs. The subdivision of the sample led to the fourth characteristic: one group carried out the project while being entirely co-located while the other group showed a greater or lesser degree of distributedness.

OPERATIONAL MEASURES

In order to test our general hypothesis, we first identified a certain number of factors characterizing the targeted practices of information exchange, planning, control, workforce management and decision making. All practices were initially measured by 26 items. We then reduced the dimensionality using Principal Components Analysis (PCA) with Varimax rotation. The analysis identified four underlying dimensions (factors) for management and two underlying dimensions (factors) related to workforce practice and communication. This initial six-factor classification then underwent further statistical testing to verify validity (convergent and discriminant) and reliability. This is recommended in the literature (Bagozzi, 1980; Bagozzi & Phillips, 1982; Venkatraman & Grant, 1986) when factors guide the constitution of variables that are subsequently used as input

Table 3. PCA of human resource management and communicational dimensions

Subdimension		
Items	C1	C2
To what extent do you agree with the following statement?		
The people in the immediate vicinity of the project were skilled communicators	0.615	
I received the information needed to get my work done on time	0.743	
Conflicts could be handled appropriately through proper communication channels	0.752	
Horizontal communications between employees were free-flowing	0.637	
The members of my work group were compatible	0.650	
Our meetings were well organized	0.758	
Written directives and reports were clear and concise	0.787	
The number of communications in the firm was adequate	0.793	
Employees were regularly given the opportunity to take on significant responsibility		0.617
Top management clearly delegated to others and left it up to them to do their work		0.771
Employees' achievements were always recognized		0.774
We participated in making decisions that affected our work		0.576
% explained variance	37.51	29.79
% cumulative variance	37.51	61.30
Reliability (Cronbach's <)	0.91	0.75

KMO = 0.92

for linear regression, as in our case. Detailed calculations are presented in the Appendix 1. Table 2 and Table 3 present the results.

- *Four management practice dimensions.* From all the items considered in this study, PCA allowed us to obtain the underlying dimensions of the company's management practices, as assessed by the respondents. The first factor (dimension G1), which we called *planning and follow-up*, represents the formal mechanisms established by the company to structure the team's approach (stage gates, financial planning, progress reports, etc.). The second factor (dimension G2) represents the mechanism by which the company tries to ensure cohesion between the various hierarchical levels involved in decision making. It could have been labeled "operational governance," but we called this factor *top management involvement* to stay in line with previous studies. The third factor (dimension G3) primarily concerns the company's use of methods, tools and standards. In other words, it involves the concrete means that the company uses to support NPD activities. Thus, we called it *tools and work methodology*. The fourth factor (dimension G4) includes a unique dimension that we called *client involvement* in project monitoring.
- *Two dimensions related to workforce management and communication.* The same approach was used to identify these two factors. The first factor (dimension C1) highlights the *communication* between the individuals involved. Quantity and quality of communication, practices as well as distribution channels are measured by this factor. The second factor (dimension C2) refers to the perceived empowerment practices of the company and is referred to as

team members' autonomy of the individuals concerned.

To these six factors, determined empirically by a PCA, we added two further measures that are central to research: a measure of the successful completion of projects and a measure of the geographic dispersion of the team members. To capture *project success*, we opted for two subdimensions: *efficiency* and *effectiveness*. The first aimed to measure the team's capacity to meet the classic parameters of deadline and budget (2 items, $\alpha_{Cronbach} = 0.73$) and the second measures the achievement of objectives and specifications (quality, technical result, goals) and customer satisfaction, but also team pride (5 items, $\alpha_{Cronbach} = 0.93$). In this way, our performance measure aimed at the project level but also included one aspect of team success.

To capture team *distributedness*, we chose to use a measure of geographic distance between the team members. In the questionnaire, the respondents were asked to rate the team on a scale between two extremes (i.e., entirely co-located team and entirely distributed team).

RESULTS

In the first analysis, we sought to identify potential differences between the main dimensions retained, depending on whether or not the teams were distributed. To do so, we divided our sample into two subgroups based on the geographic dispersion variable (co-located team vs. distributed team). Table 4 presents the results.

Overall, we observe very similar profiles across subgroups. The highest ratings were given to the *communication* and *autonomy* factors, suggesting the frequent use of information exchange practices and the granting of actor autonomy. In contrast, *tools and work methodology* and *client involvement* scored much lower than the other factors. Whether this reflects the creative context

Table 4. Mean values for the factors within the two groups [1] (co-located and distributed)

Variable	Co-located teams	Distributed teams	p-value[2]
	n = 83	n = 80	
G1: Planning and follow-up	4.63	4.68	n.s.
G2: Top management involvement	4.74	4.86	n.s.
G3: Tools and work methodology	3.84	3.93	n.s.
G4: Client involvement	3.91	4.25	n.s.
C1: Communication	5.54	5.37	n.s.
C2: Team members' autonomy	5.29	5.17	n.s.
Efficiency	5.68	5.34	**
Effectiveness	6.24	6.06	***

1. Perceptual Likert scale (1 to 7).
2. Significance levels: * p < .10, **p < .05, *** p < .01, **** p < .001 (unilateral test).

of these projects, the difficulty of involving a client who is unfamiliar with the NPD process or the team's reluctance to use tools and formal work methodology has yet to be discovered. As for the remaining factors, no significant differences were found when comparing the two subgroups (p-value column). In light of these first results, we note that the companies studied do not appear to change their behaviors with regard to team distributedness, at least for the variables studied. Lee-Kelley and Sankey (2008) found the same result at the team member level.

The only significant differences are found for the two measures of project success. Although the mean values are relatively high, we nevertheless observe significant differences between the two subgroups in favor of co-located teams. In terms of *efficiency* and *effectiveness*, these teams are more successful than distributed teams. We also note a more significant difference (p-value) in our model for the *effectiveness* than for the *efficiency* dimension, which corroborates our qualitative finding that achieving efficiency is somewhat easier for a task-driven team than achieving effectiveness (Petit et al., 2005).

The second step is illustrated by Table 5, which presents the correlation matrix. We sought to dis-

cover differences in the web of relations between variables for the two contexts.

For the most different β coefficients, we computed the significance level of Fisher's test, which helps reveal one kind of moderation: the difference in strength between the bilateral relation in the two contexts (Sharma et al., 1981). The strength of the relations between two variables seems to be significantly disrupted by virtuality: *Tools and work methodology* has β coefficients that are significantly different from *communication practices* (p = .005), *team autonomy* (p = .016) and *client involvement* (p = .027), while *client involvement* also has a different strength of relation with *top management involvement* (p = .026). This is the first indication that virtuality may have a moderating effect, and its interpretation leads us to believe that the factor *tools and work methodology* plays a more dominant role in distributed teams. Indeed, given their much stronger relationship with communication and autonomy, which are variables with the strongest link to performance, we can infer that they are even more necessary when the team is distributed. For client involvement, the strength of the relationship with *tools and work methodology* is reversed: it is stronger in co-located teams than in distributed

Table 5. Correlation matrix for both group (co-located and distributed)

Variable	1	2	3	4	5	6	7	8
Distributed								
Co-located								
1. Planning & Follow-up		0.65****	0.60****	0.15	0.59****	0.44*****	0.26*	0.31***
2. Top mgmt involvement	0.70****		0.45****	0.07	0.39****	0.44****	0.08	0.25**
3. Tools & work methodology	0.38****	0.17*		0.05	0.44****	0.40****	0.22**	0.26**
4. Client involvement	0.32***	0.38****	0.36***		0.28***	0.25**	0.28***	0.15
5. Communication practices	0.60****	0.64****	0.03	0.26**		0.55****	0.54****	0.42****
6. Team autonomy	0.51****	0.60****	0.06	0.34***	0.79****		0.44****	0.52****
7. Efficiency	0.31***	0.49****	0.02	0.23*	0.49****	0.38****		
8. Effectiveness	0.35***	0.40****	0.01	0.18*	0.51****	0.40****	0.51****	

All variables are measured with perceptual Likert scales (1 to 7)

Significance levels: * $p < .10$, **$p < .05$, *** $p < .01$, **** $p < .001$ (unilateral test)

teams, as if only the client's presence on site can "impose" such involvement, and not directives coming from afar. The relationship appears to be similar with *top management involvement*: on site, the two factors have a fairly strong relationship, but at a distance, they have none. Does this mean that management knows how to introduce clients into the NPD process on site but is unable to do so for distributed teams?

In both contexts, *workforce management* and *communication practices* are most related to the performance dimension, followed by *top management involvement* and *planning and follow-up*. Given the high correlation between variables, every precaution was taken to ensure the reliability of the results.

To more closely examine the relations between the main dimensions, *distributedness* and *project success*, we ran a set of hierarchical linear regressions to model cross-products. This corresponds to our model, which was designed to initially measure the explanatory power of the factors for the successful completion of innovation projects (H1a and H1b). We also wanted to verify with a more widely accepted procedure whether team distributedness had a moderating impact on the existing relations between the factors (independent variables) and

the measures of success (dependent variables) (H2). Hence, our approach is consistent with the literature, particularly the recommendations of Sharma et al. (1981) and Venkatraman (1989) to measure moderating effects. The introduction of cross-products would appear to be more useful than subgroup regression since it tests the form of the relation. Moreover, this approach has been used in other recent studies addressing distributed teams, notably by Hinds and Mortensen (2005). Still, not finding any significant interaction does not rule out the presence of moderation (Jaccard et al., 1990); the search for moderation is negatively affected by the imperfect data gathering instruments used. Table 6 and Table 7 present the results of the three regressions (three models), following the introduction of variable sets into the regression. Here, separate regressions were run on *effectiveness* and *efficiency*.

First, we note that all the factors obtained explain a large part of the variance for both the *efficiency* and *effectiveness* regressions. However, our model for *efficiency* appears to provide a better adjustment level, at 35.15% (R^2). A careful analysis of Model 1 for the regressions in each table reveals the importance of Factor C1 (*communication*) as an explanatory factor of the de-

Table 6. Assessment of the moderating effect of dispersion (efficiency)

Factors	EFFICIENCY					
	Model 1		Model 2		Model 3	
	β	P/2	β	P/2	β	P/2
G1: Planning & follow-up	-0.115	0.1294	-0.106	0.1489	-0.143	0.1745
G2: Top mgmt involvement	0.011	0.4516	0.013	0.4428	0.437	0.0012
G3: Tools & work methodology	0.050	0.2575	0.051	0.2523	0.070	0.2782
G4: Client involvement	**0.109**	**0.0654**	**0.107**	**0.0682**	0.162	0.0703
C1: Communication practices	**0.598**	**0.0000**	**0.583**	**0.0000**	0.546	0.0012
C2: Team autonomy	0.004	0.4811	0.008	0.4670	-0.254	0.0553
Team Distributedness (TD)			-0.052	0.2265	0.109	0.4055
TD*G1					0.183	0.3065
TD*G2					**-1.324**	**0.0001**
TD*G3					-0.087	0.3644
TD*G4					-0.223	0.1029
TD*C1					0.125	0.3938
TD*C2					**1.032**	**0.0157**
R-Squared	0.3515		0.3541		0.4292	
Adj. R-Squared	0.3241		0.3220		0.3742	
p	0.0000		0.0000		0.0000	
Delta R-Squared			0.0026		**0.0751**	
p			0.4530		**0.0100**	

pendent variables (*effectiveness and efficiency*). This result confirms previous findings (Hoegl et al., 2004) and shows the explanatory power of this dimension across the entire sample, regardless of team *distributedness*. Aside from *communication practices*, no other factors were found to be significant across the two regression sets.

In the *efficiency* regressions, a second explanatory factor, *client involvement*, shows a significant β coefficient. This result suggests that *client involvement* does indeed play a role in team effectiveness, by monitoring budgets and dead-

lines. In the *effectiveness* regressions, the second explanatory factor is *team members' autonomy*.

Model 2 for each regression set shows a non-significant contribution of team distributedness to explain overall variance (insignificant ΔR^2), which supports our initial hypothesis that team *distributedness*, although not an explanatory factor, instead acts as a moderating variable. This intuition was partly confirmed by Model 3. As explained earlier, Model 3 measures the moderating effect of the *distributedness* factor on the other factors. To confirm our hypothesis, cross-products were introduced into each regression. According

Table 7. Assessment of the moderating effect of dispersion (effectiveness)

	EFFECTIVENESS					
	Model 1		Model 2		Model 3	
Factors	β	P/2	β	P/2	β	P/2
G1: Planning & follow-up	-0.003	0.4896	-0.009	0.4155	-0.029	0.4305
G2: Top mgmt involvement	0.014	0.4432	0.011	0.3353	0.267	0.0406
G3: Tools & work methodology	0.068	0.2012	0.067	0.1680	0.033	0.3977
G4: Client involvement	0.001	0.4971	0.002	0.3858	0.108	0.1792
C1: Communication practices	**0.255**	**0.0095**	**0.265**	**0.0182**	0.518	0.0036
C2: Team autonomy	**0.281**	**0.0024**	**0.279**	**0.0069**	-0.065	0.3495
Team Distributedness (TD)			0.037	0.3295	0.597	0.1123
TD*G1					0.155	0.3471
TD*G2					**-0.931**	**0.0062**
TD*G3					0.083	0.3803
TD*G4					**-0.281**	**0.0703**
TD*C1					**-0.800**	**0.0558**
TD*C2					**1.117**	**0.0154**
R-Squared	0.2607		0.2620		0.3275	
Adj. R-Squared	0.2297		0.2257		0.2632	
p	0.0000		0.0000		0.0000	
Delta R-Squared			0.0013		**0.0655**	
p			0.6170		**0.0460**	

to Sharma et al. (1981), the potential moderator of a variable will be revealed insofar as the β coefficients obtained for the cross-products are significant, which occurs for two cross-products in the *efficiency* model and for four cross-products in the *effectiveness* model. In other words, Model 2 confers no distinct explanatory power on team *distributedness*; however, when combined with certain factors (cross-products), *distributedness* gains explanatory power in some cases. This is what Model 3 addresses.

Model 3 regressions partially confirm our Hypothesis H2. For the *efficiency* regressions,

team *distributedness* acts as a pure moderator on the main dimensions *top management involvement* and *team autonomy*, since the β coefficients of the cross-products differ significantly from 0 (β = –1.324, p < .001) and (β = 1.032, p < .05) respectively, and the β coefficient of *distributedness* in the Model 2 regressions is not significant. In other words, the introduction of *distributedness* into the regressions changes the existing relationships between the main dimensions and *efficiency*. In practical terms, this means that *top management involvement* (G2) and *team members' autonomy* (C2) do not play the same role, that is, to explain *efficiency* in the case of increasing team *distributedness*. To obtain the direction of the change, we reran the regressions on subgroups (*co-located* and *distributed*) and obtained a much more pronounced explanatory power for C2 (positive and significant β) for *distributed teams*. In other words, when *distributedness* is taken into account, *team members' autonomy* has more weight in explaining *efficiency*. The case of *top management involvement* (G2) is different because the subgroup regressions show a β coefficient sign change across groups (*co-located* and *distributed*). When teams are *co-located*, *project efficiency* is better explained by higher *top management involvement* than in *distributedness* teams, which leads to the argument that integration and decision-making in *distributed teams* are achieved by other means, for instance communication practices or team autonomy.

For the *effectiveness* regressions, team *distributedness* acts as a pure moderator on G2 (*top management involvement*), G4 (*client involvement*), C1 (*communication*) and C2 (*team members' autonomy*), since the β coefficients of the cross-products differ significantly from 0. The β coefficient of *distributedness* in the Model 2 regressions is not significant. We ran also subgroup regressions and the variables display different patterns: *top management involvement* changes signs, *team autonomy* increases markedly while *client involvement* and *communication practices* seem unchanged. We have no doubt that *distributedness* is truly a moderator of the relation between *top management involvement, team autonomy* and *effectiveness*.

Again, we ran stepwise regressions and each subgroup yielded a different parsimonious regression result, which strongly supports the hypothesis that virtuality has a moderating effect (Jaccard et al., 1990): distributed team efficiency – *communication practices* (R^2 0.37****); co-located team efficiency – *communication practices* and *top management involvement* (R^2 0.29****); distributed team effectiveness – *team autonomy* (R^2

0.26****); co-located team effectiveness – *communication practices* (R^2 0.23****). This issue clearly merits more exploration in future studies.

CONCLUDING REMARKS

To conclude the empirical section, we identify some points that should be considered. First, we found no significant differences in the practices of the project teams depending on whether they were co-located or distributed (Table 4). Does this mean that NPD projects carried out by distributed teams do not necessitate any special adjustments, and that the order of the day for such teams is "business as usual"? It appears that this conclusion is unwarranted, since the same table shows lower efficiency and effectiveness for distributed teams (slight, but significant). Communication practices had a significant influence on project performance in both co-located and distributed teams (Table 6 and Table 7, models 1 and 2). No wonder that communication stands out in every study as the most influential factor. Our study points to specific practices and to the possibility of a moderating influence of distributedness. The same tables also show the influence of *client involvement* on efficiency and of *team autonomy* on effectiveness. Both these factors have been advocated but they are not attributed a central role in project performance. Clearly, though, organizations should devote some effort to reflecting on and implementing them.

Team autonomy and *top management involvement*, or operational governance, showed a clear moderating impact of distributedness on *efficiency* (Table 6 and Table 7, models 2 and 3), while *effectiveness* presents more relations that are negatively affected by distributedness, namely *top management involvement, client involvement, communication practices* and *team autonomy*. Still there are undoubtedly other dimensions in which organizations should invest effort when running teams in a distributed context. In future research, it would be useful to investigate whether these dimensions are more explanatory than moderated by the context.

The results of this study empirically confirm the role of geographic distributedness as a moderating variable in the interrelations between certain practices applied by innovative companies and successful project completion. Among other things, our results suggest that *team members' autonomy,* which is fostered by workforce management favoring empowerment, plays a greater role in explaining efficiency when distributedness is taken into account. The autonomy of distributed team members raises an issue that is often addressed in organizational studies (the debate on centralization vs. decentralization) and discussed in human resource management (how and to what extent to foster autonomy), but is relatively neglected in studies that specifically address distributed teams. The second original result concerns *top management involvement,* essentially the operational governance structure, which also seems to contribute in ways that were not foreseen. Again, we find here a subject that requires in-depth reflection since top management members are usually not particularly aware of their influence on a project's destiny (Young & Jordan, 2008).

Like all empirical studies of this type, our results must be interpreted with caution. The relatively high number of projects in the sample leaves no doubt as to the validity of these results, but we must keep in mind certain limitations of the approach used. For instance, the fact of having a single respondent per project introduces a bias towards certain dimensions that are especially important to the particular respondent. For this reason, authors are increasingly adopting an approach involving several respondents per project (e.g., Cramton & Webber, 2005; Hoegl et al., 2003). Similarly, measures of the distributedness of activities tend to become more complicated in order to better represent the complexity of this dimension. It seems that a purely physical measure of distance

has its limitations, and this is why authors such as Hinds and Mortensen (2005) have proposed introducing subdimensions such as "structural" distributedness and "psychological" distributedness into the analysis. We plan to do the same in our next study, but the goal of this study was to introduce the moderating effect of distributedness and for this reason it was important to use the same measure as most of the previous research.

REFERENCES

AFW. (2002). *Mythos Team auf dem Prüfstand: Teamarbeit in deutschen Unternehmen.* Retrieved July 15, 2009, from http://: http://www.die-akademie.de/

Anderson, J. C., & Gerbing, D. W. (1988). Structural equation modeling in practice: a review and recommended two-step approach. *Psychological Bulletin, 103,* 411–423. doi:10.1037/0033-2909.103.3.411

Arnison, L., & Miller, P. (2000). Virtual teams: a virtue for the conventional team. *Journal of Workplace Learning, 14,* 166–173. doi:10.1108/13665620210427294

Bagozzi, R. P. (1980). *Causal models in marketing.* New York: Wiley.

Bagozzi, R. P., & Phillips, L. W. (1982). Representing and testing organizational theories: a holistic construal. *Administrative Science Quarterly, 27*(3), 459–489. doi:10.2307/2392322

Bagozzi, R. P., & Yi, Y. (1988). On the evaluation of structural equation models. *Journal of the Academy of Marketing Science, 16,* 74–94. doi:10.1007/BF02723327

Bell, B. S., & Kozlowski, S. W. J. (2002). A typology of virtual teams. *Group & Organization Management, 27,* 14–49. doi:10.1177/1059601102027001003

Bourgault, M., Drouin, N., & Hamel, E. (2008). Decision-making within distributed project teams: an exploration of formalization and autonomy as determinants of success. *Project Management Journal, 39*(S1), 97–110. doi:10.1002/pmj.20063

Christensen, C. M. (2002, June). The Rules of Innovation. *MIT Technology Review.*

Cleland, D. I., & Ireland, L. R. (2007). *Project management: strategic design and implementation* (5th ed.). New York: McGraw-Hill.

Cooper, R. G. (1979). The dimensions of industrial new product success and failure. *Journal of Marketing, 43*(3), 93–103. doi:10.2307/1250151

Cooper, R. G. (1994). New products: the factors that drive success. *International Marketing Review, 11*(1), 60–76. doi:10.1108/02651339410057527

Cooper, R. G. (2003). A research agenda to reduce risk in new product development through knowledge management: a practitioner perspective. *Journal of Engineering and Technology Management, 20*(1-2), 117–140. doi:10.1016/S0923-4748(03)00007-9

Cooper, R. G., Edgett, S. J., & Kleinschmidt, E. J. (2002). Optimizing the stage-gate process: what best-practice companies do – I. *Research Technology Management, 45*(5), 21–27.

Cooper, R. G., Edgett, S. J., & Kleinschmidt, E. J. (2004). Benchmarking best NPD practices. *Research Technology Management, 47*(1), 31–43.

Cramton, C. D., & Webber, S. S. (2005). Relationships among geographic dispersion, team processes, and effectiveness in software development work teams. *Journal of Business Research, 58*(6), 758–765. doi:10.1016/j.jbusres.2003.10.006

Duarte, D. L., & Snyder, N. T. (1999). *Mastering virtual teams: Strategies, tools, and techniques that succeed.* San Francisco, CA: Jossey-Bass Publishers.

Fisher, K., & Fisher, M. (1998). *The distributed mind.* New York: American Management Association.

Fornell, C., & Larcker, D. (1981). Evaluating Structural Equation Models with Unobservable Variable and Measurement Error. *JMR, Journal of Marketing Research, 18*, 39–50. doi:10.2307/3151312

Galbraith, J. (1973). *Designing complex organizations.* New York: Addison-Wesley.

Gibson, C. B., & Cohen, S. G. (2003). *Virtual teams that work: creating conditions for virtual team effectiveness.* San Francisco, CA: Jossey-Bass.

Gruner, K. E., & Homburg, C. (2000). Does customer interaction enhance new product success? *Journal of Business Research, 49*(1), 1–14. doi:10.1016/S0148-2963(99)00013-2

Gupta, A. K., & Wilemon, D. L. (1990). Accelerating the development of technology-based new products. *California Management Review, 32*(2), 24–44.

Hair, J. E., Anderson, R. E., Tatham, R. L., & Black, W. C. (1998). *Multivariate data analysis* (5th ed.). Upper Saddle River, NJ: Prentice-Hall.

Haywood, M. (1998). *Managing Virtual Teams: Practical Techniques for High-technology Project Managers.* Norwood, MA: Artech House.

Henry, J. E., & Hartzler, M. (1997). Virtual Teams: Today's Reality, today's Challenge. *Quality Progress, 30*(5), 108–109.

Hertel, G., Geister, S., & Konradt, U. (2005). Managing virtual teams: a review of current empirical research. *Human Resource Management Review, 15*(1), 69–95. doi:10.1016/j.hrmr.2005.01.002

Hinds, P. J., & Mortensen, M. (2005). Understanding conflict in geographically distributed teams: the moderating effects of shared identity, shared context, and spontaneous communication. *Organization Science, 16*(3), 290–307. doi:10.1287/orsc.1050.0122

Hoegl, M., & Parboteeah, P. K. (2006). Team reflexivity in innovative projects. *R & D Management, 36*(2), 113–125. doi:10.1111/j.1467-9310.2006.00420.x

Hoegl, M., Praveen, P. K., & Gemuenden, H. G. (2003). When teamwork really matters: task innovativeness as a moderator of the teamwork–performance relationship in software development projects. *Journal of Engineering and Technology Management, 20*(4), 281–302. doi:10.1016/j.jengtecman.2003.08.001

Hoegl, M., & Proserpio, L. (2004). Team member proximity and teamwork in innovative projects. *Research Policy, 33*(8), 1153–1165. doi:10.1016/j.respol.2004.06.005

Hoegl, M., Weinkauf, K., & Gemuenden, H. G. (2004). Interteam coordination, project commitment, and teamwork in multiteam R&D projects: a longitudinal study. *Organization Science, 15*(1), 38–55. doi:10.1287/orsc.1030.0053

Huxham, C., & Vangen, S. (2005). *Managing to collaborate: the theory and practice of collaborative advantage.* London: Routledge.

Jaccard, J., Turrisi, R., & Wan, C. K. (1990). *Interaction effects in multiple regression.* Newbury Park, CA: Sage.

Jarvenpaa, S., & Leidner, D. (1999). Communication and trust in global virtual teams. *Organization Science, 10*(6), 791–815. doi:10.1287/orsc.10.6.791

Katzy, B. R., & Sung, G. (2001). Information infrastructure for virtual projects requirements specification from a communication perspective. In *Proceedings of the 9th International Conference on Concurrent Enterprising,* Bremen, Germany.

Kayworth, T., & Leidner, D. E. (2000). Managing global virtual teams: a prescription for success. *European Management Journal, 18*(2), 183–193. doi:10.1016/S0263-2373(99)00090-0

Kline, R. B. (1998). *Principles and Practice of Structural Equation Modeling.* New York: Guilford Press.

Kokko, N., Vartiaine, N. M., & Lönnblad, J. (2007). Individual and collective competences in virtual project organizations. *The Electronic Journal for Virtual Organizations and Networks, 8*(1), 28-52. Retrieved June 15, 2009, from http://http://www.ejov.org

Layman, L., Williams, L., Damian, D., & Bures, H. (2006). Essential communication practices for Extreme Programming in a global software development team. *Information and Software Technology, 48*(9), 781–794. doi:10.1016/j.infsof.2006.01.004

Lee-Kelley, L., & Sankey, T. (2008). Global virtual teams for value creation and project success: A case study. *International Journal of Project Management, 26,* 51–62. doi:10.1016/j.ijproman.2007.08.010

Link, A. N., & Zmud, R. W. (1986). Additional evidence on the R&D interface. *IEEE Transactions on Engineering Management, 33*(1), 43–44.

Lipnack, J., & Stamps, J. (1997). *Virtual teams: reaching across space, time, and organizations with technology.* New York: John Wiley.

Lipnack, J., & Stamps, J. (1999). Virtual teams: the new way to work. *Strategy and Leadership, 27,* 14–18. doi:10.1108/eb054625

Lu, M., Watson-Manheim, M. B., Chudoba, K. M., & Wynn, E. (2006). Virtuality and Team Performance: Understanding the Impact of Variety of Practices. *Journal of Global Information Technology Management, 9*(1), 4–10.

Lucas, G. H. Jr, & Bush, A. J. (1988). The marketing-R&D interface: do personality factors have an impact? *Journal of Product Innovation Management, 5*(4), 257–268. doi:10.1016/0737-6782(88)90010-0

Lurey, J. S., & Raisinghani, M. S. (2001). An empirical study of best practices in virtual teams. *Information & Management, 38*, 523–544. doi:10.1016/S0378-7206(01)00074-X

Martins, L. L., Gilson, L. L., & Maynard, M. T. (2004). Virtual teams: what do we know and where do we go from here? *Journal of Management, 30*(6), 805–835. doi:10.1016/j.jm.2004.05.002

Maznevski, M. L., & Chudoba, K. M. (2000). Bridging space over time: Global virtual team dynamics and effectiveness. *Organization Science, 11*, 473–492. doi:10.1287/orsc.11.5.473.15200

Odenwald, S. (1996). Global work teams. *Training & Development, 50*(2), 54–57.

Petit, M.-C., Sicotte, H., & Bourgault, M. (2005). Investigating the enabling mechanisms for ensuring quality of communication in newly virtualized project teams. In Morel-Guimaraes, L. (Ed.), *Key success factors for innovation and sustainable development (Management of Technology Series)*. London: Elsevier.

Pinto, J. K. (2002). Project management. *Research Technology Management, 45*(2), 22–37.

Pinto, J. K., & Slevin, D. P. (1988). Project success: definitions and measurement techniques. *Project Management Journal, 19*(1), 67–71.

Pinto, M. B., & Pinto, J. K. (1990). Project team communication and cross-functional cooperation in new program development. *Journal of Product Innovation Management, 7*(3), 200–212. doi:10.1016/0737-6782(90)90004-X

Powell, A., Piccoli, G., & Ives, B. (2004). Virtual teams: A review of the current literature directions for future research. *The Data Base for Advances in Information Systems, 35*(1), 6–36.

Qureshi, S., Liu, M., & Vogel, M. (2006). The effects of electronic collaboration in distributed project management. *Group Decision and Negotiation, 15*, 55–75. doi:10.1007/s10726-005-9006-6

Reukert, R. W., & Walker, O. C. (1987). Marketing's interaction with other functional units: a conceptual framework and empirical evidence. *Journal of Marketing, 51*(3), 1–19. doi:10.2307/1251140

Rubenstein, A. H., Chakrabarti, A. K., O'Keefe, R. D., Souder, W. E., & Young, H. C. (1976, May). Factors influencing innovation success at the project level. *Research Management*, 15–20.

Schiller, S. Z., & Mandviwalla, M. (2007). Virtual team research – an analysis of theory use and a framework for theory appropriation. *Small Group Research, 38*(1), 12–59. doi:10.1177/1046496406297035

Schmidt, J. B., Montoya-Weiss, M. M., & Massey, A. P. (2001). New product development decision-making effectiveness: comparing individuals, face-to-face teams, and virtual teams. *Decision Sciences, 32*(4), 575–601. doi:10.1111/j.1540-5915.2001.tb00973.x

Sharma, S., Durand, R. M., & Gur-Arie, O. (1981). Identification and analysis of moderator variables. *JMR, Journal of Marketing Research, 18*(3), 291–300. doi:10.2307/3150970

Sicotte, H., & Langley, A. (2000). Integration mechanisms and R&D project performance. *Journal of Engineering and Technology Management, 17*, 1–37. doi:10.1016/S0923-4748(99)00018-1

Souder, W. E. (1987). *Managing new product innovations*. Lexington: Lexington Books.

Swan, B., Belanger, F., & Watson-Manheim, M. B. (2004). Theoretical foundations for distributed work: multilevel, incentive theories to address current dilemmas. In *Proceedings of the 37th Annual Hawaii International Conference on System Sciences (HICSS'04)*. Washington, DC: IEEE Computer Society.

Thomke, S., & von Hippel, E. (2002). Customers As Innovators: A New Way to Create Value. *Harvard Business Review, 80*(4), 74–81.

van Fenema, P. C., & Kumar, K. (2000). Coupling, interdependence and control in global projects. In Lundin, R. A., & Hartman, F. (Eds.), *Projects as business constituents and guiding motives.* Boston: Kluwer Academic Publishers.

Venkatraman, N. (1989). The concept of fit in strategy research: toward verbal and statistical correspondence. *Academy of Management Review, 9*, 513–525. doi:10.2307/258291

Venkatraman, N., & Grant, J. H. (1986). Construct measurement in organizational strategy research: a critique and proposal. *Academy of Management Review, 11*, 71–87. doi:10.2307/258332

von Hippel, E. (1990). Task partitioning: an innovation process variable. *Research Policy, 19*(5), 407–418. doi:10.1016/0048-7333(90)90049-C

Watson-Manheim, M. B., Chudoba, K. M., & Crowston, K. (2002). Discontinuities and continuities: a new way to understand virtual work. *Information Technology & People, 15*(3), 191–209. doi:10.1108/09593840210444746

Wehmeyer, K., & Riemer, K. (2007). Trust-building potential of coordination roles in virtual organizations. *The Electronic Journal for Virtual Organizations and Networks, 8*, 102-123. Retrieved June 15, 2009, from http:// http://www.ejov.org

Williams, T. M. (1999). The need for new paradigms for complex projects. *International Journal of Project Management, 17*(5), 269–273. doi:10.1016/S0263-7863(98)00047-7

Yahaya, S.-Y., & Abu-Bakar, N. (2007). New product development management issues and decision-making approaches. *Management Decision, 45*(7), 1123–1142. doi:10.1108/00251740710773943

Young, R., & Jordan, E. (2008). Top management support: Mantra or necessity? *International Journal of Project Management, 26*(7), 713–725. doi:10.1016/j.ijproman.2008.06.001

Zigurs, I., Evaristo, R., & Katzy, B. (2001). Collaborative technologies for virtual project management. In *Proceedings of Academy of Management,* Washington, DC.

ENDNOTES

[i] Ongoing tasks that are part of operations versus non-ongoing tasks that nevertheless fall under the project framework.

[ii] Watson-Manheim et al. (2002) introduced a new concept analogous to diversity, called "discontinuity."

[iii] Many researchers have focused exclusively on geographic diversity, for instance Maznevski & Chudoba (2000) and Odenwald (1996).

[iv] Temporal diversity arises from (1) the location of actors in different time zones (Kayworth & Leidner, 2000) and/or (2) the use of asynchronous communications (such as email), which generally limit the actors' capacity to interact in real time (Bell & Kozlowski, 2002).

[v] Note that very small companies (fewer than 20 employees) were excluded from the study.

[vi] Normed Fit Index (NFI), also known as the Bentler-Bonett Index.

[vii] Comparative Fit Index (CFI).

[viii] Root-Mean-Square Error of Approximation (RMSEA), also known as the Fit Standard Error.

[ix] Average Variance Extracted (AVE).

APPENDIX 1

Properties of validation measures:

After selecting items for each factor, we carried out the following three steps:

1. Assessment of *convergent validity*
2. Assessment of *discriminant validity* between factors
3. Assessment of *reliability*.

According to Bagozzi (1980), Bagozzi and Phillips (1982), and Venkatraman and Grant (1986), the above-mentioned properties (convergent validity, reliability, and discriminant validity) are necessary for the validation of measures to be used for subsequent regression.

In fact, as recommended by Anderson and Gerbing (1988), *convergent validity* was demonstrated by the following indicators: $chi^2/df < 3$ (Kline 1998), $NFI^{vi} > 0.9$, $CFI^{vii} > 0.9$ (Hair et al., 1998), $RMSEA^{viii} < 0.08$ (Hair et al., 1998). For each factor, Lambda contributions are highly significant. Moreover, to further support the convergent validity of the constructs, we then computed the $AVE,^{ix}$ which obtained values above 0.5 (Fornell and Larcker, 1981). High AVE (> 0.5) means a strong correlation between factor items, and each item therefore explains on average over 50% of the variance of the latent construct.

Further examination of the dimensions allowed us to assess their discriminant validity in accordance with Bagozzi and Yi's (1988) recommended procedure (constrained and non-constrained models). The results show that chi-square measures are significantly lower for non-constrained than constrained models ($\phi = 1$), which confirms the discriminant validity of the dimensions.

Finally, Cronbach's alphas and composite reliability indices (CRI) exceed the suggested levels of 0.6 and 0.7, respectively (Hair et al., 1998), showing that *the study's measures are reliable*.

Chapter 15

The Role of the Organizational Structure in the IT Appropriation:
Explorative Case Studies into the Interaction between IT and Workforce Management

Ewan Oiry
Université de la Méditerranée, France

Roxana Ologeanu-Taddeï
Université Montpellier II, France

Tanya Bondarouk
University of Twente, The Netherlands

ABSTRACT

The concept of appropriation is frequently used in IT implementation research. Rooted in the analysis of the diffusion of innovation, this concept is usually linked with characteristics of an organization's structure, size, and sector. Since the 1980s, appropriation has been actively studied by IT researchers, who linked it with technological attributions and characteristics of users. In this paper, the authors observed the application of the appropriation concept developed from the extreme of giving full credit to technology, and the other extreme of fully crediting end-users. The authors argue that to capture a full range of benefits from technology and human interaction, researchers cannot ignore organizational structure. By presenting three case studies, this paper shows that it is necessary to reintroduce this "side" to have a complete analysis of appropriation.

DOI: 10.4018/978-1-61350-465-9.ch015

INTRODUCTION

Today, the notion of appropriation is common knowledge for researchers and practitioners. They all know that users continuously reinterpret technologies in order to use them in accordance with their needs. Appropriation describes real interactions that persons develop with technologies and especially with IT. It is different from acceptance, although they have much in common. Acceptance refers to the users' perception of an IT tool without implying action (Davis et al., 1989). Thus, individuals may accept an IT tool without using it. Appropriation focuses on what actors really do with IT. The concept of appropriation was initially elaborated to explain difficulties in the diffusion of innovations within the organizational studies (Perriault, 1989; Jouet, 1993; De Certeau, 2002). Confronted with low levels of the use of innovation, researchers concluded that the structural features of innovations did not correspond to the users' expectations. In each department of an organization, persons have specific tasks and results to achieve. When an innovation is developed, users evaluate if it helps them to realize those tasks better. If that is not the case, they usually do not use the innovation. At that time, the characteristics of organizations were considered a major factor explaining the success or failure of an innovation.

Later, the concept of "appropriation" was addressed in IT implementation studies. The Adaptative Structuration Theory (AST) (De Sanctis & Poole, 1994) was one of the first to apply the concept of appropriation. The authors proposed a strong framework that links the nature of the technology used (structural features and spirit of technology) and different ways of appropriating it. While acknowledging the interpretive flexibility of the technology itself, that conceptualization underestimated the role of users in the appropriation and interaction process. In 2000 Orlikowski proposed her "theory of practice" to gain insights into the process of how users intervene in the appropriation of technology (which she names "enactment"). IT implementation studies produced two fundamental studies – AST and theory of practice – that approach the appropriation of technology from two opposite but complementary sides. On the "technological" side, AST (De Sanctis & Poole, 1994) gives lots of credit to the technologies by underlining how their structural features can explain appropriation. On the "user" side, theory of practice (Orlikowski, 2000) put forward that users permanently reinvent their uses of technologies.

In this paper, we propose integrating yet a third aspect into the process of appropriation during the interaction between technologies and actors. Although these two broadly accepted concepts are fundamental, they lose the link with the organizational structure side of the appropriation. Especially in workforce management, the "structural features" and "spirit" of technologies are directly linked to the organization where the technology is implemented. Moreover, the users of those technologies – HR professionals, line managers, and employees – are always under the organizational influence of power, rules, and cultures that affect the appropriation of a technology. Taking all of this phenomenon into account, this paper suggests refining the concept of appropriation in the process of interaction between technology and actors by adding the dimension of an organizational structure to a broadly accepted binary inclusion of technological and user characteristics.

Our paper develops this idea by presenting three different tools used in three different kinds of organizational structure. The first case study involves an HR intranet used in a professional bureaucracy. The advanced decentralisation of power, characteristic of this kind of organizational structure, directly explains the low use of this intranet. The second one is an Enterprise Resource Planning (ERP) implemented in a supermarket group of stores. In this case, the advanced centralization of power, characteristic of this kind of divisionalized structure, explains the difficulties that store managers encounter with this ERP. The last tool is a collective decision-making software used in a small and medium-sized enterprise (SME). This case study shows that the manager of the SME did not evaluate this software on the basis of what it allows employees to do but on its capacity to help him to create a new organizational structure in this enterprise.

The paper is arranged as follows. The first section contains the theoretical framework for this paper. By analysing the existing literature, we show that the concept of appropriation emerges in the studies on diffusion of innovation. It has been very much refined by AST (De Sanctis & Poole, 1994), which underlines how the structural features of the technologies play a role in appropriation, and by theory of practice (Orlikowski, 2000), which proposes a deep analysis of the role that users play in appropriation. At the end of this section, we present several studies that put forward the idea that it is also useful to take into account an "organizational" dimension in this reflection on appropriation. In the second section, we shall discuss the methodology. In the third one, we present our three case studies. In the final section, we discuss our results and present our conclusions of this research.

THEORETICAL FRAMEWORK

The Process of Appropriation and Diffusion of Innovations

Confronted with the rejection or low level of use of innovations, researchers on "diffusion of innovation" were the first to suggest the concept of appropriation (Rogers, 1964). They measured the acceptance of an innovation by measuring the adopters' perception of the new technology – for instance, "perceived relative advantage" and "perceived ease of use". Downs and Mohr (1976) initiated the work on this theme in their study on "instability" of the findings in innovation

research. In those pioneering papers, appropriation was related to the opposition between the logic of design and the logic of practice, between the prescribed uses and actual ones. Thus, Perriault (1989) argues that the logic of the designer of a technology is to provide a framework and prescribe practices, while the logic of the user, as independent from the designer, is to invent his/her own uses, according to individual representations, values and objectives.

Dedicated to adaptation (Ives & Olson, 1984) and appropriation (Clark, 1987), several studies thoroughly explored the differences in the links between technology and usage. Appropriation was considered a continuous dialogic process in which technology is modified by users, while at the same time users exert effort to adapt their work patterns to what is permitted by the technology. For example, Clark feels that appropriation requires continuous, cumulative and incremental innovation in all its aspects (Clark, 1987). For this author, appropriation is a process during which the user begins to recognize the potential value of the technology and tries to reduce the gap between the constraints of the technology and his/her own limited capabilities. The user then attempts to modify, refine, and use the technology in accordance with his/her needs. The ownership change will require continuous, cumulative and incremental innovation in all its aspects (Clark, 1987).

Overall, studies on the diffusion of innovations highlighted that the organization where all those actors work helps explain the nature of those representations, values, objectives as well as the logic of their designers. But they were insufficient in two aspects. First, they did not explain precisely what role the technology played in appropriation (technology side of appropriation). Second, they did not pay enough attention to the users' logic (user side of appropriation). More recent works explore those two aspects, but they progressively lose the link with the organizational structural side of appropriation.

The Process of Appropriation and the Adaptative Structuration Theory

The Adaptative Structuration Theory (AST) (De Sanctis & Poole, 1994) is usually considered the most powerful theory of the technology side of appropriation in the IT management literature (Markus & Silver, 2008).

The central thesis of this conceptualisation is that social structures included in the technologies are produced and reproduced by individual members of a group, by using and adapting rules and resources through the interactions.

Initially, AST was developed to study groups using electronic group decision support systems (GDSS): "it looks into the processes of human usage of computer systems and at the nature of group-computer interaction" (Poole & De Sanctis, 1989, p. 150). AST suggests that social structures serve as guides for planning and accomplishing tasks: designers incorporate such structures into the technology, with the result that the structures may be modified or reproduced (Jones, 1999). De Sanctis and Poole (1994) propose that the social structures provided by technology can be described in two ways:

- Structural features of the technology (examples of the structural features of GDSS were identified such as the voting algorithms and anonymous recording of ideas that brought meaning and control); they are classified by type of rules, resources, or opportunities for use that the technology offers to the user;
- The spirit of the technology, which is understood as the general intention of the system with regard to values and goals underlying a given set of structural features that provide a normative framework, suggesting appropriate behavior, possibly participating in the trial of domination. When technology is new, its "spirit" is defined. Designers determine how the technology

should be used, but the adoption of this technology shapes its spirit further. Over time, the mind is less open to interpretations and becomes rigid when the technology is stable and used by routines.

Since IT is only one source of structure for groups, the authors considered other ones such as work tasks and the organisational environment (De Sanctis & Poole, 1994). At this point, the concept of appropriation enters. Appropriation is considered to be the immediate and visible actions that demonstrate structuration processes. Ruël (2001) defines appropriation as "the physical and mental activities that users of technology carry out while making a selection from the potential set of structures of a technology, represented by the spirit and the technical features, for the day-to-day practices" (p. 53). There are four dimensions to appropriation:

- Appropriation moves (the ways that users choose to appropriate the available structures of technology);
- Faithfulness of appropriation (the extent to which a certain technology is appropriated in line with its spirit);
- Attitudes towards appropriation (the users' assessments of the extent to which the structures within the system are useful and easy to use);
- Instrumental uses (reasons why the system is used) (Ruël, 2001, p. 57).

To illustrate its potential, we note that AST has formed the basis of many studies (Miranda & Bostrom, 1993; Nagasundram & Bostrom, 1994; Chin et al., 1997; Majchrzak et al., 2000; Ruël, 2001; Hettinga, 2002). It has been shown that the clearer the spirit of IT to the user, the more faithfully they appropriate the technology, the more they perceive it as useful and easy to use, and the more they use the technology in a task-oriented way. The right way to make the spirit of a technology clear to its users is to: (1) achieve an agreement on the reasons for technology introduction, (2) involve the users in the process of development and implementation, and (3) provide organisational support (Ruël, 2001). Having acknowledged the great potential of AST, there are two remarks worth mentioning.

First, the epistemological framework of this theory is interactionism and social constructivism. It pays attention to the interactions at work, but it encounters difficulties when considering the global context of the organizational structure and taking into account the organizational structure as a whole in the interaction process.

Second, even when the authors feel that users play a great role in appropriation, they still emphasize the characteristics of the technology and give a smaller place to users. This is especially clear with their concept of "faithfulness of appropriation". By evaluating the appropriation from the point of view of its "faithfulness" or "unfaithfulness" to the spirit that designers inscribed in it, they ultimately do not seriously incorporate the impact of users. In contrast, some authors argue that "best appropriation" can be considered the most innovative form without taking into account whether it is faithful or unfaithful to the original spirit of the technology (Proulx, 1988; Perriault, 1989; De Certeau, 2002).

The Process of Appropriation and the Theory of Practice

To improve the analysis of the role of users, several studies have been dedicated to the investigation of the "user side" of appropriation. Users have the power and the ability to resist, to adapt and to change their work with the technology that is imposed by managers in a top-down manner. Those studies all highlight that appropriation differs from assimilation: while assimilation means "practices of accepting and regularly using a technological artefact within an organization"

(De Vaujany, 2008a), the appropriation process takes the form of continuous reinvention (Rice & Rogers, 1980), adaptation (Léonard-Barton, 1988; Tyre & Orlikowski, 1994), adjustment (Ives & Olson, 1984), improvisation, diversion (Perriault, 1989), "poaching" (De Certeau, 2002) or "coping" (Beaudry & Pinsonneault, 2005) with technology.

The theory of practice is considered the most powerful theory to analyse the user side of appropriation (Orlikowski, 2000). From Orlikowski's point of view, the concept of appropriation is too limited because its position is *related to the structure* which was embodied in the technology by the designers. Many authors demonstrate how the initially embodied structure has been sidestepped, transgressed, and changed by users. For Orlikowski (2000), users demonstrate a much greater creativity in working with the technology than "social constructivists" admit. The important point is that this creativity is not related to the structure but to numerous factors, which must be identified. To highlight this, Orlikowski (2000) suggests abandoning the term appropriation and adopting one which she takes from Weick (1969), "enactment", designating the real use that actors make of a specific technology.

Orlikowski (2000) argues that "while a technology can be seen to embody particular symbol and material properties, it does not embody structures because those are only instantiated in practice" (p. 406). In other words, Orlikowski reconsiders the AST "tradition" in IT research and states that the technology does not embody social structures because they are rules and resources that can be instantiated only in recurrent practice. Instead of analysing how the structures presumed to be embedded within technology "are used, misused, or not used by actors in various contexts", the theory of practice proposes framing what actors do with the technology not as appropriation but as enactment (Orlikowski, 2000, p. 407). Technology structures are thus not "external" to humans, simply "waiting" to be appropriated, they emerge from the actors' situated interaction with IT. These enacted structures are labelled "technology-in-practice".

When actors use a technology, they draw on:

- The properties provided by its material substance and inscribed by the designers and added by users through previous interactions (e.g., specific data content, customised features, or expanded accessories);
- Their skills, power, knowledge, and expectations about the technology, influenced mainly by training, communication, and previous experience (Orlikowski & Gash, 1994);
- The knowledge and experience of the institutional context in which they live and work.

In this way, the actors' use of technology becomes structured by their experiences, knowledge, meanings, habits, power relationships, and norms. Such structuring enacts future use as actors continue to interact with the system.

One final remark about Orlikowski's view on technology is that she also proposes expanding the understanding of a "stabilised" technology that was held by the "traditional" structurational models and social constructivism. She argues that technology cannot reach a stabilisation phase because technology-in-practice is always subject to change as humans modify their awareness, experiences, knowledge, power, etc. It is proposed that even though technology-in-practice may become institutionalised over time, this is only stabilisation "for now" (Schryer, 1993). In every use, there is always the possibility of enacting new structures. Therefore, the practice lens suggests an "open-ended set of emergent structures that may be enacted through recurrent use of technology" (Orlikowski, 2000, p. 412).

When a technology is used in recurrent social interactions, it corresponds to a "technology-in-practice": an intangible shape which intervenes in ongoing practices through facilities, norms and interpretive schemes. Each type of "technology-in-practice" therefore shapes specific facilities, norms, and interpretive schemes which in turn transform the "technology-in-practice" that individuals enact.

To analyse "technology-in-practice", Orlikowski uses the theoretical framework of structuration and considers that "technology-in-practice" is in itself influenced by the structures of the organization (hierarchy relations, remuneration/incentive system, etc.)

- All structures and the interactions between structures are instantiated in recurrent social practice that employees maintain with the other members of the organization;
- And the structures contribute to formalizing the facilities, norms, and interpretive schemes that shape their social interactions (Orlikowski, 2000, p. 409).

Therefore, a "technology-in-practice" can be explained by a precise analysis of the different structures that exist in the social environment of an individual, and it can be analyzed concretely through the facilities, norms and interpretive schemes by which the structures are instantiated in practice.

Having acknowledged the great potential of the theory of practice, there are two remarks worth mentioning. First, if the role of users is taken into account, the technology side of appropriation appears quite absent. In fact, theory of practice does not link enactment with any kind of characteristic of the technology that is used. The place of users is so important that appropriations become too close to uses (Ologeanu-Taddeï & Staii, 2008). Therefore, it appears necessary to reintroduce the technology side of appropriation in the reflection. As they belong to the same epistemological framework, it seems possible to articulate the theory of practice and AST by considering that "structural features" and the "spirit" of the technology intervene as factors to define "technology-in-practice".

The critical realist view on appropriation makes the same kind of link (De Vaujany, 2008b). In fact, this approach connects those two sides of appropriation by proposing that objects (including people, material objects and social phenomena such as institutions) and relations among objects (for instance, friendship or master-slave relations) must be taken into account to analyse appropriation.

Second, as was the case for AST, practice theory's epistemological framework is interactionism and social constructivism. Orlikowski (2000) mentions more precisely than De Sanctis and Poole (1994) that appropriation depends on the leadership, hierarchy structure and incentive systems. But she does not take into account the organizational structure as a whole. She considers that actors locally re-structure social structures through the interactions of individuals within a group, but she does not clearly link the nature of appropriation with, for instance, the repartition of powers in the organizational structure.

Those two theories on appropriation have in common their focus on the individual dimension of appropriation. They do not take into account employees' behaviours within the organizational context. Even authors who study the appropriation at the group level do not report appropriation characteristics related to the organizational context.

Appropriation of Technologies and Organizational Structure

As we mentioned above, De Sanctis and Poole (1994) consider that structures are produced and reproduced by individual members of a group when using and adapting the rules and resources for the interactions. They focused on small groups and decision-making processes within the group. Generally, authors are interested in appropriation *by users* as individuals, for example, the user

appropriation of mobile technologies (Wiredu, 2007). Thus, they disregard the organizational context. Nevertheless, in the management and organization theory field, ITs are studied in relation to organizational contexts.

In this perspective, Woodward (1958) argues that technologies directly determine differences in such organizational attributes as span of control, centralization of authority, and the formalization of rules and procedures. Leavitt and Whisler predicted in 1958 that upper management would use IT's capabilities to re-centralize their organizations. Mintzberg (1979) suggests that technology is a contingency factor that determines the structural variables of the organization. George and King (1991) and Groth (1999) look specifically at the effects of technology on the structure of organizations, and the question of whether or not the organizations become more or less centralized with the implementation of IT. Groth (1999) argues that IT can make organizations both centralized and decentralized at the same time. The author finds that IT increases the complexity a single manager can handle, but at the same time the lower levels of the hierarchy can be empowered by the information available to them through IT. This eliminates the need for mid-level management, and the organization takes on a leaner structure (Groth, 1999).

Recently, Muhlmann (2003) showed that the success (or failure) of implementation of groupware technology is intimately linked to the nature and structure of the players' games. These technologies become integrated in the "tightly coupled systems" (Perrow, 1972) and structure their operations and regulation, and then they are generally rejected by the players in "loosely coupled systems" and do not change the players' games in this type of configuration. Thus, the penetration of technology in groupware occupations is closely related to the degree of interdependence of this context (Muhlmann, 2003). According to this author, when the manager's action is supported by mechanisms of cooperation with the players, the introduction of groupware is experienced by actors as an opportunity, that is, as a new medium to help the exchange. In contrast, when the manager's action is superimposed on a structure of hardly cohesive relations, and the way of regulation is "flexible" and not integrated, the introduction of groupware technology is seen as a constraint by new actors, and it is therefore generally neglected.

In sum, when management is in a position of strength, the introduction of new technologies just maintains and even reinforces an already very cohesive exchange, while when management is in a weak position, it is faced with "self-regulation" deployed by the players on the sidelines. Moreover, Muhlmann (2003) argues that the technologies introduced by management do not shape the organizational structure but are rather systematically "digested" or "embodied" by the organizational structure.

We may interpret this result by using AST (De Sanctis & Poole, 1994). In the tightly coupled systems, employees relate IT structures to other structures. In contrast, in the loosely coupled systems, actors negate the usefulness of IT and reject it. These are two different appropriation moves dictated by the organizational structure (specifically, in the second type of situation, we may refer to non-appropriation). Furthermore, employees' attitudes toward IT are linked to the organizational structure. They perceive that the technology is of value to them in their work, while they do not perceive this value in the tightly coupled systems.

We may also connect these sentences to contingency theory and hypothesise that the perceived value (or utility) of IT by employees is connected to the perceived autonomy and control the IT provides and their need or willingness to preserve their autonomy to complete their work tasks.

In addition, we may assume that the degree of comfort associated with the use of an IT or the utility of the IT for their tasks is perceived differently by employees according to the type of organizational structure they belong to. We suggest that IT appropriation is related to the design parameters of the organizational structure.

The topic for study here is the implications of IT for organizational structures and also the consequences of IT on both organizational structures and appropriation aspects (De Sanctis & Poole, 1994). We consider that appropriation is the most suitable term to describe the behaviour of occupational groups (groups of players – Crozier & Friedberg, 1977; Mintzberg, 1979) and their stability (relative) in dealing and coping with IT.

THREE CASE STUDIES TO HIGHLIGHT THE ROLE OF ORGANIZATIONAL STRUCTURE IN THE APPROPRIATION OF IT

Methodology

This paper proposes reintroducing an organizational structure aspect along with technology and the user in the analysis of appropriation. We mentioned above that this question is quite exploratory because after several reflections linking technology and organization (Woodward, 1958), researchers usually disregarded the organizational context of technology or the uses they analysed. This phenomenon is poorly explored, and its boundary and logic are uncertain. Therefore, a case study seems to be the most accurate research method (Yin, 1994).

Nevertheless, as appropriation is assumed to be linked to the nature of the organizational structure where they appear and the technology used, we chose to conduct multiple case studies in different organizations (Miles & Huberman, 1994). This research was done as an interpretive case study. In interpretive studies, the researcher assumes that reality is socially constructed through human sensemaking and interaction (Davidson, 2002). Several semi-structured interviews were held with ensembles of highly technical and managerial-level employees within three organizations.

The interviews were transcribed, coded, and validated across the research team and subsequently with the interviewees. We also analysed secondary data in order to attempt methodological triangulation. A first level of encoding was used to reduce the diversity of the data and to sum up important elements in the interviews. Encoding then enabled us to identify the main themes arising during the interviews (Miles & Huberman, 1994).

The cases are based on the following themes (criteria):

- The organizational configuration (Mintzberg, 1979)
- The technology's spirit
- The degree of IT appropriation, especially appropriation moves.

We summarise the characteristics for these themes, in the three cases, in Table 1.

"AERO": The Role of Decentralization in the Appropriation of Technology

Aero belongs to an international group in the aeronautical and space sector (Guiderdoni-Jourdain & Oiry, 2008). In Europe, Aero has more than 12,000 employees. The group's activities cover the complete process from supplier to customer and range from R&D right through to specific hands-on training sessions for end-users. In 2000, a HR decision was taken to improve the communication policy between management and employees. One of the actions was to develop a HR intranet offering access to all employees from the company's website.

To analyse the uses of this intranet, we employed the findings from multiple data collection methods: document analysis (in particular, analysis of archival corporate information), semi-structured interviews, and screening the observation protocols of the HR intranet project. A total of 53 semi-structured interviews were held with three employee groups: department managers or equivalent, level 1 (a department has about 200

Table 1. Organisational structure, IT's spirit and appropriation moves

Case	AERO	Group of supermarkets	Caladin
Organizational configuration	Professional bureaucracy, informal communication for the operational core	Division organization	Entrepreneurial structure
IT's spirit	Communication formalization	Increase the control at the local level	- facilitate and accelerate decision-making in organizations - professional cooperation within the team (its community of practice aspect) and functional coordination with the other departments
Appropriation moves	Almost no appropriation	The ERP do not take into account the specificity of the local business units. So the department manager "forces" commands, manually.	On one hand, software is efficient because it allows employees to build collective decisions but on the other hand, the manager of the SME considers it inefficient because it does not permit him to create a new hierarchical level

people), sub-department managers or equivalent, level 2 (management of about 50 people) and team leaders, level 3 (management of about 10 people).

Among department managers who participated in the research, it was particularly interesting to analyse the case of assembly line managers. The decentralization of power due to a professional bureaucracy explained their low appropriation of the HR intranet.

Assembly line managers pushed us to enter a different world: the world of production, specifically industrial workshops and manufacturing lines (airplanes, helicopters, etc.). In "his" world, "his" workshop, the line manager is the "master". Corporate management has little hold on this world. The line manager is generally a charismatic leader, a man of action with a strong personality, respected for his integrity, an excellent technician with the ability to make "fair" decisions. Nevertheless, he is under the pressure of high production rates. Respecting final assembly dates pushes him to be very demanding (overtime, weekend shifts). The work rhythm is so intense that the balance between private and work life is often overstepped. Such a leader must be extremely close to his "guys" in order to achieve the objectives. "We are also top management's representatives in the shop, so it's our job to maintain a positive social atmosphere, which means we have to be on the field constantly, so the guys are happy to come to work every day. It's also a sensitive position, because you must be attentive: if a worker is not right or upset, you have to go and see him quickly. Talking with him, you understand that his child is sick or his wife left him … so, that's when you have to take the time and support him. You have to maintain direct contact" (William).

He is considered the guarantor of the team spirit that can be found in the sectors used to working with permanent urgency. This leader manages an average of more than 200 workers. Generally, he works his way up through the ranks. How does this person view the HR intranet? He spontaneously states: "I feel more at home in the workshop than behind a computer" (William).

Therefore, the use of the HR intranet is rare or non-existent. The tool is seen as "a waste of time" because "we can get the information elsewhere" (Jean).

Decentralization of power, pressure and the pace of work mean that managers looking for answers to HR questions prefer to contact the local HR units in workshops and assembly lines, either in person or by telephone. This quick and easy method of contact meets their needs. Since the trade unions have a greater influence in this world, these shop floor managers also maintain regular contacts with trade union representatives, who generally receive HR information before them. This state of affairs is deplored by these managers as it places them in an awkward position, but they simply have to put up with it.

This case study stresses the role of a professional culture reinforced by an organizational structure based on decentralization and pressure of time that encourages a very low use of an HR intranet.

ERP Implementation in a Group of Supermarkets: The Role of Centralization

The business units (a store) of a group of supermarkets use the same IT. The group has a divisionalized form of structure (Mintzberg, 1979). Business units enjoy some autonomy, which is greater for those franchises. However, the headquarters of the group often seeks to increase the control at the local level. The use of a computer system to aid in the store is the main way the headquarters exerts control. The ERP can manage all the elements that make up the shop (discounts, ordering, data products/suppliers/shops/customers, cost management, inventory, rates/prices, turnover). At any time it is possible to publish reports of turnover, cost per day, or promotions.

To analyse the process of appropriation of this ERP, we conducted five semi-structured interviews with the department managers (managerial level 3) in the same store and a store manager. According to both department and store managers, ERP has several advantages for the business unit: transmission of skills, strong interaction with its environment, price controls and assistance with daily tasks of the managerial department, increasing performance (powerful analytical tool, electronic data interchange and daily tasks of the business). But it also has drawbacks, as follows: proposals command not representative of the store, integration of suppliers in the SI, which reduces the flexibility and strengthens headquarters' control. Specifically, to avoid disruption of stocks, the management software assists in preparing orders for each day as a proposed order. It is based on the threshold replenishment (equal to safety stock inventory consumed during the delivery period) and the theoretical demand for each product. However, errors are frequent in these orders and proposals for several reasons:

- Inventories are recorded because of breakage, theft, omissions in registration entries, etc.
- Misinterpreting by ERP that examines each product according to its theoretical demand that is often unrepresentative of the local demand (because of strong seasonal sales). In other words, the ERP makes it difficult to take into account the specificity of the local business units. This data type must be changed manually by the department manager who "forces" commands.

In this organization the ERP is a tool for unit business performance monitoring by headquarters and, locally, for manager department performance monitoring. In addition, the store manager uses supervision control with a high degree of centralization. At the group and local level, the organization is a tightly coupled system. Managers and department managers have no choice about the organization of the work; the use of ERP is strictly obligatory. In this sense, we see an appropriation of ERP. However, if the business unit operates effectively at the local level, a degree of autonomy is necessary. ERP appropriation is manifested particularly in the way of "forcing" the order.

However, during the change of brand strategy, the business unit will in future use an information system where a command would be automatic (not assisted, allowing manual changes). The local managers are concerned about the disappearance of this degree of autonomy.

CALADIN: The Role of Managerial Deception in Appropriation of IT

The case study was carried out in CALADIN, a software and computer services company that produces and markets several software packages (registry/public records office management, mail digitisation and management, document classification). In 2006, the company's turnover was 4.5 million euros, and it employed a total of 48 people. The workforce is distributed among 6 departments: digitisation software (10 people), electronic data interchange (EDI) software (7 people), customer support (10 people), implementers (8 people), sales (10 people), and administration (3 people).

A wider presentation of this case study can be found in Oiry, Pascal and Tchobanian (2008), and it was re-analyzed for this article with the authors' permission.

In the autumn of 2007, this SME began to use the 'Think together®' software package, the purpose of which, according to its designers, is to "facilitate and accelerate decision-making in organizations". In order to understand the "spirit" of this technology, we conducted three interviews with the designers of the software. We also interviewed the SME's managing director. He told us that this software package was intended originally for use in the EDI software department. Accordingly, we interviewed 4 of the 7 members of this department. In order to extend the scope of our analysis, we also interviewed the head of the customer support department. The coding techniques presented above were used to analyse the data.

The interviews conducted in this firm revealed that some usage of 'Think together®' fit with what the designers expected. Thus, one IT developer stated: "We'd been holding meeting after meeting for four months in an attempt to solve a problem, namely how to link our 'mail' product [which digitises incoming mail] and our 'document' product [which automatically classifies documents]. Customers had been asking us for months to link the two together, and we couldn't decide on how to do it. I gathered all the e-mails we had exchanged and fed them all into ['Think together®']. That was Friday (…) This created a stir, with everybody giving their opinion… The Wednesday afterwards, we had a meeting and we came out of it with a firm decision. We really unblocked the situation thanks to ['Think together®']."

This quote shows that the structure of the "good decision" that the designers incorporated into the software may reflect the decision-making process in an organization. In this case, the actual use may be reasonably faithful to the spirit of the technology incorporated into the software by the designers.

The SME's managing director recognized that 'Think together®' allowed them to find a solution to link "mail" and "document" softwares, but he is nevertheless disappointed by 'Think together®'. To clarify this situation, we asked him further about the reasons and motivations behind the introduction of 'Think together®' in his company. His answer was slightly confusing and collated our ideas of appropriation: "…It's a rather complicated story… The Electronic Data Interchange team, which is where I wanted to use it, had not had a manager for a long time… (…) I am in charge of this team… But I've got too many things to do and I can't devote enough time to them. What's more, on the technical level,

I'm not knowledgeable enough about what they're doing. Everything changes too quickly. There's someone in the team, X (…) that I would like to promote to manager. I think he has the strength of character and the abilities, but he has to mature gradually… To my way of thinking, the use of ['Think together®'] could help him take on this new role."

As the quote shows, the SME's managing director judges 'Think together®' not only in terms of its functionality, but also in terms of its ability to change his own organization. In a certain manner, we can say that like other users, he develops the use of this software in line with the problems he encounters in his work. For him, the aim is to identify a manager for his EDI software group and to get him accepted by the team. This manager's principal role is to foster professional cooperation within the team (its community of practice aspect) and functional coordination with the other departments when decisions have to be taken collectively. This managing director is using 'Think together®' in the hope of being able to provide the future manager with a tool to assist him in carrying out his duties as well as to legitimate his managerial role.

This use accords fairly well with the initial spirit of the technology (organising exchanges of ideas with this software equates to a standard managerial activity). It is reinforced by the convergent use of other available coordination tools (for example, they hold meetings that involve all members of the team). However, this SME's managing director does not evaluate the software's contributions solely in relation to the decisions it helps to make (which is officially why it was purchased and developed) but primarily in terms of its ability to bring about organizational change. The designers developed this software around the notion of 'organizational transparency', which can be practised in various formal hierarchical organizations, if they can maintain such transparency. In this case, "transparency" was being sought by this managing director in order to legitimate a particular choice of hierarchical organization. Thus, these issues of organizational change (which are not explicitly included in the designers' offer) emerge as an important factor in the disparity between the expected uses and the actual uses.

DISCUSSION AND CONCLUSION

Our literature review showed that at the beginning, the characteristics of the organizational structure were the focus of the reflection on appropriation, especially within the realm of the diffusion of innovation literature. This concept was developed in two directions. First, the Adaptative Structuration Theory became a strong framework of the "technological side" of appropriation (De Sanctis & Poole, 1994). It explains how structural features and the spirit of technology play a role in the appropriation process. On the "user side", theory of practice (Orlikowski, 2000) is a conceptualisation that analyses precisely how users enact technology. Those two conceptualizations, being both inscribed in interactionism, fail to address the role of the organizational structure in appropriation.

In this article we insist that it is necessary to develop a new reflection on appropriation that goes beyond purely technological and user sides, and re-introduces an "organizational structure side" of appropriation. Our empirical data suggest that the organizational structure plays an important role in the appropriation of technology. With the first case study, we saw that professional bureaucracy explained the low level of use of an HR intranet. In fact, this kind of organizational structure is synonymous with a decentralisation of power. Professionalism of employees allows them to keep their hierarchy at a certain distance. If we add that those actors prefer face-to-face discussion and that they have the possibility to talk directly with the local HR manager, we can see that the organizational structure of this firm plays a great role in the explanation of the low use of the HR intranet described.

The second case is an example of the opposite phenomenon: effects of centralization of power on the use of an IT tool. We saw that the use of the ERP was obligatory, and local managers could only execute orders through the IT tool. This obligation corresponded to a high degree of centralization of power. Headquarters had the possibility to impose use of the IT tool on the lower levels of the hierarchy. But even in those highly centralised firms, the power of the headquarters must construct compromises with the different reality in stores. As we saw above, inventories are erroneous, and theoretical demands do not match the real local demands. ERP cannot take into account the specificity of the local business unit. Therefore, it appeared necessary to allow the option for orders to be changed manually by local managers. A certain degree of autonomy for local managers was indispensable if headquarters was to request all local managers to use ERP. For future research, it would be interesting to analyse how a higher level of centralization of power changes the appropriation of a system. This appropriation move is directly linked to a transformation of the organizational structure side of appropriation and, especially, the reinforcement of the centralization of power.

The third case showed how a tool can be used to try to create a new level of hierarchy. This case demonstrated that the link between the organizational structure and appropriation can be effective in both directions: the organizational structure influences appropriation, but appropriation can influence an organizational structure, too. As we saw in this case, an IT tool can be used to try to create a new organizational structure of a firm.

This study is limited. Our three case studies are only examples that underline that organizational structure side of appropriation. The foundation of this paper was a proposition: does organizational structure play a role in the appropriation processes of IT tools? Our empirical data should encourage researchers to investigate the issue of the organizational structures in more detail.

Among different tasks, those studies could create a methodological tool to measure appropriation, and a grid to analyse the degree of centralization and decentralization of the organizational structure and areas of autonomy better (linked with uses of IT tools).

As has been the case for the "technological side" and "user side" of appropriation, it appears that a strong framework is necessary to place the "organizational structure side" into the appropriation of technology.

REFERENCES

Beaudry, A., & Pinsonneault, A. (2005). Understanding user responses to information technology: A coping model of user adaptation. *MIS Quaterly*, *29*(3), 493–524.

Chin, W., Gopal, A., & Salisbury, W. (1997). Advancing the theory of adaptive structuration: the development of a scale to measure faithfulness of appropriation. *Information Systems Research*, *8*, 343–367. doi:10.1287/isre.8.4.342

Clark, P. A. (1987). *Anglo-American innovation*. New York: De Gruyter.

Crozier, M., & Friedberg, E. (1977). *L'acteur et le système*. Paris: Seuil.

Davis, F. D., Bagozzi, R. P., & Warshaw, P. R. (1989). User acceptanace of computer technology: A comparison of two theoretical models. *Management Science*, *35*(8), 982–1003. doi:10.1287/mnsc.35.8.982

De Certeau, M. (2002). *L'invention du quotidien. Arts de faire*. Paris: Gallimard.

De Sanctis, G., & Poole, M. S. (1994). Capturing the Complexity in Advanced Technology Use: Adaptative Structuration Theory. *Organization Science*, *5*(2), 121–147. doi:10.1287/orsc.5.2.121

de Vaujany, F.-X. (2008a). Capturing reflexivity modes in IS: A critical realist approach. *Information and Organization*, *18*, 51–72. doi:10.1016/j.infoandorg.2007.11.001

de Vaujany, F.-X. (2008b). Strategic Alignment: What Else? A Practice Based View of IS Value. In *Proceedings of the Twenty Ninth International Conference on Information Systems,* Paris.

Downs, G. W. Jr, & Mohr, L. B. (1976). Conceptual Issues in the Study of Innovation. *Administrative Science Quarterly*, *21*, 700–714. doi:10.2307/2391725

George, J. F., & King, J. L. (1991). Examining the Computing and Centralization Debate. *Communications of the ACM*, *34*(7), 62–72. doi:10.1145/105783.105796

Groth, L. (1999). *Future organizational design: the scope for the IT-based enterprise*. New York: John Wiley & Sons.

Guiderdoni-Jourdain, K., & Oiry, E. (2008). "Local Universe" and use of an HR Intranet. The case of Middle Management. In Bondarouk, T., & Ruël, H. (Eds.), *Electronic HRM in Theory and Practice: a Reader*. Hershey, PA: IGI Global.

Hettinga, M. (2002).*Understanding evolutionary use of groupware*. Unpublished doctoral dissertation, Telematica Instituut, Enschede, The Netherlands.

Ives, B., & Olson, M. H. (1984). User Involvement and MIS Success: A review of Research. *Management Science*, *30*(5), 583–603. doi:10.1287/mnsc.30.5.586

Jones, M. (1999). Structuration theory. In Currie, W. L., & Galliers, B. (Eds.), *Rethinking management information systems* (pp. 103–135). Oxford, UK: Oxford University Press.

Jouët, J. (1993). *Usages et pratiques des nouveaux outils de communication. Dictionnaire critique de la communication*. Paris: Universitaires de France, Paris.

Leavitt, H., & Whisler, T. (1958, November-December). Management in the 1980's. *Harvard Business Review*, 41–48.

Leonard-Barton, D. (1988). Implementation as Mutual Adaptation of Technology and Organization. *Research Policy, 17*, 251–267. doi:10.1016/0048-7333(88)90006-6

Majchrzak, A., Rice, R. E., Malhorta, A., King, N., & Ba, S. (2000). Technology adaptation: the case of a computer-supported inter-organisational virtual team. *Management Information Systems Quarterly, 24*, 569–600. doi:10.2307/3250948

Markus, M. L., & Silver, M. S. (2008). A Foundation for the Study of IT Effects: A New Look at De Sanctis and Poole's Concepts of Structural Features and Spirit. *Journal of the Association for Information Systems, 9*(3/4).

Miles, M. B., & Huberman, A. M. (1994). *Qualitative Data Analysis*. Beverley Hills, CA: Sage Publications.

Mintzberg, H. (1979). *The structuring of organizations: a synthesis of the research*. Englewood Cliffs, NJ: Prentice Hall.

Miranda, S. M., & Bostrom, R. P. (1993). The impact of Group Support Systems on group conflict and conflict management. *Journal of Management Information Systems, 10*(3), 63–95.

Muhlmann, D. (2003). *The organizational impact of new technologies. The case of groupware and knowledge management*. Unpublished doctoral dissertation, Sciences Po Paris.

Nagasundram, M., & Bostrom, R. P. (1994). The structuring of creative processes using GSS: a framework for research. *Journal of Management Information Systems, 11*(3), 87–114.

Oiry, E., Pascal, A., & Tchobanian, R. (2008). From tool to organization: uses of a collaborative application in a high-tech SME. In *Proceedings of the 8th International Conference on the Design of Cooperative Systems*, Carry-Le-Rouet, France.

Ologeanu-Taddei, R., & Staii, A. (2008). Comment analyser l'appropriation? Le défi de l'opérationnalisation empirique. In *Proceedings of the 13ème conférence de l'AIM (Association Information et Management) (pré-ICIS)*, Paris.

Orlikowski, W. (2000). Using technology and constituting structures: a practice lens for studying technology in organizations. *Organization Science, 11*(4), 404–428. doi:10.1287/orsc.11.4.404.14600

Orlikowski, W. J., & Gash, C. (1994). Technological frames: making sense of information technology in organisations. *ACM Transactions on Information Systems, 12*(2), 174–207. doi:10.1145/196734.196745

Perriault, J. (1989). *La logique de l'usage*. Paris: Flammarion.

Perrow, C. (1972). *Complex Organizations: A Critical Essay*. Glenview, IL: Scott, Foresman.

Poole, M. C., & De Sanctis, G. (1989). Microlevel structuration in computer-supported group decision making. *Human Communication Research, 19*(1), 5–49.

Proulx, S. (Ed.). (1988). *Vivre avec l'ordinateur: les usagers de la micro-informatique*. Québec, Canada: Boucherville.

Rice, R., & Rogers, E. M. (1980). Reinventing in the Innovation Process. *Knowledge: Creation, Diffusion. Utilization, 1*(4), 499–514.

Rogers, E. M. (1964). *Diffusion of Innovations*. New York: Free Press.

Ruël, H. J. M. (2001). *The non-technical side of office technology; managing the clarity of the spirit and the appropriation of office technology* (Doctoral dissertation). Enschede, The Netherlands: Twente University Press.

Schryer, C. F. (1993). Records as Genre. *Written Communication*, *10*, 200–234. doi:10.1177/0741088393010002003

Tyre, M. J., & Orlikowski, W. J. (1994). Windows of Opportunity: Temporal Patterns of Technological Adaptation in Organizations. *Organization Science*, *5*(1), 98–118. doi:10.1287/orsc.5.1.98

Weick, K. E. (1969). *The social Psychology of Organizing*. Reading, MA: Addison Wesley.

Wiredu, G. O. (2007). User appropriation of mobile technologies: Motives, conditions and design properties. *Information and Organization*, *7*(2), 110–129. doi:10.1016/j.infoandorg.2007.03.002

Woodward, J. (1958). *Management and technology*. London: Her Majesty's Stationery Office.

Yin, R. K. (1994). *Case Study Research: Design and Methods*. London: Sage.

This work was previously published in International Journal of Technology and Human Interaction, Volume 6, Issue 4, edited by Anabela Mesquita & Chia-Wen Tsai, pp. 34-48, copyright 2010 by IGI Publishing (an imprint of IGI Global).

Chapter 16
Using OLAP Tools for e-HRM:
A Case Study

Alysson Bolognesi Prado
State University of Campinas, Brazil

Carmen Freitas
State University of Campinas, Brazil

Thiago Ricardo Sbrici
State University of Campinas, Brazil

ABSTRACT

In the growing challenge of managing people, Human Resources need effective artifacts to support decision making. On Line Analytical Processing is intended to make business information available for managers, and HR departments can now encompass this technology. This paper describes a project in which the authors built a Data Warehouse containing actual Human Resource data. This paper provides data models and shows their use through OLAP software and their presentation to end-users using a web portal. The authors also discuss the progress, and some obstacles of the project, from the IT staff's viewpoint.

INTRODUCTION

Since the late 1980's and the beginning of the 1990's, Business Intelligence (BI) tools have been proposed as valuable tools for companies (Inmon, 2005; Kimball et al., 1998), helping with decision support. Inside and outside the Human Resources department there is need for information that is not delivered by traditional HR systems, such as intranets (Guiderdony, 2007). On Line Analytical

Processing (OLAP) is one of the BI proposals for making information available for managers.

Most of the literature examples of OLAP used in companies is based on financial or production data, for instance, the sales amount. According to Ngai and Wat (2004), the use of Information Systems in the HR to help make more precise decisions is only the tenth in the ranking of their perceived benefits.

In this paper we present the experience gathered during the course of a project that aimed to apply OLAP tools for HRM, targeting on employees

DOI: 10.4018/978-1-61350-465-9.ch016

demography and absenteeism. This text represents the point of view of the IT staff regarding the project progress and sequels, intending to provide an example of how such powerful technology can help the Human Resource area, and potential difficulties in this way.

The projects began in 2005 at the Human Resources department of a public Brazilian University. It offers 58 undergraduate and 127 graduate courses and is organized in 20 Institutes and Schools, one academic medical center, 23 research centers and an administrative area. The institution employs teachers and researchers, technical and bureaucratic staff, physicians and nurses, comprising about 10,000 workers.

This paper is organized as follows: in the next sections there are, respectively, an overview of the adopted Business Intelligence theory, the description of implementations of two Data Marts regarding Human Resource information and how their content can be provided to final users. In the remaining sections, we discuss the challenges faced during the project, the drawbacks, lessons learned, project follow-up and present our final remarks.

Business Intelligence Overview

The concept of Business Intelligence (BI) refers to the abilities of the corporations to retrieve information related to their operation processes and area of activity, in a flexible and dynamic way, allowing the analysis, detailing and understanding their work and providing means for decision support. The term has been popularized since the late 1980's by Howard Dresner and the Gartner Group (Power, 2002).

The data managed by Business Intelligence systems have certain specific characteristics, reflecting on the way they are gathered, stored and retrieved, which will be briefly explained in the following sessions.

EXTRACT, TRANSFORM, AND LOAD

The process of obtaining and modifying the data for feeding a Business Intelligence database is called ETL, in respect to the three steps it involves: Extract, Transform and Load.

In the Extract step data are typically queried from other systems of the company, the so-called OLTP – On Line Transactional Processing – that supports the day-by-day organization operations. Spreadsheets and plain text files can also be used as data sources for Extraction.

In the Transform step the data are handled aiming to fit in the view the users of the decision support system have of the process and of the facts they represent. This means unit conversions, codes standardization, data filtering, categorization and so forth.

In the Load step the data produced by the prior steps are stored in a special database structure called Data Warehouse, which is described as follows.

DATA WAREHOUSE AND DATA MART

The Data Warehouse (DW) is a large data repository (Inmon, 2005), obtained from all the relevant sections of the organization. The Data Warehouse contains the raw material for the management's decision support system.

When the Data Warehouse is updated from ETL, no data is deleted or overwritten. Instead, the data are accumulated, constructing the history of the data involved in the company operations.

The data structure of a DW often does not follow the common database systems techniques that use normalization to ensure data integrity and less storage space. Instead, the data are de-normalized and arranged in such a way that helps to query for reports and analysis.

From the organization Data Warehouse, the information related to each area of interest is separated, forming Data Marts. Each Data Mart (DM) is a subset of the whole DW focused on a special subject of the decision support systems (Figure 1).

Data on a DM is arranged according to the star schema: each relevant data from the organization, known as fact, is stored in a structure called cube, which can be viewed or decomposed according to pre-defined categorization of the data, known as dimensions of the cube. The dimensions are some typical meaningful attributes of the fact, such as time, customer type, products and geography of the organization.

The dimensions can have several hierarchies for classifying the facts according to many points of view, each hierarchy being composed by different levels of granularity.

ON LINE ANALYTICAL PROCESSING

Retrieving data from a DM requires specialized software that can deal with cubes and dimensions. Besides, it must be able to provide a single entry point for the managers of the organization to search for the information needed to their decision making process. This role is fulfilled by the On Line Analytical Processing systems (OLAP).

An OLAP system provides means for accessing a Data Mart, listing its cubes and related dimensions, constructing reports, regardless of the particular data it contains. This way, the user does not need to learn how to operate different systems, and also programmers do not need to develop new programs and reports for each subject addressed by the Data Marts.

Through an OLAP, a user can build reports and charts that summarize the facts retrieved from the DM according to the selected dimensions. This way, it is easy to create cross-tabulation by dragging and dropping dimensions on rows or columns.

It's also easy to change the granularity chosen by a certain dimension, in a process called drill-up or drill-down, when the user navigates trough the hierarchic levels of a dimension.

For each of these modifications on the table structure, the data on the cross-table cells are re-summarized on-line, providing immediate answers for the user and helping decision-making.

OPERATIONAL DATA STORE

Along with the use of data warehouses, companies sometimes faced situations in which the information needed to support a decision was not fully present in the BI systems, neither available nor easily retrievable from the operational systems and databases. To bridge this gap, Inmon et al. (1996) proposed the Operational Data Store – ODS.

The Operational Data Store can act as an intermediate repository for data coming from the operational and legacy systems, and going to the Data Warehouse and Data Marts. The data ODS

Figure 1. BI architecture example

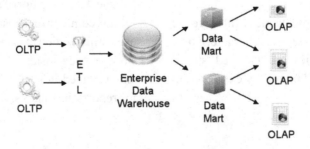

content is fine-grained, current-valued or at least often updated, and subject-oriented. The ODS is fed with operational data from several sources, which are put together to serve as a single source of information for reports and another Decision Support Systems, and for the ETL of the DW (Figure 2).

EMBEDDING OLAP VISUALIZATION INTO WEB APPLICATIONS

Sometimes managers need to see data with different levels of granularity in the same computational environment. Facing any unpredicted or suspect behavior in the operational data triggers a lookup in the BI data in order to discover a trend, prevent some future failure or explain any apparent outlier information. Having both the current and the historical data side by side is helpful to place the suspicious data in the historical scenario of the organization and take the necessary decisions and steps.

Nowadays, there are many available technologies that enterprises can adopt to bear their IT software infrastructure. Some are proprietary or customized, bought or developed exclusively for that organization. On the other hand, the growing

presence of free software that provides solutions with the same level of quality is undeniable. From the first set, we can cite the Microsoft® .Net Framework used by many organizations to support their software; from the last one, the Sun Java™ and particularly the JEE platform has a broad spread use.

Many literature sources (Few, 2009; Casati et al., 2004; Malik, 2005; Niven, 2008) refer to a need of an "enterprise dashboard" in which BI data can be promptly seen and understood. This artifact can be achieved by the use of a report generator such as Jasper Reports (http://jasperforge.org). It is a software solution that can be embedded in a large range of Java applications, both for web and desktop environments, and has both free and commercial license models.

There is a whole package of tools from the Jasper repository intended to be used with Business Intelligence and OLAP visualization, called Jaspersoft Business Intelligence Suite. Its main component is the report generator, but there is also support for interactive querying and dynamic dashboard customization for advanced users.

With the report generator, components such as the Pivot Table can be mixed with pie charts in order to obtain the desired visual information. The IT team responsible for the development and

Figure 2. ODS role in BI architecture

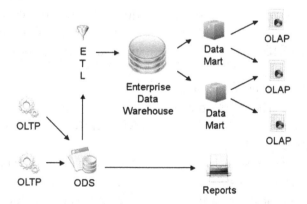

maintenance of the operational Human Resource Information System can add this functionality to the new or existing software.

As information security is always a concern in HRIS, in order to not expose unnecessary or confidential data from the employees, the BI Suite provides single sign-on integration with external security systems such as LDAP and Windows Active Directory Services, with granular access control by row, column, cell or report. It also enables an audit trail logging, with which one can know who accessed which report and when.

As a result, when someone from the HR staff uses the operational software in his or her daily activities – let us say, interview a candidate for a job or a promotion – he or she can see the necessary updated or outdated data from the person, with the background data of the whole organization or of a single department, all in a single software tool, providing better reference for comparisons and decisions.

Implementation of Data Marts

To help with the decision-making of the Human Resource area of the University we modeled the Absenteeism Data Mart and Employees Data Mart. Thus, we met the demand for information referring to workers counts and absenteeism rates distinctly. The following sections will detail each constructed Data Mart.

USING BI ON THE WORKFORCE ANALYSIS

The ability of profiling the workers of an organization is a common need in Human Resource activities. According to Burke and Ng (2006), some of the up-to-date subjects in HR are related to demographic changes of workers, such as aging and cultural diversity. In the studies presented at the United States Worker Health Chartbook (NIOSH, 2004) the major variables considered

were age, sex, ethnicity and occupation. These variables can be applied both inside and outside an organization. But specifically inside the enterprise, more attributes may be added to depict the worker's profile.

Modeling the Employees' Data Mart

The Human Resource Management Systems (OLTP) used at the organization stores the workers' enrollment data in several distinct tables. Our first challenge was to choose a set of attributes, candidates to become dimensions, which accomplish the maximum number of requirements from some Human Resource departments and other business areas of the University.

Besides, we decided to elect some extra dimensions to put in the model, trying to avoid a new modeling caused by new requirements in a short period of time. We defined the sum of employees as the fact for the cube and conclude the data model shown in Figure 3.

This cube was planned to be updated monthly, so the Time dimension contains month and year for every snapshot of an employee's situation, taken on the last day of the month. The Statute dimension stands for the legal characteristics of hiring contracts.

Workplace means the current position in the physical and organizational structure, (institutes, departments, and so on): the Journey dimension represents the nominal workday length and Frequency Situation reflects the employee availability at the workplace (still working, retired, on vacation, absent and so on). The other dimensions are self-explanatory.

APPLYING BI FOR ABSENTEEISM

According to Chiavenato (2002), Absenteeism is an expression used to designate a worker's faults or absences in the enterprise. Quick and Laper-

Figure 3. Star schema for employees' data mart

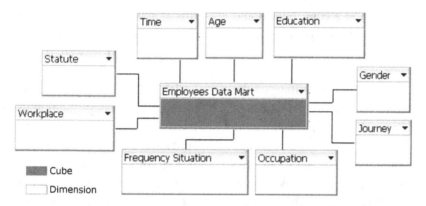

tosa (1982) suggest the following classification, regarding the cause of absence:

- **Sickness at Work Absenteeism:** originated by professional diseases or work accidents;
- **Health Absenteeism:** produced by diseases other than those related to work;
- **Legal Absenteeism:** when the absences are predicted and accepted by laws;
- **Compulsory Absenteeism:** situations beyond the worker's will, for instance, any penalty or arrest.
- **Free Will Absenteeism:** generated by personal affairs and situations without legal subsidy.

Couto (1998) emphasizes that it is very important to know how to measure and understand absenteeism rates in a corporation, based not on a single point of view, but instead involving areas as:

- **Operational Management:** focus on frequency control to detect and avoid problems with team productivity, exceeding hours on duty and overload of tasks.
- **Human Resources:** build projections to foresee the future needs of the working force.

- **Occupational Safety and Health:** aims to detect and prevent diseases produced by work situation, resulting in programs to deal with hazards and enhance life quality.

Based on these approaches, authors define several different absenteeism rate formulas, with slight variations in the input data, but all having the general rationale of quantifying the ratio between absent and expected workforces. Couto (1998) defines his rates based on the average number of employees working and the number of days that are important for each analysis: number of missed days, number of days on medical leaves, and so forth.

Couto (1998) highlights the importance of choosing a single standard of absenteeism calculation in order to make it comparable in terms of time evolution and distribution in the company geography. This convergence can be obtained by a single system that provides the data to the whole organization, however respecting particular needs, by using the tools as Business Intelligence software described below.

THE ABSENTEEISM DATA MART

From an OLTP system used in the company to store and process data related to the daily attendance of the employees, we define a star schema that uses this information in a consolidated and complete way. The information structure is modeled in agreement with the dimensions that were defined in the project.

To build the Cube, in the beginning of the project, we considered the use of the number of days of absence (Couto, 1998) as the fact for the cube. But due to characteristics of the organization, such as the variety of shift durations, and the availability of data on the HR operational system, we changed it to use the number of hours to populate the cube.

The cube thus sums the amount of hours every employee has for each frequency situation of the organization. The number of hours is obtained through the verification of the employee frequency, which is registered in a database that stores the daily amount of hours that the employee works, is absent, or is in any other exceptional situation.

To use as Dimensions, besides some historical dimensions of enrollment data like the workplace, frequency situation and gender, we created a special dimension called Absenteeism, which contains the items Integral Actuation, Partial Actuation and Long Term Absence (Figure 4).

We considered as Integral Actuation on the company all employees that worked, or were absent in accordance with the Brazilian Consolidation of the Labor Law (CLT, 2007, article 473) during the month under consideration.

Absences that were shorter than thirty days in a row or that were not legal were defined as Partial Actuation on the company. Absences exceeding thirty days in a row were regarded as Long Term Absence.

It's possible to view the amount of hours in a certain frequency situation using only the fact itself, without estimates. The number of hours is split among Integral Actuation (I), Partial Actuation (P) or Long Term Absence (LT).

Besides, we can apply a function to translate the raw number of hours into a generic absenteeism rate, r (x). To get the Integral Actuation rate in the company, we divide the amount of hours of the Integral Actuation by the total number of hours of Actuation, Integral plus Partial, or

$$r(I) = I / (I + P). \qquad (1)$$

The absenteeism rate of the Partial Actuation is obtained from the division of the amount of hours of the Partial Actuation by the sum of hours of the Integral Actuation plus the hours of the Partial Actuation, or

$$r(P) = P / (I + P). \qquad (2)$$

To get the Long Term Absence rate, just do the division of the amount of hours in the Long Term Absence by the sum of hours of the Actuation

Figure 4. Star schema for absenteeism data mart

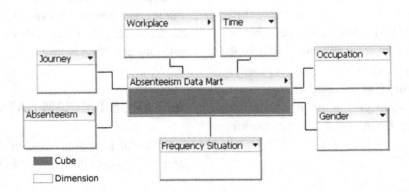

Integral plus the hours of the Actuation Partial plus the hours in the Long Term Absence.

$$r\,(LT) = LT\,/\,(I + P + LT). \qquad (3)$$

Based on these formulae we built some reports that access the absenteeism Data Mart, providing the HR staff and managers with a worker's absence information.

Spreading Knowledge

The data marts were finalized, though the information is still obscure for the end-user, then we concluded that a layer have to be created between the data mart and the end-user, because there must be means to access the data to get valuable information for analysis.

Rasmussen et al. (2002) describe five different scenarios for integrating BI tools with the data source:

a. Adopt only one BI tool to access the OLTP data source;
b. Adopt more than one BI tool to access the OLTP data source;
c. Integrate some BI tools to access the OLTP data source, by using a single web portal as a user interface to all the BI tools;
d. Use BI tools that come with the OLTP information systems by accessing its data source (e.g., functions of the HRIS that might generate analytical reports and querying.);
e. Use one or more BI tools by accessing a data warehouse.

We knew that the end-user has, not often been able to manipulate any kind of BI tool, thus some reports have been made available on a web browser. On the other hand, some users were experts at generating reports, graphics and analytical functions using a BI tool, for that reason, having an OLAP tool available was essential. Therefore, maintaining a portal where analytical reports could be accessible on the web, and disposing a BI tool for some end-user was our goal.

Having BI tools accessing the HRIS data sources was unnecessary because we had the data warehouse and data marts structured, consequently, alternatives a), b) and d) were disregarded, but c) was not, because using a web portal for some reports was a fact, then we joined options c) and d) once our goal was to build a web portal where analytical reports could be available, and in the same interface give access to the BI tool adopted to access the data marts.

USING THE OLAP TOOL

Aiming to exemplify the features of an OLAP tool, we will describe below the use of the Absenteeism Data Mart through a BI software tool. The use of the same tool for accessing the Employees Data Mart is very similar.

By accessing the Data Mart the managers can create themselves several spreadsheets and charts, or access some pre-built ones. Figure 5 shows a simple but typical table, where we can perceive the star-schema structure: dimensions in rows and columns, and a fact summarization in the center cells.

The dimension Time was used for columns in the Month hierarchy level, and the dimension Absenteeism was placed in row titles, using both levels Type and Subtype. The fact presented is the number of hours for each situation, summarized by a Sum function. The data were filtered to show only the months 01/2006, 02/2006 and 03/2006.

A common OLAP tool allows us to apply user-defined functions and calculations to the raw facts. For instance, to the same data used for Figure 5 we can apply the formulas described on the previous section for the absenteeism rate in the organization, producing the report shown on Figure 6.

Figure 5. Typical BI table, showing dimensions (gray) and facts (white)

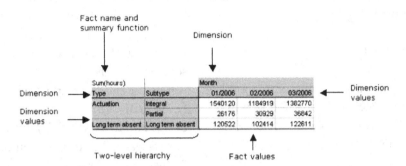

Since the users' needs for this system concern mainly the Partial Actuation index, we can plot a chart to view its behavior during all the months of 2006, as shown in Figure 7 by simply changing the filter of the Time dimension and applying the fact data to the Y axis of the chart.

If the user becomes curious about whether this behavior repeats itself every year, he or she can drill-up the Time dimension, by accessing the Year hierarchy level, and producing another report and chart (Figure 8). Managers now can get informed about possible workforce variations along the year.

Other dimensions, as the Workplace for instance, can be added to the sheet by simply dragging and dropping onto the rows or columns, and then the same procedure of drilling up and down can be applied for finding departments or offices of the organization where the absenteeism rates require more attention from the Human Resources department.

Figure 6. Processing the raw fact using Absenteeism rate formulas

% Abs.		Month		
Type	Subtype	01/2006	02/2006	03/200
Actuation	Integral	98,3%	97,5%	97,4'
	Partial	1,7%	2,5%	2,6'
Long term absent	Long term absent	7,1%	7,8%	8,0'

HR-BI PORTAL

Setting the portal as the primary point of interaction was our purpose, and then Human Resource – Business Intelligence Portal was the name granted to the web interface that made available the access to the BI tool and the analytical reports created.

The end-user community has access to this web portal according to three security levels:

1. Public: human resource quantitative reports, created in the BI software, which were chosen as a valuable information accessible to everyone;
2. Private: human resource costs and payroll reports, created in the BI software, which only the human resource area, managers and authorized users can access;
3. Restrict BI tool: qualified users able to generate analytical reports and graphics according to their needs.

Lessons Learned

When our first cubes were released to users there was great acceptance and signals of a promising future to the project (Prado et al., 2007). However, during the following months, we perceived a gradual lack of interest from users in the system. Despite many available warnings concerning BI

Figure 7. Chart for the Partial Actuation rate during the year of 2006

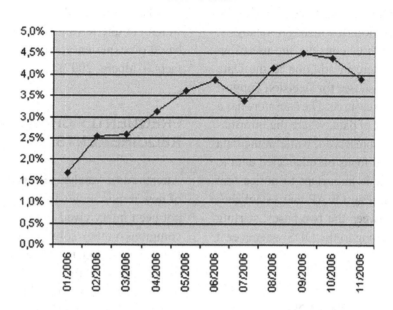

Figure 8. Drilling-up Time dimension and showing the last 3 years

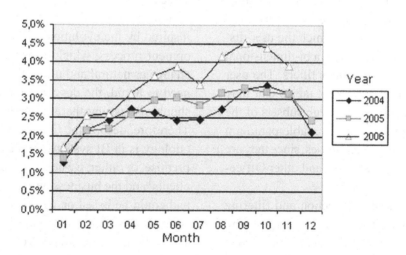

project pitfalls (Imhoff, 2005), we faced a situation in which we needed to investigate the real causes and try to correct them. The following topics summarize these findings and some considerations of the IT team.

RAW DATA HAS VALUE

A common requirement after the implantation was to allow users to see which people were placed in each cell of the fact table. This requirement shows us that data in a human resource system has a singular feature when compared with other systems, as raw data are about persons who, by themselves, are significant to a manager's analysis.

This behavior lets us consider the use of an Operational Data Store in addition to the Data Warehouse as a data source for Decision Support Systems of Human Resource. The data store has a fine-grained amount of data, where the information about people is preserved, while in the data warehouse we could focus on quantified data to manage analysis. It is important to notice that we must try to build an OLAP that establishes communication between the two bases, starting from the DW but going to the ODS whenever it is needed.

THE USERS' INTERACTION DESERVES MORE ATTENTION

The most common user interfaces for exploring multidimensional data use the table-based approaches (Siefer, 2006) in which the user displaces dimensions and facts on a bi-dimensional structure and electively applies filters. The user constructs nested or compound tables and may have navigational control through subsets of the data available in the cubes. The table paradigm fits well with the users' capabilities, since they are familiarized with spreadsheets and other Office-like software.

Nonetheless, the data selection and filtering prior to the table viewing revealed to be a problem. Sometimes the users did not apply the correct dimensions combination, leading to inappropriate results, lack of reliability on the tool, so they have abandoned its use. The purchased OLAP tool did not provide some necessary data constraints, leaving the user excessively free to handle the data.

Another drawback was the absence of a reach-trough capability of the tool, enabling the user to scrutinize the raw data (maybe in an ODS, as proposed in 4.1). Issuing a query to retrieve the underlying data became an IT task, via SQL, and the final users evaded the direct interaction with the OLAP software. Front-line employees cannot wait for IT queries, and as a result, they take action based on experience and intuition rather than in facts (Ahlberg, 2007).

FREQUENTLY CHANGED REQUIREMENTS

After the data warehouse implantation, the arousal of new requirements from some clients that had not been interviewed in the previous phase was common. A quick solution could be a data warehouse refactoring, resulting in some ETL process tuning. But, just after the new solution was found, the clients asked for more dimensions or facts that had not been provided by the data warehouse. The BI reporting has grown and changed in dramatic ways (Ahlberg, 2007), and scalability must became a concern.

Faced with this reality we believed that, inspired by the evolution of the software development process, which assumed a requirement change as natural and not as the big evil that we need to avoid, the development of a BI system should also assume that as something unavoidable. Therefore, despite the fact that the project methodology is in BI systems, evolution must be the premise, or rather, we need to understand that the clients' and the business needs will not be stable, and could be based on agile methodologies that were already concerned to it. Agile development strives to deliver small units of functionality that make good business sense (Chu, 2005).

DATA GRANULARITY VARIES AS IT AGES

In face of the requirement changes addressed by the users we observed that the variability of a requirement is totally dependent on data lifetime.

A data warehouse project needs to consider that updated data will need low granularity while outdated data will not.

Considering that, we suggest that the premise in a BI project identify not only which data are relevant, but also which data are relevant in a timeline. For example, we observed that for the last absenteeism data, the managers need to know which people are qualified to act directly with each person. On the other hand, in an older data analysis (older than 12 months) we observe the needs for statistic data that show evolutive institutional snapshots, resulting in macro decisions despite punctual decisions.

Managing data and business context together in real time and ensuring data structures are aligned to handle different levels of granularity, and the completeness of data is a key feature that we must make an effort to achieve (Rogalski, 2007).

Project Evolution and the Chase for Maturity

Despite of team's great expectation in the beginning of the project, as time went by the final product has become little helpful in making decisions related to human resources after two years of existence.

The employees' data mart has supported the statistical yearbook report, nowadays, the main usefulness of the OLAP tool. Dynamic reports were built by the team in 2006 and they have been used since then. Unfortunately this task has been executed for the IT area. The IT area has used OLAP tool to extract data, after their conversion into spreadsheets, formatting spreadsheets and finally sending data to the final user. The final user hasn't extracted data because the OLAP tool is considered very difficult to use and the IT area hasn't had top management's support to pass this task on to final users.

The absenteeism data mart was abandoned, nobody extracted data directly through the OLAP tool. The final users always need other dimensions and always need the names of employees. The IT team has extracted data from data store with SQL consults. Another problem is that a lot of missing data are edited after the ETL's day. In the future it is very important that the IT team review the ETL.

The data store has supported many other reports that are important to a Human Resource Area. These reports have been extracted from data store with SQL consults. The team's expectation was to implement improvements and develop more data marts, but urgent demands have taken all the time of the team.

We believe that the main factor to minimize problems is to form a team that is focused on Business Intelligence. This team will have primary responsibility for developing the environment of business intelligence based on the urgent demands and difficulties of users. This team would provide rapid solutions to promote quality assurance of data and the increased use of OLAP tools for users.

CONCLUSION

As highlighted by Zeleny (2007), there is a growing need for information and knowledge in the Human Resource area. Business Intelligence has been providing this information for other areas in the organization. It is time for the HR to encompass this technology in its favor.

In this paper we provided two sample models for OLAP cubes containing Human Resource specific data and showed their use through software. We also discussed the progress of the project and how some specific difficulties from HR have aroused.

Daily practice shows us that modeling HR systems for BI should not follow only the literature examples and practices, but must instead define its own methods and models, in order to address the specific issues of the Human Resources area.

We believe that the future of this project relies on making an effort to address the points covered in previous sections. We hope it can alert other projects regarding the use of BI in HRM, aiming to avoid these misfortunes and have better results.

REFERENCES

Ahlberg, C. (2007). *Disrupting the status quo: next-generation BI for the real world.* Retrieved January 14, 2009, from http://www.information-management.com/infodirect/2007_50/10000412-1.html

Burke, R. J., & Ng, E. S. W. (2006). The changing nature of work and organizations: implications for human resource management. *Human Resource Management Review, 16*(2), 86–94. doi:10.1016/j. hrmr.2006.03.006

Casati, F., Castellanos, M., & Shan, M. (2004). *Enterprise cockpit for business operation management* (LNCS 3288/200, pp. 825-827). Berlin: Springer.

Chiavenato, I. (2002). *Recursos humanos: edição compacta* (7th ed.). Sao Paulo, Brazil: Atlas.

Chu, D. (2005). *DW project management: using agile software development frameworks for data mart development.* Retrieved January 14, 2008, from www.dmreview.com/dmdirect/20050422/1025869-1.html

Couto, H. (1998). *Como evitar o absenteismo e elaborar um indice adequado.* Revista tendencia do trabalho: Administracao de Pessoal.

Decreto Lei No. 5.452. (1943, May 1). *Consolidação das Leis do Trabalho.* Retrieved February 02, 2007, from www.planalto.gov.br/ccivil_03/decreto-lei/Del5452.htm

Few, S. (2009). *Information dashboard design: the effective visual communication of data.* New York: O'Reilly Media Inc.

Guidony, K. (2007). Does local universe impact on representations, levels of utilisation of an HR intranet by the middle management user. In *Proceedings of the 1st Workshop in Human Resource Information Systems (HRIS 2007)*, Funchal, Madeira, Portugal.

Imhoff, C. (2005). *Business intelligence project pitfalls.* Retrieved December 23, 2007, from www.b-eye-network.cn/view/1519

Inmon, W. H. (2005). *Building the data warehouse* (4th ed.). New York: Wiley Publishers.

Inmon, W. H., Imhoff, C., & Battas, G. (1996). *Building the operational data store.* New York: John Wiley & Sons, Inc.

Kimball, R., Reeves, L., Ross, M., & Thornthwaite, W. (1998). *The data warehouse lifecycle toolkit.* New York: Wiley Publishers.

Malik, S. (2005). *Enterprise dashboards: design and best practices for IT.* New York: Wiley.

National Institute for Occupational Safety and Health. (2004). *Worker health chartbook, 2004.* Retrieved December 2, 2007, from http://www.cdc.gov/niosh/docs/2004-146/pdfs/2004-146.pdf

Ngai, E. W. T., & Wat, F. K. T. (2006). Human resource informatin systems: a review and empirical analysis. *Personnel Review, 35*(3), 297–314. doi:10.1108/00483480610656702

Niven, P. (2008). *Balanced scorecard: step-by-step for government and nonprofit agencies.* New York: Wiley.

Power, D. J. (2002). *Decision support systems: concepts and resources for managers.* Westport, CT: Quorum Books.

Prado, A. B., Freitas, C. E. F., & Sbrici, T. R. (2007). Business intelligence as a HRIS for absenteeism. In *Proceedings of the 1st Workshop in Human Resource Information Systems (HRIS 2007)*, Funchal, Madeira, Portugal.

Quick, T. C., & Lapertosa, J. B. (1982). Analise do absentismo em usina siderurgica. *Revista Brasileira de Saude Ocupacional, 10*(40), 62–67.

Rasmussen, N., Goldy, P. S., & Solli, P. O. (2002). *Financial business intelligence*. New York: John Wiley & Sons, Inc.

Rogalski, S. (2007). *What BI 2.0 means for data management*. Retrieved January 5, 2008, from www. dmreview.com/issues/2007_41/10000378-1.html

Siefer. (2006, October 31-November 2). User interfaces for the exploration of hierarchical multidimensional data. *IEEE Symposium on visual Analytics Science and Technology*, Baltimore (pp. 175-182).

World Health Organization. (2007). *ICD, International statistical classification of diseases and related health problems*. Retrieved February 12, 2007, from en.wikipedia.org/wiki/ICD

Zeleny, M. (2007). Data-information-knowledge-wisdom-enlightenment: towards the strategy of system integration. In *Proceedings of the 1st Workshop in Human Resource Information Systems (HRIS 2007)*, Funchal, Madeira, Portugal.

This work was previously published in International Journal of Technology and Human Interaction, Volume 6, Issue 4, edited by Anabela Mesquita & Chia-Wen Tsai, pp. 49-62, copyright 2010 by IGI Publishing (an imprint of IGI Global).

Compilation of References

AFW. (2002). *Mythos Team auf dem Prüfstand: Teamarbeit in deutschen Unternehmen.* Retrieved July 15, 2009, from http://: http://www.die-akademie.de/

Agarwal, R., & Karahanna, E. (2000). Time flies when you're having fun: cognitive absorption and beliefs about information technology usage. *Management Information Systems Quarterly, 24*(4), 665–694. doi:10.2307/3250951

Agricultural Research Service, United States Department of Agriculture. (2002). *ARS national programs, animal health.* Retrieved May 20, 2002, from http://nps.ars.usda.gov/programs/programs.htm?npnumver=103

Ahlberg, C. (2007). *Disrupting the status quo: next-generation BI for the real world.* Retrieved January 14, 2009, from http://www.information-management.com/infodirect/2007_50/10000412-1.html

Alavi, M. (1994). Computer-mediated collaborative learning: An empirical Evaluation. *Management Information Systems Quarterly, 18*(2), 159–174. doi:10.2307/249763

Alavi, M., & Leidner, D. (2001). Research commentary: Technology-mediated Learning—A call for greater depth and breadth of research. *Information Systems Research, 12*(1), 1–10. doi:10.1287/isre.12.1.1.9720

Alavi, M., Marakas, G. M., & Yoo, Y. (2002). A comparative study of distributed learning environments on learning outcomes. *Information Systems Research, 13*(4), 404–415. doi:10.1287/isre.13.4.404.72

Alavi, M., Wheeler, B. C., & Valacich, J. S. (1995). Using IT to reengineer business education: an exploratory investigation of collaborative telelearning. *Management Information Systems Quarterly, 19*(3), 293–312. doi:10.2307/249597

Alavi, M., & Yoo, Y. (2001). Media and group cohesion: Relative influences on social presence, task participation and Group Consensus. *Management Information Systems Quarterly, 25*(3), 371–390. doi:10.2307/3250922

Al-Gahtani, S. S., & King, M. (1999). Attitudes, satisfaction and usage: factors contributing to each in the acceptance of information technology. *Behaviour & Information Technology, 18*(4), 277–297. doi:10.1080/014492999119020

Allen, T., & Scott Morton, M. (1994). *Information technology and the corporation of the 1990s: Research studies.* New York: Oxford University Press.

Alonso, F., López, G., Manrique, D., & Viñes, J. M. (2005). An instructional model for web-based e-learning education with a blended learning process approach. *British Journal of Educational Technology, 36*(2), 217–235. doi:10.1111/j.1467-8535.2005.00454.x

Alquier, A-M., & Salles, M. (1997). Réflexions méthodologiques pour la conception de systèmes d'intelligence économique de l'entreprise en tant que système d'aide à la décision stratégique. *Deuxième congrès International Franco-québécois de Génie Industriel, ALBI 1997.*

Alvarez, R., & Urla, J. (2002). Tell me a good story: using narrative analysis to examine information requirements interviews during an ERP implementation. *The Data Base for Advances in Information Systems, 33*(1), 38–52.

Amabile, S. (1997). *Contribution à l'ingénierie de l'organisation: De la veille stratégique à l'attention organisationnelle.* Thèse de Doctorat en Sciences de Gestion, Université d'Aix-Marseille III, Faculté d'Economie Appliquée, GRASCE, Aix-en-Provence.

Amabile, S. (1999). De la veille stratégique à une attention réticulée. Le réseau d'attention inter organisationnel des mutuelles d'assurance automobile. *Systèmes d'information et management, 4*(2).

Amer, T. S., & Maris, J.-M. B. (2007). Signal words and signal icons in application control and information technology exception messages – Hazard matching and habituation effects. *The Journal of Information Systems, 2*(21), 1–26. doi:10.2308/jis.2007.21.2.1

American National Standards Institute. (2001). *The common industry format (ANSI/NCTS-354-2001).*

American National Standards Institute. (2002). *American national standard for product safety signs and labels.* New York: ANSI.

Amherdt, C., & Su, Z. (1997). Vers une gestion renouvelée des ressources humaines dans les organisations virtuelles. *Revue de Gestion des Ressources Humaines, 23*, 14–26.

Amit, R., & Belcourt, M. (1999). Human resources management processes: a value-creating source of competitive advantage. *European Management Journal, 17*(2), 174–181. doi:10.1016/S0263-2373(98)00076-0

Amoako-Gyampah, K. (2007). Perceived Usefulness, User Involvement and Behavioral Intention: An Empirical Study of ERP Implementation. *Computers in Human Behavior, 23*, 1232–1248. doi:10.1016/j.chb.2004.12.002

Anderson, J. C., & Gerbing, D. W. (1988). Structural equation modeling in practice: a review and recommended two-step approach. *Psychological Bulletin, 103*, 411–423. doi:10.1037/0033-2909.103.3.411

Animal Plant Health Inspection Service. (2005, April 25). *National Animal Identification System draft strategic plan.* Retrieved March 14, 2006, from http://animalid.aphis.usda.gov/nais/about/pdf/NAIS_Draft_Strategic_Plan_42505.pdf

Ansoff, H. I. (1975). Managing strategic surprise by response to weak signals. *California Management Review, 18*, 21–33.

Ansoff, H. I. (1984). *Implanting strategic Management.* Upper Saddle River, NJ: Prentice Hall.

Apple Computer, Inc. (1989). *HyperCard stack design guidelines.* Menlo Park, CA: Addison-Wesley Publishing Company, Inc. ISBN 0-201-51784-1.

Arnison, L., & Miller, P. (2000). Virtual teams: a virtue for the conventional team. *Journal of Workplace Learning, 14*, 166–173. doi:10.1108/13665620210427294

Ashby, J. A., Beltrán, J. A., Guerrero, M. P., & Ramos, H. F. (1996). Improving the acceptability to farmers of soil conservation practices. *Journal of Soil and Water Conservation, 51*, 309–312.

Aspden, L., & Helm, P. (2004). Making the connection in a blended learning environment. *Educational Media International, 41*(3), 245–252. doi:10.1080/0952398041 0001680851

Atwater, D. M. (1995). Workforce forecasting. *Human Resource Planning, 18*(4), 50–53.

Avison, D., & Elliot, S. (2006). Scoping the discipline of information systems. In King, J., & Lyytinen, K. (Eds.), *In Information Systems: The State of the Field* (pp. 3–18). Chichester, UK: John Wiley and Sons.

Axel, H. (1998). Human resources and the role of IT. *Human Resource Management International Digest, 68*(6), 30–32.

Azevedo, R., & Cromley, J. G. (2004). Does training on self-regulated learning facilitate students' learning with hypermedia? *Journal of Educational Psychology, 96*(3), 523–535. doi:10.1037/0022-0663.96.3.523

Azevedo, R., Cromley, J. G., Winters, F. I., Moos, D. C., & Greene, J. A. (2005). Adaptive human scaffolding facilitates adolescents' self-regulated learning with hypermedia. *Instructional Science, 33*(5-6), 367–379. doi:10.1007/s11251-005-1272-9

Azevedo, R., Moos, D. C., Greene, J. A., Winters, F. I., & Cromley, J. C. (2008). Why is externally-regulated learning more effective than self-regulated learning with hypermedia? *Educational Technology Research and Development, 56*(1), 45–72. doi:10.1007/s11423-007-9067-0

Bagozzi, R. P., & Yi, Y. (1988). On the Evaluation of Structural Equation Models. *Journal of the Academy of Marketing Science, 16*, 74–94. doi:10.1007/BF02723327

Bagozzi, R. P. (1980). *Causal models in marketing*. New York: Wiley.

Bagozzi, R. P., & Phillips, L. W. (1982). Representing and testing organizational theories: a holistic construal. *Administrative Science Quarterly*, 27(3), 459–489. doi:10.2307/2392322

Baillette, P., & Kimble, C. (2008, April). *The concept of appropriation as a heuristic for conceptualising the relationship between technology, people and organizations*. Paper presented at the UKAIS Conference, Bournemouth, UK.

Ball, K. S. (2001). The use of human resource information systems: a survey. *Personnel Review*, 30(5/6), 677–693. doi:10.1108/EUM0000000005979

Barendregt, W., Bekker, M. M., Bouwhuis, D. G., & Bauuw, E. (2006). Identifying usability and fun problems in a computer game during first use and after some practice. *International Journal of Human-Computer Studies*, 64, 830–846. doi:10.1016/j.ijhcs.2006.03.004

Barnes, S. J. (2002). Wireless digital advertising. *International Journal of Advertising*, 21, 399–420.

Barthélemy, J. (2004). *Stratégies d'externalisation: Préparer, décider et mettre en œuvre l'externalisation d'activités stratégiques*. Paris: Dunod.

Bartis, E., & Mitev, N. (2008). A multiple narrative approach to information systems failure: a successful system that failed. *European Journal of Information Systems*, 17, 112–124. doi:10.1057/ejis.2008.3

Barwise, P., & Strong, C. (2002). Permission-based mobile advertising. *Journal of Interactive Marketing*, 16(1), 14–24. doi:10.1002/dir.10000

Basu, V., Hartono, E., Lederer, A. L., & Sethi, V. (2002). The impact of organisational commitment, senior management involvement and team involvement on strategic information systems planning. *Information & Management*, 39(6), 513–524. doi:10.1016/S0378-7206(01)00115-X

Bauer, H. H., Barnes, S. J., Reichardt, T., & Neumann, M. M. (2005). Driving consumer acceptance of mobile marketing: A theoretical framework and empirical study. *Journal of Electronic Commerce Research, 6*(3). Retrieved April 15, 2006, from http://www.csulb.edu/journals/jecr

Baumard, P. (1997). L'information stratégique dans la grande organisation. *Systèmes d'Information et Management, 2*(2).

Beaudry, A., & Pinsonneault, A. (2005). Understanding user responses to information technology: A coping model of user adaptation. *MIS Quaterly, 29*(3), 493–524.

Becker, M. (2005, December 6). Effectiveness of mobile channel additions and a conceptual model detailing the interaction of influential variables'. *MMA Global*. Retrieved October 13, 2007, from http://mmaglobal.com/modules/wfsection/article.php?articleid=131

Bell, B. S., Lee, S., & Yeung, S. (2006). The impact of e-HR on professional competence in HRM: Implications for the development of HR professionals. *Human Resource Management, 45*(3), 295–308. doi:10.1002/hrm.20113

Bell, B. S., & Kozlowski, S. W. J. (2002). A typology of virtual teams. *Group & Organization Management, 27*, 14–49. doi:10.1177/1059601102027001003

Belmondo, C. (2002). *La création de connaissance dans les groupes de travail. Le cas d'une cellule de veille concurrentielle*. thèse de doctorat en sciences de gestion, Université Paris IX Dauphine.

Benbunan-Fich, R., & Hiltz, S. R. (2003). Mediators of the effectiveness of online courses. *IEEE Transactions on Professional Communication, 46*(4), 298–312. doi:10.1109/TPC.2003.819639

Bennet, J., & Karat, J. (1994). Facilitating effective HCI design meetings. In *Proceedings of the SIGCHI Conference on Human Factors in Computing Systems: Celebrating Interdependence*, (pp. 198-204).

Benton, A. A., Kelley, H. H., & Liebling, B. (1972). Effects of extremity of offers and concession rate on the outcomes of bargaining. *Journal of Personality and Social Psychology, 24*, 73–83. doi:10.1037/h0033368

Beyleveld, D. (1991). *The dialectical necessity of morality: An analysis and defence of Alan Gewirth's argument to the principle of generic consistency*. IL: University of Chicago Press.

Bhattacherjee, A. (1998). Management of emerging technologies: Experiences and lessons learned at US West. *Information & Management, 33*(5), 263–272. doi:10.1016/S0378-7206(98)00034-2

Bielaczyc, K., Pirolli, P., & Brown, A. (1995). Training in self-explanation and self-regulation strategies: investigating the effects of knowledge acquisition activities on problem solving. *Cognition and Instruction, 13*(2), 221–252. doi:10.1207/s1532690xci1302_3

Biocca, F., Harms, C., & Burgoon, J. K. (2003). Toward a More Robust Theory and Measure of Social Presence: Review and Suggested Criteria. *Presence (Cambridge, Mass.), 12*(5), 456–480. doi:10.1162/105474603322761270

Bishop, L., & Levine, D. I. (1999). Computer mediated communication as employee voice: A case study. *Industrial & Labor Relations Review, 52*(2), 213–233. doi:10.2307/2525163

Blackwell, A., & Green, T. (2003). Notational systems – The cognitive dimensions of notations frameworks. In J. M. Carroll (Ed.), *HCI models, theories, and frameworks: Toward a multidisciplinary science* (pp. 103-121). Amsterdam: Morgan Kaufmann Publishers. ISBN 1-55860-808-7.

Blanco, S. (2002). Sélection de l'information à caractère anticipatif: un processus d'intelligence collective. *Actes de la 11ième Conférence de l'AIMS*, Paris (pp. 1-20).

Blanco, S., & Lesca, H. (2002). Contribution à la capacité d'anticipation des entreprises par la sensibilisation aux signaux faibles. *6ème Congrès International Francophone sur la PME*, Montréal, Canada (pp. 11-19).

Blended Learning Unit. (2006). *BLU Home Page*. Retrieved October 7, 2008 from http://perseus.herts.ac.uk/uhinfo/info/blu/blu/blu_home.cfm.

Bødker, S., & Buur, J. (2002). The design collaboratorium - A place for usability design. [TOCHI]. *ACM Transactions on Computer-Human Interaction, 9*(2), 152–169. doi:10.1145/513665.513670

Bødker, S., Krogh, P. M., & Petersen, M. G. (2001). The interactive design collaboratorium. In M. Hirose (Ed.), *Proceedings of the Interact '01,* (pp. 51-58). Tokyo, Japan.

Boland, R. (1978). The process and product of system design. *Management Science, 24,* 887–898. doi:10.1287/mnsc.24.9.887

Borowski, T. (1976). *This Way for the Gas, Ladies and Gentlemen*. New York: Penguin.

Bostrom, R. P. (1989). Successful Application of Communication Techniques to Improve the Systems Development Process. *Information & Management, 16,* 279–295. doi:10.1016/0378-7206(89)90005-0

Bottino, R. M., & Robotti, E. (2007). Transforming classroom teaching & learning through technology: Analysis of a case study. *Educational Technology & Society, 10*(4), 174–186.

Bourgault, M., Drouin, N., & Hamel, E. (2008). Decision-making within distributed project teams: an exploration of formalization and autonomy as determinants of success. *Project Management Journal, 39*(S1), 97–110. doi:10.1002/pmj.20063

Boyatzis, R. E. (1998). *Transforming qualitative information: Thematic analysis and code development*. Thousand Oaks, CA: Sage.

Boyd, D., & Ellison, N. B. (2007). Social network sites: Definition, history, and scholarship. *Journal of Computer-Mediated Communication, 13*(1).

Boyd, D. (2008). Why youth (heart) social network sites: The role of networked publics in teenage social life. In Buckingham, D. (Ed.), *Youth, Identity, and Digital Media* (pp. 119–142). Cambridge, MA: MIT Press.

Boyle, T., Bradley, C., Chalk, P., Jones, R., & Pickard, P. (2003). Using blended learning to improve student success rates in learning to program. *Learning, Media and Technology, 28*(2 & 3), 165–178.

Bratton, J., & Gold, J. (2003). *Human resource management, theory and practice*. New York: Palgrave Macmillan.

Briggs, R. O., & De Vreede, G. J. (2003). Special Issue: Information Systems Success. *Journal of Management Information Systems, 19*(4), 5–8.

Brinkman, R., & Kirschner, R. (2006), *Dealing with difficult people: 24 lessons for bringing out the best in everyone*. New York: McGraw-Hill Professional.

Broderick, R. F., & Boudreau, J. W. (1992). Human resource management, information technology and the competitive edge. *The Executive, 6*(2), 7–17.

Broderick, R. F., & Boudreau, J. W. (1991). *Human resource information systems for competitive advantage: interviews with ten leaders* (CAHRS Working Paper Series). Ithaca, NY: Cornell University.

Brown, S. P., & Stayman, D. M. (1992). Antecedents and consequences of attitudes toward the ad: A meta-analysis. *The Journal of Consumer Research, 19*(June), 34–51. doi:10.1086/209284

Brown, A. D., & Jones, M. R. (1998). Doomed to failure: narratives of inevitability and conspirary in a failed IS project. *Organization Studies, 19*(1), 73–88. doi:10.1177/017084069801900104

Brown, K. M. (1996). The role of internal and external factors in the discontinuation of off-campus students. *Distance Education, 17*(1), 44–71. doi:10.1080/0158791960170105

Brown, P. J. (1983). Error messages: The neglected area of the man/machine interface. *Communications of the ACM, 4*(26), 246–249. doi:10.1145/2163.358083

Brown, S. P. (1993). A Q methodological tutorial. *Operant Subjectivity, 16*, 91-138. Retrieved October 3, 2005, from http://www.qmethod.org

Bruner, G., & Kumar, A. (2005). Explaining consumer acceptance of handheld internet services. *Journal of Business Research, 58*(5), 553–558. doi:10.1016/j.jbusres.2003.08.002

Buchanan, D., & Dawson, P. (2007). Discourse and audience: organizational change as multi-story process. *Journal of Management Studies, 44*(5), 669–686. doi:10.1111/j.1467-6486.2006.00669.x

Buchanan, R. (2007). Understanding your users: A practical guide to user requirements: Methods, tools, and techniques. *Design Issues, 23*(1), 90–92. doi:10.1162/desi.2007.23.1.92

Buellinger, F., & Woerter, M. (2004). Development perspectives, firm strategies and applications in mobile commerce. *Journal of Business Research, 57*(12), 1402–1408. doi:10.1016/S0148-2963(02)00429-0

Burke, R. J., & Ng, E. S. W. (2006). The changing nature of work and organizations: implications for human resource management. *Human Resource Management Review, 16*(2), 86–94. doi:10.1016/j.hrmr.2006.03.006

Butler, B. S. (2001). Membership size, communication activity, and sustainability: A resource-based model of online social structures. *Information Systems Research, 12*(4), 346–362. doi:10.1287/isre.12.4.346.9703

Butler, D., & Winne, P. (1995). Feedback and self-regulated learning: a theoretical synthesis. *Review of Educational Research, 65*(3), 245–281.

Byrd, T. A., Cossick, K. L., & Zmud, R. W. (1992). A Synthesis of Research on Requirements Analysis and Knowledge Acquisition Techniques. *Management Information Systems Quarterly, 16*(1), 117–138. doi:10.2307/249704

Campbell, J. (1972). *Myths to Live By*. New York: Penguin Compass.

Carlson, J. R., & Zmud, R. W. (1999). Channel Expansion Theory and the Experiential Nature of media Richness Perceptions. *Academy of Management Journal, 42*(2), 153–170. doi:10.2307/257090

Carter, P. (2007). Liberating usability testing. *Interaction, 14*(2), 18–22. doi:10.1145/1229863.1229864

Carter, P. D. (2002b). Building Purposeful Action: Action Methods and Action Research. *Educational Action Research: An International Journal, 10*(2), 207–232. doi:10.1080/09650790200200180

Carter, P. D. (2002a). *Encounters with computers: A psychodramatic adventure*. Unpublished psychodrama thesis, Auckland University of Technology, Australian and New Zealand Psychodrama Association.

Casagrande, R. (2002). Biological warfare targeted at livestock. *Bioscience, 52*(7), 577–581. doi:10.1641/0006-3568(2002)052[0577:BWTAL]2.0.CO;2

Casati, F., Castellanos, M., & Shan, M. (2004). *Enterprise cockpit for business operation management* (LNCS 3288/200, pp. 825-827). Berlin: Springer.

Cascio, W. F., & Awad, E. M. (1981). *Human resource management: An information systems approach*. Reston, VA: Reston Publishing Company.

Castells, M. (2000). *The Rise of the Network Society* (2nd ed.). Cambridge, MA: Blackwell.

Castells, M. (2004). *The Power of Identity*. Oxford, UK: Blackwell.

Cennamo, K. S., Ross, J. D., & Rogers, C. S. (2002). Evolution of a web-enhanced course: Incorporating strategies for self-regulation. *EDUCAUSE Quarterly, 25*(1), 28–33.

Chang, M. M. (2005). Applying self-regulated learning strategies in a web-based instruction - An investigation of motivation perception. *Computer Assisted Language Learning*, *18*(3), 217–230. doi:10.1080/09588220500178939

Chattratichart, J., & Brodie, J. (2004). Applying user testing data to UEM performance metrics. *CHI '04 Extended Abstracts on Human Factors in Computing Systems*, (pp. 1119-1122), *Vienna, Austria*.

Chen, H. (2000). Exploring web users' optimal flow experiences. *Information Technology & People*, *13*(4), 263–281. doi:10.1108/09593840010359473

Chen, H., Wigand, R., & Nilan, M. (1999). Optimal experience of web activities. *Computers in Human Behavior*, *15*(5), 585–608. doi:10.1016/S0747-5632(99)00038-2

Chen, C. H., & Tien, C. J. (2005). Market Segmentation analysis for taking skill test by students in an institute of technology. Retrieved October 7, 2008 from http://www.voced.edu.au/td/tnc_85.574.

Chi, M. (1997). Quantifying qualitative analyses of verbal data: A practical guide. *Journal of the Learning Sciences*, *6*(3), 271–315. doi:10.1207/s15327809jls0603_1

Chiavenato, I. (2002). *Recursos humanos: edição compacta* (7th ed.). Sao Paulo, Brazil: Atlas.

Chin, W., Gopal, A., & Salisbury, W. (1997). Advancing the theory of adaptive structuration: the development of a scale to measure faithfulness of appropriation. *Information Systems Research*, *8*, 343–367. doi:10.1287/isre.8.4.342

Chiu, C.-M., Chiu, C.-S., & Chang, H.-C. (2007). Examining the integrated influence of fairness and quality on learners' satisfaction and Web-based learning continuance intention. *Information Systems Journal*, *17*(3), 271–286. doi:10.1111/j.1365-2575.2007.00238.x

Chiu, C.-M., & Wang, E. T. G. (2008). Understanding Web-based learning continuance intention: The role of subjective task value. *Information & Management*, *45*(3), 194–201. doi:10.1016/j.im.2008.02.003

Cho, C. H., & Cheon, H. J. (2004). Why do people avoid advertising on the internet? *Journal of Advertising*, *33*(4), 89–97.

Choi, D., & Kim, J. (2004). Why people continue to play online games: in search of critical design factors to increase customer loyalty to online contents. *Cyberpsychology & Behavior*, *7*(1), 11–24. doi:10.1089/109493104322820066

Choo, C. W. (2001). Environmental scanning as information seeking and organizational learning. *Information Research*, *7*(1). Retrieved from

Christensen, C. M. (2002, June). The Rules of Innovation. *MIT Technology Review*.

Chu, T.-H., & Robey, D. (2008). Explaining changes in learning and work practice following the adoption of online learning: a human agency perspective. *European Journal of Information Systems*, *17*(1), 79–98. doi:10.1057/palgrave.ejis.3000731

Chu, D. (2005). *DW project management: using agile software development frameworks for data mart development*. Retrieved January 14, 2008, from www.dmreview.com/dmdirect/20050422/1025869-1.html

Chung, J., & Tan, F. B. (2004). Antecedents of perceived playfulness: an exploratory study on user acceptance of general information-search website. *Information & Management*, *41*, 869–881. doi:10.1016/j.im.2003.08.016

Clark, R. E. (1994). Media will never influence learning. *Educational Technology Research and Development*, *42*(2), 21–29. doi:10.1007/BF02299088

Clark, P. A. (1987). *Anglo-American innovation*. New York: De Gruyter.

Clayton, G. M., & Carter, P. D. (2004). *The Living Spirit of the Psychodramatic Method*. Auckland, New Zealand: Resource Books.

Cleland, D. I., & Ireland, L. R. (2007). *Project management: strategic design and implementation* (5th ed.). New York: McGraw-Hill.

Coats, R., & Vlaeminke, I. (1987). *Man-computer interfaces: An introduction to software design and implementation*. Cambridge, MA: Blackwell Scientific Publications, Inc.

Coble, J., Karat, J., & Kahn, M. (1997). Maintaining a focus on user requirements throughout the development of clinical workstation software. In *Proceedings of the ACM Conference on Human Factors in Computing* (pp. 170-177).

Cockton, G., Woolrych, A., & Hindmarch, M. (2004). Reconditioned merchandise: Extended structured report formats in usability inspection. *CHI '04 Extended Abstracts on Human Factors in Computing Systems, Vienna, Austria* (pp. 1433-1436).

Coffey, A., & Atkinson, P. (1996). *Making sense of qualitative data: Complementary research strategies.* Thousand Oaks, CA: Sage.

Colis, B., & Moonen, J. (2001) *Flexible Learning in a Digital World: Experiences and expectations.* Kogan-Page, London.

Collins, B. (1991). Anticipating the impact of multimedia in education: lessons from the literature. *Computers in Adult Education and Training., 2*(2), 136–145.

Collinson, D. (1992). Introducing on-line processings: Conflicting human resource policies in insurance. In Nohria, N., & Eccles, R. (Eds.), *Network and organizations: Structure, form and action* (pp. 155–173). Boston: Harvard Business School Press.

Cooper, R., & Zmud, R. (1990). Information technology implementation research: a technological diffusion approach. *Management Science, 36*(2), 123–139. doi:10.1287/mnsc.36.2.123

Cooper, R. G. (1979). The dimensions of industrial new product success and failure. *Journal of Marketing, 43*(3), 93–103. doi:10.2307/1250151

Cooper, R. G. (1994). New products: the factors that drive success. *International Marketing Review, 11*(1), 60–76. doi:10.1108/02651339410057527

Cooper, R. G. (2003). A research agenda to reduce risk in new product development through knowledge management: a practitioner perspective. *Journal of Engineering and Technology Management, 20*(1-2), 117–140. doi:10.1016/S0923-4748(03)00007-9

Cooper, R. G., Edgett, S. J., & Kleinschmidt, E. J. (2002). Optimizing the stage-gate process: what best-practice companies do – I. *Research Technology Management, 45*(5), 21–27.

Cooper, R. G., Edgett, S. J., & Kleinschmidt, E. J. (2004). Benchmarking best NPD practices. *Research Technology Management, 47*(1), 31–43.

Cooper, A., & Reimann, R. (2003). *About face: The essentials of interaction design.* Indianapolis, IN: Wiley Publishing, Inc. ISBN 0-7645-2641-3.

Couto, H. (1998). *Como evitar o absenteismo e elaborar um indice adequado.* Revista tendencia do trabalho: Administracao de Pessoal.

Cox, L. A., Popken, D. A., VanSickle, J. J., & Sahu, R. (2005). Optimal tracking and testing of U.S. and Canadian herds for BSE: A Value-of-Information (VOI) Approach. *Risk Analysis, 25*(4), 827–840. doi:10.1111/j.1539-6924.2005.00648.x

Cramton, C. D., & Webber, S. S. (2005). Relationships among geographic dispersion, team processes, and effectiveness in software development work teams. *Journal of Business Research, 58*(6), 758–765. doi:10.1016/j.jbusres.2003.10.006

Crowe, S. A. (1999). *Since strangling isn't an option...: Dealing with difficult people—Common problems and uncommon solutions.* New York: Perigee.

Crozier, M., & Friedberg, E. (1977). *L'acteur et le système.* Paris: Seuil.

Csikszentmihalyi, M. (1975). *Beyond Boredom and Anxiety.* San Francisco, CA: Jossey-Bass.

Csikszentmihalyi, M. (1993). *The evolving self: a psychology for the third millennium.* New York: Harper & Row.

Csikzentmihalyi, M. (1990). *Flow, the Psychology of Optimal Experience.* New York: Harper & Row.

Currie, G., & Kerrin, M. (2004). The limits of a technological fix to knowledge management: Epistemological, political and cultural issues in the case of Intranet implementation. *Management Learning, 35*(1), 9–29. doi:10.1177/1350507604042281

Curry, A., & Stancich, L. (2000). The Intranet: An intrinsic component of strategic information management? *International Journal of Information Management, 20*(4), 249–268. doi:10.1016/S0268-4012(00)00015-3

Czarniawska, B. (1997). *Narrating the Organization.* Chicago: The University of Chicago Press.

Dabbagh, N., & Kitsantas, K. (2005). Using Web-based pedagogical tools as scaffolds for self-regulated learning. *Instructional Science*, *33*(5–6), 513–540. doi:10.1007/s11251-005-1278-3

Daft, R. L., & Weick, K. E. (1984). Toward a Model of Organizations as Interpretation Systems. *Academy of Management Review*, *9*(2), 284–295. doi:10.2307/258441

Daft, R. L., & Lengel, R. H. (1984). Information richness: a new approach to managerial behavior and organizational design. In Cummings, L. L., & Staw, B. M. (Eds.), *Research in organizational behavior*. Homewood, IL: JAI Press.

Damsgaard, J., & Scheepers, R. (2000). Managing the crises in Intranet implementation: A stage model of Intranet technology implementation and management. *Information Systems Journal*, *10*(2), 131–149. doi:10.1046/j.1365-2575.2000.00076.x

Davidson, E. J. (1997). Examining Project History Narratives: An Analytic Approach. In A. S. Lee, J. Liebenau, & J. I. DeGross (Eds.), *Proceedings of the International Conference on Information Systems and Qualitative Research*, Philadelphia, PA (pp. 123-148).

Davis, F. D. (1989). Perceived Usefulness, perceived ease of use, and user acceptance of information technology. *Management Information Systems Quarterly*, *13*, 319–339. doi:10.2307/249008

Davis, F. D., Bagozzi, R. P., & Warshaw, P. R. (1992). Extrinsic and intrinsic motivation to use computers in the workplace. *Journal of Applied Social Psychology*, *22*(14), 1111–1132. doi:10.1111/j.1559-1816.1992.tb00945.x

Davis, F. D., Bagozzi, R. P., & Warshaw, P. R. (1989). User Acceptance of Computer Technology: A Comparison of Two Theoretical Models. *Management Science*, *35*(8), 982–1003. doi:10.1287/mnsc.35.8.982

De Certeau, M. (2002). *L'invention du quotidien. Arts de faire*. Paris: Gallimard.

De Sanctis, G., & Poole, M. S. (1994). Capturing Complexity in Advanced Technology Use: Adaptative Structuration Theory. *Organization Science*, *5*(2), 121–147. doi:10.1287/orsc.5.2.121

de Vaujany, F.-X. (2008a). Capturing reflexivity modes in IS: A critical realist approach. *Information and Organization*, *18*, 51–72. doi:10.1016/j.infoandorg.2007.11.001

de Vaujany, F.-X. (2008b). Strategic Alignment: What Else? A Practice Based View of IS Value. In *Proceedings of the Twenty Ninth International Conference on Information Systems,* Paris.

Deci, E. L., & Ryan, R. M. (1987). The support of autonomy and the control of behavior. *Journal of Personality and Social Psychology*, *53*(6), 1024–1037. doi:10.1037/0022-3514.53.6.1024

Decreto Lei No. 5.452. (1943, May 1). *Consolidação das Leis do Trabalho*. Retrieved February 02, 2007, from www.planalto.gov.br/ccivil_03/decreto-lei/Del5452.htm

Delery, J., & Doty, D. (1996). Modes of theorizing in strategic human resource management: Tests of universalistic, contingency, and configurational performance predictions. *Academy of Management Journal*, *39*(4), 802–835. doi:10.2307/256713

DeLone, W. H., & McLean, E. R. (2003). The DeLone and McLean Model of Information Systems Success: A Ten-Year Update. *Journal of Management Information Systems*, *19*(4), 9–30.

Demailly, A. (2004). *Herber Simon et les Sciences de conception", l'harmattan*.

Dennis, A. R., & Kinney, S. T. (1998). Testing Media Richness Theory in the New Media: The Effects of Cues, Feedback, and Task Equivocality. *Information Systems Research*, *9*(3), 256–274. doi:10.1287/isre.9.3.256

Derntl, M., & Motschnig-Pitrik, R. (2005). The role of structure, patterns, and people in blended learning. *The Internet and Higher Education*, *8*, 111–130. doi:10.1016/j.iheduc.2005.03.002

DeSanctis, P., & Poole, M. (1994). Capturing the complexity in advanced technology use: Adaptative structuration theory. *Organization Science*, *5*(2), 121–146. doi:10.1287/orsc.5.2.121

DeSanctis, G. (1986). Human resource information systems: A current assessment. *Management Information Systems Quarterly*, *10*(1), 15–27. doi:10.2307/248875

Desanctis, & C. Beath (Eds.), In *Proceedings of the Twelfth International Conference on Information Systems (ICIS)* (pp. 229-237). New York.

Dias, C. (2001). Corporate portals: A literature review of a new concept in Information Management. *International Journal of Information Management, 21*(4), 269–287. doi:10.1016/S0268-4012(01)00021-4

Dickey, M., & Ives, B. (2000). The impact of Intranet technology on power in franchisee-franchisor relationships. *Information Systems Frontiers, 2*(1), 99–114. doi:10.1023/A:1010054222086

Dineen, B., Ling, J., Ash, S., & Del Vecchio, D. (2007). Aesthetic properties and message customisation: Navigating the dark side of web recruitment. *The Journal of Applied Psychology, 92*(2), 356–372. doi:10.1037/0021-9010.92.2.356

Doeg, C. (2005). *Crisis management in the food and drinks industry: A practical approach* (2nd ed.). New York: Springer.

Doherty, N. F., King, M., & Al-Mushayt, O. (2003). The Impact of Inadequacies in the Treatment of Organizational Issues on Information Systems Development Projects. *Information & Management, 14*, 49–62. doi:10.1016/S0378-7206(03)00026-0

Dou, H.-M. (1996). French small business information, through the internet: a comparison with US organisations. *International Journal of Information Management, 16*(4), 289–298. doi:10.1016/0268-4012(96)00014-X

Dowling, C., Godfrey, J. M., & Gyles, N. (2003). Do hybrid flexible delivery teaching methods improve accounting student learning outcomes? *Accounting Education: An International Journal, 12*(4), 373–391. doi:10.1080/0963928032000154512

Downs, G. W. Jr, & Mohr, L. B. (1976). Conceptual Issues in the Study of Innovation. *Administrative Science Quarterly, 21*, 700–714. doi:10.2307/2391725

Drazin, R., & Van de Ven, A. (1985). Alternative forms of fit in contingency theory. *Administrative Science Quarterly, 30*(4), 514–539. doi:10.2307/2392695

Drossos, D. (2007). Determinants of effective SMS advertising: an experimental study. *Journal of Interactive Advertising, 7*(2). Retrieved from http://www.jiad.org/article90.

Duarte, D. L., & Snyder, N. T. (1999). *Mastering virtual teams: Strategies, tools, and techniques that succeed.* San Francisco, CA: Jossey-Bass Publishers.

Dumas, J. (1989, July). Stimulating change through usability testing. *SIGCHI Bulletin, 21*(1), 37–44. doi:10.1145/67880.67884

Dumas, J., & Redish, J. (1993). *A practical guide to usability testing.* Oregon: Intellect Books.

Eder, L., Arinze, B., Darter, M., & Wise, D. (2000). An analysis of Intranet infusion level. *Information Resources Management Journal, 13*(3), 14–22.

Eder, L., & Igbaria, M. (2001). Determinants of Intranet diffusion and infusion. *Omega, 29*(3), 233–242. doi:10.1016/S0305-0483(00)00044-X

Eder, L. B., & Darter, M. E. (2002). Corporate Intranet infusion. In Khosrow-pour, M. (Ed.), *Advanced topics in information resources management* (Vol. 1, pp. 223–238). Hershey, PA: IGI Global.

Efe, K. (1987). A proposed solution to the problem of levels in error-messages generation (technical). *Communications of the ACM, 11*(30), 948–955. doi:10.1145/32206.32210

Ehn, P. (1992). Scandinavian design: On participation and skill. I P. Adler, & T. Winograd, *Usability: Turning technology into tools* (pp. 96-132). New York: Oxford University Press.

Ehn, P., & Sjögren, D. (1991). From system descriptions to scripts for action. I J. Greenbaum, & M. Kyng, *Design at work - Cooperative design of computer systems* (pp. 241-268). Hillsdale, NJ: Lawrence Erlbaum.

Eiseley, L. (1946). *The Immense Journey.* New York: Vintage.

Elliot, R. H., & Tevavichulada, S. (1999). Computer literacy and human resource management: a public/private sector comparison. *Public Personnel Management, 28*(2), 259–274.

Ellison, N., Steinfield, C., & Lampe, C. (2007). The benefits of Facebook "friends": Exploring the relationship between college students' use of online social networks and social capital. *Journal of Computer-Mediated Communication, 12*(3).

EMarketer. (2006). *EMarketer*. Retrieved July 20, 2008, from http://www.find.org.tw/find/home. aspx?page=news&id=4512

Ertmer, P. A., Newby, T. J., & MacDougall, M. (1996). Students' approaches to learning from case-based instruction: The role of reflective self-regulation. *American Educational Research Journal, 33*(3), 719–752.

Fallery, B. (2004). Three visions of open learning and their propositions of norms: contents standardisation, tasks standardisation or interface standardisation? *Systèmes d'Information et Management, 9*(4), 2–24.

Feldman, D., & Klaas, B. (2002). Internet job hunting: A field study of applicant experiences with online recruitment. *Human Resource Management, 41*(2), 175–201. doi:10.1002/hrm.10030

Feldman, M. S., & March, J. G. (1991). l'information dans les organisations: un signe et un symbole. In J. G. March (Ed.), *Décisions et organisations* (Chapter 10, p. 255). Paris les éditions d'organisation.

Few, S. (2009). *Information dashboard design: the effective visual communication of data.* New York: O'Reilly Media Inc.

Fincham, R. (2002). Narratives of success and failure in systems development. *British Journal of Management, 13*, 1–14. doi:10.1111/1467-8551.00219

Fisher, K., & Fisher, M. (1998). *The distributed mind.* New York: American Management Association.

Floridi, L. (2002). What is the philosophy of information? *Metaphilosophy, 33*, 123–145. doi:10.1111/1467-9973.00221

Floridi, L. (2002a). On the intrinsic value of information objects and the infosphere. *Ethics and Information Technology, 4*, 287–304. doi:10.1023/A:1021342422699

Floridi, L. (2004). On the morality of artificial agents. *Minds and Machines, 14*, 349–379. doi:10.1023/B:MIND.0000035461.63578.9d

Floridi, L. (2005). Is semantic information meaningful data? *Philosophy and Phenomenological Research, LXX*(2), 351–370. doi:10.1111/j.1933-1592.2005.tb00531.x

Floridi, L. (2007). Understanding information ethics. *APA Newsletter on Philosophy and Computers, 07*(1), 3–12.

Floridi, L. (2008). Informational structural realism. *Synthese, 161*(2), 219–253. doi:10.1007/s11229-007-9163-z

Floridi, L. (2008a). Information ethics: A reappraisal. *Ethics and Information Technology, 10*, 189–204. doi:10.1007/s10676-008-9176-4

Floridi, L. (2007a). Global information ethics: The importance of being environmentally earnest. *International Journal of Technology and Human Interaction, 3.3*, 1-19. Retrieved April, 27, 2008, from http://www.philosophyofinformation.net/publications/publications.html#articles

Florkowski, G., & Olivas-Luján, M. (2006). The diffusion of human-resource information-technology innovations in US and non-US firms. *Personnel Review, 35*(6), 684–710. doi:10.1108/00483480610702737

Foray, D. (2000). *L'économie de la connaissance.* Paris: La Découverte Repères.

Fornell, C. R., & Larcker, D. F. (1981). Structural equation models with unobservable variables and measurement error. *JMR, Journal of Marketing Research, 18*, 39–50. doi:10.2307/3151312

Fornell, C., & Larcker, D. (1981). Evaluating Structural Equation Models with Unobservable Variable and Measurement Error. *JMR, Journal of Marketing Research, 18*, 39–50. doi:10.2307/3151312

Fornell, C. R. (1982). *A second generation of multivariate analysis methods: Vols. I and II.* New York: Praeger Special Studies.

Frappaolo, K., & Capshaw, S. (1999). Knowledge management software: Capturing the essence of know-how and innovation. *Information Management Journal, 33*(3), 44–48.

Furniss, D., Blandford, A., & Curzon, P. (2007). Usability work in professional Website design: insights from practitioners' perspectives. I E. Law, E. Hvannberg, & G. Cockton, *Maturing usability: Quality in software, interaction and value* (pp. 144-167). London: Springer.

Galbraith, J. (1973). *Designing complex organizations.* New York: Addison-Wesley.

Galitz, W. O. (2007). *The essential guide to user interface design.* Indianapolis, IN: Wiley Publishing, Inc. ISBN 978-0-470-05342-3.

Gardner, S., Lepak, D. P., & Bartol, K. M. (2003). Virtual HR: The impact of information technology on the human resource professional. *Journal of Vocational Behavior, 63*(2), 159–179. doi:10.1016/S0001-8791(03)00039-3

Garrison, R. R., & Kanuka, H. (2004). Blended learning: Uncovering its transformative potential in higher education. *The Internet and Higher Education, 7*(2), 95–105. doi:10.1016/j.iheduc.2004.02.001

Gartner Group, Inc. (1996). *Developing a powerful corporate Intranet: Issues challenges, and solution.* Stamford, CT: Gartner.

Gaski, J. F., & Etzel, M. J. (1986). The index of consumer sentiment toward marketing. *Journal of Marketing, 50*(July), 71–81. doi:10.2307/1251586

Gaski, J. F., & Etzel, M. J. (2005). National aggregate consumer sentiment toward marketing: A thirty year retrospective and analysis. *The Journal of Consumer Research, 31*(March), 859–867. doi:10.1086/426623

Gefen, D., & Straub, D. W. (1997). Gender differences in the perception and use of e-mail: An Extension to the technology acceptance model. *Management Information Systems Quarterly, 21*(4), 389–400. doi:10.2307/249720

Geib, M., Braum, C., Kolbe, L., & Brenner, W. (2005). Toward Improved Community-Supporting Systems Design: A Study of Professional Community Activity. *International Journal of Technology and Human Interaction, 1*(4), 19–36.

George, J. F., & King, J. L. (1991). Examining the Computing and Centralization Debate. *Communications of the ACM, 34*(7), 62–72. doi:10.1145/105783.105796

Gerbaix, S. (1997). Adoption logic of the videoconference. *Systèmes d'Information et Management, 2*(1), 29–50.

Gewirth, A. (1978*). Reason and morality.* IL: University of Chicago Press.

Gewirth, A. (1996). *The community of rights.* IL: University of Chicago Press.

Gewirth, A. (1998). *Self-fulfillment.* NJ: Princeton University Press.

Ghani, J. A., & Deshpande, S. P. (1994). Task characteristics and the experience of optimal flow in human-computer interaction. *The Journal of Psychology, 128*(4), 381–391.

Ghani, J. A., Supnick, R., & Rooney, P. (1991). The experience of flow in computer-mediated and in face-to-face groups. In Hair, J. F., Anderson, R. E., Tatham, R. L., & Black, W. C. (Eds.), *Multivariate data analysis with readings.* New York: MacMillan.

Gibson, C. B., & Cohen, S. G. (2003). *Virtual teams that work: creating conditions for virtual team effectiveness.* San Francisco, CA: Jossey-Bass.

Gilad, B., & Gilad, T. (1986). Business intelligence: the quiet revolution. *Sloan Management Review,* 53–61.

Gilad, B. (1989). The Role of Organized Competitive Intelligence in Corporate

Gilbert, P., & Gonzalez, D. (2000). Les progiciels intégrés et la GRH: Quand l'ambiguïté des enjeux est fonctionnelle. *Annales des Mines,* 26-33.

Goffman, E. (1981). *Forms of Talk.* Philadelphia: University of Pennsylvania Press.

Goldman, K. D. (1994). Perceptions of innovations as predictors of implementation levels: The diffusion of a nationwide health education campaign. *Health Education Quarterly, 21,* 433–444.

Gondran, N. (2001). *Système de diffusion d'information pour encourager les PME-PMI à améliorer leurs performances environnementales.* Thèse de doctorat, INSA Lyon.

Goodfellow, R. (1996). Face to face language learning at a distance? A study of a videoconference try-out. *ReCALL, 7*(1), 20–35.

Goodhue, D. L., & Thompson, R. L. (1995). Task-Technology Fit and Individual Performance. *Management Information Systems Quarterly, 19*(2), 213–236. doi:10.2307/249689

Goodman, P. S., & Darr, E. D. (1996). Exchanging best practices through computer-aided systems. *The Academy of Management Executive, 10*(2), 7–19.

Greenbaum, J., & Kyng, M. (1991). *Design at work: Cooperative design of computer systems.* Hillsdale, NJ: Lawrence Erlbaum Associates.

Greyser, S. A., & Bauer, R. A. (1968). Americans and advertising: Thirty years of public opinion. *Public Opinion Quarterly, 30,* 69–78. doi:10.1086/267382

Gribbons, B., & Herman, J. (1997) "True and quasi-experimental designs. Practical Assessment", *Research & Evaluation, 5*(14), Retrieved February 12, 2009 from http://PAREonline.net/getvn.asp?v=5&n=14.

Groe, G. M., Pyle, W., & Jamrog, J. J. (1996). Information technology and HR. *Human Resource Planning, 19*(1), 56–61.

Groth, L. (1999). *Future organizational design: the scope for the IT-based enterprise.* New York: John Wiley & Sons.

Grudin, J. (1991). Interactive systems: Bridging the gaps between developers and users. *IEEE Computer, 24*(4), 59–69.

Grundy, T. (1997). Human resource management – a strategic approach. *Long Range Planning, 30*(4), 507–517. doi:10.1016/S0024-6301(97)00030-7

Gruner, K. E., & Homburg, C. (2000). Does customer interaction enhance new product success? *Journal of Business Research, 49*(1), 1–14. doi:10.1016/S0148-2963(99)00013-2

Gu, J., & Gavriel, S. (2004). Interface methods for using Intranet portal organizational memory information system. *Ergonomics, 47*(15), 1585–1597. doi:10.1080/0014013 0412331303939

Guechtouli, M. (2007). *Contribution à l'ingénierie des systèmes d'information de veille stratégique: une approche centrée sur la motivation des acteurs. L'expérience du système de veille stratégique d'une grande entreprise technologique.* PhD. Thesis in Management, CERGAM, University Paul Cezanne, Aix en Provence, France.

Guiderdoni-Jourdain, K., & Oiry, E. (2008). "Local Universe" and use of an HR Intranet. The case of Middle Management. In Bondarouk, T., & Ruël, H. (Eds.), *Electronic HRM in Theory and Practice: a Reader.* Hershey, PA: IGI Global.

Guidony, K. (2007). Does local universe impact on representations, levels of utilisation of an HR intranet by the middle management user. In *Proceedings of the 1st Workshop in Human Resource Information Systems (HRIS 2007),* Funchal, Madeira, Portugal.

Guilloux, V., Laval, F., & Kalika, M. (2005). Les Intranets RH: de l'introduction des TIC aux nouvelles formes d'organisation. In Kalika, M., Guilloux, V., Laval, F., & Matmati, M. (Eds.), *E-RH réalités manageriales* (pp. 147–159). Paris: Vuibert.

Gulliksen, J., Boivie, I., & Göransson, B. (2006). Usability professionals - Current practices and future development. *Interacting with Computers, 18,* 568–600. doi:10.1016/j. intcom.2005.10.005

Gulliksen, J., Boivie, I., Persson, J., & Hektor, A. L. (2004). Making a difference - A survey of the usability profession in Sweden. In. *Proceedings of Nordichi, 2004,* 207–215. doi:10.1145/1028014.1028046

Guowei, J., & Jeffres, L. (2006). Understanding employees' willingness to contribute to shared electronic databases: A three dimensional framework. *Communication Research, 33*(4), 242–261. doi:10.1177/0093650206289149

Gupta, A. K., & Wilemon, D. L. (1990). Accelerating the development of technology-based new products. *California Management Review, 32*(2), 24–44.

Gurau, C., Ranchhod, A., & Gauzente, C. (2003). To legislate or not to legislate – A comparative exploratory study of privacy/personalization factors affecting French, UK and US web sites. *Journal of Consumer Marketing, 20*(7), 652–664. doi:10.1108/07363760310506184

Ha, L., & Litman, B. R. (1997). Does advertising clutter have diminishing and negative returns? *Journal of Advertising, 26*(2), 31–42.

Hage, J., & Aiken, M. (1967). Relationships of centralization to other structural properties. *Administrative Science Quarterly, 69,* 32–40.

Haider, M., & Kreps, G. L. Forty years of diffusion of innovations: Utility and value in public health. *Journal of Health Communication, 9,* 3–11. doi:10.1080/10810730490271430

Haines, V. Y., & Petit, A. (1997). Conditions for successful human resource information systems. *Human Resource Management*, 36(2), 261–275. doi:10.1002/(SICI)1099-050X(199722)36:2<261::AID-HRM7>3.0.CO;2-V

Hair, J. E., Anderson, R. E., Tatham, R. L., & Black, W. C. (1998). *Multivariate data analysis* (5th ed.). Upper Saddle River, NJ: Prentice-Hall.

Hannon, J. M. (1997). *Leveraging HRM to enrich competitive intelligence*. Human.

Hara, N., & Kling, R. (2000). Students' distress with a web-based distance education course: an ethnographic study of participants' experiences. *Information Communication and Society*, 3(4), 557–579. doi:10.1080/13691180010002297

Hassid, L., Jacques-Gustave, P., & Moinet, N. (1997). *Les PME face au défi de l'intelligence économique: le renseignement sans complexe*. Paris: Dunod.

Hassinger, E. (1959). Stages in the adoption process. *Rural Sociology*, 24, 52–53.

Hayduck, L. A. (1987). *Structural Equation Modeling with LISREL: essentials and advances*. Baltimore, MD: John Hopkins University Press.

Haywood, M. (1998). *Managing Virtual Teams: Practical Techniques for High-technology Project Managers*. Norwood, MA: Artech House.

Hedman, L., & Sharafi, P. (2004). Early use of Internet-based educational resources: effects on students' engagement modes and flow experience. *Behaviour & Information Technology*, 23(2), 137–146. doi:10.1080/01449290310001648251

Hellier, E., Wright, D. B., Edworthy, J., & Newstead, S. (2000). On the stability of the arousal strength of warning signal words. *Applied Cognitive Psychology*, (14): 577–592. doi:10.1002/1099-0720(200011/12)14:6<577::AID-ACP682>3.0.CO;2-A

Henderson, J. C., & Venkatraman, N. (1993). Strategic alignment: leveraging information technology for transforming organizations. *IBM Systems Journal*, 32(1), 472–484. doi:10.1147/sj.382.0472

Henry, J. E., & Hartzler, M. (1997). Virtual Teams: Today's Reality, today's Challenge. *Quality Progress*, 30(5), 108–109.

Hertel, G., Geister, S., & Konradt, U. (2005). Managing virtual teams: a review of current empirical research. *Human Resource Management Review*, 15(1), 69–95. doi:10.1016/j.hrmr.2005.01.002

Hertzum, M., & Jacobsen, N. (2003). The evaluator effect: A chilling fact about usability evaluation methods. *International Journal of Human-Computer Interaction*, 15(1), 183–204. doi:10.1207/S15327590IJHC1501_14

Hettinga, M. (2002). *Understanding evolutionary use of groupware*. Unpublished doctoral dissertation, Telematica Instituut, Enschede, The Netherlands.

Hiltz, S. R. (1993). *The virtual classroom: Learning without limits via computer network*. Norwood, NJ: Ablex Publishing Corporation.

Hinds, P. J., & Mortensen, M. (2005). Understanding conflict in geographically distributed teams: the moderating effects of shared identity, shared context, and spontaneous communication. *Organization Science*, 16(3), 290–307. doi:10.1287/orsc.1050.0122

Hoegl, M., & Parboteeah, P. K. (2006). Team reflexivity in innovative projects. *R & D Management*, 36(2), 113–125. doi:10.1111/j.1467-9310.2006.00420.x

Hoegl, M., Praveen, P. K., & Gemuenden, H. G. (2003). When teamwork really matters: task innovativeness as a moderator of the teamwork–performance relationship in software development projects. *Journal of Engineering and Technology Management*, 20(4), 281–302. doi:10.1016/j.jengtecman.2003.08.001

Hoegl, M., & Proserpio, L. (2004). Team member proximity and teamwork in innovative projects. *Research Policy*, 33(8), 1153–1165. doi:10.1016/j.respol.2004.06.005

Hoegl, M., Weinkauf, K., & Gemuenden, H. G. (2004). Interteam coordination, project commitment, and teamwork in multiteam R&D projects: a longitudinal study. *Organization Science*, 15(1), 38–55. doi:10.1287/orsc.1030.0053

Hoffman, D. L., & Novak, T. P. (1996). Marketing in Hypermedia Computer-mediated environments: conceptual foundations. *Journal of Marketing, 60*, 50–68. doi:10.2307/1251841

Holloway, R. E. (1977). *Perceptions of an innovation: Syracuse University's Project Advance.* Syracuse, NY: Syracuse University.

Holtzblatt, K., & Beyer, H. R. (1995). Requirements Gathering: The Human Factor. *Communications of the ACM, 38*(5), 30–32. doi:10.1145/203356.203361

Hong, J. C., & Liu, M. C. (2003). A study on thinking strategy between experts and novices of computer games. *Computers in Human Behavior, 19*, 245–258. doi:10.1016/S0747-5632(02)00013-4

Hongladarom, S. (2008). Floridi and Spinoza on global information ethics. *Ethics and Information Technology, 10*, 175–187. doi:10.1007/s10676-008-9164-8

Hornbæk, K., & Frøkjær, E. (2005). Comparing usability problems and redesign proposals as input to practical systems development. *ACM Conference on Human Factors in Computing Systems* (pp. 391-400).

Horton, R., Buck, T., Waterson, P., & Clegg, C. (2001). Explaining Intranet use with the technology acceptance model. *Journal of Information Technology, 16*(4), 237–249. doi:10.1080/02683960110102407

Hsu, C. L., & Lu, H. P. (2004). Why do people play on-line games? An extended TAM with social influences and flow experience. *Information & Management, 41*(7), 853–868. doi:10.1016/j.im.2003.08.014

Hsu, C. L., & Lu, H. P. (2007). Consumer behavior in on-line game communities: a motivational factor perspective. *Computers in Human Behavior, 23*, 1642–1659. doi:10.1016/j.chb.2005.09.001

Hubbard, J. C., Forcht, K., & Thomas, D. S. (1998). Human resource information systems: An overview of current ethical and legal issues. *Journal of Business Ethics, 17*(12), 1319–1323. doi:10.1023/A:1005735506589

Hussain, Z., Wallace, J., & Cornelius, N. E. (2007). The use and impact of human resource information systems on human resource management professionals. *Information & Management, 44*(1), 74–89. doi:10.1016/j.im.2006.10.006

Hustad, E., & Munkvold, B. E. (2007). IT-supported competence management: A case study at Ericsson. *Information Systems Management, 22*(2), 78–88. doi:10.1201/1078/45099.22.2.20050301/87280.9

Huxham, C., & Vangen, S. (2005). *Managing to collaborate: the theory and practice of collaborative advantage.* London: Routledge.

Hvannberg, E. T., Law, E., & Larusdottir, M. K. (2007). Heuristic evaluation: Comparing ways of finding and reporting usability problems. *Interacting with Computers, 19*(2), 225–240. doi:10.1016/j.intcom.2006.10.001

Iansiti, M., & MacCormack, A. (1997). Developing products on the Internet Time. *Harvard Business Review, 75*(5), 108–117.

Ichniowski, C., Kochan, T. A., Levine, D., Olson, C., & Strauss, G. (1996). What works at work: Overview and assessment. *Industrial Relations, 35*(3), 299–333. doi:10.1111/j.1468-232X.1996.tb00409.x

Iivari, N. (2006). 'Representing the user' in software development - A cultural analysis of usability work in the product development context. *Interacting with Computers, 18*, 635–664. doi:10.1016/j.intcom.2005.10.002

Imhoff, C. (2005). *Business intelligence project pitfalls.* Retrieved December 23, 2007, from www.b-eye-network.cn/view/1519

Ingold, T. (2000). *The Perception of the Environment: Essays on livelihood, dwelling and skill.* London: Routledge.

Inmon, W. H. (2005). *Building the data warehouse* (4th ed.). New York: Wiley Publishers.

Inmon, W. H., Imhoff, C., & Battas, G. (1996). *Building the operational data store.* New York: John Wiley & Sons, Inc.

ISO 9241-110 (2006). *Ergonomics of human-system interaction – Part 110 dialog principles.* Geneva, Switzerland: International Organization for Standardization.

Ivanic, R., Clark, R., & Rimmershaw, R. (2000). What am I supposed to make of this? The messages conveyed to students by tutors' written comments. In M.R. Lea & B. Stierer (Eds.), *Student Writing in Higher Education: New Contexts* (pp. 47-65). Buckingham: SHRE/Open University Press.

Ives, B., & Olson, M. H. (1984). User Involvement and MIS Success: A review of Research. *Management Science, 30*(5), 583–603. doi:10.1287/mnsc.30.5.586

Jaccard, J., Turrisi, R., & Wan, C. K. (1990). *Interaction effects in multiple regression.* Newbury Park, CA: Sage.

Jacko, J., Salvendy, G., & Sainfort, F. (2002). Intranets and organizational learning: A research and development agenda. *International Journal of Human-Computer Interaction, 14*(1), 93–130. doi:10.1207/S15327590I-JHC1401_3

Jacoby, G., & Luqi, A. (2005). Critical business requirements model and metrics, for Intranet ROI. *Journal of Electronic Commerce Research, 6*(1), 1–30.

Järvelä, S., Näykki, P., Laru, J., & Luokkanen, T. (2007). Structuring and regulating collaborative learning in higher education with wireless networks and mobile tools. *Educational Technology & Society, 10*(4), 71–79.

Jarvenpaa, S., & Leidner, D. (1999). Communication and trust in global virtual teams. *Organization Science, 10*(6), 791–815. doi:10.1287/orsc.10.6.791

Jawadi, N., & El Akremi, A. (2006). E-learning acceptance determinants: a modified technology acceptance model. *CAIS, 18*(2), 24-54.

Jenkins, A. M., Naumann, J. D., & Wetherbe, J. (1984). Empirical Investigations of Systems Development Practices and Results. *Information & Management, 1*, 73–82. doi:10.1016/0378-7206(84)90012-0

Johnson, D., & Wiles, J. (2003). Effective affective user interface design in games. *Ergonomics, 46*(13/14), 1332–1345. doi:10.1080/00140130310001610865

Johnson, D., & Johnson, F. (1990). *Joining together.* Englewood Cliffs, NJ: Prentice Hall.

Jones, M. (1999). Structuration theory. In Currie, W. L., & Galliers, B. (Eds.), *Rethinking management information systems* (pp. 103–135). Oxford, UK: Oxford University Press.

Jouët, J. (1993). *Usages et pratiques des nouveaux outils de communication. Dictionnaire critique de la communication.* Paris: Universitaires de France, Paris.

Jung, C. J. (1954). *Answer to Job.* London: Routledge.

Jung, C. G. (1921). *Psychologische Typen.* Zürich: Rascher Verlag.

Kalika, M. (1991). De l'organisation réactive à l'organisation anticipative. *Revue française de gestion,* 46-50.

Karat, C., Campbell, R., & Fiegel, T. (1992). Comparison of empirical testing and walkthrough methods in usability interface evaluation. In *Proceedings of CHI'92* (pp. 397-404).

Katz, E., & Lazarsfeld, P. F. (1955). *Personal influence.* New York: The Free Press.

Katzy, B. R., & Sung, G. (2001). Information infrastructure for virtual projects requirements specification from a communication perspective. In *Proceedings of the 9th International Conference on Concurrent Enterprising,* Bremen, Germany.

Kavanagh, M. J., Gueutal, H. G., & Tannenbaum, S. I. (1990). *Human resource information systems: Development and applications.* Boston: PWS-KENT Publishing Company.

Kayworth, T., & Leidner, D. (2000). The global virtual manager: A prescription for success. *European Management Journal, 18*(2), 183–194. doi:10.1016/S0263-2373(99)00090-0

Kayworth, T., & Leidner, D. E. (2000). Managing global virtual teams: a prescription for success. *European Management Journal, 18*(2), 183–193. doi:10.1016/S0263-2373(99)00090-0

Kearns, K. P. (1992). Innovations in local government: A sociocognitive network approach. *Knowledge and Policy, 5*(2), 45–67. doi:10.1007/BF02692805

Kennedy, S. (1989). Using video in the BNR usability lab. *SIGCHI Bulletin, 21*(2), 92–95. doi:10.1145/70609.70624

Khapova, S. (2006). *Careers in the knowledge economy and web-based career support: New challenges and opportunities* (Doctoral dissertation). Enschede, The Netherlands: Print Partners Ipskamp B.V.

Kim, A. J. (2000). *Community Building on the Web: Secret Strategies for Successful Online Communities.* Boston: Addison-Wesley Longman Publishing.

Kim, S. (1995), Interdisciplinary cooperation, *in* Baeker, R. M. (ed.), *Readings in human-computer interaction: toward the year 2000* (pp. 305-311), San Francisco: Morgan Kaufmann.

Kimball, R., Reeves, L., Ross, M., & Thornthwaite, W. (1998). *The data warehouse lifecycle toolkit*. New York: Wiley Publishers.

King, W. R., & Rodriguez, J. J. (1981). Participative design of strategic decision support systems: An empirical assessment. *Management Science*, *27*, 717–726. doi:10.1287/mnsc.27.6.717

Kleijnen, M., de Reyter, K., & Wetzel, M. (2004). Consumer adoption of wireless services: discovering the rules while playing the game. *Journal of Interactive Marketing*, *18*(2), 51–61. doi:10.1002/dir.20002

Kline, R. B. (1998). *Principles and Practice of Structural Equation Modeling*. New York: Guilford Press.

Knoke, D., & Kuklinski, J. H. (1982). *Network Analysis*. Beverly Hills, CA: Sage.

Kokko, N., Vartiaine, N. M., & Lönnblad, J. (2007). Individual and collective competences in virtual project organizations. *The Electronic Journal for Virtual Organizations and Networks, 8*(1), 28-52. Retrieved June 15, 2009, from http:// http://www.ejov.org

Konradt, U., Filip, R., & Hoffmann, S. (2003). Flow experience and positive affect during hypermedia learning. *British Journal of Educational Technology*, *34*(3), 309–327. doi:10.1111/1467-8535.00329

Korsgaard, C. M. (1983). Two distinctions in goodness. *The Philosophical Review*, *92*(2), 169–195. doi:10.2307/2184924

Korzann, M. L. (2003). Going with the flow: predicting online purchase intentions. *Journal of Computer Information Systems*, (Summer): 25–31.

Kossek, E. E., Young, W., Gash, D. C., & Nichol, V. (1994). Waiting for innovation in the human resources department: Godot implements a human resource information system. *Human Resource Management*, *33*(1), 135–159. doi:10.1002/hrm.3930330108

Koufaris, M. (2002). Applying the technology acceptance model and flow theory to online consumer behaviour. *Information Systems Research*, *13*(2), 205–223. doi:10.1287/isre.13.2.205.83

Kovach, K. A., & Cathcart, C. E. Jr. (1999). Human resource information systems (HRIS): Providing business with rapid data access, information exchange and strategic advantage. *Public Personnel Management*, *28*(2), 275–282.

Kovach, K. A., Hughes, A. A., Fagon, P., & Maggitti, P. G. (2002). Administrative and strategic advantages of HRIS. *Employment Relations Today*, *29*(2), 43–48. doi:10.1002/ert.10039

Kremer, K. S., Crolan, M., Gaiteyer, S., Tirmizi, S. N., Korshing, P. F., & Peter, G. (2000). Evolution of an agricultural innovation: The N-Track Soil Nitrogen Test: Adopt, and discontinuance, or reject? *Technology in Society*, *23*, 93–108. doi:10.1016/S0160-791X(00)00038-5

Kuzma, J., & Ahl, A. (2006). Living with BSE. *Risk Analysis*, *26*(3), 585–588. doi:10.1111/j.1539-6924.2006.00768.x

La Fasto, F., & Larson, C. (2002). *When teams work best.* Thousand Oaks, CA: Sage Publications.

Lafaye, C. (2004). *La phase de traque d'information sur Internet dans un processus de veille stratégique.* Thèse de Doctorat, Université Lyon III.

Lai, V., & Mahapatra, R. (1998). Evaluation of Intranets in a distributed Environment. *Decision Support Systems*, *23*, 347–357. doi:10.1016/S0167-9236(98)00064-5

Laval, F., Guilloux, V., & Kalika, M. (2002). Les Intranets RH: pratiques des entreprises et problématiques. In Kalika, M. (Ed.), *E-GRH: Révolution ou évolution?* (pp. 63–90). Paris: Editions Liaisons.

Law, E., & Hvannberg, E. T. (2004). Analysis of strategies for improving and estimating the effectiveness of heuristic evaluation. In *Proceedings of the Third Nordic Conference on Human-Computer Interaction NordiCHI '04* (pp. 241-250).

Layman, L., Williams, L., Damian, D., & Bures, H. (2006). Essential communication practices for Extreme Programming in a global software development team. *Information and Software Technology, 48*(9), 781–794. doi:10.1016/j.infsof.2006.01.004

Le Bon, J. (2000). *De l'intelligence économique à la veille marketing et commerciale: vers une nécessaire mise au point conceptuelle et théorique.* Papier de Recherche, Essec, Mai.

Le Moigne, J. L. (1979). Informer la décision ou décider l'information. *Economies et sociétés, 1,* 889–918.

Leavitt, H., & Whisler, T. (1958, November-December). Management in the 1980's. *Harvard Business Review,* 41–48.

Lee, S. F., Tsai, Y. C., & Jih, W. J. (2006). An empirical examination of customer perception of mobile advertising. *Information Resources Management Journal, 19*(4), 39–55.

Lee, T. H., Shen, P. D., & Tsai, C. W. (2008). Applying web-enabled problem-based learning and self-regulated learning to add value to computing education in Taiwan's vocational schools. *Educational Technology and Society, 11*(3), 13–25.

Lee-Kelley, L., & Sankey, T. (2008). Global virtual teams for value creation and project success: A case study. *International Journal of Project Management, 26,* 51–62. doi:10.1016/j.ijproman.2007.08.010

Lehmuskallio, S. (2006). The uses, roles, and contents of Intranets in multinational companies in Finland. *Journal of Business and Technical Communication, 7*(20), 288–324. doi:10.1177/1050651906287255

Lehto, M. R. (2006). Human Factors Models. In M.S. Wogalter (Ed.), *Handbook of warnings* (pp. 63-87). New Jersey/London: Lawrence Erlbaum Associates.

Leidner, D., & Jarvenpaa, S. (1993). The Information Age Confronts Education: Case Studies on Electronic Classrooms. *Information Systems Research, 4*(1), 24–54. doi:10.1287/isre.4.1.24

Leonard-Barton, D. (1988). Implementation as Mutual Adaptation of Technology and Organization. *Research Policy, 17,* 251–267. doi:10.1016/0048-7333(88)90006-6

Lepak, D., & Snell, S. (1998). Virtual HR: Strategic human resource management in the 21st century. *Human Resource Management Review, 8*(3), 215–234. doi:10.1016/S1053-4822(98)90003-1

Lesca, H. (2003). *Veille stratégique: La méthode L.E.SCAnning.* EMS.

Lesca, H., & Rouibah, K. (1997). Des outils au service de la veille stratégique. *Systèmes d'Information et Management, 2*(2), 101–131.

Lesca, H. (1996). Veille stratégique: comment sélectionner les informations pertinentes? *Concepts, méthodologie, expérimentation et résultats. Actes du colloque 5ème Conférence Internationale de Management Stratégique AIMS,* Lille.

Lesca, H. (2001). Veille stratégique: passage de la notion de signal faible à la notion de signe d'alerte précoce. *Actes du Colloque VSST'2001,* Tome 1, Toulouse (pp. 271-277).

Lesca, H., Blanco, S., & Caron-Fasan, M. L. (1997). Implantation d'une veille stratégique pour le management stratégique: proposition d'un modèle conceptuel et premières validations. *Actes de la 6ième conférence de l'AIMS,* Montréal (Vol. 2, pp. 173-183).

Levet, J. L., & Paturel, R. (1996). L'intégration de la démarche d'intelligence économique dans le management stratégique. *Actes de la 5ième conférence de l'AIMS,* Lille, Mai.

Li, H., Edwards, S. M., & Lee, J. H. (2002). Measuring the intrusiveness of advertisements: scale development and validation. *Journal of Advertising, 31*(2), 37–47.

Li, K. C., Tsai, Y. T., & Tsai, C. K. (2008). Toward development of distance learning environment in the grid. *International Journal of Distance Education Technologies, 6*(3), 45–57.

Lin, B., & Stasinskaya, V. S. (2002). Data warehousing management issues in online Recruiting. *Human Systems Management, 21*(1), 1–8.

Lincoln, Y. S., & Guba, E. G. (1985). *Naturalistic inquiry.* Beverly Hills, CA: Sage.

Lindner, R. W., & Harris, B. (1993). Teaching self-regulated learning strategies. *Proceedings of selected research and development presentations at the annual conference of the Association for Educational Communications and Technology*, (pp. 641-654).

Ling, R., & Pedersen, P. E. (Eds.). (2005). *Mobile communications: re-negotiation of the social sphere*. Surrey, UK: Springer.

Link, A. N., & Zmud, R. W. (1986). Additional evidence on the R&D interface. *IEEE Transactions on Engineering Management, 33*(1), 43–44.

Lipnack, J., & Stamps, J. (1997). *Virtual teams: reaching across space, time, and organizations with technology*. New York: John Wiley.

Lipnack, J., & Stamps, J. (1999). Virtual teams: the new way to work. *Strategy and Leadership, 27*, 14–18. doi:10.1108/eb054625

Lippert, S. K., & Swiercz, P. M. (2005). Human resource information systems (HRIS) and technology trust. *Journal of Information Science, 31*(5), 340–353. doi:10.1177/0165551505055399

Liu, C. C., & Tsai, C. C. (2008). An analysis of peer interaction patterns as discoursed by on-line small group problem-solving activity. *Computers & Education, 50*(3), 627–639. doi:10.1016/j.compedu.2006.07.002

Liu, S. (1997, July 21-22). Scanning the business environment with intelligent software agents. In *Proceedings of the 4th Conference of the International Society for Decision Support Systems (ISDSS'97)*, University of Lausanne, Switzerland.

Löfström, E., & Nevgi, A. (2007). From strategic planning to meaningful learning: diverse perspectives on the development of web-based teaching and learning in higher education. *British Journal of Educational Technology, 38*(2), 312–324. doi:10.1111/j.1467-8535.2006.00625.x

Lu, M., Watson-Manheim, M. B., Chudoba, K. M., & Wynn, E. (2006). Virtuality and Team Performance: Understanding the Impact of Variety of Practices. *Journal of Global Information Technology Management, 9*(1), 4–10.

Lucas, G. H. Jr, & Bush, A. J. (1988). The marketing-R&D interface: do personality factors have an impact? *Journal of Product Innovation Management, 5*(4), 257–268. doi:10.1016/0737-6782(88)90010-0

Lucas, K., & Sherry, J. L. (2003). *Sex Differences Among Young Adults' Video Game Use and Preference*. Paper presented at the Mass Communication Division, National Communication Association Annual Convention, New Orleans, LA.

Lurey, J. S., & Raisinghani, M. S. (2001). An empirical study of best practices in virtual teams. *Information & Management, 38*, 523–544. doi:10.1016/S0378-7206(01)00074-X

Lutz, R. J. (1985). Affective and cognitive antecedents of attitude toward the ad: A conceptual framework. In Alwitt, L. F., & Mitchell, A. A. (Eds.), *Psychological processes and advertising effects: Theory, research and application*. Hillsdale, NJ: Lawrence Erlbaum Associates.

Lynch, R., & Dembo, M. (2004). The relationship between self-regulation and online learning in a blended learning context, *International Review of Research in Open and Distance Learning, 5*(2). Retrieved October 7, 2008 from http://www.irrodl.org/index.php/irrodl/article/view/189/799.

MacInnis, D. J., & Jaworski, B. J. (1989). Information processing from advertisements: toward an integrative framework. *Journal of Marketing, 53*(4), 1–23. doi:10.2307/1251376

Mackay, D.-M. (1969). *Information, mechanism and meaning*. Cambridge, MA: MIT.

MacKenzie, S. B., & Lutz, R. J. (1989). An empirical examination of the structural antecedents of attitude toward the ad in an advertising pre testing context. *Journal of Marketing, 53*(2), 48–65. doi:10.2307/1251413

Madsen, K. H., & Petersen, M. G. (1999). Supporting collaboration in multi-media design. *Human-Computer Interaction - INTERACT'99* (pp. 185-190).

Maier, J. L., Rainer, R. K. Jr, & Snyder, C. A. (1997). Environmental Scanning for Information Technology: An Empirical Investigation. *Journal of Management Information Systems, 14*(2), 177–200.

Majchrzak, A., Rice, R. E., & Malhotra, A. (2000). Technology adaptation: the case of a computer-supported virtual team. *Management Information Systems Quarterly, 24*(4), 569–600. doi:10.2307/3250948

Maki, R. H., Maki, W. S., Patterson, M., & Whittaker, P. D. (2000). Evaluation of a web-based introductory psychology course: I. Learning and Satisfaction in On-line Versus Lecture Courses. *Behavior Research Methods, Instruments, & Computers, 32*(2), 230–239.

Malik, S. (2005). *Enterprise dashboards: design and best practices for IT*. New York: Wiley.

Mancuso, J. R. (1969). Why not create opinion leaders for new product introductions? *Journal of Marketing, 33*, 20–25. doi:10.2307/1248476

Marakas, G. M., & Elam, J. J. (1998). Semantic Structuring in Analyst Acquisition and Representation of Facts in Requirements Analysis. *Information Systems Research, 9*(1), 37–63. doi:10.1287/isre.9.1.37

Marchionini, G. (1995). *Information seeking in electronic environments*. New York: Cambridge University Press. doi:10.1017/CBO9780511626388

Marino, T. A. (2000). Learning online: A view from both sides. *The National Teaching & Learning Forum, 9*(4), 4–6.

Markus, M. L., & Silver, M. S. (2008). A Foundation for the Study of IT Effects: A New Look at De Sanctis and Poole's Concepts of Structural Features and Spirit. *Journal of the Association for Information Systems, 9*(3/4).

Marmuse, C. (1992). *Politique générale. Langages, Intelligence, Modèles et Choix stratégiques*. Economica.

Marquet, P., & Nissen, E. (2003). Distance in the languages learning through videoconferencing: dimensions, measures, consequences, *ALSIC-Apprentissage des langues et systèmes d'information et de communication, 6*(2), 3-19.

Martin, P., & Metcalfe, M. (2001). Informing the knowledge workers. *RSR. Reference Services Review, 29*(4), 267–275. doi:10.1108/00907320110408384

Martinet, B., & Marti, Y. M. (1995). *L'intelligence économique: les yeux et les oreilles de l'entreprise*. Paris: Les éditions de l'organisation.

Martinet, B., & Ribault, J. M. (1989). *La veille technologique, concurrentielle et commerciale: sources, méthodologie, organisation*. Paris: Les éditions d'organisation.

Martins, L. L., Gilson, L. L., & Maynard, M. T. (2004). Virtual teams: what do we know and where do we go from here? *Journal of Management, 30*(6), 805–835. doi:10.1016/j.jm.2004.05.002

Martinsons, M. G. (1997). Human resource management applications of knowledge-based systems. *International Journal of Information Management, 17*(1), 35–53. doi:10.1016/S0268-4012(96)00041-2

Martisons, M. G., & Chong, P. (1999). The influence of human factors and specialist involvement on information systems success. *Human Relations, 52*(1), 123–150. doi:10.1177/001872679905200107

Mathieu, J. E., Martineau, J. W., & Tannenbaum, S. I. (1993). Individual and situational influences on the development of self-efficacy: implications for training effectiveness. *Personnel Psychology, 46*(1), 125–147.

Mayfield, M., Mayfield, J., & Lunce, S. (2003). Human resource information systems: A review and model development. *Advances in Competitiveness Research, 11*(1), 139–151.

Mayhew, D. (1999). *The usability engineering lifecycle: A practitioner's handbook for user interface design*. San Francisco: Morgan Kaufmann.

Maznevski, M. L., & Chudoba, K. M. (2000). Bridging space over time: Global virtual team dynamics and effectiveness. *Organization Science, 11*, 473–492. doi:10.1287/orsc.11.5.473.15200

McGrath, J. E., Arrow, H., Gruenfeld, D. H., Hollingshead, A. B., & O'Connor, K. M. (1993). Groups, Tasks and Technology: The Effects of Experience and Change. *Small Group Research, 24*, 406–420. doi:10.1177/1046496493243007

McNaughton, R., Quickenden, P., Matear, S., & Gray, B. (1999). Intranet adoption and interfunctional coordination. *Journal of Marketing Management, 15*(5), 387–403. doi:10.1362/026725799784870270

Mehlenbacher, B., Miller, C. R., Covington, D., & Larsen, J. S. (2002). Active and interactive learning online: a comparison of Web-based and conventional writing classes. *Professional Communication. IEEE Transactions on Professional Communication, 43*(2), 166–184. doi:10.1109/47.843644

Mehrabian, A., & Russel, J. A. (1974). *An Approach to Environmental Psychology.* Cambridge, MA: MIT Press.

Meissonier, R. (1999). *NTIC et processus de décision dans les réseaux de PME-PMI.* Etudes et documents, série recherche, IAE, CEROG. Université de droit, d'économie et de sciences d'Aix-Marseille.

Merisavo, M. (2007). An empirical study of the drivers of consumer acceptance of mobile advertising. *Journal of Interactive Advertising, 7*(2). Retrieved from http://www.jiad.org/article92.

Mesulan, M. (1998). From sensation to cognition. *Brain, 121*, 1013–1052. doi:10.1093/brain/121.6.1013

Michaels, E., Handfield-Jones, H., & Axelrod, B. (2001). *The War for Talent.* Boston: Harvard Business Press.

Miles, M. B., & Huberman, A. M. (1994). *Qualitative data analysis: An expanded sourcebook* (2nd ed.). Thousand Oaks, CA: Sage.

Mills, C. (1987). Usability testing in the real world. *SIGCHI Bulletin, 18*, 67–70. doi:10.1145/25281.25285

Milne, G. R., & Rohm, A. J. (2003). The 411 on mobile privacy. *Marketing Management, 12*(4), 40–45.

Mintzberg, H., & Lampel, J. (1999). Reflecting on the strategy process. *Sloan Management Review, 40*(3), 21–30.

Mintzberg, H. (1979). *The structuring of organizations: a synthesis of the research.* Englewood Cliffs, NJ: Prentice Hall.

Miranda, S. M., & Bostrom, R. P. (1993). The impact of Group Support Systems on group conflict and conflict management. *Journal of Management Information Systems, 10*(3), 63–95.

Mobile Marketing Association. (2009). *Mobile Advertising Overview, January.* Retrieved May 12, 2009, from http://www.mmaglobal.com/mobileadoverview.pdf

Molich, R., & Nielsen, J. (1990). Improving a human-computer dialogue. *Communications of the ACM, 3*(33), 338–348. doi:10.1145/77481.77486

Mondi, M., Woods, P., & Rafi, A. (2007). Students' 'Uses and Gratification Expectancy' Conceptual Framework in relation to E-learning Resources. *Asia Pacific Education Review, 8*(3), 435–449. doi:10.1007/BF03026472

Moody, J. W., Blanton, J. E., & Cheney, P. H. (1998). A Theoretically Grounded Approach to Assist Memory Recall During Information Requirements Determination. *Journal of Management Information Systems, 15*(1), 79–98.

Moon, J. W., & Kim, Y. G. (2001). Extending the TAM for a World-Wide-Web context. *Information & Management, 38*(4), 217–230. doi:10.1016/S0378-7206(00)00061-6

Moore, G. C., & Benbasat, I. (1991). *An examination of the adoption of information technology by end-users: A diffusion of innovations perspective* (Working paper 90-MIS-012). Vancouver, BC, Canada: Department of Commerce and Business Administration, University of British Columbia.

Moreno, J. L. (1953). *Who shall survive?* New York: Beacon House.

Muehling, D. D. (1987). An investigation of factors underlying attitude-toward-advertising-in-general. *Journal of Advertising, 16*(1), 32–41.

Muhlmann, D. (2003). *The organizational impact of new technologies. The case of groupware and knowledge management.* Unpublished doctoral dissertation, Sciences Po Paris.

Mumford, L. (1966). *The Myth of the Machine: Volume One: Technics and Human Development.* New York: Harcourt.

Myers, I. B. (1962). *The Myers-Briggs type indicator.* Palo Alto, CA: Consulting Psychologists Press.

Nagasundram, M., & Bostrom, R. P. (1994). The structuring of creative processes using GSS: a framework for research. *Journal of Management Information Systems, 11*(3), 87–114.

National Institute for Occupational Safety and Health. (2004). *Worker health chartbook, 2004.* Retrieved December 2, 2007, from http://www.cdc.gov/niosh/docs/2004-146/pdfs/2004-146.pdf

Nayak, N., Mrazek, D., & Smith, D. (1995). Analyzing and communicating usability data. *SIGCHI Bulletin, 27*(1), 22–30. doi:10.1145/202642.202649

Newell, S., Scarbrough, H., & Swan, J. (2001). From global knowledge management to internal electronic fences: Contradictory outcomes of Intranet development. *British Journal of Management, 12*(2), 97–111. doi:10.1111/1467-8551.00188

Newell, S., Swan, J., Galliers, R., & Scarbrough, H. (1999). The Intranet as a knowledge management tool? Creating new electronic fences, managing Information Technology Resources. In Khosrow-Pour, M. (Ed.), *The next millennium* (pp. 612–619). Hershey, PA: IGI Global.

Ngai, E. W. T., & Wat, F. K. T. (2006). Human resource information systems: A review and empirical analysis. *Personnel Review, 35*(3), 297–314. doi:10.1108/00483480610656702

Nicol, D. J., & Macfarlane-Dick, D. (2006). Formative assessment and self-regulated learning: A model and seven principles of good feedback practice. *Studies in Higher Education, 31*(2), 199–216. doi:10.1080/03075070600572090

Niederman, F. (1999). Global information systems and human resource management: A research agenda. *Journal of Global Information Management, 7*(2), 33–39.

Niemi, H., Nevgi, A., & Virtanen, P. (2003). Towards self-regulation in Web-based learning. *Journal of Educational Media, 28*(1), 49–71. doi:10.1080/1358165032000156437

Niven, P. (2008). *Balanced scorecard: step-by-step for government and nonprofit agencies.* New York: Wiley.

Nokia Media Network. (2008). Retrieved November 13, 2008, from http://www.nokia.com/A4136001?newsid=1190110

North Dakota State University. (2005). *Agrosecurity: Disease surveillance and public health (Brochure).* Fargo, ND: Knight Printing.

North Dakota Stockmen's Association. (2005). *Comments submitted on the National Animal Identification System Strategic Plan.* Retrieved August 25, 2005, from http://www.ndstockmen.org/images/animal%20id%20comments.htm

North Dakota Stockmen's Association. (2006a). *Stockmen's Association publishes new brand book.* Retrieved October 12, 2006, from http://www.ndstockmen.org/images/Brandbook.htm

North Dakota Stockmen's Association. (2006b). *Welcome.* Retrieved March 12, 2006, from http://www.ndstockmen.org

Norzaidi, M., Chong, S., Murali, R., & Salwani, M. (2007). Intranet usage and managers' performance in the port industry. *Industrial Management & Data Systems, 107*(8), 1227–1250. doi:10.1108/02635570710822831

Novak, T. P., Hoffman, D. L., & Yung, Y. F. (2000). Measuring the customer experience in online environments: a structural modeling approach. *Marketing Science, 19*(1), 22–42. doi:10.1287/mksc.19.1.22.15184

Novak, T. P., & Hoffman, D. L. (1997). Measuring the flow experience among web users. *Interval Research Corporation.* Retrieved from http://www.find.org.tw/find/home.aspx?page=many&id=78

Noyes, J., & Baber, C. (1999). *User-Centered Design of Systems.* Heidelberg, Germany: Springer Verlag.

Nyström, C. (2006). Philosophy of technology in organizations: A foundation for Intranets. *Systemic Practice and Action Research, 19*(6), 523–535.

O'Flaherty, B., & Williams, H. (2000). Intranet adoption in Irish organisations: a survey analysis. *Systèmes d'Information et Management, 5*(2), 41–58.

Obermiller, C., & Spangenberg, E. R. (2000). On the origin and distinctiveness of skepticism toward advertising. *Marketing Letters, 11*(4), 311–322. doi:10.1023/A:1008181028040

Obermiller, C., Spangenberg, E. R., & McLahan, D. L. (2005). Ad skepticism – the consequences of disbelief. *Journal of Advertising, 34*(3), 7–17.

O'Conaill, B., Whittaker, S., & Wilbur, S. (1993). Conversation over video conferences: an evaluation of the spoken aspects of video-mediated communication. *Human-Computer Interaction, 8,* 389–428. doi:10.1207/s15327051hci0804_4

Odenwald, S. (1996). Global work teams. *Training & Development, 50*(2), 54–57.

Oiry, E., Pascal, A., & Tchobanian, R. (2008). From tool to organization: uses of a collaborative application in a high-tech SME. In *Proceedings of the 8th International Conference on the Design of Cooperative Systems*, Carry-Le-Rouet, France.

Okunoye, A., & Bada, A. (2007). Institutional drivers of Intranet use in a global context: Case of a distributed international research organisation. *World Review of Science. Technology and Sustainable Development, 4*(1), 73–85. doi:10.1504/WRSTSD.2007.012661

Ologeanu, R. (2005). Videoconferencing experiments and uses in French higher education. *Distances et savoirs, 3*(1), 11-28.

Ologeanu-Taddei, R., & Staii, A. (2008). Comment analyser l'appropriation? Le défi de l'opérationnalisation empirique. In *Proceedings of the 13ème conférence de l'AIM (Association Information et Management) (pré-ICIS)*, Paris.

Orlikowski, W. J. (1992). The duality of technology: rethinking the technology concept in organizations. *Organization Science, 3*(3), 398–427. doi:10.1287/orsc.3.3.398

Orlikowski, W. (2000). Using technology and constituting structures: a practice lens for studying technology in organizations. *Organization Science, 11*(4), 404–428. doi:10.1287/orsc.11.4.404.14600

Orlikowski, W. J., & Gash, C. (1994). Technological frames: making sense of information technology in organisations. *ACM Transactions on Information Systems, 12*(2), 174–207. doi:10.1145/196734.196745

Ozaki, S., & Taylor, C. R. (2008). What is SMS advertising and why do multinationals adopt it? Answers from an empirical study in European markets. *Journal of Business Research, 61,* 4–12. doi:10.1016/j.jbusres.2006.05.003

Panagiotis, Z. (2008). Cross-cultural differences in perceptions of e-learning usability: An empirical investigation. *International Journal of Technology and Human Interaction, 4*(3), 1–26.

Parry, E. (2008). Drivers of the adoption of online recruitment – an analysis using diffurion of innovation theory. In Bondarouk, T. V., & Ruël, H. J. M. (Eds.), *E-HRM in theory and practice*. Amsterdam: Elsevier.

Pereira, J. A., Pleguezuelos, E., Merí, A., Molina-Ros, A., Molina-Tomás, M. C., & Masdeu, C. (2007). Effectiveness of using blended learning strategies for teaching and learning human anatomy. *Medical Education, 41*(2), 189–195. doi:10.1111/j.1365-2929.2006.02672.x

Perriault, J. (1989). *La logique de l'usage*. Paris: Flammarion.

Perrow, C. (1972). *Complex Organizations: A Critical Essay*. Glenview, IL: Scott, Foresman.

Peters, C., Amato, C. H., & Hollenbeck, C. R. (2007). An exploratory investigation of consumers' perception of wireless advertising. *Journal of Advertising, 36*(4), 129–145. doi:10.2753/JOA0091-3367360410

Petit, M.-C., Sicotte, H., & Bourgault, M. (2005). Investigating the enabling mechanisms for ensuring quality of communication in newly virtualized project teams. In Morel-Guimaraes, L. (Ed.), *Key success factors for innovation and sustainable development (Management of Technology Series)*. London: Elsevier.

Pfleeger, S. L., & Atlee, J. M. (2010). *Software engineering: theory and practice*. Upper Saddle River, NJ: Prentice Hall.

Phelps, R., & Mok, M. (1999). Managing the risks of Intranet implementation: An empirical study of user satisfaction. *Journal of Information Technology, 14*(1), 39–52. doi:10.1080/026839699344737

Piccoli, G., Ahmad, R., & Blake, Y. (2001). Web-Based Virtual Learning Environments: A Research Framework and a Preliminary Assessment of Effectiveness in Basic IT Skills Training. *Management Information Systems Quarterly, 25*(4), 401–426. doi:10.2307/3250989

Pilke, E. M. (2004). Flow experiences in information technology user. *International Journal of Human-Computer Studies, 61,* 347–357. doi:10.1016/j.ijhcs.2004.01.004

Piller, C. (2004, September 12). US agriculture adds defenses against terrorism; some microbes or poisons could ruin confidence in U.S. food and devastate the farm economy. *Orlando Sentinel.* p. G1.

Pinto, J. K. (2002). Project management. *Research Technology Management, 45*(2), 22–37.

Pinto, J. K., & Slevin, D. P. (1988). Project success: definitions and measurement techniques. *Project Management Journal, 19*(1), 67–71.

Pinto, M. B., & Pinto, J. K. (1990). Project team communication and cross-functional cooperation in new program development. *Journal of Product Innovation Management, 7*(3), 200–212. doi:10.1016/0737-6782(90)90004-X

Pintrich, P. R. (1995). *Understanding Self-regulated Learning.* San Francisco: Jossey-Bass.

Plickert, G., Côté, R. R., & Wellman, B. (2007). It's not who you know, it's how you know them: Who exchanges what with whom? *Social Networks, 29*(3), 405–429. doi:10.1016/j.socnet.2007.01.007

Poole, M. C., & De Sanctis, G. (1989). Microlevel structuration in computer-supported group decision making. *Human Communication Research, 19*(1), 5–49.

Porter, M., & Millar, V. E. (1985). How information gives you competitive advantage. *Harvard Business Review, 3*(4), 149–174.

Powell, A., Piccolli, G., & Ives, B. (2004). Virtual teams: A review of the current literature directions for future research. *The Data Base for Advances in Information Systems, 35*(1), 6–36.

Power, D. J. (2002). *Decision support systems: concepts and resources for managers.* Westport, CT: Quorum Books.

Prado, A. B., Freitas, C. E. F., & Sbrici, T. R. (2007). Business intelligence as a HRIS for absenteeism. In *Proceedings of the 1st Workshop in Human Resource Information Systems (HRIS 2007)*, Funchal, Madeira, Portugal.

Preece, J. (2000). *Online Communities.* New York: John Wiley & Sons Inc.

Proulx, S. (Ed.). (1988). *Vivre avec l'ordinateur: les usagers de la micro-informatique.* Québec, Canada: Boucherville.

Quick, T. C., & Lapertosa, J. B. (1982). Analise do absentismo em usina siderurgica. *Revista Brasileira de Saude Ocupacional, 10*(40), 62–67.

Qureshi, S., Liu, M., & Vogel, M. (2006). The effects of electronic collaboration in distributed project management. *Group Decision and Negotiation, 15*, 55–75. doi:10.1007/s10726-005-9006-6

Rasmussen, N., Goldy, P. S., & Solli, P. O. (2002). *Financial business intelligence.* New York: John Wiley & Sons, Inc.

Redish, J., Bias, R., Bailey, R., Molich, R., Dumas, R., & Spool, J. (2002). Usability in practice: Formative usability evaluations - Evolution and revolution. *ACM Conference on Human Factors in Computing System,* Minneapolis, Minnesota (pp. 885-890).

Reid, D., & Reid, F. (2004). Insights into the social and psychological effects of SMS text messaging. *160characters.org,* February. Retrieved May 12, 2009, from http://www.160characters.org/documents/SocialEffectsOfTextMessaging.pdf

Reix, R. (1991). Systèmes d'information: l'intelligence en temps réel reste encore à venir. *Revue française de gestion,* 8-16.

Rettie, R., Grandcolas, U., & Deakins, B. (2005). Text message advertising: response rates and branding effects. *Journal of Targeting. Measurement and Analysis for Marketing, 13*(4), 304–312. doi:10.1057/palgrave.jt.5740158

Rettie, R. (2001). An exploration of flow during Internet use. *Internet Research, 11*(2), 103–113. doi:10.1108/10662240110695070

Reukert, R. W., & Walker, O. C. (1987). Marketing's interaction with other functional units: a conceptual framework and empirical evidence. *Journal of Marketing, 51*(3), 1–19. doi:10.2307/1251140

Revelli, C. (2000). *Intelligence stratégique sur Internet: comment développer efficacement des activités de veille et de recherche sur les réseaux.* Paris: Dunod.

Reyero, M., & Tourón, J. (2003). The development of talent: Acceleration as an educational strategy. Netbiblo, A Coruña.

Rheingold, H. (2000). *The Virtual Community: Homesteading on the Electronic Frontier.* London: MIT Press.

Rice, R., & Rogers, E. M. (1980). Reinventing in the Innovation Process. *Knowledge: Creation, Diffusion. Utilization, 1*(4), 499–514.

Riessman, C. K. (1993). *Narrative Analysis.* London: Sage.

Robey, D., & Farrow, D. L. (1982). User involvement in information system development. A conflict model and empirical test. *Management Science, 28,* 73–85. doi:10.1287/mnsc.28.1.73

Roces, C., & González Torres, M. C. (1998). Ability to self-regulate learning. In J.A. González Pienda & J.C. Núñez (Eds.), *Dificultadesde aprendizaje escolar* (pp. 239-259). Madrid: Pirámide/Psicología.

Roche, L. (2000). *Cybergagnant: Technologie, cyberespace et développement personnel.* Paris: Maxima Laurent du Mesnil.

Roche, L., & Sadowsky, J. (2000). La résistance des salariés à la high-tech. *Expansion management review, 99,* 44-50.

Rodger, J. A., Pendharkar, P. C., Paper, D. J., & Molnar, P. (1998). Reengineering the human resource information system at Gamma. *Facilities, 16*(12/13), 361–365. doi:10.1108/02632779810235681

Rogalski, S. (2007). *What BI 2.0 means for data management.* Retrieved January 5, 2008, from www.dmreview. com/issues/2007_41/10000378-1.html

Rogers, E. M. (1973). *Communication strategies for family planning.* New York: Free Press.

Rogers, E. M. (2003). *Diffusion of innovations* (5th ed.). New York: Free Press.

Rogers, E. M., & Svenning, L. (1969). *Modernization among peasants: The impact of communication.* New York: Holt Rinehart & Winston.

Rogers, E. M., & van Es, J. C. (1964). *Opinion leadership in traditional and modern Columbian peasant communities.* East Lansing, MI: Michigan State University.

Roling, N., Ascroft, J., & Chege, F. Y. (1976). The diffusion of innovations and the issue of equity in rural development. *Communication Research, 3,* 155–170. doi:10.1177/009365027600300204

Rondeau, P. J., Ragu-Nathan, T. S., & Vonderembse, M. A. (2006). How involvement, IS management effectiveness, and end user computing impact IS performance in manufacturing firms. *Information & Management, 43*(1), 93–107. doi:10.1016/j.im.2005.02.001

Rooslani, T., & Ly, F. S. (2007). The development and empirical validation of the B2E portal user satisfaction scale. *Journal of Organizational and End User Computing, 19*(3), 43–63.

Rosenbaum, S., Rohn, J. A., & Humburg, J. (2000). A toolkit for strategic usability: Results from workshops, panels and surveys. In *Proceedings of hte ACM CHI 2000 Conference on Human Factors in Computing Systems, 1,* 337-344.

Ross, J. D. (1999). *Regulating hypermedia: Self-regulation learning strategies in a hypermedia environment.* Va: Virginia Polytechnic Institute and State University.

Rovai, A. P., & Jordan, H. M. (2004). Blended learning and sense of community: A comparative analysis with traditional and fully online graduate courses. *International Review of Research in Open and Distance Learning, 5*(2). Retrieved from October 7, 2008 http://www.irrodl.org/index.php/irrodl/article/view/192/274.

Rubenstein, A. H., Chakrabarti, A. K., O'Keefe, R. D., Souder, W. E., & Young, H. C. (1976, May). Factors influencing innovation success at the project level. *Research Management,* 15–20.

Rubin, J. (1994). *Handbook of usability testing: How to plan, design and conduct effective tests.* New York: John Wiley & Sons Inc.

Ruël, H., Bondarouk, T., & Looise, J. K. (2004b). E-HRM: innovation or irritation, an explorative empirical study in five large companies on Web-based HRM. *Management Review, 15*(3), 364–380.

Ruël, H. J. M. (2001). *The non-technical side of office technology; managing the clarity of the spirit and the appropriation of office technology* (Doctoral dissertation). Enschede, The Netherlands: Twente University Press.

Ruël, H. J. M., & Bondarouk, T. (2004a). *The Web-driven individualization of the employment relationship*. Retrieved May 28, 2008, from http://exchange.usg.uu.nl/irec/papers/5_RuelBondarouk.doc

Ruël, H., & Magalhaes, R. (2008). Organizational knowledge and change: The role of transformational HRIS. In H. Ruël & R. Magalhaes (Eds.), *Human resource information systems, Proceedings of the 2nd International Workshop on Human Resource Information Systems (HRIS 2008)*, Barcelona, Spain (pp. 111-123).

Russell, T. L. (1999). *The Non Significance Difference Phenomenon*. Raleigh, NC: North Carolina State University Press.

Ruta, D. (2005). The application of change management theory to HR portal implementation in subsidiaries of multinational corporations. *Human Resource Management, 44*(1), 35–53. doi:10.1002/hrm.20039

Rutter, D. R. (1984). *Looking and seeing. The role of visual communication in social interaction*. Chichester, UK: Wiley.

Ryan, B., & Gross, N. C. (1943). The diffusion of hybrid seed corn in two Iowa communities. *Rural Sociology, 8*, 15–24.

Saade, R., & Bahli, B. (2005). The impact of cognitive absorption on perceived usefulness and perceived ease of use in on-line learning: an extension of the technology acceptance model. *Information & Management, 42*, 317–327. doi:10.1016/j.im.2003.12.013

Sabherwal, R., & Chan, Y. E. (2001). Alignment between business and IS strategies: a study of protectors, analysers and defenders. *Information Systems Research, 12*(1), 11–33. doi:10.1287/isre.12.1.11.9714

Sabherwal, R., Hirschheim, R., & Goles, T. (2001). The dynamics of alignment: Insights from a punctuated equilibrium model. *Organization Science, 12*(2), 179–197. doi:10.1287/orsc.12.2.179.10113

Saga, V., & Zmud, R. (1996). Introduction de logiciels de gestion dans des petites entreprises liées à une profession libérale. *Systèmes d'Information et Management, 1*(1), 51–73.

Saldaña, J. (2005). An introduction to Ethnodrama. In Saldaña, J. (Ed.), *Ethnodrama: An anthology of reality theatre* (pp. 1–36). Walnut Creek, CA: AltaMira Press.

Saltiel, J., Bauder, J. W., & Palakovich, S. (1994). Adoption of sustainable agricultural practices: Diffusion, farm structure, and profitability. *Rural Sociology, 59*, 333–349.

Samier, H., & Sandoval, V. (1999). *La recherche intelligente sur l'Internet et l'intranet*. Paris: Hermès Science Publications.

Sarbin, T. R. (1995). A narrative approach to repressed memories. *Journal of Narrative and Life History, 5*, 41–66.

Scharl, A., Dickinger, A., & Murphy, J. (2005). Diffusion and success factors of mobile marketing. *Electronic Commerce Research and Applications, 4*(2), 159–173. doi:10.1016/j.elerap.2004.10.006

Schell, D. (1986). Usability testing of screen design: Beyond standards, principles, and guidelines. In *Proceedings of the Human Factors Society 30th Meeting* (pp. 1212-1215), Santa Monica, CA.

Schiller, S. Z., & Mandviwalla, M. (2007). Virtual team research – an analysis of theory use and a framework for theory appropriation. *Small Group Research, 38*(1), 12–59. doi:10.1177/1046496406297035

Schindler, R. M. (1998). Consequences of perceiving oneself as responsible for obtaining a discount. *Journal of Consumer Psychology, 7*, 371–392. doi:10.1207/s15327663jcp0704_04

Schmidt, J. B., Montoya-Weiss, M. M., & Massey, A. P. (2001). New product development decision-making effectiveness: comparing individuals, face-to-face teams, and virtual teams. *Decision Sciences, 32*(4), 575–601. doi:10.1111/j.1540-5915.2001.tb00973.x

Schore, A. N. (1994). *Affect regulation and the origin of the self: The neurobiology of emotional development*. Hillsdale, NJ: Erlbaum.

Schryer, C. F. (1993). Records as Genre. *Written Communication, 10*, 200–234. doi:10.1177/0741088393010002003

Scott, J. (1994). The measurement of information systems effectiveness: evaluating a measuring instrument. In *Proceedings of the Fifteenth International Conference on Information Systems*, Vancouver, BC, Canada (pp. 111-128).

Seddon, P. B. (1997). A respecification and extension of the DeLone and McLean model of IS success. *Information Systems Research, 8*(3), 240–253. doi:10.1287/isre.8.3.240

Sellen, A. J. (1995). Remote conversations: the effects of mediating talk with technology. *Human-Computer Interaction, 10,* 401–444. doi:10.1207/s15327051hci1004_2

Severin, W. J., & Tankard, J. W. (1997). *Communication theories: Origins, methods, and uses in the mass media* (4th ed.). White Plains, NY: Longman Publishing Group.

Shang, R. A., Chen, Y. C., & Shen, L. (2005). Extrinsic versus intrinsic motivations for consumers to shop on-line. *Information & Management, 42,* 401–413. doi:10.1016/j.im.2004.01.009

Sharma, S., Durand, R. M., & Gur-Arie, O. (1981). Identification and analysis of moderator variables. *JMR, Journal of Marketing Research, 18*(3), 291–300. doi:10.2307/3150970

Shen, P. D., Lee, T. H., & Tsai, C. W. (2007b). Facilitating students to pass certificate tests via blended e-learning with self-regulated learning: A quasi-experimental approach, *WSEAS Proceedings on Multimedia, Internet & Video Technologies,* Beijing, China.

Shen, P. D., Lee, T. H., Tsai, C. W., & Ting, C. J. (2008). Exploring the effects of Web-enabled problem-based learning and self-regulated learning on vocational students' involvement in learning. *European Journal of Open, Distance and E-Learning,* 2008(1). Retrieved October 7, 2008 from http://www.eurodl.org/materials/contrib/2008/Shen_Lee_Tsai_Ting.htm.

Shen, P.D., Lee, T.H., & Tsai, C.W. (2007a). Applying Web-enabled problem-based learning and self-regulated learning to enhance computing skills of Taiwan's vocational students: A quasi-experimental study of a short-term module. *Electronic Journal of e-Learning, 5*(2), 147-156.

Shneiderman, B. (1982). Designing computer system messages. *Communications of the ACM, 9*(25), 610–611. doi:10.1145/358628.358639

Shneiderman, B., & Plaisant, C. (2005). *Designing the user interface: Strategies for effective human-computer interaction.* Pearson Publishing, Inc., ISBN 0-321-19786-0.

Sicotte, H., & Langley, A. (2000). Integration mechanisms and R&D project performance. *Journal of Engineering and Technology Management, 17,* 1–37. doi:10.1016/S0923-4748(99)00018-1

Siefer. (2006, October 31-November 2). User interfaces for the exploration of hierarchical multi-dimensional data. *IEEE Symposium on visual Analytics Science and Technology,* Baltimore (pp. 175-182).

Simon, H. A. (1996). *The Sciences of the Artificial* (3rd ed.). Cambridge, MA: MIT Press.

Simon, H. (1983). *Administration et processus de décision.* Paris: Economica.

Simon, H. (1986). Il devient tout aussi passionnant de rechercher l'organisation des processus de pensée que de découvrir l'organisation du mouvement des planètes. *Commentaires et réponses présentées par H.A. Simon au Colloque de la Grande Motte, Sciences de l'intelligence, sciences de l'artificiel, publié dans les actes édités par les PUL.* ISBN 7297 0287 3.

Simon, H. (1991). *Sciences des systèmes, sciences de l'artificiel* (pp. 148-169).

Singh, H. (2003). Building effective blended learning programs. *Educational Technology, 43*(6), 51–54.

Singhal, A., & Rogers, E. M. (2003). *Combating AIDS: Communication strategies in action.* New Delhi, India: Sage.

Skadbert, Y. X., & Kimmel, J. R. (2004). Vistors' flow experience while browsing a Web site: its measurement, contributing factors and consequences. *Computers in Human Behavior, 20,* 403–422. doi:10.1016/S0747-5632(03)00050-5

Smith, A. D., & Rupp, W. T. (2004). Managerial challenges of e-recruiting. *Online Information Review, 28*(1), 61–74. doi:10.1108/14684520410522466

Souder, W. E. (1987). *Managing new product innovations.* Lexington: Lexington Books.

Sparshott, J. (2004, February 24). Outbreak points out vulnerability of U.S. food supply. *The Washington Times.* p. A01.

Speck, P. S., & Elliott, M. T. (1997). Predictors of advertising avoidance in print and broadcast media. *Journal of Advertising, 26*(3), 61–76.

Spence, E. (2006). *Ethics within reason: A neo-Gewirthian approach*. Lanham: Lexington Books (a division of Rowman and Littlefield).

Spence, E. (2007, July 12-14). What's right and good about Internet information? A universal model for evaluating the cultural quality of digital information. In L. Hinman, P. Brey, L. Floridi, F. Grodzinsky, & L. Introna E.,) *Proceedings of CEPE 2007, The 7th International Conference of Computer Ethics: Philosophical Enquiry*, University of San Diego, USA.

Stenmark, D. (2003). Knowledge creation and the web: Factors indicating why some Intranets succeed where others fail. *Knowledge and Process Management, 10*(3), 207–216. doi:10.1002/kpm.173

Stenmark, D. (2006). Corporate Intranet failures: interpretating a case study through the lens of formative context. *International Journal of Business Environment, 1*(1), 112–125.

Stephenson, W. (1935). Correlating Persons instead of Tests. *Character and Personality, 4*, 17–24.

Stephenson, W. (1953). *The study of behavior: Q-technique and its methodology*. Chicago: University of Chicago Press.

Stoffels, J. D. (1982). Environmental scanning for future success. *Managerial Planning, 31*(3), 4–12.

Strategy. *Columbia Journal Of World Business*.

Straus, S. G., Weisband, S. P., & Wilson, J. M. (1998). Human Resource Management Practices in the networked organization: Impact of Electronic Communication Systems. In Cooper, C. L., & Rousseau, D. M. (Eds.), *Trends in Organizational Behavior* (pp. 127–154). New York: John Wiley & Sons Ltd.

Strauss, A., & Corbin, J. (1998). *Basics of qualitative research - Techniques and procedures for developing grounded theory*. California: Sage Publications.

Stroh, L. K., Grasshoff, S., Rudé, A., & Carter, N. (1998). Intergraded HR systems help develop global leaders. *HRMagazine, 43*(5), 13–17.

Strohmeier, S. (2007). Research in e-HRM: Review and implications. *Human Resource Management Review, 17*(1), 19–37. doi:10.1016/j.hrmr.2006.11.002

Suder, G., & Inthavong, S. (2008). New health risks and sociocultural contexts: Bird Flu impacts on consumers and poultry businesses in Lao PDR. *Risk Analysis, 28*(1), 1–12. doi:10.1111/j.1539-6924.2008.00997.x

Swan, B., Belanger, F., & Watson-Manheim, M. B. (2004). Theoretical foundations for distributed work: multilevel, incentive theories to address current dilemmas. In *Proceedings of the 37th Annual Hawaii International Conference on System Sciences (HICSS'04)*. Washington, DC: IEEE Computer Society.

Swart, J., & Kinnie, N. (2003). Knowledge-intensive firms: the influence of the client on HR systems Systems. *Research and Behavioral Science, 23*(6), 839–844.

Swimme, B., & Berry, T. (1992). *The Universe Story*. New York: Harper Collins.

Szmigin, I., Canning, L., & Reppel, A. E. (2005). Online community: Enhancing the relationship marketing concept through customer bonding. *International Journal of Service Industry Management, 16*(5), 480–496. doi:10.1108/09564230510625778

Tähti, M., Väinämö, S., Vanninen, V., & Isomursu, M. (2004). Catching emotions elicited by mobile services. In *Proceedings of the Australian Conference on Computer-Human Interaction*. Wollongong, Australia (CD-ROM).

Tang, X., & Lu, Q. (2002). Intranet-extranet-internet based quality information management: system in expanded enterprises. *International Journal of Advanced Manufacturing Technology, 20*(11), 853–858. doi:10.1007/s001700200226

Tannenbaum, S. I. (1990). Human resource information systems: User group implications. *Journal of Systems Management, 41*(1), 27–26.

Tansley, C., Newell, S., & Williams, H. (2001). Effecting HRM-style practices through an integrated human resource information system: An e-greenfield site? *Personnel Review, 30*(3), 351–370. doi:10.1108/00483480110385870

Targowski, A. S., & Deshpande, S. P. (2001). The utility and selection of an HRIS. *Advances in Competitiveness Research, 9*(1), 42–56.

Tarondeau, J.-C., Jolibert, A., & Choffray, J.-M. (1994). *Le management à l'aube du XXIe siècle*. Revue Française de Gestion.

(2004). An SMS history. In Taylor, A., & Vincent, J. (Eds.), *Mobile World, Computer Supported Cooperative Work* (pp. 1431–1496). London: Springer.

Taylor, S. J., & Bogdan, R. (1998). *Introduction to qualitative research methods* (3rd ed.). New York: John Wiley & Sons.

Thomke, S., & von Hippel, E. (2002). Customers As Innovators: A New Way to Create Value. *Harvard Business Review*, *80*(4), 74–81.

Torben, A., Eriksen, B., Lemmergaard, J., & Povlsen, L. (2006). The many faces of fit: An application to strategic human resource management. In Burton, R., Døjbak Håkonsson, D., Eriksen, B., & Snow, C. (Eds.), *Organization Design - The Evolving State of the Art* (pp. 85–101). New York: Springer.

Townley, B. (1994). *Reframing human resource management: Power, ethics and the subject at work*. London: Sage Publication.

Townsend, A. M., & Hendrickson, A. R. (1996). Recasting HRIS as an information resource. *HRMagazine*, *41*(2), 91–94.

Trevino, L. K., & Webster, J. (1992). Flow in computer-mediated communication. *Communication Research*, *19*(5), 539–573. doi:10.1177/009365092019005001

Tsang, M. M., Ho, S. C., & Liang, T. P. (2004). Consumer attitudes toward mobile advertising: an empirical study. *International Journal of Electronic Commerce*, *8*(3), 65–78.

Turkle, S. (1995). *Life on the screen: Identity in the age of the Internet*. New York: Simon & Schuster.

Turnbull, P. W., & Meenaghan, A. (2001). Diffusion of innovation and opinion leadership. *European Journal of Marketing*, *14*(1), 3–33. doi:10.1108/EUM0000000004893

Tyre, M. J., & Orlikowski, W. J. (1994). Windows of Opportunity: Temporal Patterns of Technological Adaptation in Organizations. *Organization Science*, *5*(1), 98–118. doi:10.1287/orsc.5.1.98

Uldall-Espersen, T., & Frøkjær, E. (2007, July 22-27). Usability and software development: Roles of the stakeholders. In [*Beijing, China.*]. *Proceedings of, HCI2007*, 642–651.

Uldall-Espersen, T., Frøkjær, E., & Hornbæk, K. (2007). Tracing impact in a usability improvement process. *Interacting with Computers*, 48–63.

USDA-APHIS. (2008). *National Animal Identification System*. Retrieved April 16, 2008, from http://animalid.aphis.usda.gov/nais/

Vaast, E. (2004). O Brother, where are thou?: From communities to networks of practice through Intranet use. *Management Communication Quarterly*, *8*(18), 5–44. doi:10.1177/0893318904265125

Vakratsas, D., & Ambler, T. (1999). How advertising works: what do we really know? *Journal of Marketing*, *63*(1), 26–43. doi:10.2307/1251999

Valacich, J. S., Mennecke, B. E., Watcher, R. M., & Wheeler, B. C. (1994). Extensions to Media Richness Theory: A Test of the Task-Media Fit Hypothesis. In *Proceedings of the Hawaii International Conference on Systems Science*, Maoui, HI (pp. 11-20).

Van der Linden, G., & Parker, P. (1998). On paradoxes between human resources management, postmodernism and HR information systems. *Accounting. Management and Information Technology*, *8*(4), 265–282. doi:10.1016/S0959-8022(98)00014-9

van Dijk, J. (2005). *The Network Society: Social Aspects of New Media*. Thousand Oaks, CA: Sage.

van Fenema, P. C., & Kumar, K. (2000). Coupling, interdependence and control in global projects. In Lundin, R. A., & Hartman, F. (Eds.), *Projects as business constituents and guiding motives*. Boston: Kluwer Academic Publishers.

Van Maanen, J. (1995). An End of Innocence: The Ethnography of Ethnography. In Van Maanen, J. (Ed.), *Representation in Ethnography* (pp. 1–35). Thousand Oaks, CA: Sage.

Vellerand, R. J. (1997). Toward a hierarchical model of intrinsic and extrinsic motivation. *Advances in Experimental Social Psychology*, *29*, 271–360. doi:10.1016/S0065-2601(08)60019-2

Venkatesh, V., & Morris, M. G. (2000). Why don't men ever stop to ask for directions? gender, social influence, and their role in technology acceptance and usage behavior. *Management Information Systems Quarterly, 24*(1), 115–139. doi:10.2307/3250981

Venkatesh, V., Morris, M. G., Davis, G. B., & Davis, F. D. (2003). User acceptance of information technology: Toward a unified view. *Management Information Systems Quarterly, 27*(3), 425–478.

Venkatraman, N. (1993). Continuous strategic alignment: Exploiting information technology capabilities for competitive success. *European Management Journal, 11*(2), 139–149. doi:10.1016/0263-2373(93)90037-I

Venkatraman, N. (1989). The concept of fit in strategy research: toward verbal and statistical correspondence. *Academy of Management Review, 9,* 513–525. doi:10.2307/258291

Venkatraman, N., & Grant, J. H. (1986). Construct measurement in organizational strategy research: a critique and proposal. *Academy of Management Review, 11,* 71–87. doi:10.2307/258332

Vidal, P., & Planeix, P. (2005). *Systèmes d'information organisationnels.* Upper Saddle River, NJ: Pearson Education.

Voiskounsky, A. E., Mitina, O. V., & Avetisova, A. A. (2004). Playing online games: flow experience. *Psych-Nology Journal, 2*(3), 259–281.

von Hippel, E. (2007). Horizontal innovation networks—by and for users. *Industrial and Corporate Change, 16*(2), 293–315. doi:10.1093/icc/dtm005

von Hippel, E. (1990). Task partitioning: an innovation process variable. *Research Policy, 19*(5), 407–418. doi:10.1016/0048-7333(90)90049-C

Walker, A. J. (1982). *HRIS development: A project team guide to building an effective personnel information system.* New York: Van Nostrand Reinhold.

Walker, A. J. (1993). *Handbook of human resource information systems: Reshaping the human resource function with technology.* New York: McGraw-Hill.

Walther, J. B. (1995). Relational Aspects of Computer-Mediated Communication: Experimental Observations Over Time. *Organization Science, 6*(2), 186–203. doi:10.1287/orsc.6.2.186

Wan, C. S., & Chiou, W. B. (2006). Psychological Motives and Online Games Addiction: A Test of Flow Theory and Humanistic Needs Theory for Taiwanese Adolescents. *Cyberpsychology & Behavior, 9*(3), 317–324. doi:10.1089/cpb.2006.9.317

Wan Hooi, L. (2006). Implementing e-HRM: The readiness of small and medium sized manufacturing companies in Malaysia. *Asia Pacific Business Review, 12*(4), 465–485. doi:10.1080/13602380600570874

Wasson, C. R., Sturdivant, F. D., & McConaughy, D. H. (1970). The social process of innovation and product acceptance. In Britt, S. H. (Ed.), *Consumer behaviour in theory and in action* (pp. 252–255). New York: John Wiley & Sons.

Watson-Manheim, M. B., Chudoba, K. M., & Crowston, K. (2002). Discontinuities and continuities: a new way to understand virtual work. *Information Technology & People, 15*(3), 191–209. doi:10.1108/09593840210444746

Weatherly, L. A. (2005). HR technology: Leveraging the shift to self-service – it's time to go strategic. *HRMagazine, 50*(3), 1–11.

Webster, J., & Ho, H. (1997). Audience engagement in multi-media presentations. *The Data Base for Advances in Information Systems, 28*(2), 63–77.

Webster, J., Trevino, L. K., & Ryan, L. (1993). The dimensionality and correlates of flow in human-computer interactions. *Computers in Human Behavior, 9,* 411–426. doi:10.1016/0747-5632(93)90032-N

Webster, B., & Hackley, P. (1997). Teaching effectiveness in Technology-mediated Distance Learning. *Academy of Management Review, 40*(6), 1282–1309. doi:10.2307/257034

Wehmeyer, K., & Riemer, K. (2007). Trust-building potential of coordination roles in virtual organizations. *The Electronic Journal for Virtual Organizations and Networks, 8,* 102–123. Retrieved June 15, 2009, from http:// http://www.ejov.org

Weibel, D., Wissmath, B., Habegger, S., Steiner, Y., & Groner, R. (2008). Playing online games against computer-vs. human-controlled opponents: Effects on presence, flow, and enjoyment. *Computers in Human Behavior*, *24*(5), 2274–2291. doi:10.1016/j.chb.2007.11.002

Weick, K. E. (1969). *The social Psychology of Organizing*. Reading, MA: Addison Wesley.

Weinstein, C. (1989). Teacher education students' preconceptions of teaching. *Journal of Teacher Education*, *40*(2), 53–60. doi:10.1177/002248718904000210

Weir, T. (1999). Innovators or news hounds? A study of early adopters of the electronic newspaper. *Newspaper Research Journal*, *20*(4), 62–81.

Wellman, B., Boase, J., & Chen, W. (2002). The networked nature of community on and off the Internet. *IT and Society*, *1*(1), 151–165.

Wellman, B., & Haythornthwaite, C. (2002). *The Internet in everyday life*. Oxford, UK: Blackwell. doi:10.1002/9780470774298

Wellman, B., Quan-Haase, A., Witte, J., & Hampton, K. (2001). Does the Internet increase, decrease, or supplement social capital? Social networks, participation, and community commitment. *The American Behavioral Scientist*, *45*(3), 436–455. doi:10.1177/00027640121957286

West, J., & Berman, E. (2001). From traditional to virtual HR. *Review of Public Personnel Administration*, *21*(1), 38–64. doi:10.1177/0734371X0102100104

Wheelis, M., Casagrande, R., & Madden, L. V. (2002). Biological attack on agriculture: Low-tech, high-impact bioterrorism. *Bioscience*, *52*(7), 569–576. doi:10.1641/0006-3568(2002)052[0569:BAOALT]2.0.CO;2

White, M. (2000). Corporate portals: Realizing their promise, avoiding costly failure. *Business Information Review*, *12*(17), 177–184. doi:10.1177/0266382004237737

Williams, T. M. (1999). The need for new paradigms for complex projects. *International Journal of Project Management*, *17*(5), 269–273. doi:10.1016/S0263-7863(98)00047-7

Windows Vista Development Center. (2008). *MSDN library*. Retrieved August 2008, from http://msdn.microsoft.com/en-us/library/aa511267.aspx

Windows XP Design Team. (2001). *Windows XP visual guidelines*. Microsoft Corporation. Retrieved June 2004, from http://www.microsoft.com/whdc/hwdev/windowsxp/downloads/default.mspx

Winer, M., & Ray, K. (1994). *Collaboration handbook: Creating, sustaining, and enjoying the journey*. Lafond, St. Paul, MN: Amherst H. Wilder Foundation.

Wiredu, G. O. (2007). User appropriation of mobile technologies: Motives, conditions and design properties. *Information and Organization*, *7*(2), 110–129. doi:10.1016/j.infoandorg.2007.03.002

Wixon, D., & Wilson, C. (1997). The usability engineering framework for product design and evaluation. In M. Helander & T. Landauer (Eds.), *Handbook of human computer interaction* (p. 653–688). North-Holland: Elsevier Science.

Wogalter, M. S., Conzola, V., & Smith-Jackson, T. (2002). Research-based guidelines for warning design and evaluation. *Applied Ergonomics*, *3*(33), 219–230. doi:10.1016/S0003-6870(02)00009-1

Wogalter, M. S. (2006a). *Handbook of warnings*. New Jersey/London: Lawrence Erlbaum Associates.

Wogalter, M. S. (2006b). Purposes and scope of warnings. In M.S. Wogalter (Ed.), *Handbook of warnings* (pp. 3-9). New Jersey/London: Lawrence Erlbaum Associates.

Wolters, M. (2006). The Effectiveness of job board Internet Recruitment. In *Proceedings of the First European Academic Workshop on e-HRM*, The Netherlands.

Woodward, J. (1958). *Management and technology*. London: Her Majesty's Stationery Office.

World Health Organization. (2007). *ICD, International statistical classification of diseases and related health problems*. Retrieved February 12, 2007, from en.wikipedia.org/wiki/ICD

Woszczynski, A. B., Roth, P. L., & Segars, A. H. (2002). Exploring the theoretical foundations of playfulness in computer interactions. *Computers in Human Behavior*, *18*, 369–388. doi:10.1016/S0747-5632(01)00058-9

Wulf, W. A., Haimes, Y. Y., & Longstaff, T. A. (2003). Strategic alternative responses to risks of terrorism. *Risk Analysis*, *23*(3), 429–444. doi:10.1111/1539-6924.00325

Yahaya, S.-Y., & Abu-Bakar, N. (2007). New product development management issues and decision-making approaches. *Management Decision, 45*(7), 1123–1142. doi:10.1108/00251740710773943

Yang, S. C., & Tung, C. J. (2007). Comparison of Internet addicts and non-addicts in taiwanese high school. *Computers in Human Behavior, 23*(1), 79–96. doi:10.1016/j.chb.2004.03.037

Yates, J., & Orlikowski, W. J. (1992). Genres of Organizational Communication: A Structurational Approach to Studying Communication and Media. *Academy of Management Review, 17*, 299–326. doi:10.2307/258774

Yin, R. K. (2003). *Case Study Research: Design and Methods* (3rd ed.). Thousand Oaks, CA: Sage.

Yoo, Y., & Alavi, M. (2001). Media and group cohesion: Relative influences on social presences, task participation, and group consensus. *Management Information Systems Quarterly, 25*(3), 371–390. doi:10.2307/3250922

Young, R., & Jordan, E. (2008). Top management support: Mantra or necessity? *International Journal of Project Management, 26*(7), 713–725. doi:10.1016/j.ijproman.2008.06.001

Yukselturk, E., & Bulut, S. (2007). Predictors for student success in an online course. *Educational Technology & Society, 10*(2), 71–83.

Yushau, B. (2006). The effects of blended e-learning on mathematics and computer attitudes in pre-calculus algebra. *The Montana Math Enthusiast, 3*(2), 176–183.

Zaltman, G., Duncan, R., & Holbek, J. (1973). *Innovations and organizations*. New York: John Wiley & Sons.

Zanot, E. (1984). Public advertising towards advertising. *International Journal of Marketing, 3*, 3–15.

Zeleny, M. (2007). Data-information-knowledge-wisdom-enlightenment: towards the strategy of system integration. In *Proceedings of the 1st Workshop in Human Resource Information Systems (HRIS 2007)*, Funchal, Madeira, Portugal.

Zhao, H. (2006). Expectations of recruiters and applicants in large cities of China. *Journal of Managerial Psychology, 21*(5), 459–475. doi:10.1108/02683940610673979

Zigurs, I., Evaristo, R., & Katzy, B. (2001). Collaborative technologies for virtual project management. In *Proceedings of Academy of Management,* Washington, DC.

Zimmerman, B. J. (1990). Self-regulated learning and academic achievement: An overview. *Educational Psychologist, 25*(1), 3–17. doi:10.1207/s15326985ep2501_2

Zimmerman, B. J., & Martinez-Pons, M. (1986). Development of a structured interview for assessing student use of self-regulated learning strategies. *American Educational Research Journal, 23*(4), 614–628.

Zimmerman, B. J. (1998). Developing self-regulation cycles of academic regulation: An analysis of exemplary instructional model. In D.H. Schunk & B.J. Zimmerman (Eds.), *Self-regulated learning: From teaching to self-reflective practice* (pp. 1-19). New York: Guilford.

Zmud, R., & Apple, L. (1992). Measuring information technology infusion. *Production and Innovation Management, 9*, 148–155. doi:10.1016/0737-6782(92)90006-X

Zusman, R., & Landis, R. (2004). Applicant preferences for web-based versus traditional job posting. *Computers in Human Behavior, 18*, 285–296. doi:10.1016/S0747-5632(01)00046-2

About the Contributors

Anabela Mesquita is a professor at the School of Administration and Accountancy (ISCAP)/Polytechnic School of Porto (IPP), Portugal. She is also an invited researcher at the Algoritmi R & D Center, Information Systems Group, at the University of Minho (Portugal). She lectures courses related to business communication, information society, and digital storytelling. Dr. Mesquita's research interests include knowledge and innovation management, impact of information systems in organization, life long learning at higher education levels, and e-learning. She also has been involved in several European and national research projects. Dr. Mesquita has published numerous papers in various international journals and conference proceedings. She has been a member of the programme committee and scientific committee of several national and international conferences, in most cases also serving as referee. She serves as Member of the Editorial Board and referee for IGI Global. She also serves as Associate Editor of the *Information Resources Management Journal*. She serves as referee for the *Journal of Cases of Information Technology*. She has also been evaluator and reviewer for European commission projects.

*** *** ***

T. S. Amer is a professor of accounting in the W. A. Franke College of Business at Northern Arizona University. He received his PhD from The Ohio State University in 1989. Professor Amer teaches accounting information systems, managerial and cost accounting. His current research interests include the implications of information technology on human decision making and human/computer interactions. Amer has published in *Contemporary Accounting Research, Auditing: A Journal of Practice and Theory, The Journal of Information Systems, and Advances in Accounting Information Systems.*

T. Bondarouk is an Assistant Professor of Human Resource Management at the University of Twente, the Netherlands. She holds two PhDs: in Didactics (1997) and Business Administration/HRM (2004). Since 2002 she has been busy with the emerging research area of Electronic HRM. Her main publications concern an integration of Human Resource Management and social aspects of Information Technology Implementations. Her research covers both private and public sectors and deals with a variety of areas such as the implementation of e-HRM, management of HR-IT change, HRM contribution to IT projects, roles of line managers in e-HRM, implementation of HR Shared Service Centers. She has conducted research projects with the Dutch Ministry of Interior and Kingdom Relations, Dow Chemical, Ford, IBM, ABN AMRO bank, Shell, Unit4Agresso. Among her current research projects are Implementation of HR Shared Service Centers at the Dutch Ministry of Defense, Large Non-academic Hospital, and the Belgian Federal Public Health Service. Since 2006 she is involved in organizing European Academic Workshops on e-HRM, and International Workshops on HRIS.

Mario Bourgault is a full professor at École Polytechnique, Montreal, Canada. He has conducted over a decade of research in the field of innovation and project management. Dr. Bourgault has held the Canada Research Chair in Technology Project Management since 2004. His work has been published in a number of journals, including *Project Management Journal, International Journal of Project Management, R&D Management* and *International Journal of Managing Projects in Business*. In addition to his academic credentials, he spent several years in the field working as a professional engineer, and he maintains close ties with the industry by participating in various research projects and acting as an expert consultant. He also holds Project Management Professional (PMP®) certification.

Phil Carter is a psychodramatist and co-author with Max Clayton of *The Living Spirit of the Psychodramatic Method*. He taught English as a second language for seven years in the 1980s in Taiwan and tutored Mandarin at Massey University in New Zealand in the 1990s. He has a PhD in information systems and is currently teaching computer usability and research methods to post-graduate students in the School of Computing and Mathematical Sciences at the Auckland University of Technology. In recent years, he has offered training in leadership and group work.

Jaouad Daoudi is a PhD student in Industrial Engineering at École Polytechnique, Montreal, Canada, where he received a Master's of Engineering (MEng) in Technology Project Management. Since 2004, Mr. Daoudi has been a research assistant under the Canada Research Chair in Technology Project Management, where he conducted a number of theoretical and empirical studies on project maturity, new product development, and distributed teams. Currently, his main research interests are in the area of critical success factors in distributed and collaborative technological projects. Prior to returning to graduate school, he spent several years in the industry as a Project Control Analyst.

Nathalie Drouin started her academic career in 2002 after several years in the private sector. She specializes in strategic management and project management. She holds a Ph.D. from Cambridge University and completed postdoctoral studies at École Polytechnique de Montreal, where she conducted various projects on organizational capabilities and innovation. Since 2003, she has been a professor at the Université du Québec à Montréal (UQAM) in the Master's Program in Project Management. In 2004, she became a principal researcher of the Canada Research Chair in Technology Project Management. The Chair is held by Professor Mario Bourgault, École Polytechnique de Montréal. She is also a member of the Research Board of the Project Management Research Chair (UQAM) and is responsible of the research axis named: Competencies and Transfer of Learning.

Bernard Fallery is Professor in Management Sciences at the University of Montpellier 2. Since 2000 he has published 53 papers in scientific journals, books and conferences. He teaches at the Department "Computer Science and Management " in Polytech'Montpellier (www.polytech.univ-montp2.fr) and head of the research group "Information Systems" CREGOR. His research has always focused on the appropriation of information and communication technologies (SIM Journal, No. 2, Vol 6, 2001), whether in the e-learning (SIM Journal No. 1, vol 10, 2005) or in the knowledge management (SIM Journal No. 4, vol 11, 2007).

Carmen Freitas is a Systems Analyst at State University of Campinas, Brazil. She received a Bachelor's degree in Computer Science from the University College of Para, Brazil and post-graduate degree in Quality Management System from the State University of Campinas, Brazil. She has been active in the Human Resources Information Systems area for over 5 years and she works on projects related with staffing, occupational health, human resources processes, strategic planning, business intelligence and metrics. His current work involves the portal corporate development with a focus on human resource management with researches on knowledge management, content management systems, human resources strategy, among others.

Elfi Furtmueller is an Assistant Professor at the Department of Information Systems & Change Management at the University of Twente (UT), the Netherlands. Prior to joining the UT, she worked at the Institute of Management, Innovation and Organization at the Haas School of Business, University of California, Berkeley. She obtained her doctorate in Organizational Behaviour from the University of Linz, Austria. She currently teaches in the Master's program Information Systems & Service Management. She also has gained several years of professional experience in human resource management. While her research is theoretically grounded in social-psychology and service management theory (commitment, identification, customer bonding and retention), she applies these concepts to e-recruiting services research. Dr. Furtmueller is also actively engaged in e-recruiting practice involving the realization of information systems design for career management. She co-founded an Austrian-wide e-recruiting service for university graduates http://absolventen.at.

Claire Gauzente is a university professor of marketing and organisation at the Institute of Political Sciences of Rennes, Researcher at GRANEM University of Angers, France and an affiliate professor at ESC Rennes School of Business. Her research interests include: interactive marketing, relationship marketing, ethical and privacy issues. Dr. Gauzente's work has been published in, among others, *Electronic Markets, International Journal of Electronic Business, Journal of Electronic Commerce Research, Journal of Small Business Management, Journal of Consumer Marketing, International Journal of Retail and Distribution Management, Academy of Marketing Science Review.* She was a guest editor for the special issue entitled "A consumer stance at search engine marketing" of the *International Journal of Internet Marketing and Advertising* and serves on editorial boards of academic journals such as *International of Business and Emerging Markets, International Journal of Advanced Decision Sciences.*

Sylvie Gerbaix is an assistant professor in Management Science at the University of Montpellier 2 and at the University, Paul Cézanne, of Aix-en-Provence. She obtained a Ph D in Information System Management from the University of Montpellier. Her research topics are related to the role of information and communication systems for organizations. She is the author of books and participates to chapters of books on Management Control and on Information Systems Management. Her research articles and communications include themes such as: use and diffusion of videoconferencing system within organizations, E-training, management control, Internet security, e-payment. More generally, her research themes deal with the effect analysis of Information and Communication Technologies (ICT).

Manelle Guechtouli is teaching information systems and competitive intelligence at the ESCEM business school (France). She received a PhD in management at Paul Cezanne University in Aix en Provence (France) and her thesis has been qualified by the CNU (French university council). Her research topics are basically linked to information systems' management in a general way. In a more specific way, she has been working on organizational, motivational and strategic aspects of Business Intelligence (BI). She also has been teaching strategy Management and BI at Paul Cezanne University and at Avignon University (France).

Véronique Guilloux is assistant professor in Paris 12 University. She teaches HRM, organization & behaviours, e-management in an "international management" master. Interorganizational relationships, information systems and HRM are her research themes. She has written several articles and has coordinated a French book on Intranets. She is currently working on the impact of Web2.0 on recruiting policy and on organizational improvisation in multinationals.

Kasper Hornbæk is an associate professor in human-computer interaction at the Department of Computer Science, University of Copenhagen. He earned a PhD in computer science from University of Copenhagen in 2002. His research interests include usability engineering, interfaces for information access, eye-tracking, and information visualization. He is a member of the editorial boards of the *Journal of Usability Studies and International Journal of Human-Computer Studies*, and is involved in national and European research projects on usability research. He has published in ACM Conference on Computer-Human Interaction, *International Journal of Human-Computer Studies*, and *Transaction on Computer Human-Interaction.*

Chin-Lung Hsu is an associate professor of Information Management at Da-Yeh University, Changhua, Taiwan. He received BS, MBA and PhD degrees from National Taiwan University of Science and Technology, Taipei, Taiwan in 1997, 1999 and 2004, respectively. Dr. Hsu's articles have appeared in *Information & Management, Omega, Computers in Human Behavior, International Journal of Mobile Communications, International Journal of Technology and Human Interaction, International Journal of Computer Applications in Technology, Information Management & Computer Security*, and His research interests include electronic commerce, internet marketing, and innovation adoption.

Michel Kalika is Professor in Management Sciences since March 2008, and the Dean of EM Strasbourg business school, the school of management of the University of Strasbourg. Former Professor at Paris-Dauphine University, he is the author or co-author of twenty books and approximately a hundred various other publications: articles, communications, books chapters and case studies. He directed 48 PhD theses (two prizes of best thesis in information systems: 2002/2005, one Chancery prize: 2006) and is currently directing 10 PhD students in information systems.

Florence Laval is assistant professor in Human Resource Management at the Poitiers' Institut d'Administration des enterprises. HRM, e-management and Organizational theories are her teaching themes. She works currently on HRM and network. She analyses the impact of information technology on Human Resources. She considered IT with a strategic, organizational or human lens. She currently is analyzing e-HRM according to interpretative methodology. Working on two case studies, she is writing articles on e-HRM in a big public office (ie City Council of Paris) and on a private small company.

Joe-Mae B. Maris is an associate professor of computer information systems in the W. A. Franke College of Business at Northern Arizona University. She received her DBA from Louisiana Tech University in 1989. Professor Maris teaches programming, operations management, and management information systems. Her research interests include systems development, web design, and human/computer interaction. Maris has published in *The Journal of Information Systems, IEEE Transactions on Education, and the Systems Research Journal.*

Mie Nørgaard holds a PhD in human computer interaction from the University of Copenhagen. Her research interests include collaborative and organizational aspects of user research and experienced-focused HCI. To explore new aspects of cross-professional collaboration she currently teaches and practises visual facilitation in various Danish companies. With a background in prehistoric archaeology Nørgaard is curious about how technology changes the way humans live, work and interact with the world. Currently, she is exploring this topic through a number of critical design projects.

Ewan Oiry is the author is currently an associate professor in Human Resource Management in the University of Mediterranée and in the LEST. He is currently responsible of an MBA and a national thematic think tank on the subject of « competencies management ». He published several books and articles on HRM, appraisal systems, etc. Currently, he works on the theme of construction and uses of management tools (especially electronic management tools). He is also member of the Organizing Committee of the *European Academic Workshop on e-HRM.*

Roxana Ologeanu-Taddei is currently an associate professor in Communication studies and Information and Communication Technologies. She is researcher in Information Systems at the Research Centre on Management of Organizations, University Montpellier 2, France. Her area of research consists on questions arising from the use and appropriation of information and communication technology, related to professional training. She has begun a research program on the professional uses of Internet forums. She has published especially in the field of communication studies. She is also participated to the 3rd International Workshop on Human Resource Information Systems (HRIS 2009), in Milan, Italy.

Hilkka Poutanen has graduated in information systems science from the University of Oulu, the department of Information Processing Science in 1988. Since then she has worked as an Adp Analyst, a Systems Analyst and as a Human Resource Analyst in different organizations for twenty years. She has started her research career in the 2000s. At the moment she is finishing her PhD thesis titled 'Developing the Role of Human Resource Information Systems for the Activities of Good Leadership'. Hilkka Poutanen will defense her thesis at spring in 2010.

Alysson Bolognesi Prado is a Computer Engineer and received M.Sc. degree in Human-Computer Interaction, when he studied Semiotic Engineering for user interfaces and Geographical Information Systems. Since 2002, he works as System Analyst at State University of Campinas, Brazil, designing and developing systems for the Human Resources Department, using On Line Analytical Processing, report generators and web technologies such as Java and Ajax, building and evolving an application framework that allows programmers to focus the business rules of the Human Resources team despite of technical idiosyncrasies. His current research interests are HCI, Business Intelligence, workflow systems, Organizational Semiotic, collaborative design and end-user programming.

Vesa Puhakka is a professor of entrepreneurship at University of Oulu. He is doing research especially on ICT-business and trying to understand the emerging mechanisms of becoming an ICT-entrepreneur, business opportunity-creating processes and development and change processes of ICT-ventures. The Academy of Management and the NFIB Education Foundation awarded his doctoral dissertation for outstanding research in the fields of entrepreneurship and independent business in 2003.

Thiago Ricardo Sbrici is a Systems Analyst at State University of Campinas, Brazil. He is graduated at Pontificia Universidade Catolica de Campinas, Brazil. His main function is as Database Administrator at the Human Resource Department of the University. Since 2007, he has been active as research assistant for The International Research on Permanent Authentic Records in Electronic Systems (Inter-PARES) 3 Project. Nowadays, he is working in a project for the University researching the architecture and development of a digital repository for archival storage. His current work in business intelligence area refers to the conception of the infrastructure of a web portal for the human resource data warehouse.

Pei-Di Shen now works as director of the Teacher Education Center and professor of Graduate School of Education, Ming Chuan University, Taipei, Taiwan. Shen is one of the editors-in-chief of International Journal of Online Pedagogy and Course Design, which will be published by IGI-Global in 2011. Her primary interest areas are e-learning, knowledge management, virtual community, and management information systems. Her research focus is the distance education in higher education. Readers can contact her by email: pdshen@mcu.edu.tw

Hélène Sicotte is an associate professor at the Department of Management and Technology and currently teaching in the Graduated Project Management Programs at the École des sciences de la gestion of UQAM, accredited by PMI's Global Accreditation Center. She is also a member of Project Management Research Chair of UQAM. She conducts research on project management, NPD, and innovation in the private and public sectors. Her research results have given her the opportunity to participate in several international conferences on innovation and technology management, including RADMA, IRNOP, PICMET, IAMOT and PMI. Some of her research is accepted for publication in international journals such as the *Journal of Engineering and Technology Management, International Journal of Technology Management.*

Edward Spence, BA (Hons), PhD, is a senior lecturer in moral philosophy and applied and professional ethics in the School of Communication, Charles Sturt University, Senior Research Fellow at the Centre for Applied Philosophy and Public Ethics (CAPPE), Canberra, Australia and Research Fellow at the 3TU. Centre for Ethics and Technology, The Hague, Netherlands. He is currently working as a Research Fellow (2006 to 2009) on a nationally funded research project on New Media and the Good Life in the Department of Philosophy, University of Twente, Netherlands. He is author of Media, Markets and Morals (forthcoming) Blackwell, Advertising Ethics (2005) and Corruption and Anti-corruption: A Philosophical Approach (2005), Pearson/Prentice Hall, and Ethics within Reason: A Neo-Gewirthian Approach (2006) Lexington Books.

Chia-Wen Tsai is an assistant professor in the Department of Information Management, Ming Chuan University. Tsai is one of the editors-in-chief of International Journal of Online Pedagogy and Course Design. He is also the associate editor of *International Journal of Information Communication Technologies* and *Human Development,* and *International Journal of Innovation in the Digital Economy.* He is interested in the online teaching methods and knowledge management. Readers can contact him by email: jawen12b@gmail.com

Rolf van Dick is a Professor of Social Psychology at the Goethe-University Frankfurt (Germany) and currently serves as Associate Dean. Prior to his current position Rolf van Dick was Professor of Social Psychology and Organizational Behavior at Aston Business School Birmingham (UK). He received his Ph.D. in social psychology from Philipps-University Marburg (Germany). His research interests center on the application of social identity theory in organizational settings. In particular, he is interested in identity processes in teams and organizations which are highly diverse, he is applying identity research in the area of mergers and acquisitions and is currently investigating leadership and identity in the field and the laboratory. Rolf served as associate editor of the European Journal of Work & Organizational Psychology and is editor-in-chief of the British Journal of Management and the Journal of Personnel Psychology. He has published and edited seven books, over 20 book chapters and more than 60 papers in academic journals published in outlets including the Academy of Management Journal, Journal of Marketing, Journal of Applied Psychology, Journal of Organizational Behavior, Journal of Vocational Behavior, and Journal of Personality and Social Psychology.

Shari R. Veil, PhD, North Dakota State University, is the Coordinating Director of the Center for Risk and Crisis Management at the University of Oklahoma where she teaches crisis communication and public relations as an assistant professor in the Gaylord College of Journalism and Mass Communication. Dr. Veil was previously a research fellow with the Risk and Crisis Communication Project investigating agrosecurity concerns for the United States Department of Agriculture and the Department of Homeland Security National Center for Food Protection and Defense. Her research focuses on organizational learning in high-risk environments, community preparedness, and communication strategies for crisis management.

Celeste P. M. Wilderom holds the chair in Management and Organizational Behaviour in the Private and Public Sector at the University of Twente (UT), the Netherlands. She obtained her Ph.D. from the State University of New York at Buffalo (USA). She is the chair of the European Group of Organization Studies (EGOS) workgroup on professional service organizations and professionalization at work (from 2003-2006 with Royston Greenwood, University of Alberta, Canada; from 2007 till 2011 with Huseyin Leblebici, University of Illinois, Urbana Champaign, USA). Dr. Wilderom is one of the three editors of the award-winning Handbook of Organizational Culture & Climate (Sage: 2000 and (soft cover) 2004). Currently she serves as a senior editor of the British Journal of Management and is a member of editorial boards of various international journals. Previously, she was an associate editor of the Academy of Management Executive and the International Journal of Service Industry Management. She held posts at the University of Tilburg, Department of Strategy & Organization, the Netherlands; did a sabbatical at the University of Cambridge, Judge Institute of Management Studies, UK and at the Free University, Amsterdam, Economic and Social Institute (ESI), Netherlands.

Index